NEW HONG KONG CINEMA

NEW HONG KONG CINEMA

TRANSITIONS TO BECOMING CHINESE IN 21ST-CENTURY EAST ASIA

BY RUBY CHEUNG

Berghahn on film

Published in 2016 by
Berghahn Books
www.berghahnbooks.com

Library of Congress Cataloging-in-Publication Data
Cheung, Ruby.
New Hong Kong Cinema: transitions to becoming Chinese in 21st-century East
Asia / by Ruby Cheung.
pages cm
Includes filmography.
Includes bibliographical references and index.
ISBN 978-1-78238-703-9 (hardback: alk. paper) -- ISBN 978-1-78238-704-6
(ebook)
1. Motion pictures--China & Hong Kong--History--21st century. 2. Chinese in
motion pictures. I. Title.
PN1993.5.C4C44218 2015
791.43095125--dc23

2015002053

British Library Cataloguing in Publication Data
A catalogue record for this book is available from the British Library

ISBN 978-1-78238-703-9 (hardback)
ISBN 978-1-78238-704-6 (ebook)

For Mama and Thomas

Contents

Illustrations

Acknowledgements

It has been a long time coming. Now it is here.

Many people have been involved over the course of the years; without their invaluable input and support there would be no book. Special thanks are due: for intellectual inspiration – Dina Iordanova, who started all this in the first place, and has fiercely supported me and my work throughout, David Martin-Jones' clarity of thought and advice on my research career; for reading early versions of relevant research and giving invaluable comments – Robert Burgoyne, Mette Hjort, Robert A. Rosenstone, Julian Stringer and Belén Vidal; for sharing film industry inside information at various research stages –Thomas Gerstenmeyer, Chris Harris and Li Cheuk-to; for language use suggestions at various stages of writing-up: Valerie Holmes, Alex Marlow-Mann and Vladimir Vladov; for those at or via Berghahn Books – Adam Capitanio for his editorial support, Mark Stanton, who first showed interests in my project, and the anonymous reviewers for their invaluable comments; all my friends for sharing laughs and tears with me; my students at the United International College (UIC), Zhuhai, China for being truly inspirational regarding the use of new media in mainland China in the forthright way only young people can be; all colleagues at universities over the past decade of work on this project – St Andrews (United Kingdom), Dundee (United Kingdom), Lingnan (Hong Kong) and UIC (China).

Part of the research I conducted on the Hong Kong International Film Festival (including the personal interview with its Artistic Director, Li Cheuk-to) was within the context of the 'Dynamics of World Cinema' project, spearheaded by Dina Iordanova at the University of St Andrews and funded by The Leverhulme Trust. Also, I am grateful to Routledge (publisher) and Robert Burgoyne (editor) for allowing me to reprint two tables of statistics that are carried in my essay 'Red Cliff: The Chinese-language Epic and Diasporic Chinese Spectators' in The Epic Film in World Culture (pp. 192–94). A part of Chapter Four in this book is based on the primary research data listed in these two tables. They are now included here as Tables A.2 and A.3 (in Appendix) respectively, in a slightly modified format.

I am grateful to my family for being there and for tolerating my long-term absence – Terence, Vivian, Aunt Helen, Father; 'the girls' Ava, Constance, Lynn and Nina; most importantly – Mama (I would be nowhere without you) and Thomas (for keeping me on course, fed, watered and warm in all climates and seasons).

Notes on Romanization, Terminology and Information Source

This book mainly follows the pinyin system of Romanization, the conventional one for Chinese-language film studies in the English-speaking world. On specific occasions, Cantonese-language terms Romanized according to the general practice prevailing in Hong Kong (initially employed by the local government) are also provided. Except for cases when an Anglicized name and/or an English given name is adopted, in general East and South East Asian names (in particular, Chinese, including mainland Chinese and Chinese diaspora, Japanese and Korean names) are Romanized in this book with the surname placed first and the given names second. This is to reflect the original form and the specific manner of Romanization of the names when they are used in their places of origin. To be more specific, names of filmmakers, actors, actresses, other film industry practitioners and so on are presented as they are widely known, e.g., John Woo where Woo is the surname (instead of Wu Yusen in pinyin (Mandarin) or Ng Yu-sum in Hong Kong Cantonese). Authors' names, if already Romanized when used in publications, are presented as they are printed in relevant publications, e.g., Yiu-Wai Chu and Laikwan Pang (the in-text citations of their works in this book are Y-W. Chu and L. Pang respectively).

Film titles are italicized and are used in their English version in the main text and notes. Information on film director(s), country(ies) of origin and year of general release in the main audience market is given in parentheses immediately following a film title at its first appearance in the text (except in those cases with relevant information in the text nearby); for example: *A Simple Life* (Ann Hui, Hong Kong, 2012). A Filmography is included at the end of the book. For Chinese-language films, information about the pinyin and the Chinese film title (in both traditional and simplified scripts) is given in the Filmography in addition to the English title of the films. For each major role in the films under close analysis, the name of the actor/actress is given in parentheses immediately following the protagonist name at its first appearance in the text.

Proper names such as the 'New Hong Kong Cinema' or 'New Taiwan Cinema' are used to refer to specific cinematic traditions, film industries and relevant institutional aspects, and individual films made in the mentioned places. These proper names are capitalized in this book.

The information on individual films' country (or countries) of origin, company credits, release places and dates comes mainly from IMDb (www.imdb.com), unless referenced otherwise in the text.

Abbreviations

In general, full names of companies/entities in this book will be cited on the first mention, and in abbreviated form from the second mention onwards. On occasions, the same full names are mentioned again after their first appearance in the book.

China-related

Beijing Film Academy (BFA)
Beijing Film Market (BFM)
Beijing International Film Festival (BJIFF)
Central Academy of Drama (CAD)
China Film Group Corporation (CFGC)
Economic Cooperation Framework Agreement (ECFA)
Mainland and Hong Kong Closer Economic Partnership Arrangement (CEPA)
National Film Capital Company Limited (NFC)
People's Republic of China (PRC)
Shanghai Film Group (SFG)
Shanghai International Film Festival (SIFF)
Shanghai Media & Entertainment Group (SMEG)
Shanghai Media Group (SMG)
SMEG Special Events Office (SSEO)
State Administration of Press, Publication, Radio, Film and Television (SAPPRFT)
State Administration of Radio, Film and Television (SARFT)

Hong Kong-related

British National (Overseas) (BN(O))
Create Hong Kong (CreateHK)
Film Services Office (FSO)
Home Affairs Department (HAD)
Hong Kong-Asia Film Financing Forum (HAF)

Hong Kong Film Development Council (HKFDC)
Hong Kong International Film & TV Market (FILMART)
Hong Kong International Film Festival (HKIFF)
Hong Kong International Film Festival Society (HKIFFS)
Hong Kong Trade Development Council (HKTDC)
Independent Commission Against Corruption (ICAC)
Mainland and Hong Kong Closer Economic Partnership Arrangement (CEPA)
Office for Film, Newspaper and Article Administration (OFNAA)
Office of the Communications Authority (OFCA)
Radio Television Hong Kong (RTHK)
Special Administrative Region (SAR)
Television and Entertainment Licensing Authority (TELA)
Television Broadcasts Limited (TVB)

International

Asian Film Commissions Network (AFCNet)
International Federation of Film Producers Associations (FIAPF)
World Trade Organization (WTO)

Japan-related

Japan Association for International Promotion of the Moving Image (UNIJAPAN)
Japan Broadcasting Corporation (NHK)
Japan Film Commission Promotion Council (JFCPC)
Tokyo International Anime Festival (TIAF)
Tokyo International Film Festival (TIFF)
Tokyo International Music Market (TIMM)

South Korea-related

Asian Film Market (AFM)
Asian Project Market (APM)

Busan International Film Commission & Industry Showcase (BIFCOM)
Busan International Film Festival (BIFF)
Korean Film Council (KOFIC)
Pusan International Film Festival (PIFF)
Pusan Promotion Plan (PPP)

Taiwan-related

Central Motion Picture Company (CMPC)
Central Pictures Corporation (CPC)
Economic Cooperation Framework Agreement (ECFA)
Government Information Office (GIO)

United Kingdom-related

British Broadcasting Corporation (BBC)

U.S.-related

Motion Picture Association of America (MPAA)

Introduction
The New Hong Kong Cinema, Cinema of Transitions and East Asia

Made on a 'mid budget' of RMB30 million (£2.8 million or U.S.$4.8 million),[1] *A Simple Life* (Ann Hui, Hong Kong, 2012) does not belong to any Hong Kong mainstream genres (Bordwell 2000; FILMART 2007). It tells a very simple story between an elderly, loyal housemaid Tao Jie of a Hong Kong Chinese migrant family and her young master Roger. Their love and care for each other makes them no different from any blood-related family. The director Ann Hui acknowledges that one of the main themes of *A Simple Life* – the sociopolitical issues of ageing – was rarely explored in Hong Kong films.[2] She admits that making this film was a risky endeavour, for she employed stars to play major roles while shooting the film like a documentary.[3] After Hui and the film's writer/producer Roger Lee (whose real-life story was the blueprint of the film) showed the synopsis to Hong Kong superstar Andy Lau and Deanie Ip (playing Tao Jie), the two actors were not just interested in playing the key roles, but Lau was also willing to find finances for the film (H. 2012). *A Simple Life* turned out to be emotionally touching, garnering multiple important awards (such as the best actress and best director awards) when it travelled along the international film festival circuit in 2011 and 2012. The film's international glory meant it soon became the talk of the town. It was also one of the highest box-office grossing films (ranked number five) in Hong Kong in the first half of 2012 (Shackleton 2012b), becoming the most bankable film Hui had made in decades (Sek 2013: 124). Its mainland China box-office takings doubled the film's initial budget.[4]

Being *A Simple Life*'s lead actor and executive producer, Lau promotes the film in its 'Making of' programme.[5] Upon finishing it, he chants loudly in Cantonese,[6] 'Hurray, Hong Kong Cinema!' Lau is internationally famous for his role as the triad mole inside the Hong Kong Police Force in the *Infernal Affairs* trilogy (directed by Hong Kong filmmakers Andrew Lau and Alan Mak, and released in 2002 and 2003 respectively).[7] Much less known outside Hong Kong is Lau's active support (in terms of both finances and human resources) for independent Hong Kong films, especially those made on low budgets. The star often assumes the role of producer of these films, such as for Fruit Chan's *Made in Hong Kong* (Hong Kong, 1997). Lau's wholehearted support for Hong Kong Cinema is indisputable.

What these filmmakers show us is more than their success and perseverance in helping Hong Kong films survive. Reading between the lines of their comments on this non-genre Hong Kong film *A Simple Life* and Hong Kong Cinema more generally in different media interviews, we can detect a number of concerns that Hong Kong filmmakers are carrying with them. Most notable are the struggles of the once-prosperous mainstream film industry in Hong Kong. The filmmakers reveal the limitations of the filmmaking environment within Hong Kong in recent years and the uncertainty of the future of the Hong Kong film industry when East Asia moves towards a pan-Asian, China-led co-production era.[8] Lau, for example, could have chanted 'Hurray, Chinese Cinema!' instead of 'Hurray, Hong Kong Cinema!' in promoting *A Simple Life*, which is technically a China–Hong Kong co-production that has received serious investment from China. On top of concerns on the industry level, these filmmakers continue to place themselves at the forefront, fighting for a distinct identity of local Hong Kong films that help to define the identity of their fellow Hongkongers.[9]

This book is a treatise on the New Hong Kong Cinema (including the cinematic tradition, film industry and relevant institutional aspects, and individual films) that has developed over the past three and a half decades from the 1980s to the mid 2010s. Hong Kong films made during this era often directly or indirectly concern the 1997 sovereignty handover (or just 'Handover' in short) of the city, whether they belong to mainstream genre traditions or lean towards experimental and non-commercial practice. My main argument is that these films should be discussed, and can be understood more fully, from the angle of 'transitions' in the renewed and continuously changing East Asian regional context in the age of China's rise. Hence, I highlight three related areas of concern here: (1) the New Hong Kong Cinema, (2) its relationship to 'Transitions', and (3) its positioning vis-à-vis China and within East Asia. In turn, they will inform my critical analysis in this book. Situating my argument at the intersection of these three related angles, this book goes beyond the parameters of other theoretical paradigms such as transnational, national or local cinema, in which Hong Kong Cinema is often explored.

The New Hong Kong Cinema

I use the term 'New Hong Kong Cinema' by building on cultural theorist Ackbar Abbas' ideas. Abbas uses this expression to refer to Hong Kong films made since 1982, in order to highlight a special stage of development of Hong Kong Cinema as a response to a specific sociopolitical, historical situation and a cultural space of disappearance related to the 1997 political handover (Abbas 1997: 16–17). Abbas moves on to use this term as the umbrella title of a book series (published by the Hong Kong University Press) under the general editorship of himself and his colleague Wimal Dissanayake (they were joined by film scholars Mette Hjort, Gina Marchetti and Stephen Teo).[10] Each volume presents a close analysis by a scholar or critic of one Hong Kong film (an exception is Marchetti's (2007) study on all three films of the *Infernal Affairs* trilogy in a single book). In the preface of the books in this publication series, Abbas and Dissanayake (no original date; see for example Marchetti 2007, E. Cheung 2009 and Yue 2010) identify further the qualities of the New Hong Kong Cinema:

> *In the New Hong Kong Cinema ... it is neither the subject matter nor a particular set of generic conventions that is paramount. In fact, many Hong Kong films begin by following generic conventions but proceed to transform them. Such transformation of genre is also the transformation of a sense of place where all the rules have quietly and deceptively changed. It is this shifting sense of place, often expressed negatively and indirectly – but in the best work always rendered precisely in (necessarily) innovative images – that is decisive for the New Hong Kong Cinema.*

While Abbas and Dissanayake focus their attention on the cultural and historical importance of these Hong Kong films (on a par with Italian neorealist films, French New Wave and New German Cinema) in a disappearing cultural space in Hong Kong, my usage of the term here in capitals is an extension slightly modified from their concept. Firstly, I stress the fact that new Hong Kong mainstream films offer cinematic representations of residents in Hong Kong (especially of the Hong Kong Chinese). These films are related primarily to a population called 'Hongkongers' on screen, off-screen and/or behind the screen. Given the volatility of different qualifiers that have been applied to the Hongkongers' sense of being, it is logical to think that the identities represented in many Hong Kong films during the Handover transition, which is still ongoing as I will discuss below, should be better understood on multiple levels. Vantage points of reference may include the narrative structures, subject matter, visual and audio styles and so on of these films. Secondly, the commercialism in the Hong Kong mainstream film industry has pushed the boundaries of the New Hong Kong Cinema. Whereas new Hong Kong mainstream films cannot be too formulaic and convey their messages via certain genres only (as Abbas and Dissanayake point out), the filmmakers cannot be extremely auteurist or artistic, especially in Andrew Sarris' sense (1981), and ignore the commercial side of their film projects. Moreover, although most of the films under discussion in this book are considered components of the commercial Hong Kong mainstream film industry, many of them in fact are not indigenous Hong Kong films, because they have significant financial investments and human resources coming from outside Hong Kong. Depending on the contexts in which they are mentioned and explored, these films can be classified as 'Hong Kong films', 'China-Hong Kong co-productions', 'pan-East Asian films' or all of the above at the same time. Prime examples are John Woo's *Red Cliff* and *Red Cliff II* (China/Hong Kong/Japan/South Korea/Taiwan/United States), released in 2008 and 2009 respectively (they are in fact two instalments of a single film; I will thus refer them to as Part I and Part II of *Red Cliff* hereafter) (see my discussion in Chapter Four of this book). To avoid confusion over the origin of these co-produced Hong Kong films, in this text I call them Hong Kong-related Chinese-language films.

To maintain these two characteristics, the New Hong Kong Cinema must engage with (and in) the empirical environs and people of Hong Kong. My first experience of Hong Kong films, unlike that of many of their admirers, did not occur in a movie theatre but at home in Hong Kong when I watched television reruns of small-budget old Cantonese films made within relatively short production periods in the late 1950s and the 1960s.[11] These were a major source of enjoyment in my childhood, but I should admit that these Hong Kong films meant more than pure entertainment to me when I was growing up in my native Hong Kong. Through them, I acquired some snapshot knowledge of the city and people's lives in a recent past of Hong Kong. The more I understand this place and the more Hong Kong-made or Hong Kong-related Chinese-language films from different periods I see, the more I feel these films should be watched and understood not just for the sake of their aesthetic or industrial value, but as a combination of various factors intrinsic and extrinsic to them and to the place they are concerned with.

Therefore, besides being a critical study of recent Hong Kong-related Chinese-language films, this monograph is based on a particular take of how Hong Kong has developed as a city newly under Chinese rule amid new regionalization in East Asia. Those films belonging to the New Hong Kong Cinema I scrutinize here are not only treated as parts of the mass media, nor do they only serve as a sort of lens through which Hong Kong society can be explored. They are also viewed and critically examined as channels, facilitators, catalysts (in some cases), meaning producers and redevelopers influencing the social, cultural, economic, political and historical spheres of Hong Kong. Moreover, in exerting influences on these spheres of Hong Kong, the New Hong Kong Cinema (especially in the senses of film industry and cinematic tradition) has transcended, is transcending and will most likely continue to transcend the interfaces between Hong Kong, China, East Asia and the rest of the world. In particular, I would like to ask throughout this book: (1) Over the past three and a half decades, have Hong Kong films made use of any specific subject matter, plots, aesthetics, characterization, etc., to construct an on-screen world that would reflect the impact of the sovereignty change in real life? (2) How have the target audiences of these films (especially those in East and South East Asia) responded to changes – if such there are – to these filmic elements (in question 1) in Hong Kong-related Chinese-language films? (3) Has the Handover had any direct or indirect political-economic effects on the changes taking place in Hong Kong's mainstream film industry in the context of the rise of China and the rearrangement of East Asia's international relations after the Asian Financial Crisis (1997–98)? (4) How have these changes, as mentioned in the above questions, interplayed with one another, and what lessons might other parts of the globalized world learn from the developments in contemporary Hong Kong Cinema? In the following I will first discuss some special times, places and people, which I believe are so significant to the development of the New Hong Kong Cinema that my analysis of these films would be incomplete without them.

Hong Kong: A Revisit to the 'Borrowed Time' and the 'Borrowed Place'

Firstly, the *time*. The period from the late 1960s to the late 1970s marked the penultimate stage of the 151-year-old British colonial governance of Hong Kong (excluding the three years and eight months of Japanese occupation of Hong Kong during the Second World War). As Richard Hughes opens his famous book *Hong Kong: Borrowed Place – Borrowed Time* (1968: 9) with a snapshot of

Hong Kong in the postwar period: 'A borrowed place living on borrowed time, Hong Kong is an impudent capitalist survival on China's communist *derriere*, an anachronistic mixture of British colonialism and the Chinese way of life, a jumble of millionaires' mansions and horrible slums, a teeming mass of hard-working humans, a well-ordered autocracy' (italics in original). The very same period also saw some of the major incidents elsewhere that are still having repercussions and lingering consequences today: the Cold War (1947–89), the Vietnam War (1956–75), China's Cultural Revolution (1966–76), the 1973 oil crisis ... None of these *seemed* to have any lasting negative impacts on the island in the grand scheme of things. Contrary to the trend in the world's major events, the British Crown Colony as a whole enjoyed a prosperous period in the late 1970s and the 1980s, and would even become one of the Four Asian Tigers.[12] Stock exchanges repeatedly hit historic highs of transactions. The properties and real estate sectors of the city's economy soared to incredible levels. Banking, finances and other service industries also enjoyed their heydays. The whole society followed suit at a rapid pace. Wealth was being seriously accumulated, while the gap between the rich and the poor began to widen quickly. Starting from that period, the Hong Kong Chinese saw they might be quite different from other Chinese communities. They began to explore in other sectors as well, most notably in political and cultural areas, their identity as 'Hongkongers' – an identification that distinguished them from their British colonizers and definitely from their still backward and poor mainland Chinese neighbours.

The *place* itself indeed helps to create this kind of hope and mentality. Geographically Hong Kong is located at the south-eastern tip of China's territory. This location had been doing the place a huge injustice throughout the long history of development of the Chinese governance system, dating back to around 1700 BC. As journalist and historian Martin Jacques (2012) argues in his book *When China Rules the World*, China is in itself a civilization-state, whose central governance operates somewhere in the middle of its vast territory. Thus, Beijing, Nanjing, Louyang and Xian were chosen to be the country's capitals in different periods. The physical location of the governance centre suggests that the Chinese territories located along the country's geographical borders might not have enjoyed the same importance as regards the governance of the whole nation. Located on the country's geographical periphery, Hong Kong has never fallen under the strict and direct administration of the central authorities ever since China was officially united as one nation by Qin Shihuang (the First

Emperor of the Qin Dynasty, 221–206 BC).[13] Arguably, this was also one of the reasons why Qing China (under the Qing Dynasty, which ruled from 1644 to 1912, and was the last in the country's history) ceded Hong Kong, albeit reluctantly, to the British as part of the compensation after the country's defeat in the two Opium Wars (in 1842 and 1860 respectively). Towards the end of the British colonial empire in the late 1960s, Hong Kong as a British Crown Colony benefited from the non-interventionist policy of the Hong Kong British government, which enabled the city to utilize its natural strengths to develop as an entrepôt and a bridge between China and the outside world. It has gradually consolidated its indispensable position as a global city transcending the national and geopolitical confines of its hinterland (Sassen 2001).

Towards Identification with Hong Kong and the Hongkongers' Identity

Finally, the *people*. The specific history and geographical location of Hong Kong have strongly contributed to what makes up the community living there over the years. According to the 2011 Hong Kong government census (released on 4 May 2012), ethnic Chinese residents in Hong Kong stood at a total of 6.6 million, accounting for 93.6 per cent of the territory's entire population of 7.07 million.[14] The majority of the Hong Kong Chinese residents were immigrants or descendants of immigrants from mainland China. They had been regarded by their mainland counterparts and the People's Republic of China (PRC) authorities as members of the overseas Chinese communities (known as *hai wai qiao bao* in Mandarin) before Hong Kong reunited with China politically. In studying the sojourn patterns of overseas Chinese over the past 200 years, Chinese immigration scholar Wang Gungwu (1991a) classifies Chinese emigrants into several categories, including 'trader', 'coolie', 'sojourner' and 'descent or re-migrant'; these categories are based mainly on the various primary reasons for people leaving China. Although Wang arranges these migration patterns chronologically, in reality these kinds of migrations could also be found in periods other than the ones in which they were the predominant kinds.

Due to the convenient geographical proximity, many Chinese emigrants from the south of China might find themselves residing in Hong Kong at some point without the initial intention of staying there forever. During the post-Second World War period, these previous refugees or emigrants witnessed the negative changes in China after the establishment of the PRC. They also saw how the colonial government began a series of beneficial sociocultural policies that

turned out to be useful for the Hong Kong residents to build their local consciousness after the 1967 pro-communist riots and anti-colonialism demon-
strations. With other locals, they have begun to enjoy the effects of economic
prosperity in Hong Kong since the 1970s. They realized their stay in Hong Kong
might be much longer than originally envisaged (Curtin 2003: 215–16; Y-W. Chu
2013: 125). Economically, if not necessarily culturally, they began to identify with
Hong Kong more than with their places of origin in mainland China.

Hence, although many Hongkongers are ethnic Chinese and culturally also
very Chinese,[15] their Chineseness – itself a problematic, controversial, cultural
essentialist and ethnic deterministic concept (Tu 1994; Chun 1996; Ang 1998,
2001; R. Chow 1998: 17) – is inevitably different from that of their co-nationals
in mainland China (see further discussion on 'Chineseness' in Chapter Two).
Cultural critics have found various stages of change taking place in the identification, mentality and worldview of the Hong Kong Chinese throughout the
years (Skeldon 1994c; Tu 1994; Wang G. and J. Wong 1999; Jacques 2012). Over
the colonial history and the post-reunification period, the sentiments and
ways of thinking of the Hong Kong Chinese have been closer to those of the
Chinese descendants settled far from Chinese soil. Theirs can be regarded as
the direct effect of exposure to colonial and postcolonial influences, although it
may depend on individuals how deep such influences can go. The postcolonial
effects they undergo, however, may not necessarily result in nationalist sentiments, as film scholar Laikwan Pang (2007) observes when writing about postcolonial Hong Kong Cinema. The author argues that it is more and more difficult
for the recent Hong Kong Cinema to fit into the postcolonial model, in which
local films are supposed to be employed to assert the newly gained national
status (2007: 423–24). Such ethno-centric nationalist sentiments, nonetheless,
are lacking in many Hong Kong Chinese. Likewise, Hong Kong as a society does
not display such sentiments often.

One might even say that the Chineseness that the Hongkongers display often
changes depending on circumstances. Many Hong Kong Chinese may choose
to align with the mainland Chinese and the Chinese living in other territories (or
countries) when a suitable political, cultural or economic environment prevails.
Recent incidents, such as the fighting for territorial rights over Diaoyu Island,
show that the ethnic Chinese in Hong Kong do align themselves with China on
international relations issues. Yet, many of them also feel uneasy about their
own status as 'Chinese nationals' after the political handover. They fight hard for

their own local distinctiveness, something that might not be deemed appropriate elsewhere on the mainland under the PRC rule.

The identity complex of many Hong Kong Chinese comes to a certain extent from their self-awareness of being 'overseas Chinese' or themselves once being part of the Chinese diaspora (Safran 1991; R. Chow 1993; Ang 2001; W. Cheung 2007: 66–69). As diaspora scholar William Safran (1991: 87) regards, 'diasporic consciousness' is 'an intellectualization of an existential condition'. Seen in the above context, I argue that ideas related to the 'diaspora' paradigm can provide us with an informative starting point for understanding the complicated identification issues of the Hong Kong Chinese, and the pre- and post-reunification Hong Kong. It allows us to be better informed with regard to Hong Kong's relationship with a 'China' that tends to exert its deeply rooted civilization-state posture, to revive its position as a regional big brother in East Asia, and to behave as a country that will become a true world power in the foreseeable future (Katzenstein 2000; Jacques 2012).

Yet, I also believe there are limitations to deploying the strict ideas of this paradigm when analysing the Hongkongers' ever-changing identity negotiations. Media historian and social theorist John Durham Peters (1999: 39) defines diaspora as those people who have to be tolerant of the 'perpetual postponement of homecoming and the necessity ... of living among strange lands and peoples'. In writing about exilic and diasporic filmmakers from Third World countries now residing in the West, diaspora and film scholar Hamid Naficy (2001: 14) defines 'diaspora' as follows:

> People in diaspora have an identity in their homeland before their departure, and their diasporic identity is constructed in resonance with this prior identity. However ... diaspora is necessarily collective, in both its origination and its destination. As a result, the nurturing of a collective memory, often of an idealized homeland, is constitutive of the diasporic identity ... People in diaspora, moreover, maintain a long-term sense of ethnic consciousness and distinctiveness. (emphasis in original)

If the original idea of homeland and home country is not very clear and has at times become a hegemonic 'other', as in the case of many Hong Kong Chinese with their love-hate relationship with 'China',[16] with the current Chinese authorities and with their mainland Chinese counterparts, then perhaps 'diaspora' as a concept does not work perfectly. Still, there is no reason to believe the diasporic paradigm is completely inappropriate here. As cultural theorist Ien Ang (1998: 225) puts it concisely:

> Central to the diasporic paradigm is the theoretical axiom that Chineseness is not a category with a fixed content – be it racial, cultural, or geographical – but operates as an open and indeterminate signifier whose meanings are constantly renegotiated and rearticulated in different sections of the Chinese diaspora ... There are, in this paradigm, many different Chinese identities, not one.

Therefore, we must and should be prepared to use this concept open-mindedly in order to interrogate the very nature of the centre-prone, vertically integrated 'China' influences and 'China' factor when studying the identity issues of the Hong Kong Chinese. At the same time, we can appreciate and highlight the tendency towards a hybridity that diasporic dispersal might result in (Ang 1998: 236).

From People to Films: Local Chinese, Ex-British Subjects, or East Asians?

Understanding how the Hong Kong Chinese perceive themselves and are perceived by others (other Chinese communities and the non-Chinese) is important for us to construct a comprehensive picture of the roles Hong Kong as a society plays in a complex system of international relations, in which China is emerging as a world power. This background also helps me examine the functions and dimensions of Hong Kong films made recently, especially in an era in which the Hong Kong film industry has been declining continuously. For most of its history, the local film industry has operated without assistance from the Hong Kong government (see Chapter Five for an analysis of Hong Kong's film policy). The demise of the studio system that supported most of the film outputs in Hong Kong from the 1960s to the mid 1980s further aggravated the difficulties in filmmaking there. After the last Hong Kong-based production studio Shaw Brothers stopped financing and producing film projects in 1986 and concentrated its investments on its television station, Television Broadcasts Limited (TVB), film productions in Hong Kong have been typically run by small companies with limited investment capital in a form not much different from a cottage industry (except for a few larger independent companies including Cinema City

(1980–91), D&B Films (1984–92) and Golden Harvest (since 1970)[17]) (Bordwell 2000: 1, 70; Chan C. 2000: 9–10, 599–606; S. Chung 2003: 13–14). Hong Kong Cinema enjoyed its heyday in the 1980s and the early 1990s. Domestic box-office earnings and overseas revenue from Hong Kong-made films reached the highest record of HK$3.1 billion in 1992 (£246 million or U.S.$400 million) (J. Chan, Fung and C. Ng 2010: 13). The film industry turned out 239 films in 1993 at its apex (Chan C. 2000: 457), selling films to the domestic as well as overseas markets in East/South East Asia and North America. Hong Kong films had a close to 80 per cent gross local market share in the early 1990s. There were about 15,000 people working in film production in Hong Kong during that period (Szeto and Y. Chen 2013).

Small companies were able to enjoy the film industry pinnacle throughout the late 1980s and in the early 1990s when the economy of Hong Kong was booming. However, in 1994 a recession of the whole film industry began. Critics blame the recession of Hong Kong's film sector on a combination of causes, which occurred at around the same time, such as piracy, overproduction of low quality films, threatening rivalry of Hollywood blockbusters, brain drain of creative labour from the local film industry to the West (mainly Hollywood), changing consumption habit of film audiences and shrinking of both local and traditional overseas markets, e.g., Taiwan (Chung H. 1999: 21–23). It was noted that between 1992 and 1998 overseas revenue of Hong Kong film production dropped 85 per cent. Many small, local film companies in Hong Kong suffered as a result of this recession that turned out to be long term (G. Leung and J. Chan 1997: 147–48). After the local film industry representatives had lobbied for governmental help, it was only in the post-Handover period that the Hong Kong Special Administrative Region (SAR) government set up two funds (the Film Development Fund and the Film Guarantee Fund in 1999 and 2003 respectively) to help the ailing film industry (see discussion on these funding schemes in Chapter Five).[18] And it was as late as 2007 that the local government officially established the Hong Kong Film Development Council (HKFDC) to administer these two film funds, which are notoriously difficult to apply for due to the specific requirements of the funding schemes. On the other hand, the 'return' to Chinese rule, and the signing of the Mainland and Hong Kong Closer Economic Partnership Arrangement (CEPA) in 2003 between Hong Kong and the mainland authorities gave the Hong Kong film industry in the new millennium a hope of penetrating the vast mainland Chinese audience market, which was not available to Hong Kong in the colonial period. The CEPA, in particular, allows Hong Kong film projects to bypass China's strict quota on foreign film import and enter China by way of co-producing films with China-based companies and/or film talent. Working in the discipline of comparative literature, Yiu-Wai Chu (2013: 100–1) notes the difference between contemporary China-Hong Kong co-productions that started to appear in the 1990s, and the 'Mainland-Hong Kong cooperative films' made before the Cultural Revolution and after the open-door policy in communist China. The latter often involved left-wing, pro-communist film companies in Hong Kong and their special relationship with mainland Chinese organizations. These 'cooperative films' are mostly period dramas and were produced outside Hong Kong's mainstream film industry. The more recent China-Hong Kong film co-productions came into being when the mainland Chinese filmmakers began to work with the commercial Hong Kong film industry to produce such critical successes as Chen Kaige's *Farewell My Concubine* (China/Hong Kong, 1993). Their birth coincided with the start of the decline of the Hong Kong film industry.

Lamenting the difficult situation of Hong Kong film professionals, Hong Kong actor Chapman To comments that previously Hong Kong filmmakers might only have cared about how to make good Hong Kong films; now, since 1997, because of the co-productions with the mainland Chinese filmmakers and the gradual integration of Hong Kong cinematic practice into the mainland Chinese one, Hong Kong filmmakers have to care about whether a film can pass China's censorship mechanism.[19] His comments echo Pang's remarks (2007: 424): 'If we consider 1997 the moment when Hong Kong merged back into China to become a city of a nation, the nation is welcomed most wholeheartedly by Hong Kong people on economic grounds, but, culturally, Hong Kong filmmakers continue to see the mainland market as a foreign one'. Like many other film scholars who focus on Hong Kong Cinema and how its functions are going to play out when China's influences are indeed becoming stronger and stronger, Pang's observation has a certain truth (and also hidden worries) in it. Pang is confident enough to say that Hong Kong Cinema will continue to retain its certain place-based local characteristics, as she sees that 'the local is at the core of the transnational' (L. Pang 2007: 427). Yet, like many other film scholars, Pang mobilizes the binary enquiries of local/transnational to study the situation of Hong Kong Cinema.

We can find other similar binaries such as local/national, national/transnational, local/global, colonial/postcolonial presented in scholarly literature on Hong Kong films by other film scholars. For example, Stephen Teo's *Hong Kong Cinema: The Extra Dimensions* (1997) gives a thorough record of how Hong Kong Cinema has developed in both historical and local/national filmmaking respects. Similarly, Yingchi Chu's *Hong Kong Cinema* (2003) uses the national cinema paradigm (see Higson 1989, 1997) to discuss locally made Hong Kong films in relation to China and the United Kingdom. Vivian P.Y. Lee's *Hong Kong Cinema since 1997* (2009) gives an update on Hong Kong films from a cultural studies perspective. Her analysis also emphasizes heavily the 'local' and 'global' (see also Fu and Desser 2000). In light of the ever-changing filmmaking and film consumption contexts of Hong Kong-related Chinese-language films, employing only binary sets of concepts for enquiry will not be sufficient for us to fill in the blanks that might be left as we try to understand Hong Kong's cinematic practice and what it might mean to those who regularly produce and consume the relevant films.

Moreover, being a global city that has been regarded by some as more successful economically than its former colonizer, Hong Kong and its film industry do enjoy a status that cannot fit comfortably within the 'local' category. Grouping Hong Kong Cinema under the category of postcolonial or even global does not work perfectly either. I should also note that for most of these Hong Kong-related films made recently, the national cinema paradigm is not appropriate. As Pang (2010: 140) points out rightly, Hong Kong Cinema has never been 'national' in any direct sense, although other media or film scholars argue otherwise that Hong Kong Cinema 'practically' functions 'as a national cinema in quantity, quality, and stylistic distinctiveness' (Shih 2007: 14). The variety of views among different researchers of Hong Kong Cinema stems partially from the personal theoretical underpinnings of the scholars and partially from the versatile yet ambiguous nature of the distinct Hong Kong cinematic tradition. Hong Kong Cinema never really contributed to the British national cinema when Hong Kong was a British Crown Colony. It had a more intriguing relationship with the cinematic practice in mainland China before the establishment of the PRC in 1949, and later with Taiwan Cinema during the 1960s to the early 1980s.[20] The recent contributions of Hong Kong Cinema to the Mandarin-speaking national cinema of the PRC can best be regarded as a form of commercial partnership and by no means a hard-core 'nationalist' move.

Other existing studies on Hong Kong Cinema, individual Hong Kong filmmakers or films tend to focus on a single area of concern to explore critically, such as the formalistic appreciation, the search for identity, philosophical and literary interpretation, or industrial aspects. Film scholar David Bordwell's *Planet Hong Kong* (2000), for instance, emphasizes the formal techniques used in mainstream Hong Kong films, making a hidden comparison of these films with Hollywood products. For those scholars who deal with the identity and cultural issues in film, they characterize contemporary Hong Kong Cinema as a 'crisis cinema' or as a major part of a 'disappearing culture' right before and/or immediately after the 1997 Handover (Abbas 1997; E. Cheung and Chu Y-w. 2004). When the use of these terms is confined to a specific time frame, they seem to be correct. There is, however, doubt as to using these terms to acknowledge Hong Kong Cinema appropriately when the latter continues to evolve beyond that specific time frame.

While these perspectives may be useful in initiating analysis of Hong Kong Cinema as part of world cinemas,[21] we should be alert to the subtleties of Hong Kong Cinema and the ways different Hong Kong films are produced, distributed, exhibited and received in different highly politicized, spatial-temporal environments. Analysing contemporary Hong Kong films, especially those made after the 1990s, in terms of the above-mentioned paradigms is thus too easy a way of shying away from more in-depth interrogation of the complexity of transnational, (trans-)cultural, political and economic relationships that are still emerging within the geopolitical boundary of East Asia. The latter is a geopolitical context that is still under-studied in existing research of Hong Kong films. Hong Kong Cinema has been playing a paramount role in the region's mediascapes, a role far better recognized in East Asia than in other parts of the world (Appadurai 1990, 1996). This is the reason why this book aims to fill in this gap to understand the New Hong Kong Cinema from the East Asian regional perspective.

The Model of 'Cinema of Transitions'

With the benefit of hindsight, and after years of observing the dramatic evolution of the New Hong Kong Cinema since 1997, I argue for and choose to use the model of 'Cinema *of* Transitions' instead in this book. I seek to obtain better understanding of the most recent developments in Hong Kong Cinema and film culture in multiple areas of concern, and in relation to Hong Kong's transitions over the past few decades in an East Asian setting (Abbas 1997; Y. Chu 2003; L.

Pang 2007: 424, 2009: 84). The term 'Cinema of Transitions' is defined here as any cinema practice, tradition or film industry that demonstrates the ability to *reflexively* adjust and continuously readjust itself in *proactive* response to multiple types of transitions taking place in the surrounding world, whether they be cultural, social, political, economic, historical or religious. The cinematic adjustment could result in a change in the messages films convey, in the quest for human identity the films present, or even just in the transitional restructuring of the film industry of concern.

The manner in which I use the concept thus allows our discussion to embrace more aspects and kinds of transitions than how 'transition' in singular (or as a mass noun) is often used, for example, in denoting newly emerged national cinemas of the post-socialist nations in Europe. Eastern European cinemas, such as the Polish and Slovenian ones, are considered to be 'cinemas *in* transition' (my emphasis) predominantly within the national cinema paradigm or its variants (Sosnowski 1996; Mazaj 2011). Naficy (2008) uses the term 'cinema of transition' (i.e., transition without plural form) to depict those Iranians in film who are in transit in third spaces or third countries. On the other hand, cultural historian Jessica Stites Mor (2012: 9) uses 'transition cinema' to identify those Argentine political films that reflect the transition (to democracy) culture in Argentina. 'Transition' in their cases is mainly related to the change of the political-economic system in the countries concerned and how such change is imprinted on the cultural imagination in films.

Many contemporary Hong Kong mainstream films do depict in their diegetic scenarios the multitude of sociocultural and political transitions in the wider context. First and foremost, part of the society's transition is related to Hong Kong's status change from being a British Crown Colony to a Chinese special administrative region. There are numerous scholarly volumes and monographs devoted to Hong Kong's political transition from British to Chinese rule. Many of them are aligned closely with the perspectives of law and sociology. Not surprisingly, most of these publications came out right before or in the year 1997, during which the actual political handover took place.[22] A few of them were published after 1997.[23] What is particularly interesting is not the fact that these publications were written by scholars studying politics and have a strong focus on the political effects of the city's sovereignty shift, but how these authors regard the 1997-related transition of Hong Kong as something that stopped right at the point when Hong Kong became a Chinese special administrative region.

Transitions

I prefer to adopt a broader and pluralistic understanding of transitions. Hong Kong society had undergone a prolonged process of transitions before and after 1997 that have had multilayered, lingering effects. We have to understand what these 'transitions' actually mean to Hong Kong economically, politically and socioculturally. From an *economic* perspective, Wang Gungwu and John Wong (1999: 8) point out that, due to China's open-door policy, Hong Kong in its last stage as a British Crown Colony had already started to build a closely knit economic relationship with China. Hence, even though there was no formal economic integration arrangement in place before the political handover, the economic transition from the colonial into the postcolonial period has, on the whole, been a smooth one. With China's accession to the World Trade Organization (WTO) in 2001 and its skyrocketing gross domestic product (GDP) in the first ten years after the accession,[24] Hong Kong is one of those China-administrated cities that have harvested economic benefits. For example, it has weathered the effects of the Asian Financial Crisis much better than other South East Asian territories, and is enjoying stronger protection against the Global Financial Crisis that began in 2007. Yiu-Wai Chu (2013), however, expresses his worries for Hong Kong in transition in the age of China's rise as one of the superpowers in a globalized world. The author builds his opinion on Abbas' idea about the 'disappearance' of Hong Kong culture and explores it from a different perspective, highlighting the negative aspects of the changes Hong Kong has been experiencing since the Handover. There was, for example, an overemphasis on the top-down 'Central District Values' (Y-W. Chu 2013: 43–68) caring for 'profitability', 'efficiency', rather than other human aspects of the population during Donald Tsang's administration (the successor of Tung Chee-hwa as the head of the Hong Kong SAR government). In 2001, the local government launched the 'Brand Hong Kong' marketing programme to promote Hong Kong as 'Asia's World City' on a par with London and New York. The programme was updated in 2010. This move, however, ended up marginalizing other core values that truly define the Hongkongers, especially those struggling in the grass-roots social stratum (Y-W. Chu 2013: 70, 74). To Chu, Hong Kong has been 'lost in transition'– the title of his book, in part due to the incompetence of the newly established SAR government (Y-W. Chu 2013: 12–14). In Chu's opinion, Hong Kong can no longer maintain its uniqueness as a capitalist city on Chinese soil after the Severe Acute Respiratory Syndrome (SARS) outbreak in 2003. Many mainland Chinese cities have since been striving to become as 'capitalist' as Hong Kong (or 'Hong Kong-ized' in Chu's words), while Hong Kong has been relying more and more on mainland Chinese capital to sustain its economic well-being (Y-W. Chu 2013: 9–12). Hong Kong's economic transition from being the only capitalist city under Chinese rule to becoming heavily reliant on the huge capital support from the supposedly socialist China has in turn tremendously influenced Hong Kong's political and sociocultural spaces.

Politically, Hong Kong's transitions are manifest in at least two different ways. On the one hand, both the British and Chinese authorities see the Handover as the point when the British transferred Hong Kong's sovereignty to the Chinese at midnight on 30 June 1997. Hence, the official transition was the period that started when both countries signed the Sino-British Joint Declaration in 1984, thereby nailing the destiny of Hong Kong up to the point when the Handover would be completed, that is, 1 July 1997. Yet, on the other hand, we also need to bear in mind that Deng Xiaoping, who was the chief engineer on the Chinese side behind the sovereignty change, advocated an as yet unheard of 'one country, two systems' principle for Hong Kong's supposedly smooth political reunification with China.[25] Under this principle, Hong Kong would be allowed to enjoy a high degree of autonomy to continue having the capitalist system in place, and to have its own political framework and institutional structure for fifty years after 1997, without the interference by the socialist system of the PRC. Operating institutions from colonial years, such as the legal and educational systems, have continued to function in Hong Kong after the Handover. Wang Gungwu and John Wong (1999: 8) emphasize that 'there is neither a clear-cut institutional mechanism nor a firm timetable' for how the 'two systems' will eventually become one. There is also no institutional arrangement for any conflicts that might arise between the two systems (Kuan 1999: 24).[26] Giving the impression of playing it by ear, the political transition (and uncertainty) of Hong Kong is de facto still going on; Wang and Wong (1999: 10) call it 'limbo'.

Socioculturally, as noted by well-known government officials and scholars as well as by ordinary citizens of Hong Kong, the 'real transition' is not about sovereignty but about the identity of the people involved (Wong S. 1999: 182). And to this note I would add that many Hong Kong Chinese have some sort of diasporic experience (first-hand experience or learned knowledge from their parents and grandparents), which further complicates the Hongkongers' identity negotiations at any given time.[27] The Hongkongers' identity transitions thus have countless dimensions and directions. Sociologist Wong Siu-lun (1999: 186–88) in a longitudinal survey (1991–97) identifies four identity transitions: Loyalists (to China), Locals (focusing on Hong Kong), Waverers (wanting to emigrate but being rejected by the countries they are aiming at), and Cosmopolitans (planning and having the resources to emigrate). Irrespective of how much money they earn, how much education they have had and what social class they are in, those who undergo identity transitions from British subjects or stateless Chinese to (involuntary) Chinese nationals[28] are often inarticulate when it comes to expressing the intense emotional complexities that they have to deal with. Not to mention that such emotional conditions often range from cultural embracing or resistance, to psychological readjustment. Constantly changing with situations and circumstances, this identity complex is also interrelated with how a unit of individuals (family or community) feel about themselves and how others perceive who and what they are (Wong S. 1999: 186).

As an example of Cinema of Transitions, the New Hong Kong Cinema entails another level of transition in the society, especially in the commercial film industrial practice that is concerned with film finance, production, distribution, exhibition and reception. There have been several stages of *structural adjustment in the mainstream Hong Kong film industry* since the late 1970s when a clearer direction of genuine local productions addressing concerns of local Hongkongers (and not the 'Chinese nationals' living in Hong Kong) was introduced into the field. In brief, we can characterize contemporary Hong Kong film industry as having started as a local and global-oriented one in the late 1970s and the 1980s. This was the time when the first Hong Kong New Wave directors began their filmmaking career, often using international film festivals as their première platforms. Cultural studies scholars Mirana M. Szeto and Yun-chung Chen (2013) observe that there was a 'mixed system' going on in the film sector of Hong Kong during that period. The system was characterized by 'satellite systems, director subcontracting, and major-minor relations that reflect different power relations between the studios and the independents' (Szeto and Y. Chen 2013). The local film industry then went through shrinkage in the input (finances and human resources in particular), and the amount and quality of output in the 1990s. The 'mixed system' of film production was giving way to a flexible 'independent system', characterized by highly networked, non-contracted film labourers and small companies of less than ten staff members. It then passed to a stage of polarization in terms of types of films (blockbusters versus small-budget indies) in the 2000s and the 2010s. Since the late 2000s, the industry has landed on another mode, where East Asia is both the input source and the output channel. Not only have the types of film output changed rapidly over the last few decades, but likewise the ways of production, distribution, exhibition and reception of Hong Kong-related Chinese-language films. It is expected that Hong Kong Cinema (if this term is to be in use continuously to describe the cinematic practice of films made in Hong Kong) will undergo further transformation again in the near future in order to find a niche of its own in the larger screen industry environments, whether those of China, East Asia or the world. Through stages of structural adjustment of the Hong Kong film industry, we can see that external transitions have not bogged down or worsened the cinematic practice. At times they even become a driving force that impels the constant reinventions, growth and prospering of the cinema of concern. External transitions and the Cinema of Transitions, as in the case of the New Hong Kong Cinema, are therefore working partners (metaphorically speaking) that mutually sustain each other. As long as there are external transitions, the Cinema of Transitions will reflect and respond to these changes internally.

In addition, within the model of Cinema of Transitions, the cinema of concern may itself become a factor intervening in the external transitions. There are numbers of instances of recently made Hong Kong films attempting to intervene in the changes of the city's sociopolitical arena. For example, Herman Yau's *From the Queen to the Chief Executive* (Hong Kong, 2001) questions the hypocrisy of the local law system in handling the cases of twenty-three juvenile delinquents who committed serious crimes (e.g., murder) before 1997 (B. Lee 2002: 26). In real life, these delinquents were supposed to be 'detained at Her Majesty's pleasure' during the colonial era due to their young age, and to wait for the British monarch's final decision on their sentences. However, these young criminals were completely forgotten by the British colonizers when the latter left after Hong Kong's sovereignty change. The new chief executive of the Hong Kong SAR government did not show much concern for these juvenile delinquents either. Ultimately, these young criminals might have to spend an even longer, indeterminate period in prison as opposed to what adult criminals committing similar crimes would have to undergo.

The Cinema of Transitions may even proactively extend its influences to other cultural forms, such as television, animation, video games and comics. Tsui Hark's *A Chinese Ghost Story* (Hong Kong, 1987) is a typical example of film contents 'flowing' across different screen-based media during the time when the Hong Kong film industry was going through structural adjustment in response to the changes in wider sociocultural and political contexts. Tsui's film was loosely based on a short story within the Chinese classic collection of supernatural stories *Strange Tales from a Chinese Studio* (written by Pu Songling approximately in the late 1600s and the early 1700s), and was inspired by Li Han-hsiang's film adaption *The Enchanting Shadow* (Hong Kong, 1960) of the same story. Both 1960 and 1987 films share the same Chinese title *Qian Nu You Hun* (倩女幽魂 in both traditional and simplified Chinese scripts). They tell the fight between a good Taoist and an evil spirit amid the love story between a young man and a beautiful female ghost. Tsui's 1987 film is believed to have spawned three other films under the same family title: *A Chinese Ghost Story II* (Ching Siu-tung, Hong Kong, 1990), *A Chinese Ghost Story III* (Ching Siu-tung, Hong Kong, 1991) and *A Chinese Fairy Tale* (aka *A Chinese Ghost Story*) (Wilson Yip, China/Hong Kong, 2011). Tsui was the producer of the 1990 and 1991 films but was not involved in the 2011 version. In 1997, Tsui directed an animated film based on the same series and entitled it *A Chinese Ghost Story: The Tsui Hark Animation* (Tsui Hark, Hong Kong, 1997). This film series also inspired a 2003 television series of forty episodes under the same title. It was produced and broadcast in Taiwan (then broadcast in Hong Kong in 2006). The television series features Hong Kong, mainland Chinese and Taiwanese actors, who were not involved in any of Tsui's *A Chinese Ghost Story* films.

Cinema of Transitions and Interstitiality

An essence of the Cinema of Transitions is its quality of being interstitial. The New Hong Kong Cinema and the transitions it has been reflecting in the past thirty-plus years since the Handover news was announced come closest to an interstitial style of cinema in Naficy's accented cinema theory (proposed in 2001), despite the obvious place-specific differences between Hong Kong and the accented filmmakers' places of origin. In Naficy's proposition (2001: 10), the accented films are made by filmmakers predominantly from 'Third World and postcolonial countries (or from the global South)' who have gone into exile or diaspora because of decolonization and other political changes taking place in their home countries since the 1960s. They have managed to find their ways to make films again within the mainstream filmmaking systems of the West after migrating to the United States and various European countries. Owing to the specific political-cultural transitions of their identities, their filmmaking style and filmmaking process have also undergone drastic changes. As Naficy argues:

> If the dominant cinema is considered universal and without accent, the films that diasporic and exilic subjects make are accented ... the accent emanates not so much from the accented speech of the diegetic characters as from the displacement of the filmmakers and their artisanal production modes. (Naficy 2001: 4)

> To be interstitial, therefore, is to operate both within and astride the cracks of the system, benefiting from its contradictions, anomalies, and heterogeneity. It also means being located at the intersection of the local and the global, mediating between the two contrary categories, which in syllogism are called 'subalternity' and 'superalternity'. As a result, accented filmmakers are not so much marginal or subaltern as they are interstitial, partial, and multiple. (Naficy 2001: 46–47; my emphasis)

According to Naficy, diasporic and exilic filmmakers making films in the West often refer to their places of origin and displacement experience. These films are therefore 'accented' (Naficy 2001: 4). Here, Naficy uses the linguistic term 'accent' in order to suggest a distinctive particularity of certain cinemas: if the classical and the new Hollywood cinemas are free from any overt ideology and accent (i.e., the neutral one), then by extension all alternative cinemas are accented (Naficy 2001: 23). We may adapt Naficy's idea of accented cinema to the case of the New Hong Kong Cinema where we can find cinematic expressions of the Hongkongers' diasporic experience and interstitiality: *if the dominant film industry is becoming a China market-oriented film industry that is based in mainland China and is heavily charged with the Sinocentric ideology, then the New Hong Kong Cinema is accented in the sense that it is transitional and interstitial.*

The sense of interstitiality in the case of the New Hong Kong Cinema has been a troubled one, precisely because it is hidden under a thick veneer of commercialism (Abbas 1997: 17–18; M. Berry 2005). Yet, the more this cinematic practice's interstitiality lies hidden below the surface, the more it is betrayed by all sorts of clues contained in the films and picked up effortlessly by target audiences who have similar concerns. Far from leading to ghettoization or marginalization, the interstitiality of the New Hong Kong Cinema tends to work for proactive transcendence, enabling the cinematic practice, and what it depicts, to circumvent the orthodox geopolitical constraints of particular locales, cities or nations. Ultimately the New Hong Kong Cinema firmly maintains an advantageous position, as it reaps rich harvests in good times and weathers adversities in bad times.

Hence, Abbas' (1994: 65) mention that Hong Kong Cinema 'is both a popular cinema and a cinema of auteurs' is not entirely correct. Many Hong Kong mainstream filmmakers, including those whom critics praise as being auteurs, would always have, first and foremost, the goal of surviving in the film business by securing financial resources and maintaining sufficient box-office income (Ngai and Wong K. 1997: 97; M. Berry 2005: 422–542). It follows that even when these mainstream filmmakers have wished to address some sociopolitical issues of Hong Kong, instead of the constraint of political censorship, their concern has mostly been the financial conditions of their film projects and their livelihood (Sek 1988: 15; Teo 1988; Lo Y. 1997; K. Ng 2009). These two seemingly contrasting concerns have been haunting Hong Kong filmmakers for a long time. Striking a balance between caring for ideological, society-related topics in films and playing by the rules of the game in the commercial filmmaking industry has become one of the most imperative tasks of many Hong Kong mainstream filmmakers. At the same time, their success stories in filmmaking offer us abundant material for exploring and appreciating film practices in different places.

Naficy's theory covers a wide range of areas that are the components of the 'accented style' (in the author's words) the accented filmmakers employ to reflect their diasporic and exilic identity after re-establishing their filmmaking careers in the West (Naficy 2001: 289–92). These areas of concern include accented films' visual style, narrative structure, characters and characterization, subject matter, structures of feeling, accented filmmakers' own location and authorship, as well as their specific mode of film production, distribution, exhibition and reception activities. This theory and its areas of discussion thus serve as a highly adaptable theoretical framework that we can utilize to examine the New Hong Kong Cinema as an example of the Cinema of Transitions. It also informs the structure of this book and the realignment of several seemingly separate issues regarding Hong Kong-related Chinese-language films. I will return to this point in the last section 'About the Research and the Book' of this 'Introduction'. For now, we will discuss how the New Hong Kong Cinema has remained firmly an identifiable unit against the backdrop of recent developments in China and East Asia.

East Asia in the Twenty-first Century: Concepts and Perspectives

While Hong Kong film culture has come to reflect the economic, political, social and cultural concerns of the Hong Kong Chinese, we can no longer confine Hong Kong-related Chinese-language films to 'local', 'global' or a portmanteau 'glocal' that consists of the two. Instead, we should turn to an already emerging new direction that makes more visible the understated component within the global-local paradigm, i.e., the redefined regional film cultures in an 'East Asia' that is undergoing the latest round of regionalism. This reconsideration is especially necessary in view of the dramatic international relations triggered by the rise of China, U.S. preoccupation with Middle Eastern issues and its interests in the Asia-Pacific region in the twenty-first century (Campbell 2011), and the Global (mainly Western) Financial Crisis.

The New East Asian Regionalism

The regionalism and regionalization characteristics of East Asia should not be confused with that of the European Union or the two Americas. International relations expert Peter J. Katzenstein distinguishes between 'regionalism' and 'regionalization'. According to Katzenstein (2000: 354), 'Regionalisation describes the geographic manifestation of international or global economic processes. Regionalism refers to the political structures that both reflect and shape the strategies of governments, business corporations and a variety of non-governmental organisations and social movement'. When Katzenstein wrote about East Asia's 'new regionalism' in 2000, in East Asia there were two political-economic centres, China and Japan. In little more than ten years, however, the situation in East Asia changed drastically. Jacques (2012) stays away from a Euro-American perspective and looks at East Asia's (in particular China's) progress from the historical perspective of Chinese civilization. He notes that China will soon become the single most important power in East Asia, first, through its economic prowess in the post-WTO accession years and, second, through revitalized cultural influences. Jacques' assumption represents a still somewhat homogenous approach to treating and understanding Chinese people, especially as he does not delve deep into the cultural and racial conflicts between different Chinese communities or into the Hong Kong Chinese community's uneasiness about returning to the rule of PRC. However, his emphasis on China's being a civilization-state (and not a nation-state in the modern sense) offers strong support to his arguments that China's approach to the entire world is going to be very different from what the West (of which Europe and the United States are the two cornerstones) is familiar with. Jacques reminds his readers that China is not just the nation-state it has 'recently' become (in the last one hundred years approximately). It is, in the author's words, 'the oldest continuously existing polity in the world' (Jacques 2012: 244). He also notes that:

> When the Chinese use the term 'China' they are not usually referring to the country or nation so much as Chinese civilization – its history, the dynasties, Confucius, the ways of thinking, the role of government, the relationships and customs, the guanxi (the network of personal connections), the family, filial piety, ancestral worship, the values, and distinctive philosophy, all of which long predate China's history as a nation-state ... Chinese identity is overwhelmingly a product of its civilizational history. The Chinese think of themselves not as a nation-state but as a civilization-state ... its multitudinous layers comprising the civilization-state, with the nation-state merely the top soil. (Jacques 2012: 244)

Understanding how China works and thinks as a civilization-state, rather than just a nation-state, is important, as it will help us understand how the Chinese (particularly those of the mainland) behave towards one another and towards the non-Chinese. Jacques detects the often overlooked racial discriminatory attitudes the ethnic Chinese generally have towards peoples of darker complexion,[29] combined with ignorance of racial difference within China. He also discusses the possibility that China's rise might lead to a renewed expression of the age-old China-centred tributary system (encompassing some of the past East Asian tributary states, such as Japan and Korea), the modern East Asia (ASEAN+3) summit in the late 1990s and the 2000s being an important hint of such a tendency (Jacques 2012: 347, 374–405).

Rey Chow (1993: 9), herself a Hong Kong-raised cultural theorist now living in the United States, also protests against the Chinese 'hegemony' in her book *Writing Diaspora*. Chow disapproves of the cultural essentialism that results from Chinese 'hegemony', and of the Chinese identity being imposed upon those people of Chinese descent who hold a culturally pluralistic view. The author argues that such moves demonstrate a focus on consanguinity that violently demands total submission of the ethnic Chinese to a hollow Sinocentrism

(Chow 1993: 24–25). Chow advocates that people should 'unlearn' their sub-mission to their ethnicity and acknowledge the more realistic cultural identity negotiations often demonstrated by her fellow Hong Kong Chinese.

What is common to Jacques' and Chow's writing is their acknowledgement of Sinocentrism (or 'the Middle Kingdom mentality') (Jacques 2012: 294–341), an ideology rarely discussed and taken for granted in scholarly works. It focuses on 'China' as a modern nation-state, a civilization, a race and even a cultural concept. The concept of 'cultural China' put forward by neo-Confucian Tu Wei-ming in *The Living Tree* (1994: 1–34) provoked much controversy. He argues the need for those who live and work on the 'periphery' of China (i.e., those Chinese descendants who do not live on the mainland) to replace the traditional 'centre' (mainland Chinese) in cultural and intellectual discussions. This should lead to a rethinking of the concept of 'China'. On the surface, Tu's argument looks like a kind of nonconformist disapproval of the absolute cultural elitism in which the mainland Chinese intellectuals are dominant. Ien Ang, however, points out that Tu's definition of three symbolic universes comprising 'cultural China' represents yet another Sinocentric ideology. It highlights the 'periphery' (where Chinese intellectuals in diaspora dominate) instead of the 'centre', and precludes the possibilities of cultural pluralism and diversity among these overseas Chinese (Ang 1998: 228–33). Why, after all, do the overseas Chinese have to think and act only like 'Chinese', and why does the thinking of 'cultural China' have to be initiated by intellectual communities? A strong marginalization of non-intellec-tual ethnic Chinese communities who think and act otherwise but most likely form the great majority of the Chinese diaspora is easily detected here. As we shall see in my discussion in Chapter Four, the cultural Sinocentrism and feeling of superiority could be as dangerous as any other essentialist ideology, such as German Nazism or Italian Fascism, that glorifies one's own culture and history while potentially marginalizing, ignoring and, in the extreme case, killing off other cultures and peoples.

The awareness of the possible effects of cultural Sinocentrism is very impor-tant if we are to understand how modern China, attempting to be a continu-ity of its civilizational past, is proactively influencing its own nationals and the overseas and returned Chinese communities to perceive themselves and others. This in turn influences the ways these different ethnic Chinese communities construct *a* Chinese identity more on the basis of Chinese culture and history than on the modern notions of nationality and citizenship (Wu 1994: 148–49).

The cultural-political effects also extend to the interactions of these communities and individuals within and beyond cultural-industrial sectors like the film industry, practitioners of which are often involved in working with colleagues from various countries. As Jacques (2012: 343) notes, 'The way in which China handles its rise and exercises its growing power in the East Asian region will be a very important indicator of how it is likely to behave as a global power'.

The New Hong Kong Cinema as One of the Most Prominent Components of the East Asian Film Industries

To reiterate, this book has chosen to focus on Hong Kong Cinema of the last thirty-plus years. Special attention is paid to this cinematic tradition's relation to China on the rise in an East Asian setting. It explores the manner in which the New Hong Kong Cinema has been influenced by a love-hate relationship with the cultural Sinocentrism at home (in Hong Kong and elsewhere in mainland China) and, more significantly, in other parts of East Asia.

Why do we shift Hong Kong Cinema from the usual transnational or national cinema paradigms and reposition it instead in the (new) East Asia paradigm – a regional and cultural concept that was perhaps less important for Hong Kong Cinema in the Cold War period than after the Asian Financial Crisis? In other words, why is it essential for us to understand how contemporary Hong Kong Cinema has been moulded to become a part of China-led, East Asia-oriented film business?

With more and more archival materials being explored and published in different scholarly studies in recent years, we can now understand that the film industries in East Asia have been prone to working and doing business interdependently in different historical periods, including the most recent one (see, for example, Yau S. 2010; Sugawara 2011; DeBoer 2014). The phenomenon in today's East Asian collaborative film business world finds a surprising parallel in the 1950s and the 1960s as well as in much earlier periods. Initiated by key players in the film scene in the East Asian region, this kind of interrelationship among different East Asian film industries has gone beyond individual East Asian film industries' aim of fighting against the invasion of Hollywood products. It has also accomplished more than just the promotion of national film products of each country in East Asia. The Shaw family, for example, has been one of the dominant players in the region (see, for example, Wong A. 2003; Fu 2008). Throughout the years, the Shaws have changed from their earliest form,

Tianyi (aka Unique) Film Productions in Shanghai (established in 1925), through to a reincarnation in Hong Kong as Nanyang (established in 1937; renamed as Shaw and Sons Limited in 1950), and the establishment of Shaw Brothers (HK) Limited (1958–2011), to its present mode of producing films under various companies of the Shaw conglomerate. By the 1950s and the 1960s, Shaw Brothers had firmly established branches of production, distribution and exhibition across East/South East Asia, becoming the biggest film studio in the region. Besides building a film kingdom with branches operational in various places, the Shaws also worked with some of the biggest players (film studios) in East Asia (most notably Japan's Shochiku, Toho, Daiei (acquired by Kadokawa in 2002), Toei and Nikkatsu) to weave a tight regional film business network. Together they launched in 1954 the first film festival in East/South East Asia chiefly for film marketing purposes (see K. Yau 2003; R. Cheung 2011c: 203–4; Iordanova 2011: 11).[30] Initially known as the Southeast Asian Film Festival, the event was renamed in 1957 as the Asian Film Festival; then in 1982 it was further renamed as the Asia-Pacific Film Festival, the title that is still in use today (S. Lee 2011: 242–46).

Therefore, from a historical point of view, the late 1990s to 2010s actually witnesses a revitalized, rather than a completely new, phenomenon of collaboration (in the areas of film financing, production and marketing) and resources sharing within East Asia. We see it happening in some of the most successful mainstream East Asian films of the new millennium, the latest being Wong Kar-wai's *The Grandmaster* (China/Hong Kong, 2013) on the biographic story of martial arts master Ip Man. Successful projects do not involve key film companies only. There are also profitable co-produced films that are made on smaller budgets. They find their niches and enjoy positive box-office/critical reception. We can easily find some examples among those made and distributed by Peter Chan's Applause Pictures (established in 2000) (Davis and Yeh 2008: 93–99).[31]

Several East Asian and Chinese-language cinema experts have considered using East Asia as the main vantage point of their studies. From an industrial-cultural point of view, Darrell William Davis and Emilie Yueh-yu Yeh (2008: 1) argue that a discussion of East Asian screen industries as a whole will better reflect the significant restructuring and transformation of all film industries in specific East Asian localities involved. The authors consider aspects of film industries in the region, ranging from film policies and funding opportunities to trans-border production and talent sharing. What they have found to be the latest trend in the 2000s is 'increasing decentralisation, deregulation, and regional cooperation'

(Davis and Yeh 2008: 3). In writing about the political economy of the first genuine co-produced China-Hong Kong blockbuster, Zhang Yimou's *Hero* (2002), Anthony Fung and Joseph M. Chan (2010: 203) discover a rational economic calculation in the production of the film. The authors believe *Hero* follows an international market structure: the Asian, including the Chinese, audience market serves as a barometer for the American market, which in turn influences either positively or negatively the film buyers in Europe (see also Curtin 2007: 25). From a cultural studies point of view, as suggested by Jonathan D. Mackintosh, Chris Berry and Nicola Liscutin (2009: 8–9), a regional perspective underscores the ongoing cultural negotiations between the dichotomy of 'global' and 'local'. It also intervenes in postcolonial approaches to globalization, which has been seen as a Western-led ideology to be followed by the rest of the world. Similar to its ever-changing geopolitical parameters, 'East Asia' as a cultural entity and ideological concept is bound to undergo continuous constructions and deconstructions (Mackintosh, C. Berry and Liscutin 2009: 21–22; see also R. Cheung 2011a: 42–43).

The regional interdependence in film and other screen industries is not without problems. It raises the question of industrial biases and the consolidation of the more powerful film business players in the region. As media and cultural studies scholar Kōichi Iwabuchi (2009: 26–27) observes, instead of de-Westernizing the media cultural flows, what has been happening in East Asia in the past fifteen years or so places the United States again in the dominant position. This is made possible by the growing dominance of multinational media conglomerates that have connections with the country. However, with the rise of China, the government of which is keen on developing the nation's cultural and creative industries, there is increasing evidence that the key players of East Asian film industries are of Chinese origin and are mostly based in Beijing. Cases such as China Film Group Corporation (CFGC), Bona Film Group, Huayi Brothers and Wanda Group have enviable financial power of influence, and are usually permitted and backed in various ways by the Chinese central government in operating their film business.[32] As a sanctioned gateway of China's domestic film industry, at least one of these key players, the state-run CFGC, also holds almost absolute control of foreign imported film distribution within China.[33] Moreover, these key industry players do not just aim at selling Chinese film products to domestic and neighbouring markets in East Asia. They are also using East Asia as their hinterland to engage in collaboration with Hollywood to produce English-speaking films, thereby skimming off the most profitable markets, which

Hollywood products used to dominate for decades. As Bruno Wu, the founder of ChinaWood Film and Media Hub in China, says: 'We want to participate in English-language global content, but with Chinese elements and talent that Chinese audiences relates [sic] to' (China's New Global Strategy 2012).

This situation of asymmetrical interdependence (and power relations), with Chinese film companies that are operating at certain economic and political advantages, seems to echo the China-centred tributary system in the realm of international relations I discussed above. Some might argue that this bears a similarity to the marginalization and oppression already prevailing in the bipolar world (Mackintosh, C. Berry and Liscutin 2009: 15–16). However, we should also have in mind that such an asymmetrical relationship among film industry players in East Asia is not imposed single-handedly by China. Neither does it imply that there are no big film business players in other parts of East Asia: we can see that South Korea and Japan have their own 'big shots', like CJ E&M Film Division (formerly CJ Entertainment) in South Korea and Toho in Japan. The way that other East Asian film business players have chosen to benefit from the success of their Chinese counterparts may suggest that: (1) these other East Asian players are content to work under the leadership of those leading players from China at the dawn of the twenty-first century, (2) they are accumulating and saving up their own resources before coming to the fore again, (3) they are looking at other markets besides those in their own countries and East Asia, (4) they do not mind imitating China's ways of operating its film business for specific reasons, even to the extreme extent of being Sinicized in various ways. Whichever is the case, the picture is bound to be very complicated and intriguing.

In these seemingly Chinese-dominated situations, as far as film industries in East Asia are concerned, Hong Kong Cinema's role in the industrial, cultural, geopolitical and economic arenas of China and East Asia has not only been well maintained, it has also been highlighted in official records. For example, in 2003, the Centre for Cultural Policy Research of the University of Hong Kong published a 'Baseline Study on Hong Kong's Creative Industries' for the Hong Kong SAR government. Hong Kong's film and video industry was highlighted among the eleven creative industries under study (The Centre for Cultural Policy Research of the University of Hong Kong 2003: 104–11). Moreover, there have been more and more signs of the reinvention of Hong Kong's cinematic practice in the twenty-first century amid China's rise, and the latest development of East Asian and global film business (see, for example, A Description of China's Film

Industry 2007; Coonan 2009; Shackleton 2012c). Some recent phenomena with regard to Hong Kong-related Chinese-language films since the turn of this millennium include:

1. Appealing to a pan-Chinese film market is apparently the most popular way for the China-Hong Kong as well as pan-East Asian co-production projects to maintain a strong regional and international presence. The subject matter and talent employed also show a deliberate consideration of the Chinese audience market.[34]

2. Hong Kong local films test the regional water with their local relevance in the use of visual elements and their audio distinctiveness before going beyond East Asia (for example, insistence on the use of Cantonese language to maintain Hong Kong's local identities, despite full awareness that Cantonese-speaking films may have linguistic and cultural limitations in reaching Mandarin-speaking film audience communities in China).

3. In the Hong Kong film industry, between the level of co-produced blockbusters and that of low-budget local film productions there is one other film-making stratum, albeit a much less visible one. In it we find some Hong Kong directors occasionally making films that are not characteristics of their typical oeuvres (for example, big-budget filmmakers making low-budget films, or inexperienced filmmakers participating in expensive co-productions).

4. Hong Kong has made itself an excellent candidate for illustrating communications scholar Michael Curtin's argument (2003, 2007: 14–19) about 'media capital', which attracts immigration of creative labour. It has a well-established community of filmmakers, actors and other kinds of talent. Moreover, Hong Kong film viewers are one of the major sounding boards of Hong Kong-related Chinese-language films.

5. Hong Kong film financiers and film executives have a forward-looking attitude and flexible operational modes. They are the chief cultural-industrial representatives of Chinese-language films. They are also the first collaborators of foreign film executives who might want to take advantage of Hong Kong's signing of the CEPA with China, so as to enter the huge mainland Chinese audience market (Petkovic 2009; Fung and J. Chan 2010: 205–6).

6. The Hong Kong SAR government has made the decision to promote the film industry as one of the core cultural industries. This in turn inspires the mainland Chinese film industry's changing mode of doing business.

7. The Hong Kong International Film Festival (HKIFF) and its related events (e.g., Hong Kong International Film & TV Market (FILMART), the Hong Kong-Asia Film Financing Forum (HAF) and the Hong Kong Film Awards) together form one of the main regional film hubs with regard to film trade, marketing and distribution.

Hence, while Hollywood remains the biggest film industry player in a more and more globalized world, the once homogenized East Asia deserves a closer study as the Chinese film industry now becomes the powerhouse of the region while Hong Kong Cinema is one of the most distinct frontiers of East Asia's film sector.

About the Research and the Book

In discussing the transitions that are closely related to Hong Kong as a society and how the Hong Kong film industry operates under such circumstances, I strongly believe that an analysis pertaining not just to one or two facets but various different ones of the New Hong Kong Cinema can anatomize the issues more thoroughly than otherwise. Here we do not only deal with the human identity quest often revealed in film, but we also explore how underlying ideologies of individual films and filmmakers have influenced the actual operation of film as a cultural and creative industry. My purpose is to display the interlocking manner of these facets of the New Hong Kong Cinema. In doing so, I do not intend to highlight or downplay any particular area of this cinematic practice. To achieve this purpose, my multidimensional methodology has helped me carry out the research tasks. Over more than eleven years of investigations of the New Hong Kong Cinema, I have conducted numerous rounds of textual analysis of films. I have also conducted online and offline study of old newspapers and film trade press, archival research, field surveys at film festivals, personal interviews with film industry insiders, and online surveys of written chat room conversations. These research activities have been helpful for me to understand the contexts of the making, distribution, exhibition and reception of Hong Kong related Chinese-language films. They also allow me to examine critically how the New Hong Kong Cinema has accumulated its cultural and economic values via these various functions along its 'value chain', to borrow the concept from business management. Although my research approach to the New Hong Kong Cinema is mainly qualitative, I have also employed quantitative data in certain parts of my analysis.

As I mentioned earlier, Naficy's accented cinema theory and the areas it regards as components of the accented style (Naficy 2001: 289–92) inform the way I see apparently separate issues of Hong Kong films as parts of a closely integrated entity within the model of Cinema of Transitions. For the purpose of easily presenting these issues that intertwine with each other in reality, I will deal with them as a structure. The first three chapters in this book can be viewed as the book's pivot. They cover interrogations pertinent to the matters of the films themselves and the film production, as a consequence of the diasporic and interstitial experience of the Hongkongers (Hong Kong Chinese being the majority of this population) over the course of colonial and postcolonial history. In order to show the extent of the issues of concern found across a wide range of films, I select an array of film examples to illustrate and illuminate my points within the confines of each chapter.

Chapter One critically examines the use of 'journeys' and 'journeying' in Hong Kong-related Chinese-language films. As Naficy observes (2001: 4–6), the accented filmmakers are often preoccupied with place and displacement. Various kinds of journeys become cinematic tools with which filmmakers express struggles over identities. Naficy chooses specific places, spaces and vehicles as his 'privileged' sites to investigate journeys and related subject matter in accented and exilic films. Similar to these accented films, the New Hong Kong Cinema often features journeys and journeying. Extending from Naficy's ideas, I focus my discussion not only on the journeys per se, but on three stylistic areas – subject matter, way of developing characters and narrative structure, where journeys and journeying are typically employed in new Hong Kong films to unveil the Hongkongers' identity negotiations.

According to Naficy (2001: 275, 290), accented films tend to feature foreigner or outsider characters to show the films' and the filmmakers' interstitiality. The typical characteristics of these characters include speaking the dominant language in film with an accent. They carry with them an air of alienation and loneliness. Many of these roles are played by non-actors or amateur actors. Bearing in mind the interstitial quality of accented films, in Chapter Two I look at several types of outsider characters that are often featured in new Hong Kong films. These characters are from Vietnam, mainland China and other parts of South East Asia; some of them are hand-drawn, non-human animated figures. Not only are they fluent in the Cantonese Chinese language, which is the mother tongue of most of the Hong Kong Chinese residents, these outsider characters are able to speak the language without any accent. Their presence in film raises questions, such as: why are they the lead characters in the first place, if the New Hong Kong Cinema is supposed to be about the city and people of Hong Kong? What roles do they play in helping the Hong Kong Chinese to look inwardly to their own qualities being 'Chinese'? I explore in this chapter how these supposedly non-Chinese characters provide an indirect route for the Hong Kong Chinese (filmmakers and audience alike) to perceive themselves from a different angle during periods of transitions.

Chapter Three draws on the idea of accented filmmakers' authorship to discuss the vision of four different types of Hong Kong filmmakers and their self-inscription in film in the context of Hong Kong's transitions. Naficy's original idea on the accented filmmakers' authorship (2001: 34) is to 'put the locatedness and the historicity of the authors back into authorship', as 'authors' are free from a definite expression in pre-structuralism and post-structuralism. Filmmakers of accented films assume multiple roles, mostly as a way to perform their selves. They can be the author, narrator or simply a subject in film (Naficy 2001: 291). Borrowing Naficy's concept, the 'locatedness' and the 'historicity' of filmmakers in the New Hong Kong Cinema refer to the place Hong Kong and the Handover respectively. Yet, unlike the archetypal accented filmmakers identified by Naficy, many Hong Kong filmmakers cannot show their existence directly on screen, due to the commercial nature of their films. The demand of senior film executives, film distributors and viewers may be more influential than the filmmakers themselves in determining how filmmakers inscribe or do not inscribe themselves in film, and the image filmmakers create for themselves inside and beyond their films. Ann Hui represents those who work between commercial and art-house productions. Johnnie To is a firm believer of film commercialization. Fruit Chan presents himself as a grass-roots independent filmmaker with a highly skilled marketing mind. The 'New Generation Directors' are still struggling with their filmmaking endeavours. For this reason, it is interesting to study the authorial concerns and vision of these different Hong Kong filmmakers when they feature the life of the under-privileged or social underdogs – a common theme that shows their love of the city and people of Hong Kong, and their worries amid the place's historical transitions.

In the field of film studies, the film audience is often under-explored or is not usually deemed a core research area. In Chapter Four I bring the film audience into my consideration by interrogating the New Hong Kong Cinema's state of transitions and interstitiality from the perspective of film audiences. I believe it is important to unearth audience reception information of Hong Kong-related Chinese-language films that the box-office data or professional film critics would not be able to provide. To accomplish my task, I trace the reception of the Chinese-language mega blockbuster *Red Cliff* (Part I in 2008 and Part II in 2009), as a representative of the New Hong Kong Cinema, among its various ethnic Chinese film viewing communities in East and South East Asia. These audiences in the region are traditionally Hong Kong Cinema's major target markets (Hau 2012). I give details of a series of original online surveys and a follow-up survey of their viewing experience. In this research, I found that the command of spoken and written Chinese languages, and the knowledge of Chinese history, did help many of these film viewers articulate their diverse opinions on the film, which are quite different from the director John Woo's initial directorial vision. These audiences' existential conditions and their spectatorial responses thus add one more dimension to our discussion of the state of diasporic mentalities and transitions found in the New Hong Kong Cinema.

In Chapter Five I explore the newest East Asian film business network that has evolved since the Asian Financial Crisis attacked the region. There, we can see the combined influences of the political-economic frameworks of different East Asian territories on shaping the region's film industries and business. My purpose is to find out how the New Hong Kong Cinema operates astride and within the interstices found in this regional context, in which several cinematic hubs interact, collaborate and compete with each other in conducting film-related activities. These cinematic hubs, which I call nodes, include Beijing, Shanghai, Tokyo, Busan, Taipei and Hong Kong. My discussion focuses on the respective national/sub-regional film policies affecting these East Asian film business nodes, and these nodes' complicated relationships in maintaining their network of activities. In this regional film landscape, the New Hong Kong Cinema's role during transitions is again highlighted when China is increasing its influence in East Asia and throughout the rest of the world.

This book concludes with a summary of my arguments for looking at the New Hong Kong Cinema as a Cinema of Transitions. Hong Kong Cinema's ever-increasing importance as one of the sharpest frontiers of the East Asian film arena makes it a natural engine, and a prime example, for the regional and international development of other cinematic practices.

Notes

1. According to the Hong Kong International Film & TV Market (FILMART) (2007), films made with a budget between U.S.$1 million and U.S.$5 million (i.e., between £615,000 and £3 million) are considered 'mid-budget films' in Asia.
2. Source: interview with Ann Hui in 'No Regrets', *A Simple Life* (DVD) (Hong Kong version, bonus track).
3. Source: interview with Ann Hui in the 'Making of', *A Simple Life* (DVD) (Hong Kong version, bonus track).
4. The mainland China box-office figures for *A Simple Life* were reported in *China Film News* (in pinyin, *Zhongguo Dianyin Bao*), and quoted in another entertainment-related website ent.163.com (How Bad n.d.). *China Film News* is under the governance of the State Administration of Press, Publication, Radio, Film and Television (SAPPRFT; formerly the State Administration of Radio, Film and Television (SARFT)) of the People's Republic of China (PRC).
5. Source: interview with Andy Lau in the 'Making of', *A Simple Life* (DVD) (Hong Kong version, bonus track).
6. The specific Chinese language a person uses discloses his/her geopolitical origin. The Cantonese language is the mother tongue of most Hong Kong Chinese. It is spoken as the everyday language there. Unlike the mainland Chinese, the Hong Kong Chinese are still taught to write traditional Chinese written characters in school, although more and more Chinese residents in Hong Kong can also read texts in simplified Chinese characters (which were introduced by the government of the PRC in mainland China in the 1950s). Today, traditional written Chinese is used by the Hong Kong Chinese, the Taiwan Chinese, the Macau Chinese and earlier generations of overseas Chinese living in Europe and the United States. Simplified written Chinese, on the other hand, is used by the mainland Chinese and Chinese communities living in South East Asia, such as those in Singapore and Malaysia.
7. Film information: *Infernal Affairs* (Andrew Lau and Alan Mak, Hong Kong, 2002); *Infernal Affairs II* (Andrew Lau and Alan Mak, Hong Kong, 2003); *Infernal Affairs III* (Andrew Lau and Alan Mak, Hong Kong, 2003).
8. To conform with the general recognition of the status of the nation of China, by the name 'China' here I refer to the PRC, set up by the Chinese Communist Party in 1949 in mainland China. Regarding the Republic of China that was established in 1912 in mainland China and that later resettled in Taiwan by the Kuomintang (i.e., the Chinese Nationalist Party) in 1949, I will refer to it in this text as 'Taiwan'. It also claims to be the true China.
9. The words 'Hongkonger' and 'Hong Kongese' were officially included in the Oxford English Dictionary in March 2014 to refer to a 'native or inhabitant of Hong Kong', although the use of the word 'Hongkonger' dates back to 1870 (Lam 2014). 'Hong Kongese' can also be used as an adjective, 'Of or relating to Hong Kong or its inhabitants'.

10. For a complete list of this series of books, see Hong Kong University Press' official website, www.hkupress.org (accessed 5 May 2015).

11. The local mass media in Hong Kong nicknamed some of these postwar Cantonese films as *tsat yat sin* in Cantonese (or *qi ri xian* in Mandarin; literally, seven-day works) because they were completed over production periods that were in some cases as short as a single week. Not surprisingly, many of them are not of high quality.

12. Hong Kong together with Taiwan, Singapore and South Korea are referred to as Asia's Four Little Dragons (aka Asian Tigers) due to their intense economic growth between the 1960s and the 1990s.

13. There is archaeological evidence of human presence in Hong Kong dating as far back as 39,000 years ago.

14. See 'Nationality and Ethnicity' (released on 4 May 2012) under 'Interactive Visualisations', results of the 2011 Population Census, conducted by the Census and Statistics Department of the Hong Kong Special Administrative Region (SAR) government, www.census2011.gov.hk (accessed 5 May 2015).

15. Jacques (2012: 535, 567–68) highlights the influence of Confucian tradition as one of the persistent and long-lasting cultural influences on ethnic Chinese, as well as on former tributary states to China, such as Japan and Korea (see also Straubhaar quoted in Curtin 2003: 221).

16. 'China' is used here to denote both the country and a cultural-political concept.

17. Golden Harvest was renamed as 'Orange Sky Golden Harvest' in August 2009 after the single largest shareholder Wu Kebo joined the group through Orange Sky Entertainment Group (International) Holding Company Limited. Source: 'About Us', Orange Sky Golden Harvest Entertainment's official website (English), www.osgh.com.hk (accessed 5 May 2015).

18. For details of the two film funds, see 'Film Development Fund' and 'Film Guarantee Fund', the Hong Kong Film Development Council (HKFDC)'s official website (English), www.fdc.gov.hk (accessed 5 May 2015).

19. Interview footage in *News Magazine*, Jade Channel, Television Broadcasts Limited (TVB), Hong Kong. Broadcast on Saturday, 1 December 2012, from 7 PM to 7.30 PM Hong Kong time.

20. For a detailed account of that part of the history of Hong Kong Cinema, see the studies by Stephen Teo (1997), David Bordwell (2000) and Yingchi Chu (2003). Mainland China and Taiwan both claim that their respective cinemas are the real Chinese national cinema. While mainland China still treated locally made, non-co-produced, Hong Kong films as foreign films after the Handover, Taiwan had accepted Hong Kong films as part of its national cinema long before Hong Kong returned to Chinese rule.

21. I refer to 'world cinemas' in the plural in this book, instead of 'world cinema', in order to acknowledge the emergence of different cinematic practices within the once homogeneous 'world cinema' in the discipline of film studies.

22. See the works by, for example, Peter Wesley-Smith (1993) (subject: law), Michael Sida (1994) (subject: history, politics and government), David Newman (1995) (subject: politics and government), Enbao Wang (1995) (subject: politics and government), and Wang Gungwu and Wong Siu-lun (1995) (subject: politics and government).

23. See the works by, for example, Wang Gungwu and John Wong (1999) (subject: interdiscipline), Robert Ash et al. (2000) (subject: economics, politics and government), Robert Ash et al. (2003) (subject: politics and government) and Ralf Horlemann (2003) (subject: history).

24. In 2012, China's GDP stood at U.S.$8,226,885 million (£5,060,000 million). Source: National Bureau of Statistics of China, 22 February 2013.

25. The 'one country, two systems' principle was also planned to apply to Macau (whose sovereignty change from Portuguese to Chinese rule happened in 1999) and Taiwan as well (see Y-W. Chu 2013: 4–6).

26. In practice, however, Hong Kong is not entirely free from China's political interference. Occasional incidents (e.g., the Hong Kong SAR sought interpretation of the Basic Law by the Standing Committee of the National People's Congress of the PRC after the judiciary passed a judgement in 1999 regarding right of abode issues) have led observers to suspect the judiciary independence of Hong Kong in the 'one country, two systems' framework. On 10 June 2014 the Chinese State Council issued a white paper on the practice of the 'one country, two systems' policy in Hong Kong, alerting the pro-democracy camp in Hong Kong of China's intention to further narrow Hong Kong's political freedom (China Media 2014; Hume 2014). The white paper stresses that 'the central government exercises overall jurisdiction over the HKSAR [Hong Kong SAR]' and 'the powers delegated to the HKSAR by the central government ... enable it to exercise a high degree of autonomy in accordance with the law' in the section on 'Establishment of the Special Administrative Region System in Hong Kong' (Full Text 2014).

27. Even after more than seventeen years (at the time of writing) since the official Handover, sociocultural alienation between the mainland Chinese and the Hong Kong Chinese, and between their respective identifications, has not subsided and has influenced a wide array of aspects of people's everyday lives.

28. According to the official information of the Hong Kong SAR government, notwithstanding that a Hong Kong resident had obtained the British National (Overseas) (BN(O)) passport before the 1997 Handover, he/she is a Chinese national in the Hong Kong SAR after the Handover if he/she is of Chinese descent and was born in Chinese territories (including Hong Kong). He/she is, however, not required to give up his/her BN(O) passport, which was the result of a special political arrangement put in place by the British government for Hong Kong citizens before the British gave up sovereignty of Hong Kong. The choice of not having the Chinese nationality status is out of the question, unless one officially applies for renouncement of one's Chinese nationality. See 'Frequently Asked Questions about Chinese Nationality',

the Hong Kong Immigration Department of the Hong Kong SAR government's official website (English), www.gov.hk/en/residents/immigration/chinese/faqnationality.
htm (accessed 5 May 2015).

29. Jacques refers to several such examples in his book. In particular, the author mentions the tragic death of his wife Harinder Veriah, a young Malaysian lawyer of Indian
descent, in Hong Kong in 2000, as being a direct result of serious racial discrimina-
tion at a local hospital. In 2008, this case led the Hong Kong SAR government to
introduce anti-racist legislation for the first time (Jacques 2012: 325). Racial issues
have not gone completely unnoticed by the Hong Kong Chinese population. The
Chinese-language mass media occasionally mention such issues, but usually in connection with other pressing sociopolitical matters. For example, one of the in-depth
news programmes of TVB Jade channel (a Cantonese-language channel), *Sunday
Report*, presented a half-hour broadcast on 25 November 2012 on the topic of foreign children's schooling in Hong Kong. The programme showed that the Hong Kong
mainstream education system had not made any provisions or special arrangements
for the children of expatriates (who lack Chinese language skills) to take lessons in
Chinese if they wished. This indirectly touched upon the problem of the local government's insufficient awareness of the needs of ethnic minorities in Hong Kong.

30. Personal interview with Li Cheuk-to, Artistic Director of the Hong Kong International
Film Festival (HKIFF), conducted by the author in Hong Kong on 7 July 2010 (within
the context of the 'Dynamics of World Cinema' project at the University of St
Andrews).

31. While expensively made East Asian films are usually staples of the mainstream movie
theatres throughout East Asia, they are marketed and exhibited as art-house films
in Europe and the United States. The reverse happens when European mainstream
films and American indies are screened in East Asia's art houses.

32. China Film Group Corporation (CFGC) is the largest and most influential state-run
film enterprise in China. Bona Film Group is the largest privately owned film distributor in China. It develops an integrated business model that encompasses film distribution, film production, film exhibition and talent representation. Huayi Brothers
is China's leading independent television and film production company, which also
diversifies into producing music labels and building movie theatres. The Dalian
Wanda Group operates in the cultural industry as well as in commercial properties,
luxury hotels, tourism investment and department store chains (See China's Wanda
Group Buys AMC Entertainment 2012; Davis and Yeh 2008: 27–28; see also Fung and
J. Chan 2010: 204 (on *Hero*, a film that enjoyed exceptionally privileged promotion
and marketing due to its close connection with the Chinese government)).

33. At the time of writing, CFGC and a smaller film distributor, Huaxia Film Distribution
(CFGC owns 20 per cent of Huaxia's shares), are the only two officially approved film
distributors in China allowed by the Chinese authorities to distribute foreign films
in China on a revenue-sharing basis. According to film trade magazine *Variety*, there

will soon be one more Chinese film distributor allowed to achieve their calibre and release foreign films (China Opens up 2012).

34. There have been worries that Hong Kong filmmaking might soon lose its distinctiveness once it is thoroughly blended with other cinematic practices in the East Asian region, most notably mainland Chinese filmmaking. Counter-comments from both Hong Kong and mainland China uphold that, instead of being 'mainlandized', Hong Kong filmmaking is influencing mainland Chinese commercial films with its specific style of shooting (Sek 2013: 123–24; it is also noted in renowned mainland Chinese actor-director Zhang Guoli's thank-you speech when he received the Best Film from Mainland and Taiwan Award for the film *Back to 1942* (Feng Xiaogang, China, 2012) in the thirty-second edition of the Hong Kong Film Awards in 2013).

CHAPTER ONE

Cinematic Journeys and Journeying in New Hong Kong Films

Hong Kong's relationship to China has always been intriguing. Physically located at the south-eastern tip of China's territory, Hong Kong had not been of key political and cultural significance to China during most of the country's 5,000 years of history. It was not until the British colonizers took over political control of Hong Kong after China's defeat in the two Opium Wars (1839–42 and 1856–60 respectively) that Hong Kong,[1] as a geographical outpost of China and a remotely located colony of the British Empire, began to assume its historical, cultural, and, much later on, economic distinctiveness. Thanks to this distinctiveness from the development of its supposed motherland China after the collapse of the Qing dynasty, Hong Kong has played a very important role in the social redevelopment of the country, especially due to the population mobility that has gone on in China throughout most of the late nineteenth, twentieth and early twenty-first centuries. Unlike the familiar northward movement of the population that has occurred within many Western countries during their periods of national development, Chinese migrants have been moving from the north to the south of China, Hong Kong being the last point of departure of many of these migrants before they finally leave Chinese soil. These moves have predominantly been triggered by major historical incidents, natural and/or human-made disasters and the economic needs of the people to go elsewhere to make their living.

In his book on *China and the Chinese Overseas* (1991a), Chinese immigration scholar Wang Gungwu traces the trajectory patterns of overseas Chinese over the last two centuries, classifying them into the categories of 'trader', 'coolie', 'sojourner', 'descent or re-migrant'. In addition to these four categories, there are at least two other kinds of Chinese emigrants: student (Pan 1999: 62) and illegal emigrant (R. Cheung 2013). These migrant groups and their moves have certainly inspired many Chinese-language films produced on the mainland or elsewhere. In particular, there are Hong Kong-related Chinese-language films, which have been made over the last thirty-plus years, that testify to a sudden increase in the outgoing migration from Hong Kong to Western countries right before and shortly after the 1997 Handover.

This chapter employs the long history of Chinese people journeying across the national border as a major point of departure for the discussion of the New Hong Kong Cinema as a Cinema of Transitions. I would like to raise two questions here to guide the discussion: How have these human migrations changed the self-perception of Chinese descendants as being genuine, or not so genuine, Chinese people? Have they had any profound impacts on the ways different groups of Chinese communities have perceived, loved and despised one another throughout the long history of Chinese civilization? I start with a review of the specific migration experience of the Hong Kong Chinese during the period that led up to the official Handover, and their return migrations. Drawing on diaspora and film scholar Hamid Naficy's argument of journeys and journeying as important elements of accented films, I use 'journeys' and 'journeying' here as the connecting thread to align several Hong Kong-related Chinese-language film examples – *Floating Life* (Clara Law, Australia, 1996); *Happy Together* (Wong Kar-wai, Hong Kong/Japan/South Korea, 1997); *Exiled* (Johnnie To, Hong Kong, 2006); *Days of Being Wild* (Wong Kar-wai, Hong Kong, 1990); *Echoes of the Rainbow* (Alex Law, Hong Kong, 2010); *Bruce Lee, My Brother* (Manfred Wong and Raymond Yip, China/Hong Kong, 2010); and *Song of the Exile* (Ann Hui, Hong Kong/Taiwan, 1990). Regardless of their official places of origin, all these films are about residents of Hong Kong and how they deal with the constant moves in their lives. I further identify three major types of situation whereby journeys and journeying are strongly emphasized in these films: journeys and journeying being dealt with as the subject matter, characters in the film being developed during their journeys or revisits to the past, and films employing 'journeying' as their unconventional narrative structure. My close analysis of these films shows how they can serve as a testimony to the direct and indirect sociocultural effects of the 1997 Handover on Hong Kong society, in particular, in the area of human mobility. By telling us what kind of decisions characters make with regard to their travels and by showing how their decisions might in turn affect their transitional perspectives, these films prove to us that they are not just witnesses but, arguably, also active members of the New Hong Kong Cinema to intervene in the public discourses and shape the public imagination at this historical-political crossroads in Chinese history. Through them, we can also see how 'journeys' and 'journeying' have become significant elements of the New Hong Kong Cinema.

When Journeys Begin

As excellent lenses for studying social lives in Hong Kong over the last three and a half decades, new Hong Kong films are characterized, first and foremost, by the theme of human migrations. More precisely, 'moves', 'migrations', 'journeys', 'sojourns' are among the indispensable elements of these films. Moves into and away from Hong Kong are featured through subject matter, character development and/or narrative structure, which reflect and magnify this reality. In 1994, geographer Ronald Skeldon charted the migration history of the Hong Kong Chinese. In his studies he highlights that Hong Kong itself has been a product of migration, with more than 90 per cent of its Chinese population having their places of origin in mainland China (although by 1981, 57 per cent of the population consisted of people born in Hong Kong) (Skeldon 1994a: 22). The sudden influx of mainland refugees into Hong Kong immediately following the establishment of the PRC on the mainland in 1949, as the author argues, provided the foundation of the 'refugee mentality' of many Hong Kong Chinese and their children/grandchildren. There would still be a few waves of migration out of China into Hong Kong triggered by economic factors, or by major political events, such as China's participation in the Korean War (1950–53), the Cultural Revolution (1966–76) and the June Fourth Incident (aka Tiananmen Square Massacre) (1989). The main consequence of this 'refugee mentality' was that those Chinese migrants who seemed firmly settled in Hong Kong were prepared to move again with the approach of the 1997 Handover, even though their children or grandchildren had been born in the local territory (Skeldon 1994a: 23).

Elsewhere I have termed this mentality 'situational, diasporic consciousness' (W. Cheung 2007) – meaning that many Hong Kong Chinese are aware of their status and mentality as being one of a diaspora in situ, and that they can never become the real PRC Chinese as long as they are legitimate Hong Kong citizens.[2] Their diasporic mindset may be downplayed as long as they are allowed to live the so-called Hong Kong way of life and enjoy Hong Kong's core values in terms of human rights and freedoms, as promised in the Basic Law of the Hong Kong SAR for their lives after 1997. But their diasporic consciousness immediately comes to the forefront whenever their Hong Kong core values are endangered. This was evident in occurrences, such as the Hong Kong SAR government's forceful introduction of Basic Law Article 23 (the basis of a security law) in 2003 and the mainland Chinese way of moral and national education in Hong Kong in 2011 and 2012 (Textbooks Round the World 2012). A great majority of the Hong Kong general public felt that Hong Kong society was being oppressed in these incidents. They responded to these SAR governmental actions, allegedly backed by the Beijing government, by participating voluntarily in sizeable, peaceful street protests and various kinds of public debates (J. Cheung and K. Lee 2003; Fitzpatrick 2003; In the dock 2003). The decision by the Beijing government in August 2014 to set the limits of Hong Kong's electoral reform, in which only a small group of local elite and professionals will be allowed to nominate the city's future government head, further aggravated the situation. This incident led directly to the sizeable civil disobedience movement the Umbrella Movement, which started in Hong Kong on 28 September 2014 and lasted for seventy-nine days. Although the local government cleared the movement forcibly on 11 December 2014, since then the protestors have continued the rally in different formats.

Hence, emigrations occurring just before 1997 can be understood as a specific kind of sociopolitical response of ordinary Hong Kong citizens to the changes in the wider context. With the 'refugee mentality', many of them felt that their circumstances might be adversely affected by the uncertain political, social and economic conditions that the sovereignty change might bring about. Official government estimates in Hong Kong show an annual average of more than 48,600 Hong Kong residents emigrating to other countries between 1987 and 1997, compared to an annual average of 20,000 Hong Kong emigrants in the early 1980s. The number peaked at 66,000 in 1992 before 1997 arrived (Hong Kong 1990, 1991, 1992, 1993, 1994, 1995, 1996, 1997, 1998, 1999, 2000; Skeldon 1994a: 30). The latest data from various countries suggest that the emigration from Hong Kong between 1984 and 1997 could have been as high as 800,000 in total (Sussman 2011: 21–22). Such emigration figures have more significant implications than their purely numerical indications might suggest: in this most recent surge of emigration from Hong Kong, most of the emigrants were university educated, highly skilled and wealthy. They were from the elite of Hong Kong society. Their departure thus meant a serious brain drain from Hong Kong just before 1997. Many of them left Hong Kong as families comprising two or three generations, rather than as the single emigrants in indentured labour typical of earlier waves of Hong Kong emigrations (Sussman 2011: 22). Skeldon highlights that emigration from Hong Kong before the Handover was not triggered by political anxieties alone. There were certainly other reasons that can largely be seen as push factors – such as the Hong Kong Chinese's fears of the imminent Chinese communist rule, or pull factors – for instance, the changing immigration policies in major destination countries, such as the United States, Canada and Australia, which welcomed these Hong Kong elites (Skeldon 1994a: 34–37, 1994b: 4).

Hong Kong's 1997-related emigration was, however, much more complicated than the estimated figures above can show. One reason for this complexity is that available figures are very often only rough estimates, as the Hong Kong government did not gather precise migration statistics (Wong S. 1997). Another reason is that many Hong Kong emigrants did not actually settle down for good in their destination countries. Very often they landed with their families in the host countries and then went back to Hong Kong on their own almost immediately, in order to benefit from the booming economic conditions there, which Western countries were not enjoying. These returnees were commonly nicknamed 'astronauts' (Skeldon 1994a: 39–41, 1994b: 11). A third complexity of emigration trends is that while Hong Kong seemed to have suffered from brain drain during the lead-up period to 1997, there was also an increase in the number of immigration cases into Hong Kong, with many skilled labourers coming in (Skeldon 1994a: 38).

Return migrations to Hong Kong and further north into China additionally complicate this already intricate picture of the most recent migration patterns and the identity layering of the Hong Kong Chinese, a picture not commonly found among remigrants in other territories (Sussman 2011: 7). The Hong Kong Chinese returning after having secured their foreign passports is a trend that many scholars consider to be an economic decision aimed at obtaining better job and entrepreneurship opportunities in Hong Kong and the big cities of China, rather than something related to political attitudes or Chinese nationalism (Ley and Kobayashi 2005: 116). As anthropologist Aihwa Ong (1999: 20, 112) identifies, this kind of 'flexible citizenship' of these returnees had much to do with their economic calculation and was facilitated by the Hong Kong SAR government's immigration policy. Under such policy, these returnees and their families were (still are) allowed to maintain their foreign passports, and to preserve their permanent right of abode in Hong Kong. Arguably, this political arrangement played a primary role in the decision-making process of these Hong Kong returnees when they were pondering the possibility of their return migration. Geographers David Ley and Audrey Kobayashi (2005: 115) estimate that by the mid 1990s, Hong Kong residents holding foreign passports who had returned to live and work in Hong Kong amounted to some 500,000–700,000 people in a local population of 6.5 million. Moreover, such return migration to Hong Kong may not be considered a finality; rather, it might be just one of the many expected or unexpected moves along the 'continuing itinerary' of their lives in a transnational context (Ley and Kobayashi 2005: 113).

The perennial openness to moves makes the Hong Kong Chinese migrants conform to the argument made by Skeldon (1994b: 17) before 1997 that these Hong Kong Chinese migrants are 'exiles, but they are not impelled to move'. His use of the term 'exile' is somewhat in line with the use of the term 'diaspora' put forward by scholars who work in the larger field of diaspora studies. For example, media historian and social theorist John Durham Peters (1999: 39) argues that people in 'diaspora' have to endure the difficult reality of not being able to return 'home' over a long period of time, while the status of 'exile' signifies a desire for 'earthly home' that is estranged (Peters 1999: 39). Naficy has a similar interpretation of the concepts of 'diaspora' and 'exile', and their intriguing relationship with 'homeland'. Where 'exile' traditionally implies banishment or prohibition of return, Naficy distinguishes 'exile' from 'diaspora' as follows:

> *Diaspora, like exile, often begins with trauma, rupture, and coercion, and it involves the scattering of populations to places outside their homeland. Sometimes, however, the scattering is caused by a desire for increased trade, for work, or for colonial and imperial pursuits. Consequently, diasporic movements can be classified according to their motivating factors ... Unlike the exiles whose identity entails a vertical and primary relationship with their homeland, diasporic consciousness is horizontal and multisited, involving not only the homeland but also the compatriot communities elsewhere. (Naficy 2001: 14)*

Unlike the conventional use of the term 'exile', 'diaspora' is then often associated with the collective action of the diasporic subjects (Tölölyan 1996: 24; Cohen 1997: 25). Making reference to different generations of the South Asian diaspora, historian Dipesh Chakrabarty (1998: 472) points out that 'diasporas are internally differentiated around constellations of shared memories'. In other words, diasporas would be understood more comprehensively if the periods and the historical conditions that caused the movement of people out of their places of origin are taken into account. Some scholars of diaspora studies equate such places of origin of diasporas with their homelands or home-nations, which might become part of the identity problems for future generations of diasporas born and living as natives in their host countries (Hall 1990 [1989]; Tölölyan 1991; Clifford 1994; Robbins 1995; Braziel and Mannur 2003: 7–9). As different countries of origin have produced diasporas of different categories, such as expellees, exiles, overseas settlers, refugees, voluntary and involuntary migrants, emigrants, immigrants, etc., in different periods of time, an orthodox definition of 'diaspora' is unlikely to cover all kinds of empirical experiences that global diasporas have had (Safran 1991: 83; Cohen 1997: 21).

While there is certainly a hidden concern with the homeland, Skeldon's term 'reluctant exiles' for describing emigrants from Hong Kong deviates from the conventional use of the terms 'exile' as well as 'diaspora', for these 'reluctant exiles' carry with them complicated economic considerations on top of socio-political reasons that have generated other diasporas, such as the Jewish. They are also different from other segments of the Chinese diaspora, which have a much clearer idea of what 'homeland' means. To these Hongkongers, an imagined homogenous 'China' may not be as important as their actual lives in their real home(land) Hong Kong (S. Chan 1999: 81; Y. Huang 1999: 145). This makes the Chinese diaspora from Hong Kong distinctive when they are represented in films.

Accented Filmmaking and Film Journeys

The prototype of accented films in Naficy's theory places great emphasis on the transitional and transnational places or spaces, in which 'journeys of and struggles over identity' happen (Naficy 2001: 5). These films certainly reflect to a large extent the filmmakers' own unpleasant and marginalized situation in diaspora and exile. According to Naficy, a majority of these filmmakers are from 'Third World and postcolonial countries (or from the global South)' (Naficy 2001: 10). They were displaced from their homelands as a result of decolonization, post-nationalization and/or other kinds of sociopolitical changes at home. Different diasporic or exilic filmmakers often share the commonalities of being liminal subjects when located interstitially in societies and film industries after migrating to the West. We should bear in mind that films featuring journeys may not necessarily be 'accented', but accented films will have to involve certain journeys or journeying to signify the displacement of the filmmakers and/or the characters, and to qualify as products of accented filmmaking. Often initiated by the places of concern, journeys in accented films are either 'deterritorializing' or 'reterritorializing' (Naficy 2001: 222). Once journeys start, they are bound to shape and affect profoundly the experience and, very possibly, the identities of the filmmakers and the characters. The nature of the journeys may sometimes also change along the way. Many journeys depicted in accented films involve not just geographical, but also psychological, metaphorical and philosophical journeys. Among them, home-seeking journeys, journeys of homelessness and homecoming journeys are highlighted by Naficy (2001: 5–6, 33, 222–23). Borders, tunnels, seaports and airports, hotels and motels, trains and buses, and suitcases are typical icons of accented films.

Naficy's discussion of journeys and journeying in the accented cinema with specific film examples is inspiring for our discussion of new Hong Kong films and the journeys they feature. As I discussed above, many segments of the New Hong Kong Cinema depict and reflect on journeys, moves and migrations of the Hongkongers. Such human mobility was triggered by historical-political trans-formations in the city and the subsequent economic concern of the residents. The latter, however, is less of a concern in accented films made by displaced filmmakers from Third World and other postcolonial territories. Be they com-mercial or film festival-oriented art-house in nature,[3] these Hong Kong-related Chinese-language films have as their organic parts actual and cinematic jour-neys and journeying. These moves are components of the films, but, equally important, their presence shapes how the films are presented and received.

Journeys and Journeying as Subject Matter

As a direct reflection of what is going on in Hong Kong society, travels in films, regardless of their nature, often generate mixed feelings and advance different power relations and meanings (Cresswell and Dixon 2002: 4). Arguably one of the very few films of its kind, *Homecoming* (Yim Ho, Hong Kong, 1984) poetically depicts the self-rediscovery of a Hong Kong woman who returns to her ancestral home in mainland China for a short sojourn, which before long rekindles her love for her people and the harmonious country life. *Just Like Weather* (Allen Fong, Hong Kong, 1986) is a docudrama following a Hong Kong couple before, during and after their migration from Hong Kong to the United States. The film was one of the first to deal directly with the topic of the Hongkongers' westward migration when the sovereignty change began to loom large in people's lives. Parts of the story in *Crossings* (Evans Chan, Hong Kong, 1994) take place in Hong Kong. The film features several protagonists of Chinese descent. They are portrayed as sojourners who meet in Hong Kong. Their individual stories end up intertwining with one another on a more emotional level. *Once upon a Time in China and America* (Sammo Hung, Hong Kong, 1997) portrays a fictitious trip of the legendary martial arts master Huang Feihong and several of his pupils. Set in the late 1800s, the master crosses the Atlantic to establish an American-based branch of his traditional Chinese medical clinic. However, he is caught up in the conflicts between the European settlers and native Americans. The film reflects the real-life migrations of the Hongkongers, who made their own destinies after being denied any part in the British and Chinese negotiations and determination of the return of Hong Kong to Chinese rule. It also mirrors the filmmaking career of the film's director Sammo Hung and the male lead Jet Li. Before making this film, Hung and Li had left their base in Chinese-language film industries to work in Hollywood.

Whereas the above films have a clear country of origin in Hong Kong, more and more films made since the 1990s entail investments of film executives and financiers who are based in Hong Kong, China, Taiwan and other East Asian territories. Depending on the projects' requirements, the production of these films may only be accomplished through filmmakers going on long business trips to shoot the films elsewhere from Hong Kong. Journeys and journeying thus start even before the films are made. This is especially typical for those films that are made with the pan-East Asian co-production mode and have dual, triple or even multiple countries of origin officially. For example, the Pang Brothers prefer Thailand as the shooting location for their films such as *The Eye* (Oxide and Danny Pang, Hong Kong/Singapore, 2002), although Thailand is not mentioned in the film's official places of origin. Once a member of the Hong Kong New Wave, Patrick Tam made a major comeback and won the Best Director Award at the twenty-sixth edition of the Hong Kong Film Awards (the Hong Kong equivalent of the Oscars) in 2007 for his father-and-son drama *After This Our Exile* (Patrick Tam, Hong Kong, 2006), which is set entirely in the rural area of Kuala Lumpur and Perak in Malaysia. Edmond Pang Ho-cheung, a well-liked and bankable 'New Generation Director' (L. Pang 2009: 84) from Hong Kong, had major parts of his comedy *Love in the Buff*

(China/Hong Kong, 2012) shot on location in China. A significant part of the story in his *Vulgaria* (Hong Kong, 2012) is also set in China. The protagonists in both films have to expand their professional circles to include investors and customers from mainland China following the country's economic rise. As we shall see in Chapter Five, the mainland Chinese partners play an extremely important part in many of these Hong Kong-related film projects. Their presence, based on the requirements of the CEPA signed between the central government of the PRC and the Hong Kong SAR government, allows the China-Hong Kong co-produced films to enter the mainland Chinese audience market without being subject to China's annual quota on importing foreign films.[4] In addition, the Hong Kong partners of these co-produced films are likely to rely on the personal and business networks of their mainland Chinese partners to open up for them the biggest single audience market on earth. In such circumstances the situation of Hong Kong filmmakers comes closest to that of the accented filmmakers with respect to their survival (be it political or economic) within the interstices of a much larger film industry in China. I will devote the following paragraphs to discussing journeys and journeying as the subject matter of three feature films that fictionalize the Hong Kong Chinese's migrations, long-term sojourns (with or without a specified return date) and return migrations (resettlements) in the context of Hong Kong's intriguing relationship with China.

Floating Life: *Home-Seeking Journeys and Migrations*

Produced by the Australian-based production company Hibiscus Films (focusing on quality specialist films) and funded partially by the Special Broadcasting Service of Australia, *Floating Life* is Hong Kong immigrant director Clara Law's first Australian film after she migrated with her family to Australia. According to the director, her move was partly due to the impacts of the sovereignty change on the Hong Kong Chinese's self-identification and to her aspiration to further pursue her filmmaking career in a more diversified environment (Tan S., Clemens and Hogan 1994–95: 51). The film is hence labelled 'Australian', although its story is entirely devoted to documenting the life of a Hong Kong immigrant family before, during and after their settlement in Australia just prior to 1997. This Hong Kong-related film has thus been chosen here to start our discussion of 'journeys' in film. As a product of the Australian government's multiculturalism policy and a cinematic mirror of Law's real-life move from China, via Macau and Hong Kong, to Australia, *Floating Life* has much of its concern focused on how immigrants turn into settlers, and the changes this might bring about in their lives and their psychological conditions (Files 1997; Teo 2001; Louie 2003: 98). The film's cast includes many Chinese-Australian actors and actresses who are not well-known in Hong Kong or in other Chinese communities in East Asia. The major language spoken in the film is Cantonese and not English.

Floating Life tells the story of the Chans led by a pair of elderly parents – retired tea merchant Pa (Edwin Pang) and his wife Mum (Cecilia Lee). They have two adult daughters, one adult son and two teenage sons. There are nine sections in the plot, indicated by eight intertitles: 'A house in Australia', 'A house in Germany', 'A house in Hong Kong', 'A house in China', 'A house without a tree', 'A house in turmoil', 'A big house' and 'Mui Mui's house' respectively. The film opens with Pa and Mum's last day in Hong Kong before they migrate to Australia. They are taking the two teenage boys with them, while their second daughter, Bing (Annie Yip), has already settled in Australia for a few years and has a professional job in a local office. The Chans' third child (and the eldest son), Gar Ming (Anthony Brandon Wong), is still waiting for his immigration papers in Hong Kong. The Chans' enthusiasm for reunion in Australia soon turns into a nightmare for the whole family. Bing, after spending seven years living alone in Australia and later joined by her husband from Hong Kong, appoints herself as the matriarch of the family. Under Bing's strict domestic regime, Pa, Mum and their teenage sons soon start living a socially withdrawn life in the suburban house of Bing and her husband. The two boys secretly describe themselves as living in 'illegal custody' and in a 'concentration camp'. Conflicts frequently arise among the Chans, mostly provoked by Bing's unyielding attitude.

Meanwhile, the Chans' eldest daughter, Yen (Annette Shun Wah), is happily married to her German husband. The couple and their young daughter, Mui Mui, reside in Germany. Feeling responsible for her parents' family, and learning about their uncomfortable situation, Yen decides to pay them a visit in Australia. She transits in Hong Kong to see Gar Ming, who works as a foreign currency broker and is living a spiritually empty life in the cosmopolitan city. Yen's visit to Australia does not help resolve the family conflicts. The situation even worsens, culminating in Pa and Mum's purchase of a new house and moving out of Bing's. Feeling betrayed, Bing falls into clinical depression and cuts all ties with her family, but later on is helped by her mother to gradually resume a normal life. The film ends with Mui Mui's unsubtitled voice-over (spoken in Cantonese with a strong German accent) wishing the family to be reunited in the years to come.

Without showing the move itself, the plot of the entire film is triggered by the protagonists' longing to settle down in a place they can regard as their 'real home'. Dialogues between the characters suggest their move is provoked, to a certain extent, by their fears of intangible things: the fear of the new communist rulers in Hong Kong, the fear of having their house confiscated (something not uncommon in mainland China immediately after the establishment of the PRC) and so on. For example, Bing emphatically reminds her parents that they should not regard their lives in Australia as an enjoyment. In Bing's words in Cantonese, they are in Australia for *chau nan* (in Mandarin, it would be *tao nan*) – literally becoming refugees in order to flee or run away from disasters in their place of origin. '*Chau nan*' as their supposedly main purpose of emigrating from Hong Kong is however not subtitled and can only be understood by Cantonese speakers. Similar exchanges are charted in the opening sequence of the film, where Pa chats with the noodle shop owner about the family's 'running away' once again, just when they have started to 'warm up their seat' in Hong Kong. It is only hinted in the film that the older generation underwent maltreatment by the Chinese communists on the mainland before migrating to Hong Kong. They probably fled the country along with hundreds of thousands of mainland Chinese refugees who sought political refuge in Hong Kong in the 1950s (as a result of China's participation in the Korean War, 1950–53), or in the 1960s (as a result of the notorious Cultural Revolution, 1966–76).

Geographical mobility between old and new homes/houses, on the other hand, offers the transnational migrants the possibility to choose a life they desire. Mobility encompasses the physical, psychological and emotional activities the migrants are involved in. More importantly, mobility enables these migrants to escape from the difficult conditions at home. Film scholar Gina Marchetti (2006: 197) reads the allegory of this film, arguing that it moves in the direction of 'embracing a new homeland'. The move can then be viewed as the 'tactics of intervention' in the trajectory of the migrants. As cultural theorist Rey Chow (1993: 25) argues, 'These are the tactics of those who do not have claims to territorial propriety or cultural centrality. Perhaps more than anyone else, those who live in Hong Kong realize the opportunistic role they need to play in order, not to "preserve", but to negotiate their "cultural identity"'. Furthermore, the move per se could easily become an end in itself instead of the means by which the characters try to solve their problems. This is when the state of being mobile can be thought of as a space/site where migrants physically and spiritually linger on for a long time, seeking comfort in a self-constructed and a self-confined emotional limbo while trying to adjust to their new lives (Teo 2001; see also Stein 2002).

Happy Together: *Journeys of Homelessness and Long-Term Sojourns*

Whereas the Chans in *Floating Life* portray the Hong Kong Chinese as 'reluctant exiles' (in Skeldon's sense), Wong Kar-wai, who is a Hong Kong-based director, conveys his diasporic sentiments and the 1997-related anxiety of his fellow Hongkongers in the Cannes award winner *Happy Together* (Rayns 1995: 14; Stephens 1996: 17). Like many of his peers in the Hong Kong film industry, Wong was a Chinese immigrant who moved with his mother to Hong Kong from Shanghai when he was only five years old. At that time he did not speak any Cantonese at all. Most of Wong's films, according to the director, are influenced by his childhood experience of being completely uprooted from his hometown in Shanghai (Ngai and Wong K. 1997: 88). *Happy Together* is the director's sixth feature film, and entirely scripted by himself. It was co-produced by Wong's Jet Tone Production in Hong Kong, and its Japanese and South Korean filmmaking partners, Prénom H and Seowoo Film Company respectively. The story in *Happy Together* was inspired by Argentine author Manuel Puig's novel *The Buenos Aires Affair* (1973) and the film was mainly shot on location in Argentina. It was completed with footage taken in Taipei and Hong Kong. The prolonged shooting period of three months in Argentina stirred up in Wong (as well as in his whole crew and cast from Hong Kong) a feeling of being exiled and of homesickness for Hong Kong (Havis 1997: 15; Ngai and Wong K. 1997: 107–9).[5] Although the film is generally considered an art-house film even by Hong Kong films' standards, the main cast includes three of the most famous East Asian stars, Tony Leung Chiu-wai, the late Leslie Cheung and Chang Chen, who are mainstays of the East Asian commercial cinemas. *Happy Together* was theatrically released in Hong Kong in the summer of 1997 prior to the official Handover, a timing that suggests a certain degree of political sensitivity of the film.

The film is packaged as a gay romance story, set between mid 1995 and early 1997, between Fai (Tony Leung Chiu-wai) and Wing (Leslie Cheung), who have left Hong Kong on a long journey without any specific return date. Unlike Wong's previous films, which are narrated from multiple angles by the films' main characters, the story in *Happy Together* is mainly told from the angle of Fai. The viewer is not told much about Wing's background. The film starts with the two men arriving in Argentina in mid May 1995 in hopes of restarting their deteriorating relationship afresh, but the journey itself brings them more conflicts. They soon lead separate lives after entering the country. Fai is getting tired of his self-exilic life in Argentina and hopes to return to Hong Kong to be reconciled with his estranged father. The father and son stopped talking to each other after Fai stole a sum of money from his former boss, who is a friend of his father's. In order to save up money for the return journey, Fai takes up several odd jobs in Argentina, first as a receptionist at a Tango bar, then as a kitchen helper in a Chinese restaurant, and finally as an abattoir worker. Contrarily, Wing does not think much about returning to Hong Kong. After separating from Fai, he lives a promiscuous lifestyle in Argentina and makes his living by occasionally prostituting himself to the locals. Whenever he encounters any difficulties (such as being beaten up by his clients), he goes back to Fai knowing that Fai will take good care of him.

Amid Fai and Wing's series of break-ups followed by make-ups during their prolonged Argentine sojourn, a third man Chang (Chang Chen) comes into the picture. Chang is from Taipei and works at the same Chinese restaurant kitchen where Fai works. It is implied that Fai and Chang are attracted to each other but they never develop a relationship, for Chang soon leaves the restaurant to return to Taiwan. After Chang is gone, Fai also saves up enough money to return to Asia, leaving Wing completely on his own in Argentina.

Fai chooses to transit to Taiwan to see Chang, whom he is unable to find, before the planned return to Hong Kong. While in Taiwan, Fai learns that Deng Xiaoping has just passed away at the age of ninety-two on 19 February 1997. Deng was the chief engineer of the 'one country, two systems' political framework for Hong Kong to rejoin China. The film ends with Fai taking a night train in Taipei. His journey still seems to be continuing, but moving towards an unknown future. It is not revealed whether Fai finally returns to Hong Kong.

The series of journeys that form the backbone of *Happy Together* has been seen by film scholars working on Hong Kong and other Chinese-language cinemas as a political allusion (to the 1997 Handover), no matter how hard Wong tries, as he claims, to stay away from the topic (Ngai and Wong K. 1997: 112; Pang Y. 1997). For example, Jeremy Tambling (2003: 11) argues that 'allegory' is the key to understanding this film. Stephen Teo (2005: 100) thinks that *Happy Together* is Wong's 'most political movie to date – it is conditioned by the 1997 deadline, highlighting its spiritually debilitating effects on two Hong Kong men'. Sheldon Lu (2000: 280) thinks that the national identity issue of the Hongkongers is brought up early in this film. Taiwan-based film producer and critic Peggy Chiao

Hsiung-ping (1997: 18) believes that the film is about three cities: Beijing, Taipei and Hong Kong.

Fai's story looks unfinished at the end of *Happy Together*. With the benefit of hindsight, nonetheless, it is quite safe to assume that Fai's role and his journey into an unknown future (as well as his identity quest) would soon continue in another of Wong's films, *In the Mood for Love* (France/Hong Kong, 1999), via another protagonist. In this 1999 film, which was also a Cannes award winner, the emotionally lost main character Chow Mo-wan (also played by Tony Leung Chiu-wai) seems to be a 1960s version of Fai of *Happy Together*. Here, Chow is a professional writer penning mainly serialized martial arts novels for local newspapers in Hong Kong. The film tells us that he has been cheated on by his wife but later finds his true love, albeit unrequited. At the end, the sad Chow moves to Singapore to continue his writing career (Nochimson 2005: 16–17).

The role of Chow would reappear in Wong's newer film, *2046* (China/France/Germany/Hong Kong/Italy, 2004), which nonetheless was not supposed to be the direct sequel of *In the Mood for Love*. The main events of *2046* happen in the Hong Kong of the 1960s. Although the name of the main character of this newer film, Chow Mo-wan, is the same as that of the male lead in *In the Mood for Love*, and the role is played by the same actor, the Chow in *In the Mood for Love* has very different personality traits from that of the Chow in *2046*. The former Chow is sort of a family man; the latter Chow is a typical playboy. The former Chow is hurt by his cheating wife but he is able to move on to pursue a new relationship; the latter Chow does not want to love anybody. At first, the Chow in *2046* mainly writes pornography stories for newspapers. He later begins to devote himself to writing a saddening science fiction novel. This diegetic novel tells a futuristic story in which lonely persons attempt to take a train to a mysterious place called 2046 where they may regain their loves; but it is impossible to know the outcome for them as no one has ever returned from 2046.

Within the film text of *2046*, travelling to the place 2046 is an imaginary journey created by the character Chow. This diegetic novel is visualized as an insertion into the film. However, if we read this futuristic novel within the film as an intertextual continuation of the journey that Fai in *Happy Together* has started, and if we understand all the journeys in Wong's three consecutive films (i.e., *Happy Together*, *In the Mood for Love* and *2046*) within the political context of Hong Kong after the Handover, the number 2046 will evoke another level of meaning. This is because 2046 is the last year of the transitional period given as a grace period to Hong Kong by the Chinese government, before Hong Kong will be completely absorbed into the PRC's political and economic systems. This play on number in Wong's film, advanced through using the narration of the same actor featured in different films and a visualization of a seemingly imaginary journey within the diegetic environment, cleverly creates the effect of a lingering political allusion underneath the more noticeable, aesthetic achievements of Wong's works (Brunette 2005; Teo 2005). Arguably, the director's own worries about the 1997-related transitions of Hong Kong have never really diminished since he started his subtle way of including political allegory in *Days of Being Wild* in 1990 (see below), as no one knows what will happen to Hong Kong after the year 2046 in a political environment in which China dominates. To a certain extent, we can also see that Wong's worries echo, and continue from, the Hong Kong Chinese's fears of the Handover – the fears that had started long before the year 1997 arrived.

Exiled: *Homecoming Journeys and Return Migrations (Resettlements)*

As one of the most prolific genre film directors locally trained in Hong Kong (starting his career at Hong Kong's local television station TVB), Johnnie To (whose family name is pronounced *toe* in its English Romanized version, *dou* in Cantonese, and *du* in Mandarin) insists on having his filmmaking career firmly established in his native Hong Kong. Most of his firms were produced through his co-owned independent production house Milkyway Image, based in Hong Kong (Bordwell 2003). While his films are internationally famous for visually poetic action scenes (Asch 2007; Camper 2007; see also the detailed background of Johnnie To in Chapter Three in this book), the stories are mainly related to the place Hong Kong. However, To's *Exiled*, made in 2006 and marketed as a Hong Kong film, is set entirely in Macau in a period shortly before the territory's return to Chinese rule in 1999. A former Portuguese colony located right next to Hong Kong, Macau has long been regarded as a backwater of Hong Kong; before its return to China, the small peninsula was a haven for gambling and local gangster activities. Although *Exiled* tells a story that is not directly related to Hong Kong, the chaotic social situation depicted in it clearly suggests a similar state in Hong Kong before its Handover (V. Lee 2009: 84; He 2012: 304).

The Chinese title of *Exiled* is *Fang • Zhu* (放 • 逐), which has a double meaning. Ignoring the period sign between the two Chinese characters, the two words form the Chinese equivalent of its English translated title. Literally, it means being in exile or going into exile. However, with the magic of the period punctuation set between the two Chinese words, we can see another layer of meaning: to let go • to chase after. This points directly at the on-the-run situation that the entire film is about. The story opens with Wo (Nick Cheung), who wants to quietly rebuild his home with his wife (Josie Ho)[6] and their newborn son in a deserted neighbourhood in Macau after a long absence from the place. Four hitmen come to Wo's flat to look for him. Blaze and Fat (played by Anthony Wong and Lam Suet respectively) have been sent by Wo's corrupt former boss Fay (Simon Yam), whom Wo attempted to assassinate some time earlier but failed. It is now Fay's turn to seek revenge by sending his two hitmen to chase after Wo and kill him (hence, 'to chase after'). Tat and Cat (played by Francis Ng and Roy Cheung respectively) come to help Wo run away again (hence, 'to let go'). As it turns out, Wo and the four hit men were close childhood friends.

When Wo comes back to the flat from being outside, the visitors follow him in and start a minor gunfight. The group of friends are soon reconciled with each other. The next morning the group of friends go to a hitman agent, Jeff (Eddie Cheung), to ask for a job that would pay off handsomely, for Wo wants his wife and baby son to be left with some money in case he is killed. Jeff informs them of the possibility of hijacking a ton of genuine gold owned by corrupted government officials. Meanwhile, aware that Wo is still alive, Fay avenges himself on Wo and soon kills him. He also captures Wo's wife and baby. The group of friends go to rescue Wo's surviving family, ignoring the dream life that they would soon have with the hijacked gold. The final gunfight results in almost all of the male characters being killed, leaving alive only Wo's wife, her baby and a prostitute working nearby. This home-return journey of Wo and his family has thus resulted in a tragic end.

Many commentators believe that the male bonding in this film echoes that found in To's earlier films, such as *The Mission* (Hong Kong, 1999), *PTU* (Hong Kong, 2003), *Election* (Hong Kong, 2005) and *Election 2* (aka *Triad Election*) (Hong Kong, 2006), and some of his later films such as *Sparrow* (Hong Kong, 2008) (Sanjek 2007; V. Lee 2009: 95–100). The Hong Kong-born director's love for his native territory that he declares explicitly as regards his film *Sparrow*,[7] however, is rarely associated with *Exiled* and discussed extensively by critics. For example, film scholar Vivian P.Y. Lee feels that the setting in Macau could mean 'a changing perception of Macau in Hong Kong's cultural imagination' (2009: 95). But there is no further analysis as to the motivation for To in treating this 'changing perception' of a place in his unique way. There is also no analysis as to why the characters in *Exiled* remind each other of their long-term friendship, growing up together at '*gai liu*' (in Cantonese; 雞寮 in written script), when they are now in Macau. '*Gai liu*' is mentioned in their dialogues and shown clearly in Chinese subtitles, but not English, about five minutes into the film. The term is commonly used by many Cantonese-speaking Hongkongers to refer to the Kwun Tong Resettlement Estate built in the 1960s on the Kowloon side of Hong Kong for new immigrants and low-income families. The place has now become Tsui Ping Estate, a public high-rise housing estate in Hong Kong, after several decades of district redevelopment. '*Gai liu*' in the case of the characters in *Exiled*, then, refers to a childhood rendezvous that is gone forever. It suggests their (and the director's) nostalgia for the past and places in Hong Kong, as well as their resistance to both political and cultural changes of the territory they once called 'home' (Nochimson and Cashill 2007). Yet, the new 'home' in Macau is also a 'no-go area' under uncontrollable circumstances: just like the exilic character Wo, who was coerced to leave and has to die on returning 'home' in Macau. Wo's connection to this Macau 'home' is built more on the rekindled friendship with his friends than with the place that is as dangerous and undesirable as anywhere else (Braziel and Mannur 2003: 6; Mannur 2003: 286). On the basis of this understanding, I read the final showdown in *Exiled* as an expression of the director's unarticulated anxiety and doubt over Hong Kong's political reunification with China (the new 'home' for Hong Kong natives) and the return migrations of many Hong Kong emigrants since the Handover.

Developing Characters through Journeys (to the Past)

Naficy (2001: 27) remarks that many characters featured in diasporic and exilic films are sad, lonely and alienated because they are displaced from their homelands. They are often multilingual while speaking the dominant language with an accent. These characters are performed by professional and non-professional actors and actresses, and can be regarded as on-screen self-representations of the filmmakers themselves (Naficy 2001: 290). If journeying in these films involves not just geographical and textual, but also historical, biographical and/ or psychological journeys, we should expect they will very likely become major catalysts for the transformation of the characters and their identities (Naficy 2001: 223). In this regard, I find three Hong Kong films especially appropriate for our discussion of the characters' development via journeying where this involves not just textual journeys but also historical ones to a recent past, and whereby the protagonists and the filmmakers themselves attempt to reinvent their feelings for their (absent) homelands.

Days of Being Wild: *Multiple Character Development*

Days of Being Wild is Wong Kar-wai's second feature film. It was festively released in Hong Kong in 1990 right before the Christmas holidays, and expected to appeal to a young audience with its superstar cast. But it turned out to be a box-office disappointment to its investor In-Gear, which had previously produced Wong's first feature film *As Tears Go by* (Hong Kong, 1988) (Ngai and Wong K. 1997: 97). *Days of Being Wild* is set in 1960. The film was planned to have a sequel set in 1966. But the dissatisfactory box-office record of *Days of Being Wild* triggered a quick commercial decision to abort production of the second part (which arguably became the background of Wong's two other films, *In the Mood for Love* and *2046*) (Ngai 1990: 38–39; Abbas 1997: 50; Amato and Greenberg 2000). Despite its box-office failure, *Days of Being Wild* brought Wong his first Best Director Award at the tenth Hong Kong Film Awards in 1991 (Abbas 1997: 50; Dissanayake and D. Wong 2003: 12; Brunette 2005: 5; Teo 2005: 32–33, 68). Over the course of time, this film has gathered many positive reviews and is now regularly ranked as one of the best Chinese-language films ever produced.[8]

Wong uses an unconventional (by Hong Kong films' standards in the 1990s), episodic way to tell the story of six young adults. Among them, Yuddy (Leslie Cheung) steals most of the spotlight as a character evoking the role of James Dean in *Rebel Without a Cause* (Nicholas Ray, United States, 1955),[9] though the other five characters all take turns in the film to tell their sides of the story (and show their feelings). These six characters represent six different types of self-centred, lonely persons, who feel their love for others remains unrequited. According to Wong, however, these characters are also imbued with various feelings experienced by the Hong Kong Chinese about leaving or staying behind in Hong Kong. Such feelings were particularly strong when the sociopolitical uncertainty related to the imminent 1997 Handover began to loom larger and larger in the early 1990s (Rayns 1995: 14).

The handsome, playboy-like Yuddy opens the film by flirting with Lizhen (Maggie Cheung), a shy tuck shop worker who later becomes his first lover in the film. Understanding that Lizhen wants eventually to marry him, Yuddy refuses to make a commitment and the two break up. Yuddy quickly becomes sexually involved with another woman, Mimi (aka Lulu) (Carina Lau), who is a dance hall courtesan.[10] It is later revealed in the film that Yuddy is in fact the illegitimate child of a very rich Philippine woman who has paid Yuddy's foster mother Rebecca (Rebecca Pan), a former dance hall courtesan, to take care of the boy over the years. Both Yuddy and Rebecca do not have to work, being supported by Yuddy's rich biological mother. The real identity of Yuddy's biological mother has long been a mystery to the boy. After pestering Rebecca for years to give him information about his biological parents, whom he has never met, Yuddy finally gets the answer from Rebecca when she decides to emigrate to the United States. Yuddy then breaks up with Mimi and travels alone to the Philippines hoping to meet with his biological mother. But she refuses to see him.

Meanwhile, Yuddy's unemployed best friend Zeb (Jacky Cheung) is secretly in love with Mimi. Mimi does not share Zeb's feelings. She later leaves Hong Kong, going to the Philippines in hopes of reuniting with Yuddy. Yuddy's previous lover Lizhen has by now developed a special friendship with the policeman Tide (Andy Lau), who later changes his job to that of sailor and leaves Hong Kong. He runs into the drunken Yuddy in the Philippine Chinatown. The two spend a night together as drinking buddies, but in the following morning Yuddy is shot dead by Philippine gangsters in the course of an illegal passport deal. Like Yuddy's reincarnation, an unidentified man (Tony Leung Chiu-wai) is featured in a non-dialogued, two-and-half-minute long take in the finale; he is grooming himself meticulously in his small, dimly lit room before going out. This character and his gestures have a strong association with the image of Chow Mo-wan in 2046 (though Wong never admits both characters in the two films are the same person).

Through their voice-overs, conversations and decisions made in the film, these six lonesome spirits tell the audience about their dissatisfaction with their situations. All of them do (or are revealed to have done) some travelling in order to move on to the next stage in their lives: Lizhen travelled from Macau to settle in Hong Kong; Yuddy leaves Hong Kong to go to the Philippines; Mimi follows him; Shanghainese-speaking Rebecca relocated from Shanghai to Hong Kong where she further emigrates to the United States; Tide leaves Hong Kong for his sailing job; while Zeb stays behind in Hong Kong. With every journey they make, they acquire completely new dimensions of perception of their existence and new ideas about their lives. More importantly, Wong employs these characters in order to travel, together with the audience, back to a past period in Hong Kong. It was a period when Wong was a new Hong Kong immigrant (or a diasporic subject newly from Shanghai) – a period that gave him more pleasure than suffering (Ngai 1990: 38; Rayns 1995: 14; Ngai and Wong K. 1997: 85, 88; Marchetti 2006: 10). Wong's experience in his motherland, China, on the other hand, does not seem to have any lingering effect on the director's worldview after Hong Kong has become the director's new home(land) and not just a host territory. Wong's personal experience and the way he conveys it through the characters in *Days of Being Wild* thus attests to interdisciplinary scholar James Clifford's idea (1994) that diaspora may sometimes challenge the very idea of nation-state. As Clifford (1994: 322) points out: 'The empowering paradox of diaspora is that dwelling *here* assumes a solidarity and connection *there*. But *there* is not necessarily a single place or an exclusivist nation' (italics in original).

Echoes of the Rainbow: *To Be Strong and Happy*

Echoes of the Rainbow is considered a small-budget film, with a production cost of HK$3.6 million (£283,000 or U.S.$464,000) provided by the Film Development Fund of Hong Kong (Film Development Fund 2012; Hong Kong Government's Sponsorship 2012). It was directed by Alex Law, who scripted many of the well-known films on the topic of 'migrations' that his partner Mabel Cheung made, such as *An Autumn's Tale* (Hong Kong, 1987) and *Eight Taels of Gold* (Hong Kong, 1989). *Echoes of the Rainbow* was distributed by Mei Ah Entertainment, a major media distribution company in Hong Kong. The film explores the story of a family that has fled the south of China to settle joyfully in Hong Kong. It became an unexpected box-office sensation locally, winning the Best Director and Best Actor Awards in the twenty-ninth Hong Kong Film Awards in 2010, as well as the Crystal Bear for the Best Film in the Children's Jury 'Generation Kplus' at the sixtieth Berlin International Film Festival (also in 2010).

The plot of *Echoes of the Rainbow* is set in Hong Kong in the 1960s. It is narrated as a nostalgic adventure to the recent past of the territory through the eyes of the protagonist, the eight-year-old Jin-er Law (aka Big Ears; played by child actor Buzz Chung), who is modelled on the director's own childhood image.[11] Despite having limited financial means after migrating to Hong Kong, the Laws are a loving and united family residing in a friendly neighbourhood in Sham Shui Po on the Kowloon side of Hong Kong. Jin-er is the second son of the Laws and a naughty brat in the eyes of adults. His father, Mr Law (Simon Yam), is a conservative, reticent and hard-working shoemaker who opens a side street shoe shop in the ground floor area of the little zinc hut where the family lives. Mrs Law (Sandra Ng) is an optimistic, energetic and chatty housewife who also helps her husband at the shoe shop. Jin-er's older brother, the sixteen-year-old Desmond (Aarif Rahman aka Aarif Lee), is a polite, top-grade student of a reputable missionary school. Desmond is also a talented musician and a champion runner. Jin-er's Big Uncle (Paul Chiang) and Grandma (Ha Ping aka Teresa Loo) also live in the same neighbourhood.

From Jin-er's perspective, the Hong Kong of the 1960s is memorable and full of treasurable human feelings. He immerses himself in different exciting hobbies, such as watching Cantonese films and gathering (or more precisely, stealing) odd objects of the period as his collectibles. Even dealing with a corrupted British police officer is so much fun. However, Jin-er also goes through incidents that speed up his growth. He witnesses Desmond falling in love for the first time. The gap between Desmond and the girl, who comes from a wealthy family, however, makes the love impossible. Jin-er also sees Desmond falling prey to Leukaemia and later his death, as well as the whole family's hopelessness over the entire course of Desmond's illness. Yet, no matter how bad the situation is, Jin-er remains strong and cheerful in his adolescence, and continues to look on the bright side of life.

Jin-er's personal development in different incidents allows the audience to get involved nostalgically in a filmic journey back to the past and the disappearing space of Hong Kong (Abbas 1997). The experience may not necessarily be upsetting. In fact, different parts of the film join together to create an atmosphere that guarantees a warm and enlightening viewing. A positive feeling for one's family, home and homeland, present and future, is often felt. For Jin-er, the ancestral land in China is, at best, only a myth that Grandma always talks about. More important for him is his present home in Hong Kong, where he was born, raised and will continue to prosper in the future. This somehow also tells us that there is no need for diasporic people to always look back at the past and feel sad, as a bright future is waiting for them.

Bruce Lee, My Brother: *Uncertain Development*

Bruce Lee, My Brother focuses on the biographical story of action superstar Bruce Lee from his childhood and teenage years in Hong Kong until he left for the United States to start his kung fu career there. It was made mainly to commemorate the seventieth anniversary of the birth of the late eponymous star (Shackleton 2010b), co-directed by Manfred Wong and Raymond Yip. Both of these experienced Hong Kong filmmakers are often associated with the *Young and Dangerous* series made in Hong Kong in the 1990s.[12] The film is a China-Hong Kong co-production between Shanghai TV Media, Beijing Antaeus Film, Beijing Meng Ze Culture & Media, and J' Star Group in China, and Media Asia Films in Hong Kong. This biopic is praised as the most accurate portrayal of Bruce Lee's early life, with endorsements from his younger brother, Robert Lee, and two elder sisters (Hung and Z. Li 2010). Seeing how Bruce Lee's early life is presented in the film, we notice that it was intertwined with the fate of Hong Kong between the Japanese occupation and the time of Western popular culture's impact on the territory in the late 1950s. In this respect, Bruce Lee can also be read as a representative of those Hong Kong Chinese residents who have gone through identity changes while on the verge of choosing to move away from Hong Kong.

The film depicts several major physical and metaphorical journeys that affect Bruce Lee's life. It commences with a brief commemoration by Robert Lee and his eldest sister, and is later narrated on and off by Robert Lee. The first journey in the film is set in 1940. It is a physical journey taken by Bruce Lee's father, the renowned Cantonese operatic comedian Lee Hoi-chuen, who is on a performance tour in San Francisco. On 27 November that year, the wife (Christy Chung) of Lee Hoi-chuen (Tony Leung Ka-fai) gives birth to their second son (the fourth child) whom the couple name Bruce. As a second journey in the film, the Lees return to Hong Kong a year later, shortly before the Japanese occupation of Hong Kong begins (in real life, Bruce Lee was about three when the Lees returned to Hong Kong).

During the postwar era in Hong Kong, Bruce Lee, now a young boy, has grown healthily but is not interested in school. His acting talent is discovered and highly praised by director Fung Fung (aka Feng Feng; played by Cheung Tat-ming). Fung recruits Bruce Lee to be the child protagonist in the film *The Kid*, released in 1950 (in real life, Bruce Lee's Chinese screen name, Lee Xiaolong, was first used in this film). As a teenager, Bruce Lee (Aarif Rahman aka Aarif Lee) spends much time playing around, partying and getting into trouble. The film also re-enacts how, in order to win a boxing competition, Bruce Lee starts to study Wing Chun martial arts under master Ip Man. Bruce Lee treasures friendship highly. One of his friends, Lau Lin-kong, has become a drug addict and gets involved in drug dealing. In order to save Lau, Bruce Lee and his two close friends go to look for him in the den but end up fighting with the drug dealers. The drug gang is later busted by the police. This incident alarms Lee Hoi-chuen, who then decides to send Bruce Lee to the United States in order to keep the young man from getting into more serious trouble (in real life, Bruce Lee left for the United States in April 1959 with U.S.$102 (£62) in his pocket). The final scene of the film consists of a pull-back shot of Bruce Lee running alone towards the ship that will soon take him to the United States (an implied third major physical journey in the film).

Readers may argue that this film is about Bruce Lee's personal life and has nothing to do with other Hongkongers' diasporic sentiments over the decades. But as the directors deliberately incorporate a bygone era of Hong Kong and the on-screen re-enactment of the production of some of the most popular old Hong Kong Cantonese films made by and for postwar diasporic subjects from mainland China, such as *Thunderstorm* (directed by Ng Wui in 1957) and *Wong Fei-hung's Fight at Henan* (directed by Wu Pang in 1957), this film cannot be read as just a biopic (Y. Chu 2003: 22–41; Fu 2008: 12–15). With the insertion of these re-enacted filmmaking scenes, the directors of *Bruce Lee, My Brother* have turned this recollection about the star into a restaged history of Hong Kong as well as a revisit of Hong Kong's film industry in the 1950s.

Beyond developing the main characters alongside the journeys they take in the diegetic environment, the filmmakers of the three nostalgia films I just discussed convey a strong yearning for a past of Hong Kong – the ultimate homeland of the main characters. But that was a Hong Kong under British colonial rule, which has disappeared since the Handover and to which they cannot return in reality. When shooting *Days of Being Wild*, Wong Kar-wai could only reinvent a 1960s Hong Kong from his childhood memories and impressions, which he did with a sense of loss (Rayns 1995: 14; Ngai and Wong K. 1997: 88). Alex Law of *Echoes of the Rainbow* was lucky to find a very old street, Wing Lee Street, in Sheung Wan district in Hong Kong that could be used as the setting for the neighbourhood where the protagonist Jin-er lives. Comparative literature scholar Yiu-Wai Chu (2013: 80–83) notes that Wing Lee Street later escaped demolition under the original urban renewal plan due to the success of the film. The author regards the street preservation not as part of the government's plan to conserve local cultural heritage, but as a 'spectacle' under the 'Brand Hong Kong' marketing programme that lacks the real 'personality' or the soul of the city. *Bruce Lee, My Brother* was shot partially in an old building in Guangzhou,

China, and not in Hong Kong where that kind of old establishments could no longer be found. The production of the nostalgia films made in the 2000s, as in the case of *Echoes of the Rainbow* and *Bruce Lee, My Brother,* are closely linked to the preservation of local cultural heritage for such monuments as the Star Ferry Pier and the Queen's Pier under the challenge of a globalized economy and the local government's failure to see the values of the local culture (Y-W. Chu 2013: 117–18, 165). Yiu-Wai Chu (2013: 117–18) believes that these 'new nostalgia' films are different from those made in the 1990s, such as *Arrest the Restless* (Lawrence Ah Mon, Hong Kong, 1992) and *He Ain't Heavy, He's My Father* (Peter Chan, Hong Kong, 1993), because the 2000s films do not just address the golden past but also the future. I would like to add that even though these films may have projected hope for the future, the hope is heavily overwhelmed by the present grief of the Hong Kong locals, which is felt under the double shadow of China's dominance and the globalized economy. A metaphorical time travel to the Hong Kong homeland in a past period as shown in the three films discussed here can only generate temporary relief but not ultimate resolution to spare the Hongkongers from their sense of loss and uncertainties about their existential conditions.

'Journeying' Narrative Structure

Naficy focuses his discussion of journeys in diasporic and exilic films mainly in terms of how different types of journeys have enriched the films and been incorporated into the films' subject matter. If journeys are indeed defining features of accented films, then we may deduce that journeys and journeying can happen not only within these films' diegetic worlds, but may also be found in the way films and their narratives are organically structured. After all, every film can be considered a visual 'journey' that the audience takes while it sits through the motion picture. What makes an accented film different from other feature films in this respect might include how the filmmaker incorporates the diasporic or exilic sentiments into the telling of the story. It is in this regard that I believe *Song of the Exile,* a semi-autobiographical film by director Ann Hui, is a prime illustration of 'accentedness' and transitions (in every possible sense) in new Hong Kong films.

Song of the Exile: *Flashbacks*

Hui is famous for making films concerned with stories about women (E. Ho 1999, reprinted 2001). Arguably, in *Song of the Exile*, Hui uses the film medium to revisit her own self in a fictional story. This semi-autobiography was supported by Taiwan investment. It tells the story of a daughter and her mother, based on Hui's own diasporic life: Hui was born in mainland China, spent her childhood in Macau and then moved to settle in Hong Kong (see Chapter Three here for her personal background). Hui came up with this story during a trip back to Japan with her Japanese mother (Hui 2012b: 141). Both characters in the story of *Song of the Exile* have self-identification problems while living in places they cannot regard as their real homes.

The plot is structured principally around multiple on-screen and off-screen expeditions of different duration to the United Kingdom, Hong Kong, Macau, China and Japan respectively, which have all taken place in the diegetic past. The film starts with a voice-over recollection by the main protagonist Hueyin (Maggie Cheung) of her situation in the summer of 1973 after she has just finished her master's degree in the United Kingdom.[13] Unable to find a job there even with a British nationality (her Chinese background is hinted in the film as a reason why she cannot get a job interview at the British Broadcasting Corporation (BBC)), the 25-year-old Hueyin returns to Hong Kong to attend her younger sister Huewei's wedding. There, she once again confronts her estranged mother Aiko (played by Taiwanese actress Lu Hsiao-fen). This confrontation evokes some deep-seated misunderstandings and miscommunications dating back through the years to Hueyin's childhood. The plot thereafter oscillates across the 1950s, the 1960s and the 1970s, unveiling the causes of the deep estrangement between the mother and the daughter, who actually love each other dearly.

With a flashback to the 1950s, the audience is introduced to the young mother Aiko. Aiko, a Japanese, is not a welcome daughter-in-law because of the strong Chinese nationalist thinking of her parents-in-law. Ignorant of the fact that her mother Aiko is of Japanese ethnicity, the little Hueyin is totally on her grandparents' side and feels that her mother always behaves strangely. Eventually Hueyin chooses to stay with her grandparents when her parents move to Hong Kong. It is only when Hueyin, at fifteen years old, relocates to join her parents in Hong Kong in 1963 that she finds out about her mother's Japanese nationality. Learning about this personal background does not help improve the difficult relations with her mother. The teenage Hueyin soon decides to move to a local boarding school, and later to the United Kingdom for university studies, in order to escape from her mother.

Back to 1973 after sister Huewei and her newly wedded husband have migrated to Canada, Hueyin and Aiko take a short trip together to Japan, which Aiko has been absent from for decades. During this trip Hueyin finally understands and empathizes with her mother's miserable diasporic situation in China, and then in Macau and Hong Kong. The mother and the daughter are reconciled, and agree that Hong Kong is their current home. At the finale, the 25-year-old Hueyin visits her ageing grandparents in Guangzhou, China, during the notorious Cultural Revolution (the old couple have been impelled by their love for their country to return to the mainland). It is suggested at the ending that Hueyin is still confused about who she really is in a place that is supposed to be her motherland (Chua S. 1998; Williams 1998: 100; Naficy 2001: 33, 127).

In order to tell this complex story about mother and daughter, home and homeland, and unarticulated identity issues of the Hong Kong Chinese, Hui has adopted Wu Nien-jen's suggestion of using flashbacks as the film's main structural framework (Hui 2012b: 142–43). Wu is the film's screenwriter; he is also one of the mainstays of the New Taiwan Cinema movement (1982–86), which includes works by famous directors Hou Hsiou-hsien and Edward Yang (see M. Berry 2005). The flashbacks not only chart the characters' physical travels, but more importantly also visualize their psychological journeys and the structural journeying in the film's narration. In order of appearance within the plot, major journeys and journeying are:

1. The 25-year-old Hueyin returns to Hong Kong from the United Kingdom after graduating with a master's degree (hinted journey not shown on screen; as part of the first layer of flashbacks set in 1973 and recollected by the adult Hueyin in voice-over in the 'present' in an unknown period).
2. In 1973 right after returning home to Hong Kong, Hueyin reminisces about episodes of her early childhood in Macau (as sets of flashbacks set in the 1950s from the perspective of the first layer of flashbacks set in 1973).
3. Hueyin's parents relocate from Macau to Hong Kong (actual journey shown on screen; as a flashback set in the 1950s from the perspective of the first layer of flashbacks set in 1973).
4. The fifteen-year-old Hueyin moves from Macau to Hong Kong to join her parents (actual journey shown on screen; as a flashback set in the summer of

1963 and recollected by the adult Hueyin in voice-over in the 'present' in an unknown period).

5. Grandparents return to mainland China from Macau (hinted journey in the summer of 1963 not shown on screen; recollected by the adult Hueyin in voice-over in the 'present' in an unknown period).

6. The fifteen-year-old Hueyin moves from home in Hong Kong to a local boarding school (actual move shown on screen; as a flashback set in 1963 continued from the perspective of the adult Hueyin in the 'present' in an unknown period), and later to the United Kingdom to study at university (journey skipped).

7. Hueyin's newly wedded sister Huewei migrates from Hong Kong to Canada with her husband (hinted journey not shown on screen; as part of the first layer of flashbacks set in 1973).

8. The 25-year-old Hueyin and the middle-aged mother Aiko travel from Hong Kong to Japan (actual journey shown on screen; as part of the first layer of flashbacks set in 1973).

9. While in Japan, the middle-aged Aiko reminisces about her own past in Manchuria, China (from the perspective of the first layer of flashbacks set in 1973).

10. The young adult Aiko leaves Japan to join her brother's family in Manchuria (hinted journey in the late 1930s to the early 1940s not shown on screen; recollected by the middle-aged Aiko in dialogue with other characters in the first layer of flashbacks set in 1973).

11. Aiko's brother and his family are deported from Manchuria back to Japan after the Second World War (hinted journey in the 1940s not shown on screen; recollected by the middle-aged Aiko in dialogue with the 25-year-old Hueyin in the first layer of flashbacks set in 1973).

12. Aiko and her husband (that is, Hueyin's father; played by Waise Lee) move from Manchuria to Macau after getting married (hinted journey in the 1940s not shown on screen; recollected by the middle-aged Aiko in dialogue with the 25-year-old Hueyin in the first layer of flashbacks set in 1973).

13. The middle-aged Aiko and the 25-year-old Hueyin complete the Japan trip and return to Hong Kong (hinted journey not shown on screen; as part of the first layer of flashbacks set in the autumn of 1973 and recollected by the adult Hueyin in voice-over in the 'present' in an unknown period).

14. The 25-year-old Hueyin visits her ageing grandparents in Guangzhou, China (actual journey shown on screen; as part of the first layer of flashbacks set in the late autumn of 1973).
15. In Guangzhou, Hueyin reminisces about her early years living with her grandparents in Macau (a short flashback set in the 1950s from the perspective of the first layer of flashbacks set in 1973).

The structural journeying of this film is often triggered by family conflicts and quarrels between the mother and the daughter, while the journeys are shot mostly from Hueyin's viewpoint (see W. Cheung 2007: 157–58). On-screen journeys in any given sequence in the film may start in 1970s Hong Kong and end in 1950s Macau, etc., so that the audience and the characters can revisit the causes of the long-term misunderstandings between mother and daughter in relation to Hueyin's situation in 1973. They also show different dimensions of the characters' identity issues (Abbas 1997: 38; Yue 2010: 63). As Hui says:

> There is endless mobility in the structure ... It starts at a certain point and stops at another but never really returns to the original point. Fragmented structure occurs in the middle of the film. There are also changes in the primary and the secondary structures. That makes the film very interesting and unconventional. (Ann Hui 1990: 13; my translation)

Film scholar Audrey Yue situates Hui in the conventions of Hong Kong filmmaking and argues that the flashbacks among other stylistic devices in *Song of the Exile* can be considered strategies of 'corrective realism', challenging the 'dominant (usually classical and patriarchal) modes of authenticity' (Yue 2010: 56). The purpose of such filmic strategies, according to Yue, is to deconstruct and redress ideologies that are 'naturalized' in dominant filmic styles featuring such elements as linear plot, classical realism and continuity editing. Literary scholar Elaine Yee Lin Ho (1999: 167, 177–79) also thinks that *Song of the Exile* manifests women's struggles in a patriarchal world. By invoking the past via flashbacks, this film and many others in Hui's oeuvre show how the female characters' present is energized and reaffirmed. Film scholar Patricia Brett Erens (2000a: 49–53) argues that Hueyin's recollections or memories of her early years via flashbacks in the film are constructed with relevance to the present, and that there are no literal returns to the past. Naficy (2001: 233–34) remarks that the flashbacks in this film are forms of symbolic return (to a past as well as to a place of origin) for the diegetic mother and daughter, for the director Hui and her own mother, and for Hong Kong residents and China to be reconciled. Hui admits that *Song of the Exile* is relevant to a historic period when the Hongkongers (in particular the Chinese descendants) were considering emigrating to other countries. They had to think about what kind of attitudes they needed to hold when adjusting to their new lives (Hui 2012b: 142). Going along this line, I believe these flashbacks also serve the function of changing the audience's vantage points, which are not confined to those of the domestic environment at 'home' (Chua S. 1998), of mother and daughter, or of Hong Kong and China. As the main narrative structure of this film, the layering of flashbacks allow the viewers a holistic exploration of the problems and the situations in which diasporic persons living in different time periods, with Hong Kong as their current home, suffered in a similar manner. It seems to speak directly to those Hong Kong Chinese watching this film in the 1990s and beyond in the transitional Hong Kong, and asks them to calm down a bit to search introspectively for what they actually hoped to have had in the bigger transitional political environment at the historical crossroads.

Concluding Remarks

Naficy highlights journeys and journeying as some of the main qualities that we can use to identify accented films. In this chapter I have used this point of departure to examine seven Hong Kong-related Chinese-language films that deal with, directly or indirectly, the migration decisions of the Hong Kong Chinese via the films' subject matter, character development and narrative structure. Deciding whether to move or not, which may or may not be told straightforwardly through the films, permeates every single element in these films. They reflect the 'refugee mentality' and diasporic sentiments of many Hong Kong Chinese. Unlike other global diasporas (Cohen 1997, 2008) such as the Jews or the Africans, the segments of the Chinese diaspora residing in Hong Kong practise their diasporic lives and relate to their 'homeland(s)' in multiple ways. Some still think of 'China' (it may or may not be the one under the communist rule) as their homeland; others regard their current home Hong Kong as their real homeland without reference to it being part of the geographical China. Still others lament that not even the present Hong Kong is their real homeland. The city has become a place that they do not know anymore because of the drastic sociopolitical deteriorations since the Handover. Many Hongkongers' diasporic sentiments have continued to this day.

These chosen films have been considered the components of the New Hong Kong Cinema because of their specific concerns with Hong Kong's political and sociocultural developments with regard to the Handover. They also allow us to see that journeys and journeying in film have become the special features in the New Hong Kong Cinema, which I have used to exemplify the Cinema of Transitions. Not only do these diegetic and non-diegetic journeys and journeying give a visual impression of the transitions on which new Hong Kong films are based, but they are also helping to define what the New Hong Kong Cinema is.

As global citizens, the Hong Kong Chinese cannot single themselves out as living alone on an isolated island. They will certainly need to build up their self-perception by identifying the difference between themselves and others, especially other segments in the Chinese diaspora living elsewhere. Sometimes the process of the Hongkongers' self-identification as 'Chinese' can itself be an emotional trauma. In the next chapter, we will discuss those new Hong Kong-related Chinese-language films that attempt to answer the nationality question of the Hong Kong Chinese from the angle of the Chinese people not belonging to Hong Kong society. This angle of exploration in film is arguably useful to prevent the filmmakers and the target viewing community in Hong Kong from facing the emotional and psychological distress relevant to their self-identification.

Notes

1. Hong Kong Island was ceded to Britain when China signed the 'Treaty of Nanking' in 1843, as part of the indemnity paid to Britain after the First Opium War. In 1860, after its second disgraceful defeat in the Second Opium War, China signed the 'Convention of Peking' and ceded the Kowloon Peninsula (the part south of Boundary Street in Kowloon Peninsula) to Britain. Both Hong Kong Island and Kowloon Peninsula were ceded in perpetuity. In 1898, China and Britain signed the 'Convention Between Great Britain and China Respecting an Extension of Hong Kong Territory' (aka the Second Treaty of Peking), which allowed Britain to gain a rent-free lease over the New Territories part of Hong Kong for a period of ninety-nine years. As a result of the signing of the 'Sino-British Joint Declaration' in 1984, all three parts of Hong Kong were returned by the United Kingdom to China in 1997. The actual 'Handover' ceremony took place at midnight, 30 June 1997.

2. The Hong Kong Chinese have never had an equal national status with their mainland counterparts, not even since the Handover. For example, they hold the Hong Kong SAR passports while their mainland counterparts hold the PRC passports. The locals in Hong Kong are often still referred to as Hong Kong *qiao bao* (overseas Chinese living in Hong Kong) by their neighbours on the mainland.

3. The distinction between commercial and art-house cinemas used in Euro-American contexts is not suitable for understanding the nature of Hong Kong and Hong Kong-related Chinese-language films, when the latter are released domestically or in neighbouring East Asian territories. Due to a lack of governmental subsidies, most of these films, if they are lucky to get theatrical release, aim to earn a certain amount from the box-office sales and post-theatrical sales through DVD, online and other channels in order to recoup initial investments in their production. For example, John Woo's mega-budget film *Red Cliff* was released as an art-house film in Europe and the United States, even though it was screened as a genuine blockbuster in East Asia. For more exploration on *Red Cliff*, see Chapter Four in this book (see also Bordwell 1979).

4. Foreign films are required to be subjected to China's strict foreign film import quota before they can enter the country's domestic market. Upon the WTO's request, in February 2012 China increased the annual number of revenue-sharing foreign films, from twenty to thirty-four, to enter China (Jaffe 2011; China Agrees 2012; China Eases 2012). See also note 20 in the Introduction to this book about Hong Kong films' foreign status vis-à-vis mainland Chinese films.

5. See also *Buenos Aires Zero Degree: The Making of Happy Together* (Kwan Pun-leung and Amos Lee, Hong Kong, 1999).

6. Ho in real life is one of seventeen children of the Chinese tycoon, Stanley Ho, who has built a gambling empire in Macau.

7. Source: interview with Johnnie To, *Sparrow* (DVD) (Hong Kong version, bonus track).

8. At the twenty-fourth Hong Kong Film Awards in 2005, *Days of Being Wild* was ranked third among one hundred best Chinese films made during the first century of Chinese-language cinemas.

9. The film's Chinese title (*A Fei Zheng Zhuan*, literally, the story of rebels) is the same as the Chinese translated title given to *Rebel Without a Cause* when the latter was released in Hong Kong.

10. This character, Mimi, reappears in Wong's *2046* as a more mature version of herself, but without direct reference to *Days of Being Wild*.

11. Source: information given by Alex Law in *Echoes of the Rainbow* (DVD) (Hong Kong version, bonus track).

12. The *Young and Dangerous* series is directed by Andrew Lau. There were six instalments altogether of this film series made between 1996 and 2000; it features a young gangster group whose characters are based on the local comic book series entitled *Teddy Boy*. The young triad members in the films are all depicted as heroes, although they are involved in criminal activities. Information about each instalment

is as follows: *Young and Dangerous* (Andrew Lau, Hong Kong, 1996) (Manfred Wong as the co-producer and the writer); *Young and Dangerous 2* (Andrew Lau, Hong Kong, 1996) (Manfred Wong as the co-producer and the co-writer); *Young and Dangerous 3* (Andrew Lau, Hong Kong, 1996) (Manfred Wong as the producer and the writer); *Young and Dangerous 4* (Andrew Lau, Hong Kong, 1997) (Manfred Wong as the producer and the writer); *Young* and Dangerous 5 (Andrew Lau, Hong Kong, 1998) (Manfred Wong as the producer and the writer); *Born to be King* (Andrew Lau, Hong Kong, 2000) (Manfred Wong as the co-producer and the writer). After this series, Andrew Lau moved on to co-direct with Alex Mak the *Infernal Affairs* series in 2002 and 2003. During the late 1990s, other similar Hong Kong gangster films were made. They have themes and characters derived from the *Young and Dangerous* series, or are spin-offs; for example, *Portland Street Blues* (Raymond Yip, Hong Kong, 1998). Manfred Wong worked again as the producer and the writer of this film.

13. Maggie Cheung was a typical Chinese diasporic subject from Hong Kong. She was born in Hong Kong and moved to the United Kingdom with her family when she was eight. Cheung returned to Hong Kong when she was eighteen and entered the entertainment business through being the first runner-up at the Miss Hong Kong beauty pageant in 1982.

CHAPTER TWO

Outsider Characters
Chineseness, and Hong Kong Screen Imagination and Imageries

In November 2012, the Chinese University of Hong Kong's Centre for Communication and Public Opinion Survey released its latest public opinion poll 'The Identity and National Identification of Hong Kong People' conducted in October 2012. This was the ninth poll of a series launched by the research centre in 1996 (Chan S-I. 2012a, 2012b). The 2012 survey showed that among 819 telephone respondents (chosen through random sampling) who were Hong Kong residents and could speak fluent Cantonese, only 12.6 per cent identified themselves as 'Chinese' (the lowest registered percentage of identification with the nation 'China' since 1996), whereas 65.2 per cent of the respondents highlighted they were 'Hongkongese' ('Hongkongese' and 'Hongkongers' are often used interchangeably).[1] The survey results not only attracted unprecedented Hong Kong mass media attention for this kind of poll, but they also received challenges and criticism from the representatives of the Chinese authorities. To the mainland Chinese officials, the shortcomings of this survey were not related to its methodology or interpretations. What they strongly disapproved of was the survey questions that asked ordinary Hong Kong citizens about their choice between being 'Hongkongese' or being 'Chinese'. From the Chinese authorities' point of view, national status is something that should not be questioned. The mainland Chinese officials interpreted that, worst of all, these public opinion polls would encourage people to think about Hong Kong's independence, and therefore challenge the absolute rule and control of the Beijing government over its territory. Similar criticism was addressed to well-known public opinion researchers, such as Robert Chung who had spearheaded a public opinion programme at the University of Hong Kong concerning the Hongkongers' ethnic identification (R. Chung 2012). These kinds of conflicts between the mainland Chinese officials and Hong Kong-based scholars conducting public opinion polls are by no means single incidents but are part of the long-standing cultural differences between various Chinese communities (England 2012). At the same time, the events inevitably expose one of the root causes of many ongoing social and political disputes between Hong Kong and the mainland – the concept of 'being Chinese' could be interpreted from more than one angle and on different levels.

In film, the ambiguous and unclear definition of 'Chinese' and 'Chineseness' has resulted in multiple manifestations of Chinese identification in Hong Kong Cinema over the past several decades. This chapter seeks to find out what these filmic manifestations are and what implications they might have for the filmmakers and their target audiences. My discussion starts with a summary of differing opinions on the concept of Chineseness. The discourses of the theorists and scholars I highlight give us an idea that the said concept is complex and multi-layering. There are indeed numerous interpretations of what, who and how to be 'Chinese'. I am particularly interested in knowing how Hong Kong filmmakers have dealt with the topic in their works. With the support of an array of film examples, I examine why, and how, Hong Kong filmmakers have employed the non-Hong Kong Chinese characters as the featured roles in their films. The characters of Vietnamese refugees, mainland Chinese illegal immigrants, Chinese migrants living in South East Asia and animated figures are of special significance in Hong Kong's context, although the personalities they represent all seem to be unrelated to Hong Kong society. Moreover, they also have certain ethnic and linguistic connections with the Hong Kong Chinese viewers, who are some of the target audiences of these films. I argue that these outsiders' on-screen existence is not random. It has the effect of helping the Hong Kong Chinese revisit the issues of their own ethnic-cultural identity through an indirect route (Abbas 1997: 28).

'Chineseness', 'Being Chinese' and 'Becoming Chinese'

Cursory library and online research reveals that scholars from various disciplines, critics, observers and the general public have different understandings of the concept of Chineseness. Should Chineseness be defined culturally, politically or nationally? Should it be dealt with differently with respect to different times and locales? Should it be treated according to the specific circumstances of individuals or communities? Should it be subdivided into cultural Chineseness, political Chineseness, social Chineseness, economic Chineseness, etc.? Or is it pointless to discuss it at all, because if Chineseness means different things to different people, it may simply be a meaningless term? Who should define it and for whom?

While critics have attempted to make sense of what Chineseness is, more and more of them argue that defining Chineseness is a daunting task because this is not a fixed and stable concept. Nonetheless, one thing in common among their views is that the definition of the concept and what it might mean to those it concerns have evolved through time. Ideas about it broadly range from those that support the wide applicability and pluralization of Chineseness, to those that argue Chineseness is an empty term. The views often oscillate from one extreme to the other on the explanation scale of Chineseness. From this angle, Chineseness per se is not only a place- or culture-specific notion (see, for example, Y-W. Chu 2001, 2013: 38–39), but it also involves the much less discussed element of 'time' as related to the manifestations, meanings, interpretations and discussions of the notion. Let me make a brief summary of scholarly debates throughout the years about the concept of Chineseness. As there are indeed various views from critics who have discussed this topic, the summary here can only provide highlights of different comments and is by no means exhaustive. This overview is important for understanding why Hong Kong films made in different decades may carry tints of Chineseness, transitional Chineseness or non-Chineseness.

Born in Indonesia and raised in Malaysia, Chinese immigration scholar Wang Gungwu was one of the first scholars to systematically discuss the concept of Chineseness: he did this as early as 1957 (Wang G. 1991b: vii). Wang highlights that Chineseness is a 'shared historical experience whose record has continually influenced its growth' (Wang G. 1991b: 2). This opinion points to the first written record of Chinese civilizational thinking, Confucianism, supported by the unifying language of signs and symbols. The author acknowledges that the kind of Chineseness manifested in mainland China after 1949 (the year of the establishment of the PRC) is different from that found in Taiwan, Hong Kong and among large Chinese communities in South East Asia and North America respectively (Wang G. 1991b: 7).

Hong Kong-raised cultural theorist Rey Chow argues that the resort to Chineseness, or Sinicization, is illusory and manipulative in a sociopolitical sense. It amounts to merely submitting oneself to the empty myth of consanguinity (R. Chow 1993: 23–24). Underlying Chow's argument, and in her usage of the term in the early 1990s, is the condition of Chineseness being related to the Chinese ethnicity (R. Chow 1993: 25). Is Chineseness restricted to those born Chinese, or is it not?

In the Introduction to this book, I showed that Chinese-American Neo-Confucian scholar Tu Wei-ming advocates an imaginary overarching universe called 'cultural China'. In this sphere, Tu envisions that Chinese diasporic people should come to the fore to spearhead discourses concerned with Chinese matters. Within the third universe of 'cultural China', Tu includes non-Chinese descendants who are mostly intellectuals of other nationalities and who have strong research interests in Chinese matters. His idea seems to be based on a wider understanding of what Chineseness could mean and involve. But the inevitable implication is that Tu's idea assumes the superiority of Chineseness. It forces people to think and discuss only from the angle of Chineseness and it is thereby restrictive. Openly challenged by cultural theorist Ien Ang in 1998 and 2001 in two of her famous publications, Tu's idea however does add an extra dimension to the debates about Chineseness.

Born to Chinese parents in Indonesia, educated in the Netherlands and now settled in Australia, Ang does not deny the concept of Chineseness. Instead, Ang (1998: 225) advocates that Chineseness should be treated as an open and indeterminate signifier, and used with caution. How one deals with one's Chineseness remains a personal political choice (Ang 2001: 35–36, 44–51). Ang's disagreement with Tu's 'cultural China' thesis is shared by Chua Beng Huat (2012), a Chinese-Singaporean sociologist. In his writing about East Asian pop culture being used by the regional powers as a tool of exerting 'soft power', Chua dismisses the concepts of Confucian greater China and Chinese diaspora. Chua (2012: 34) argues that 'the cultural definition of Chineseness has been unavoidably and increasingly marked by local politics'. He recalls the rupture that took place between cultural-ethnic Chineseness and Chinese nationality when in 1955 Zhou Enlai, then Prime Minister of the PRC, encouraged overseas Chinese communities (except those in Hong Kong, Macau and Taiwan) to take up their local citizenship (Chua 2012: 36). This fully indicates the multiple layering in the concept of Chineseness and what it might mean to be 'Chinese' to different individuals and communities. The author also cites the case of Singapore as an example of counteracting the monolithic term 'Chinese', as Singapore adopts the nationality-neutral term 'Huaren' to refer to those cultural-ethnic Chinese people who are Singaporean citizens (Chua 2012: 37). In Mandarin, 'Huaren' literally means 'ethnic Chinese people' without denoting any specific nationalities of the group.[2] Although built on a disputable assumption that Mandarin is the lingua franca of ethnic Chinese, 'Huaren' can be regarded as a better label to replace the term and concept of 'Chinese' when 'Chinese' is used with essentialist intention on the individuals and groups concerned.[3] From a historical perspective, Asian studies scholar Caroline S. Hau (2012) revisits the ways in which the Chinese communities and individual countries in South East Asia have related to 'China'. Hau argues that Chineseness is multi-sited and the signifier 'China' is floating. According to the author, 'In *practice*, no single political entity/regime embodies or exercises ultimate authority on "China," "Chinese," and "Chineseness"' (italics in original). She disagrees that China has played the role of the 'preeminent cultural arbiter of Chineseness'. Instead, Britain (one of the most aggressive colonizers in Asia in the colonial period), the United States, Japan, Hong Kong, Taiwan and South East Asian countries (and the Chinese communities they host) that have had an ongoing economic and cultural-political relationship with mainland China, and the governments of these territories in different historical periods, have all had a part in defining what 'China', 'Chinese' and 'Chineseness' mean. Over the years, regional 'de-Sinicization' and 're-Sinicization' of ethnic Chinese communities in East and South East Asia, triggered by various political, economic and cultural reasons, have gone far beyond the reach of the Chinese state. In fact, the hybrid Chineseness manifested at times at grass-roots level in mainland China may not necessarily coincide with, and sometimes even challenge, the Chineseness officially sanctioned by the Chinese state.

In a similar vein, Hong Kong-based cultural theorist Kwai-Cheung Lo writes about the Chineseness of the Hongkongers in his *Chinese Face/Off* (2005). Lo calls it a 'potential Chineseness' (2005: 3), and regards Hong Kong's culture as operating 'an articulation of "transitional Chineseness"' (2005: 4). His idea then serves as another alternative to the so-called proper and 'real' Chineseness represented by China. Lo (2005: 4, 8) also argues that 'Hong Kong's Chineseness is a site of performative contradictions'. Hong Kong serves as a sounding board by which the meanings of Chineseness, which have been evolving through time, can be tested. Like Chow (1993, 1998), Lo (2005: 6) agrees that Chineseness, a supposed master signifier of the so-called Chinese nation, is nothing but an empty sign. He applies his idea about Chineseness and its manifestations to the diasporic situation of Tibetans. Here, Lo (2009: 2) reminds us that the diaspora concept is used by the Chinese state to promote nationalism under the empty notion of Chineseness among different races of people who are now considered 'Chinese' politically, if not culturally. Besides the prevalent Han race, there are fifty-five ethnic minorities (including the Tibetans that Lo discusses) identified under the Chinese Communist Party's ethnic classification scheme. These ethnic minorities reside in places that have now come under Chinese state governance. Due to historical and political reasons, these groups of populations have become 'Chinese' even though they may not be willing to be designated as such. To them, the 'Chinese' status is an imposed nationality.

The rejection of the imposed identity is certainly shared by many Hongkongers, who do not wish to be labelled as 'Chinese'. The social feelings involved are regarded by the mass media as 'negative expressions of Hong Kong people's "Chineseness"' (A. Zhang 2012). These Hongkongers find online channels to express their dissatisfaction with the imposed national and cultural identity, and their difference from their mainland counterparts. Meanwhile, local grass-roots organizations, such as 'We Are Hong-kongian, Not Chinese' and 'Scholarism', organize regular street protests and establish online forums to discuss the issues of being or not being 'Chinese', and the invasion of 'mainlanderism' in Hong Kong. Writing on the postcolonial identity crisis as reflected in the Hong Kong cop-and-gangster *Infernal Affairs* trilogy, Ohio-based Chinese culture and literary scholar Howard Y.F. Choy (2007: 55) adds the consideration of the Hongkongers' Britishness to the discussion of the Hongkongers' re-Sinicization, or the state of becoming 'Chinese'. Writing against the 'orthodox Chineseness' promoted by the PRC, Hilary Hongjin He (2012: 299), who was educated in Australia and is now based in Fujian, China, argues that Hong Kong demonstrates 'the cosmopolitan side of Chineseness' against a broad notion of 'Greater China', and not just the 'China' as located on the mainland or the 'China' as represented by the Republic of China in Taiwan.

Among all these discussions of Chineseness and the Hongkongers' kind of Chineseness, I find psychologist Nan M. Sussman's discussion of the Hongkongers' identity inspiring, in that the author takes into account the East Asian aspect and multiple migration experience of the Hong Kong Chinese. Based on the historical legacies of Hong Kong's past and present political and cultural experience, the author dissects the identity of the Hongkongers into layers in order to understand the returned Hong Kong Chinese. They had emigrated from Hong Kong before 1997 and have then remigrated back to the city. The author traces the identity of the Hong Kong Chinese as starting to develop only in the 1840s, when Hong Kong became a British Crown Colony. The author argues that the Hongkongers' Chinese identity has evolved in relation to four particular historical incidents and eras, with each newer stratum of identity demonstrating particular historical and cultural concerns laying on top of the older ones. The historical eras that Sussman identifies are: (1) the time prior to the Opium Wars, (2) the postwar British sovereignty period, (3) the pre-Handover period (1984–97) and (4) the post-Handover, remigration period (Sussman 2011: 12).

Sussman sees the resulting Hong Kong Chinese identity as composed of three nested layers. At the core is a Chinese identity (inherited from the ancestors or coming from the persons themselves, who have brought the typical Chinese cultural values from their places of origin in mainland China). This core is then surrounded by a layer of Western cultural and civic values (resulting from the British colonial influence, and other daily interactions between the Hong Kong Chinese and their Western neighbours living in the same society). Further out, these two layers of the Hong Kong Chinese identity are encompassed by a regional, geographical identity (Sussman 2011: 18). Although Sussman does not articulate it clearly, this third layer is understood as directed towards the East Asian status that forms part of the Hong Kong Chinese's sense of identification. As for those migrants who have returned to Hong Kong, their identities are bound to be even more complex. The corresponding layering in Hong Kong Chinese identity that Sussman highlights thus sets the author's idea apart from that of other researchers, who argue that the Hongkongers' Chineseness is transitional, flexible or subject to contextual determination.

Two things are worth noticing. On the one hand, it is not surprising to see that Chineseness as a cultural marker indeed has multiple layers of interpretation depending on its manifestations in different time periods, locales and social-cultural-political contexts. The concept's openness is perhaps most pronounced when the historical burden of Chinese civilization interacts with other cultures and societies. Hence, we see different researchers, especially those ethnic Chinese researchers around the world who have empirical experience of 'being Chinese' culturally and ethnically, analysing it differently. On the other hand, the topics of 'Chineseness', 'being Chinese' and 'becoming Chinese', as developed by ethnic Chinese researchers outside mainland China in non-Chinese languages, should not be taken as something coincidental. Rather, they are the by-products or long-tail effects of two hegemonies, the Western (mainly European and American) and the Chinese. Most cases of the treatment of these topics are responses against the 'chauvinistic sinocentrism' or 'sinochauvinism'

(R. Chow 1998: 6) of the mainland Chinese intellectuals, which in turn has been aimed against earlier Western hegemony. We should not forget that, politically, the Chinese authorities do not encourage open discussions of Chinese nationality status, as evident in the conflicts between the mainland Chinese officials and Hong Kong-based identity researchers mentioned in the introduction to this chapter. Here, we can see the internal conflicts of the Chinese hegemony – that is, the official, authoritative Sinocentrism on top of the cultural Sinocentrism – that have inadvertently impacted the discourse on Chinese-related matters in various fields.

Outsider Characters: The Hong Kong Chinese's Imaginary Stand-ins and Alter Egos

Given that there is no clear definition of Chineseness or what it means to be Chinese nowadays, it is arguably convenient for Hong Kong film directors to make use of the non-Hong Kong Chinese roles as metaphors and allusions to develop their cultural, social and political comments on the surrounding environment. In interrogating why non-Hongkonger actors/actresses are employed to play Hong Kong natives in Hong Kong films and why a particular past is emphasized, comparative literature scholar Yiu-Wai Chu argues that the purpose of such cinematic representations is to 'develop an autonomous imaginary free from the domination of the China factor' and to resort to a 'hybridized' cosmopolitanism (Y-W. Chu 2013: 98–99). According to the author, the use of a local narrative in Hong Kong's 'cultural imaginary' can subvert this cosmopolitanism simultaneously. Applying the same logic, we can consider those Hong Kong Kong-related Chinese-language films featuring Hong Kong actors/actresses to be non-Hong Kong Chinese characters as cases of offsetting the influence of the places of origin. The purpose is also to stress the 'hybridity' quality of the films, especially those made immediately before and after the Handover.

What specific kinds of non-Hong Kong Chinese characters to be featured depended heavily on the prevailing sociopolitical circumstances at any particular point in the recent past. For example, films portraying Vietnamese boat people (referring to those refugees fleeing Vietnam in crudely built big boats), who are usually ethnic Chinese in the diegetic settings, saturated Hong Kong screens in the early to mid 1980s when Hong Kong was under international pressure to be a refuge port in real life for Vietnamese refugees. Besides everyday news coverage and television drama series, moving images such as *The Story of Woo Viet* (Ann Hui, Hong Kong, 1981); *The Man from Vietnam* (Clarence Fok, Hong Kong, 1982); *Hong Kong, Hong Kong* (Clifford Choi, Hong Kong, 1983); *To Liv(e)* (Evans Chan, Hong Kong, 1991); and *Run and Kill* (Billy Tang Hin-sing, Hong Kong, 1993) feature main protagonists who hail from Vietnam but speak Cantonese fluently and without any accent. Another troupe of so-called outsiders – new or illegal immigrants from mainland China – is featured as the main characters in Hong Kong films that were made in the mid 1980s, the 1990s and the early 2000s. It was a time when Hong Kong society had to face the economic-sociopolitical transitional uncertainty of the Handover. Hong Kong films such as *Long Arm of the Law* (Johnny Mak, Hong Kong, 1984); *Love in a Fallen City* (Ann Hui, Hong Kong, 1984); *Her Fatal Ways* (Alfred Cheung, Hong Kong, 1991); and *Comrades, Almost a Love Story* (Peter Chan, Hong Kong, 1996) are some of the classics that famously make use of the mainland Chinese characters and their sojourns to reflect sociopolitical realities the Hongkongers would need to face once the nationality on their passports changed from British National (Overseas) to Chinese.

There are practical advantages for filmmakers to use outsider characters in film, as they could serve as imaginary stand-ins and alter egos for the Chinese audience in Hong Kong to experience indirectly the vicissitudes of life and the changes in time and place. The audience could empathize with these characters and share their different diegetic structures of feeling, such as melancholia, fear and loneliness (Naficy 2001: 291), without the need of going through these feelings in real life. Outsider characters and their diegetic experience also help minimize and rehearse the impacts of what might be severe blows to the sense of being of the local target audience (see discussion below on *Boat People* (Ann Hui, Hong Kong, 1982), *Durian Durian* (Fruit Chan, China/France/Hong Kong, 2000) and *Going Home* (in *Three*) (Peter Chan, Hong Kong, 2002)[4]). They highlight an escapist function that many Hong Kong mainstream genre films perform (see discussion below on *The Detective* series and the *McDull* series).

No matter what the practical advantages are, Hong Kong filmmakers have been in a similar position to that of the accented filmmakers in employing outsiders as main protagonists and adopting the characters' vantage points to tell the stories. Typical foreign characters in accented films, as suggested by diaspora and film scholar Hamid Naficy (2001: 70, 290), have ambiguous identities. They often speak the dominant language in film with an accent and are usually played by non-actors. Although we may find the outsider characters in Hong Kong-related Chinese-language films deviating from those in accented films (e.g., speaking Cantonese fluently and without any accent, and blending into the dominant society if they so wish), the presence of these outsider characters in the New Hong Kong Cinema often offer, on top of other conveniences, an association to Chineseness. At any given point in time, they give an alternative angle for the filmmakers and the target audiences to look into their quality of being or not being 'Chinese'. To the filmmakers/target audiences/dominant environment, these characters are foreign but they also look strangely familiar. The ambiguity of these outsider characters thus heightens the interstitial quality that many new Hong Kong films project.

Chinese-Vietnamese-turned-Hong Kong Chinese?

Although the arguments I present in this book are largely concerned with the sociocultural-political situations of the ethnic Chinese population in Hong Kong, which represents a majority of around 93.6 per cent of the total population of 7.07 million, I would like to mention that the minority groups in Hong Kong are not ignored in my discussion. These groups amount to around 6.4 per cent of the total Hong Kong population. They are categorized under 'Other Ethnicities' in Hong Kong in the 2011 Population Census conducted by the government. Within this 6.4 per cent of the Hong Kong population, there are Indonesian (1.89 per cent), Filipino (1.88 per cent), White (0.78 per cent), Indian (0.40 per cent), Pakistani (0.26 per cent), Nepalese (0.23 per cent), Japanese (0.18 per cent), Thai (0.16 per cent), Korean (0.07 per cent), other Asian (0.10 per cent) and others (0.43 per cent). In other words, apart from the local community of white European descent (including people hailing from the United Kingdom, the United States, Canada, continental Europe, Australia, New Zealand and South Africa), who may serve to support Cohen's imperial diaspora proposition (1997, 2008), minorities in Hong Kong consist mostly of other Asians. The census indicates that 98.7 per cent of these ethnic minorities are 'Usual Residents', while 1.3 per cent are 'Mobile Residents'. A majority (86.7 per cent) of them were not born in Hong Kong. The census results provide no further information on the category of 'Other Asian' in the section on 'Ethnicity of Population', or about 'Other Nationalities' in the section on 'Nationality of Population'. The only exception is the category 'Vietnamese'. While there is no mention of 'Vietnamese' in the 'Thematic Report: Ethnic Minorities' (2012) published by the 2011 Population Census Office of the Census and Statistic Department of the local government, the category 'Vietnamese' is included in the 'Ethnicity' item in the demographic fact sheets for individual districts in Hong Kong. Whether these Vietnamese are in fact Vietnamese by descent, or whether they are Vietnamese by nationality remains uncertain.[5]

Vietnamese illegal immigration into Hong Kong was a heated topic in the local public debates and mass media reports between the mid 1970s and the late 1980s. The first Vietnamese refugees arrived at Hong Kong in May 1975. The influx of boat people from Vietnam was caused by their fear of the new Vietnamese Communist government and by subsequent ethnic cleansing carried out by the government in the major cities of Vietnam. Many of the victims were ethnic Chinese, who then fled the country to neighbouring territories such as Hong Kong, Malaysia, Singapore and Thailand. Whereas Malaysia and Singapore prohibited the Vietnamese refugees from entering their territories, in 1979 Hong Kong declared itself a 'port of first asylum', effectively absorbing all the Vietnamese refugees who might have planned to go to South East Asian countries but were turned away. It is estimated that more than 210,000 Vietnamese have reached Hong Kong since the first boat arrived in 1975. As a result, during the time when Hong Kong was taking in the Vietnamese refugees, Hong Kong had one of the highest boat people populations in the region. Over the years, the nature of these refugees has changed from political to mainly economic (D. Wong 1983; C. Cheung 1998; Williams 2000).

Between the years 1975 and 2011, 143,714 Vietnamese refugees in Hong Kong re-settled overseas. Some 57,344 Vietnamese illegal immigrants were repatriated from Hong Kong back to Vietnam under the 'UNHCR Voluntary Repatriation Programme' (1991–97). Another 19,210 Vietnamese migrants and illegal immigrants were repatriated under another scheme, the 'Orderly Repatriation Programme', introduced in Hong Kong in 1991 (Immigration Department Annual Report 2011). A 'Widened Local Resettlement Scheme' was implemented by the Hong Kong SAR government in February 2000, allowing some 973 Vietnamese refugees and 435 eligible Vietnamese migrants stranded in Hong Kong to be assimilated into Hong Kong society.

The Vietnamese illegal immigrants have been a huge social and financial burden for Hong Kong society during the pre- and post-Handover period. While local mass media in Hong Kong reported on the negative impact of Vietnamese refugee flow on Hong Kong society, international mass media focused more on the human rights issues related to these boat people, such as the closed refugee camps in which they were held and, later, the repatriation policy that received serious international criticisms of Hong Kong's ways of treating these outsiders (Chugani 1984). The tense international relations between the United Kingdom and China over the handling of the Vietnamese refugee problem during the period leading up to the Handover was also a news topic in the international mass media (Gittings 2000).

Boat People

Ann Hui was famously one of the first Hong Kong directors to explore the theme of Vietnamese illegal immigrants in television programmes and cinematic works in the late 1970s and the early 1980s. Hui became an assistant to the Hong Kong martial arts film guru King Hu after she had graduated from London Film School in the 1970s. Her own directorship took off while working at the local television station TVB. She also worked for a short while for the Independent Commission Against Corruption (locally known as the ICAC), which is an independent governmental unit combating corruption in society. Most of her works display strong humanist concerns from a female perspective, something rare in the male-dominated local film industry. Cultural studies scholar Mirana M. Szeto (2011) celebrates Hui's success in dealing with 'cinematics of everyday life' in a way that allows the director to connect with the local audience. Media culture scholar Cindy Hing-Yuk Wong (2011: 14) identifies Hui among a small group of female auteurs worldwide. Hui and her films have earned awards and praise from international film festivals that they themselves may at times demonstrate gender bias. Over a directorial career spanning more than three decades, Hui has used her films as powerful tools to show sympathy for the underprivileged and to attend to what might generally be regarded as insignificant topics and/or characters. This may explain why Hui was drawn to the topic of the Vietnamese and their lives in Hong Kong in the 1970s. In 1978, she explored the issue of Vietnamese boat people in a television episode entitled 'The Boy from Vietnam' ('來客') as part of the *Below the Lion Rock* (獅子山下) series sponsored by the government-funded but independently operated Radio Television Hong Kong (locally known as the RTHK). The story reflects the difficult life of a teenage Vietnamese boy who has landed in Hong Kong and awaits resettlement to his final destination in the West. In 1981, Hui tackled a similar topic in a fictional film, *The Story of Woo Viet*, featuring the up and coming Chow Yun-fat as an ethnic Chinese refugee from Vietnam, who, instead of resettling in the United States, ends up being a hired killer in the Chinatown of the Philippines.

Moving from the small screen to the big screen, again with the heated topic of Vietnamese refugees, Hui made *Boat People* in 1982 (Shu 1988: 47; Hui 1998: 21). The project was initiated by the film's producer Miranda Yang and funded by a leftist Hong Kong-based company, Bluebird Movie (M. Berry 2005: 428).[6] The film was released mainly in Hong Kong, although it also enjoyed limited international release in the United States, France and Japan. It was screened to selected audiences at major international film festivals such as the Cannes Film Festival (as a selection film) and the New York International Film Festival in 1983 (Erens 2000b: 184; Stringer 2003: 17).

Boat People was shot on location in Hainan, China, which was meant as a stand-in of Vietnam (M. Berry 2005: 429). Strictly speaking, the film is not about Vietnamese refugees but about the hardships of their lives in Vietnam before they choose to become boat people (Szeto 2011: 51). The film is set mainly in 1978, a time when the united communist Vietnam was in an incipient stage, and tells the story of the Japanese photojournalist Akutagawa (George Lam), who is invited by the Vietnamese government to be the witness of the country's new reforms. During the time when Akutagawa is in Vietnam, he makes friends with several locals, including the family of the fourteen-year-old Cam Nuong (Season Ma), To Minh (Andy Lau), Officer Nguyen (Qi Mengshi) and Nguyen's mistress (Cora Miao). All of them are leading a difficult life. Except Officer Nguyen, they all hope to leave the country. Their experience shows the dark side of Vietnam that is completely opposite to what the Vietnamese government wants Akutagawa to see. After Cam Nuong's mother, an illegal prostitute, has committed suicide, Akutagawa decides to help Cam Nuong and her young brother to board the big boat and flee the country; in doing so he can save them from being sent to the New Economic Zones where many people died of hard labour. The plot ends with Akutagawa tragically sacrificing his life, albeit unintentionally, in order to allow the Vietnamese siblings to flee successfully.

Although most of the major characters in the film are supposedly local Vietnamese, they are played by popular Hong Kong Chinese actors and actresses, such as George Lam, Cora Miao, and the then up and coming Andy Lau and Season Ma. These characters in *Boat People* are supposedly outsiders to Hong Kong society, yet bear certain linguistic similarities to the target audience in Hong Kong. All of them, including the main Japanese character, speak fluent Cantonese to one another, but not the Vietnamese language. If not for the opening scene portraying communist soldiers marching triumphantly on main streets in Vietnam after the Vietnam War (1955–75), the viewers could indeed be easily confused and think they were watching a Hong Kong Chinese-related film (Sek 1988: 20). Hui's reluctant admission that *Boat People* serves to dramatize the Hongkongers' perception of life and their fear of an uncertain future could support this confusion (Stokes and Hoover 1999: 181, 347; see also Szeto 2011: 54–55). The timely (or one may say in hindsight, untimely) release of the film in Hong Kong in mid October 1982, shortly after the commencement of a series of negotiations regarding Hong Kong's return to Chinese rule, quickly spurred the local audience's interest in the film (Hui 1998). Instead of the featured topic of Vietnamese refugees, many local Chinese viewers saw the film as an allusion to their own imminent destiny under the authoritarian rule of communist China. The subsequent local box-office success (grossing more than HK$15 million (£1.2 million or U.S.$1.9 million), and ranked number four among ninety-nine Hong Kong films in that year's Hong Kong box-office chart) brought to Hui both her first major directorial success and, later on, much trouble on a political level (Snapshots 1986: 7; Teo 1988: 41; Li C. 1994: 167; Chan C. 2000: 509; Leung P. 2000: 242; W. Cheung 2007: 207). In Chapter Three, I will explore more the director's possible political stance.

In particular, the fact that the male lead Akutagawa is Japanese may have further problematized the sense of identification and identity among the Hong Kong viewers in the early 1980s. One may even argue that Akutagawa represents Hui's alter ego exploring an imagined world that the filmmaker had never actually been to, but had done a great deal of research on before starting the film's production (Cheuk 2012: 470). Not much information on Akutagawa's background is given in the film. Through his conversations with other characters, we learn that he is an orphan and a Tokyo resident. He was married by the age of eighteen but he does not mention anything about his wife or children. Comparable with other lonesome characters often featured in accented films (Naficy 2001: 27, 290), Akutagawa as a character speaking Cantonese (Lam pretending to have a Japanese accent) and coming from a developed country stands in strong contrast with the main Vietnamese characters in this film. Yet, the characterization made by Lam, a popular Cantopop singer and seasoned actor, not only helps ease the incongruity and foreignness of Akutagawa, but also rouses the audience's sympathy for him and for those he cares about (W. Cheung 2007: 208–10; see also Bhabha 1994: 227–28). Akutagawa complicates this poignant, semi-political drama by his own geographical, national and cultural displacement: he starts out as a genuine outsider to the communist Vietnamese society (as well as to the target audience's familiar environment in Hong Kong), passes through disillusionment with the country's superficial stability, and assumes a foster-father role for Cam Nuong and her brother after their mother's death. The penultimate scene illustrates this fully. It is enhanced by a dissolve from a close-up of Cam Nuong (now aboard the big boat, her status changing from a Vietnamese citizen to one of the Vietnamese boat people) to an extremely long shot of Akutagawa (being burnt alive at the pier after the policemen have shot him). On the one hand, this on-screen transit emphasizes both characters' *displacement*, and on the other hand it *re-places* Akutagawa in this foreign country through Cam Nuong, who by this scene becomes Akutagawa's cinematic extension visually and metaphorically. At the ending, the freeze frame of a close-up showing Cam Nuong looking blankly at the sea works effectively to fix forever the images of another set of identity *displacement* (out of Vietnam) and *re-placement* (into a rough sea, as the film's Chinese title *Tou Ben Nu Hai* suggests) that are shown simultaneously. Despite being banned for political reasons in China and Taiwan (and for ten years in Hong Kong), this Hong Kong New Wave pioneer film, with the timeliness and multi-placement of its characters, remains in the canon of important films in the New Hong Kong Cinema (*Boat People Reappears* 1992: 26; Li C. 1994: 168–69; Hui 1998: 24; Stringer 2003: 20).

Mainland Chinese vs Hong Kong Chinese?

The dramatized incident in *Boat People* serves to fill in some of the blanks in the public awareness and imagination in Hong Kong about how Vietnamese outsiders might have ended up in the immigrant city. Since the early 1980s, another kind of outsider coming from mainland China has quickly been made visible as a secondary agenda to the discourses of Hong Kong's political, economic, social, cultural and historical contexts amid the city's preparation for the Handover. Interestingly, unlike the Vietnamese (who usually occupy the public imagination in Hong Kong as refugees or boat people), what the mainland Chinese nationals and new mainland Chinese immigrants stand for in the imagination of the Hong Kong public has changed over time. This change has gone hand in hand with Hong Kong's development over the last three and a half decades as a global city (similar to London and New York, especially in the realms of economic and cultural interaction) (Sassen 2001), as well as with China's economic reform.

Different mass media (e.g., newspapers,[7] television dramas, novels and novellas, Cantopop, radio talk shows and, of course, films) play a significant role in influencing how the Hong Kong public has formed its impressions of this unavoidable 'other' from the mainland. Although biased at times, the mediated images of the mainlanders are not always negative. They are in fact very diverse. They might be nondescript, laid-back sons, daughters and cousins, such as the role of Ah Caan in the 1979 TVB drama series *The Good, the Bad and the Ugly* (網中人), and of Choi Sum in the 2013 TVB drama series *Inbound Troubles* (老表, 你好嘢!). They might also be acquaintances (or people one has never met before in real life) on Facebook or Twitter, members of one's WhatsApp instant messaging groups and Skype contacts. Sometimes, the mainlanders impress the Hong Kong locals with the image of the worldly-wise *lao xiong* (pronounced in broken Mandarin by the Cantonese-speaking Hongkongers; literally meaning 'old big brother from the North'). At other times, they are represented as illegal immigrants, for instance, in the role of Fan in *Little Cheung* (Fruit Chan, Hong Kong, 2000) and *Durian Durian*, and of the female helper at the butcher's in *Hollywood Hong Kong* (Fruit Chan, France/Hong Kong/Japan/United Kingdom, 2001). They could also be hard-working middle-class office workers, such as the role of Yen in *Don't Go Breaking My Heart* (Johnnie To and Wai Ka-fai, China/Hong Kong, 2011). The mainlanders are often found among intellectuals. But they might also be associated with some of the biggest criminals the city has ever had. Many Hong Kong-produced mainstream cop-and-gangster films have the major role of villain from the mainland, e.g., in *Long Arm of the Law, Intruder* (Tsang Kan-cheung, Hong Kong, 1997) and *The Stool Pigeon* (Dante Lam, Hong Kong, 2010). The mainlanders might be found among those mainland Chinese pregnant women abusing Hong Kong's medical system, as in the role of Wong Fei-fei in the 2012 TVB drama series *Friendly Fire* (法網狙擊). In other settings, they could also be carers, such as the role of Pearl in *Homecoming*, and of Miss Choi in the nursing home in *A Simple Life*. The mainlanders might also be among the elite, wealthy venture capitalists and business executives, such as the role of Chen Handong in *Lan Yu* (Stanley Kwan, China/Hong Kong, 2001), and of

Brother Tyrannosaurus in *Vulgaria*. They might be part of the authorities, Hong Kong-based People's Liberation Army members and mainland Chinese policemen (or other kinds of mainland Chinese uniformed officials). We can see them in the cameo of the soldiers in *The Longest Summer* (Fruit Chan, Hong Kong, 1998), and in the role of Inspector Shen Chen in *Infernal Affairs III*, of Li in *The Floating Landscape* (Carol Lai, Hong Kong, 2003), of the mainland Chinese police captain in *Election 2*, and of Fang Zhengdong in *A Beautiful Life* (Andrew Lau, China/Hong Kong, 2011). In a lot of Hong Kong-related Chinese-language films, the mainlanders are represented as victimized females, such as prostitutes, femme-fatale figures or battered new immigrants. For example, we can find them in the role of the prostitute in *Intruder*, of Yan in *Durian Durian*, of Hung Hung (aka Tong Tong) in *Hollywood Hong Kong*, of Mary in *Mary from Beijing* (Sylvia Chang, Hong Kong, 1992), of Li Qiao in *Comrades, Almost a Love Story*, of Vivian in *Chinese Box* (Wayne Wong, France/Japan/United States, 1996), of Bai Ling in *2046*, of Mei in *Dumplings* (Fruit Chan, Hong Kong, 2004), of Sun Na (aka Xiaoyu) in *Perhaps Love* (Peter Chan, China/Hong Kong/Malaysia, 2005), of Chung Chun-lei in *Sparrow* and of Wong Hiu-ling in *Night and Fog* (Ann Hui, Hong Kong, 2009). But the mainland Chinese are also portrayed in films as practitioners of various cultural and creative industries, such as the major characters in *Shaolin Soccer* (Stephen Chow, China/Hong Kong, 2001) and *Beijing Rocks* (Mabel Cheung, Hong Kong, 2001). They might also be seen in films in the roles of heroes, stars and celebrities, and so forth. Over the years, the images of mainland Chinese counterparts have formed an inseparable part of the real, as well as the imaginary, state of existence of Hong Kong – a city located on the southern edge of China's territory, and which itself is a composite product of multiple waves of migrations from mainland China (and other territories). The mainlanders are, one may even argue, a kind of alter ego that suggests to Hong Kong society what a 'Chinese' city is like or not like.

Durian Durian

Still, stereotypes of this prominent 'other' from the mainland have abounded in Hong Kong-related Chinese-language films over the past thirty-plus years since the Hongkongers started to seriously consider and construct their own identity through visual images. In *Durian Durian*, we see two kinds of images of this mainland 'other'– illegal mainland prostitute and child immigrant. The mainlanders in Hong Kong-related Chinese-language films may not be put in marginalized positions. Yet, they are often given the kind of spotlight that does not do them justice either. In the cases of illegal mainland prostitutes and child immigrants, they are often discussed in a negative manner in the sociopolitical contexts of Hong Kong. Being an independent Hong Kong production, *Durian Durian* strives to redress this problem, but the film ends up in a self-knitted web of complicated and unanswered questions that perhaps only time can resolve.

This docudrama is the fourth feature film made by Hong Kong independent director Fruit Chan after he has turned away from the mainstream Hong Kong film industry (see Chapter Three for Fruit Chan's biographical background). Before *Durian Durian*, Fruit Chan made his Handover Trilogy, which includes *Made in Hong Kong* (1997), *The Longest Summer* (1998) and *Little Cheung* (2000). These three films portray various archetypal Hong Kong locals, especially those born and raised under the British colonial system, in order to explore and scrutinize the effects of the Handover on the Hongkongers. *Durian Durian* (2000) is the first of Fruit Chan's Prostitute Trilogy (still unfinished), which also includes *Hollywood Hong Kong* (2001). The third film in this supposed trilogy has not been made; for a long time, Fruit Chan's *Public Toilet* (Hong Kong/Japan/South Korea, 2002) has been mistakenly thought of by critics as this third one (E. Cheung 2009: 152 note 17). *Public Toilet* marks a halt in the director's annual production of independent films that he started to make in 1997.[8]

Durian Durian obtained financial support from Wild Bunch, the French film distribution and international sales company that has handled the international sales of many award-winning films, such as *Spirited Away* (Miyazaki Hayao, Japan, 2001) and *4 Months, 3 Weeks and 2 Days* (Cristian Mungiu, Belgium/Romania, 2007) (Gan 2005: 23). The film reached its audiences mainly through the international film festival circuit, moving from Venice, Toronto, London, Hong Kong in 2000 to Rotterdam in 2001, before selected international release in other territories such as Tokyo and Malaysia, and DVD sales much later on.

Durian Durian follows the stories of two different mainland Chinese characters who stay in Hong Kong temporarily, each for their own specific reason. The first half of the film is about the story of Fan, the same illegal child immigrant from *Little Cheung* (Ye 2000: 22). *Little Cheung* is about the eponymous nine-year-old boy who has lived all his life in Mongkok, one of the old districts in Hong Kong, and the sociopolitical changes of the society he has witnessed over about a year. *Durian Durian* picks up what is left untold about Fan in *Little Cheung* (Fan in both films is played by nine-year-old amateur actress Mak Wai-fan from Hong

Kong). Through Fan's voice-over, we learn that she was born to a Hong Kong father and a mainland Chinese mother, and that she regards mainland China as her real home. Fan is a typical example of tens of thousands of children who are not given the right of abode in Hong Kong by birth due to the non-citizenship of one or both of their parents (HK Government 2001). In order to reunite with her whole family in Hong Kong, the girl overstays in the city after her three-month entry visa has expired. Yet, during the time in Hong Kong, she is confined at home for fear of being caught overstaying. Going to school is unfortunately also out of the question. Often shot at low camera height from the subjective point of view of Fan, the city to her, as an outsider, looks different from what it is often associated with: glamour, progress, civilization and prosperity. All Fan can see (and all that the audience can see through Fan's eyes) are dark alleyways, the small flat in which she is cramped up with the whole family, and other illegal immigrants or migrant workers. There is no place for Fan in Hong Kong and, naturally, she is not happy there.

Half way through the film, Fan meets the 21-year-old Yan (played by professional mainland Chinese actress Qin Hailu). From then on, the vantage point of the film changes from that of Fan to that of Yan. Yan, who is also from China, works illegally as a prostitute while she is on a three-month travel visa in Hong Kong. She represents another kind of outsider to Hong Kong society. Yan's main goal is to stay in Hong Kong to earn quick money through prostitution before returning home in a post-industrial town in the north-east of China. Although Yan is from a middle-class family and has received proper training in the Beijing opera performing arts, like everyone else from her generation she struggles to make a living in her hometown.

The stories of Fan and Yan subvert the stereotypical images of these two types of mainlanders in the minds of many Hongkongers (V. Lee 2009: 172). To Fan and Yan, China is their ultimate home no matter how harsh their lives there have been. Hong Kong, in contrast, is the unapproachable 'other'. Their improvised lines and dialogues in the film make their unpleasant situations in Hong Kong stand out in sharp relief against Hong Kong's *seeming* prosperity after 1997 (F. Chan 2000; M. Berry 2005: 472, 476). Their presence in the city seems also to ask the audience to look at Hong Kong and the characters' own situations from a double-alternative angle, in that late capitalism has gradually taken its toll on both China and Hong Kong (Tsui 2000). Moreover, the two females' illegitimate status during their temporary stays in Hong Kong also questions the effectiveness and the limitations of the 'one country, two systems' political framework, as well as other intertwining cultural, economic and psychological relationships between Hong Kong and China (Acquarello 2001; Cheng S. 2002; Gan 2005: 2; V. Lee 2009: 176–77). As film scholar Esther M.K. Cheung (2008: 90) argues, the 'realistic' traits of this docudrama are better understood in specific historical and cultural contexts. To the author, Fruit Chan employs a realistic film style (e.g., he uses quasi-realistic mise en scène) to enhance 'the impressions and effects of the "real"' (E. Cheung 2008: 90) in a film that is, after all, fiction and is reliant on the use of symbolism to explore the themes of 'homelessness' and 'dislocation' (M. Berry 2005: 474, 477). Talking about the symbolism of the eponymous fruit durian that is described in the Chinese title of the film as the 'floating durian' (E. Cheung 2008: 92), Fruit Chan comments: 'Durian is a strange fruit. People who like it thinks [sic] it's the greatest, people who don't think it really stinks' (Ye 2000: 23). Much like the fruit's ambiguous position in the minds of its consumers, the ambivalent view of reunification of Hong Kong and China, and the exacerbated atmosphere of homelessness and helplessness in Hong Kong society after 1997, are still bothering many Hong Kong and mainland Chinese.

Going Home (*in* Three)

Not surprisingly, the mainland 'other' is often met with in Hong Kong genre films, such as the widely celebrated kung fu films and the more recent pan-Asian horrors (Choi and Wada-Marciano 2009). The latter were revitalized in the late 1990s under the inspiration of successful Japanese horror films (aka J-horror), e.g., *Ringu* (Nakata Hideo, Japan, 1998). Peter Chan's *Going Home*, part of the first omnibus pan-Asian horror, *Three*, explores the sensitive issues of mainland Chinese immigrants. The mainland 'other' here is the male lead, played by one of the most bankable East Asian stars, Leon Lai (who was born in Beijing and raised in Hong Kong). The cast certainly poses challenges to the imagery often used in Hong Kong-related Chinese-language films to represent the mainlanders.

The film segment of *Going Home*, which runs for around fifty minutes, tells the tragic love story of Yu (Leon Lai) and his wife Hai'er (Eugenia Yuan).[9] It is set in a rundown, almost deserted public housing complex.[10] Widowed policeman Wai (Eric Tsang) moves into the area with his eight-year-old son. The young boy is scared by the ghostly atmosphere in the neighbourhood, and claims he keeps seeing a young girl in a red dress. Wai does not pay much attention to his son's complaint until one day the boy disappears after school. Wai searches around for his son but to no avail. He goes to his only neighbour Yu, who lives in another block right across from Wai's. After Yu has denied having seen the boy, Wai sneaks into Yu's flat and discovers that Yu is keeping his wife's corpse in the flat. Yu hits and ties up Wai the intruder. In the conversations thereafter, Yu reveals that he and his wife are from Changsa, China. Both of them are qualified Chinese medical doctors, yet both developed cancer. Yu is trying to resurrect Hai'er from death by bathing her dead body with Chinese herbal medicine every day. He hopes that, once Hai'er wakes up, they can go back home to mainland China. When Wai's colleagues come to look for Wai, they take Yu as a lunatic and remove the corpse of Hai'er from the flat. In the finale, Yu is knocked down by a car when he attempts to chase after the vehicle carrying his wife's body away. Yu also dies eventually. It is later revealed that Hai'er used the same method to resurrect Yu from death three years ago. The (ghostly) girl in a red dress turns out to be their aborted child.

Going Home highlights and blurs the boundaries between Hong Kong natives and their mainland counterparts both inside and outside the film story (Li C. 2012: 201; Wong C-f. 2012: 203). Yu is perfectly bilingual in both Mandarin and Cantonese. When he speaks to Hai'er's dead body in Mandarin, he is at 'home' in the mental sphere that he creates for himself and Hai'er. Wai, who intrudes in their sphere, is the outsider. But when Yu is talking to Wai in Cantonese, he is aware of his outsider's location in Hong Kong society. This is visually presented by the almost vacant residential complex where only the lowly paid policeman and the unemployed mainland Chinese medical doctor would consider living. The casting of Leon Lai and Eric Tsang as the main characters, and the Mandarin-speaking Eugenia Yuan as the supporting actress, adds one more dimension to the blurry boundaries between the Chinese of Hong Kong and those of the mainland. Yuan was a newcomer in the Hong Kong film industry. Born and raised in the United States, she is the eldest daughter of Cheng Pei-pei, who is the martial arts star famous for her connections with Shaw Brothers and her performance in *Crouching Tiger, Hidden Dragon* (Ang Lee, China/Hong Kong/Taiwan/United States, 2000). According to Peter Chan, *Three* was one of the first ambitious strategies of Asian-based filmmakers gathering Asian talent and investments to capitalize on the regional markets in recent years. If so, in addition to Lai and Tsang's bankability with the East Asian audience markets (especially those of Chinese-language films), the ambiguity of boundaries between the mainland Chinese and the Hong Kong Chinese is indeed necessary to please the audiences on both side of the border (Frater 2000; Mazurkewich 2000). While paving the way to the successful pan-Asian *Three... Extremes* (2004)[11] and *The Eye* series (2002, 2004, 2005),[12] Peter Chan's *Going Home* arguably gave the director/producer a confident poise to penetrate further the Chinese-language audience markets (especially on the mainland) in the years to come (Shackleton 2009b). After co-founding Applause Pictures in 2000 in Hong Kong to develop his concept of pan-Asian productions, and after producing an array of financially and critically successful pan-Asian projects, Peter Chan moved on to establish We Pictures in 2008. The company is aimed at producing and selling 'China-centric' films, in the hope of changing the vista of Chinese-language cinemas.[13] From this perspective, the mainland Chinese 'other' in Peter Chan's films (from *Comrades, Almost a Love Story* to *Going Home*) can be viewed as an important element in the filmmaker's course to ultimate success.

South East Asian-Chinese and Animated Chinese

So far I have discussed two main types of outsiders to Hong Kong society that filmmakers present in Hong Kong-related Chinese-language films. In real life, these so-called outsiders have brought to the Hong Kong citizens, at worst, social and economic strain, and at best, a chance to revisit the Hongkongers' own existence as being 'Chinese'. As anthropologist David Yen-ho Wu (1994: 150–51) puts it concisely when explaining the multi-layering of perceptions of the concept of 'Chinese' among the Chinese:

> Both Zhonguoren *[literally, people from the China country]* and zhonghua minzu *[literally, the Chinese people clan]* represent an identity based on concepts of cultural and historical fulfillment rather than the more conventional modern notions of nationality or citizenship. Since most Chinese have believed that the Han people were the race of China, one that had absorbed people of all languages, customs, and racial and ethnic origins, the meanings of being Chinese in the sense of ethnicity, culture, citizenship, or residence were almost never addressed. (emphasis in original)

Over the years Hong Kong filmmakers have not just portrayed Vietnamese boat people and the mainland Chinese as the two most visible groups of outsiders.

In some instances films have presented characters that come from other social and cultural minorities living at the margin of Hong Kong society. These might not be refugees, like the Vietnamese; or illegal immigrants, like some of the mainland Chinese. Many of the other minorities found in Hong Kong, such as Thais, Singaporeans, Malaysians, Indonesians, Filipinos, Nepalese, have gained legal status in Hong Kong through the official channels of migration, work or personal connections (e.g., marriage to Hong Kong citizens). Even though they account for less than 6.4 per cent of the total population in Hong Kong, they are rarely given the limelight in Hong Kong mainstream films, which are still filled with mostly Chinese or Chinese-like faces.

Recent Hong Kong-related Chinese-language films shot on location in South East Asia tend to feature Cantonese-speaking Chinese immigrants to these countries (e.g., Thailand, Malaysia). These films, which cater mainly to the viewers in Hong Kong, then offer an opportunity of empathy, rather indirectly, to the target audience to understand the situations of new immigrants and minority groups hosted by Hong Kong. The setting of their stories is justifiably not in Hong Kong but in South East Asian countries. Employing Hong Kong Chinese actors and actresses to play the roles of diasporic Chinese living in South East Asia can further enhance these films' appeal to their target audience in Hong Kong. On the other hand, Hong Kong-led runaway productions have benefited from the long-existing East and South East Asian film production and distribution networks. These film business connections were first established prominently by the Shaws (operating under the company name Tianyi (aka Unique) Film Productions at the beginning) in the 1920s and maintained throughout the years. In the early 2000s, the film business connections in the region were revitalized by Peter Chan's pan-Asian co-production concept through his co-owned Applause Pictures. Affordable production costs in South East Asian territories also facilitate the proliferation of these runaway productions during the new millennium. Some of the most recent ones include Patrick Tam's award-winning *After This Our Exile*, which was shot on location in Perak and Kuala Lumpur in Malaysia, and the Pang Brothers' *The Detective* series, which was shot mainly in Thailand.

The Detective *Series*

Oxide Pang (the elder of the twin brothers) directed all three films in *The Detective* series. They include *The Detective* (Oxide Pang, Hong Kong, 2007),

The Detective 2 (Oxide Pang, Hong Kong, 2011) and *Conspirators* (Oxide Pang, Hong Kong, 2013; aka the last instalment of *The Detective* series). The twin brothers also had the roles of the producers of *The Detective* and *The Detective 2*, and Oxide Pang was the co-producer of *Conspirators*. The younger of the twins, Danny Pang, did not work on the final instalment. The series was produced by Universe Entertainment (Hong Kong), while the first two instalments were produced in association with several other companies, including Sil-Metropole and Magic Head Film Production. All the films in this series belong to a new generation of Hong Kong noirish crime thrillers with a Thai flavour. Although they were mainly shot in Bangkok, Thailand (the final instalment was also shot on location in Malaysia and in Guangzhou, China), Hong Kong, not Thailand, is regarded as the films' sole country of origin. Also, the films did not have theatrical release in Thailand. *The Detective* was released in Hong Kong, China, Malaysia, Singapore and South Korea. *The Detective 2* and *Conspirators* had similar places of theatrical release to that of *The Detective*, except the list included Taiwan instead of South Korea.

The Pang Brothers themselves are ethnic Chinese born in Hong Kong in 1965. They started their involvement in film production by working, respectively, as colourist (Oxide Pang) and editor (Danny Pang). Their film production and directorial careers, nonetheless, did not start in Hong Kong but in Thailand, after they moved there in the early 1990s. There the Pangs directed television commercials for a while. Their co-directorial debut was *Bangkok Dangerous* (Oxide and Danny Pang, Thailand, 1999), which was shown at major international film festivals, such as Toronto and Rotterdam. It was subsequently remade by the Pangs in 2008 into the Hollywood-style, action-packed *Bangkok Dangerous* (Oxide and Danny Pang, United States, 2008). This 2008 film was shot on location in Bangkok, starring Hollywood actor Nicolas Cage in the male lead role and Hong Kong actress Charlie Yeung as the female lead. The remake is labelled an American film. It has enjoyed much wider international theatrical release than its Thai version. The success of *Bangkok Dangerous* showered sudden fame and wide recognition on the Pangs; this caught the attention of Peter Chan, who around that time was developing his concept of pan-Asian co-production at Applause Pictures. Peter Chan, whose parents are Thailand-born Chinese, spent his formative years in Thailand, and has developed personal and professional ties with the country. He invited the Pangs to return to Hong Kong from Thailand to make *The Eye* in 2002. It was a financially and critically successful ghost film

(E. Liu 2004a, 2004b; Li C. 2012: 196–97). The connection between pan-Asian productions, Hong Kong, Thailand and horror stories thus arguably forms the backbone of *The Detective* series and its basis for success on the Hong Kong commercial cinema scene (Martin 2007; *The Detective 2* 2011).

The films tell the story of Chan Tam (Aaron Kwok), an ethnic-Chinese private detective living and doing most of his detective work in the Chinatown of Bangkok. A dropout from the Thai police academy, Chan Tam is evidently no genius as a detective. The Cantonese title of the *The Detective, C+ Zing Taam* (a play on words denoting both a private detective and a grade C detective) indicates Chan Tam's mediocrity and, at times, poor performance in his profession. Chan Tam's clumsiness has made it hard for him to sustain his business and has led him into conflicts with the local police force, though he has a good police friend Fung Chak (Liu Kai-chi). In *The Detective* Chan Tam is suddenly commissioned by a local bully to find a missing girl. Several murder cases are uncovered during the search, eventually revealing the presence of a supernatural force and the cause of the mysteries – the missing girl is already dead and has returned to the mundane world to take her revenge. In *The Detective 2* (with a Cantonese title *B+ Zing Taam* to indicate Chan Tam's professional improvement in this second instalment), Chan Tam again gets involved in mysterious serial murders. He uncovers the identity of the murderer, who is an ethnic Chinese orphan living in Thailand. Also revealed in the course of this search are the possible causes of the murder of Chan Tam's parents and his subsequent troubled childhood. *Conspirators* continues the story that is told in the two previous instalments. It unveils the real cause of the death of Chan Tam's parents and the identity of their murderer.

From the start in the series, Chan Tam is portrayed as a lone character. He is an orphan and lives alone in the attic of a cinema house he inherited from his parents after their disappearance (the fact that they were murdered is only revealed to him much later in life). To the Thai police force, and by extension, to Thai society, he is a complete outsider. Although he speaks Thai, he prefers to speak in his mother tongue, Cantonese, with his Chinatown neighbours. This language choice shows his Chinese diaspora status and his possible ancestral roots in the south of China where Cantonese is spoken. Yet, his expression of Chineseness is by no means a direct reference to mainland China alone, exemplifying Hau's idea of multi-sited Chineseness (2012). The fact that Chan Tam has been orphaned since childhood also suggests to the audiences his lack of real national/parental roots. Although rootless, Chan Tam as a private detective knows his position in Chinatown inside-out, which is that of someone who somewhat defines and confines his own marginalization in his host country Thailand. His involvement with the unexplained supernatural power (in instalment 1) and the dark side of human nature (in instalments 2 and 3) adds further dimensions to the mysterious past of this anti-hero-type character. To the target audiences, especially those in Hong Kong, the role of Chan Tam seems also to serve as an on-screen image for those Thai natives residing in and hosted by Hong Kong. It may raise the question as to who the hosts and the hosted actually are. The lonesome character of Chan Tam thus multiplies the interstitial qualities of this Hong Kong series produced astride the filmmaking environments of Hong Kong and Thailand in a film business network where China is exercising its unprecedented power (Naficy 2001: 46–47). Chan Tam's isolated state of existence and psychology blend in well with the coarse and edgy visuals of the films, which are saturated with a bleached colour tone and a heavy use of chiaroscuro. Such visuals strike a stark contrast to the more vibrant and robust depictions of Bangkok city life often found in the mass media. These aesthetic qualities thus further enhance the mysterious and noirish atmosphere of this Hong Kong thriller series.

Although the instalments in *The Detective* series are commercial Hong Kong films, the lonesomeness of the main character certainly echoes the displacement situations of many similar outsider characters we find in the New Hong Kong Cinema, and more generally in different accented films (in Naficy's sense). All the Chinese-Thai characters in *The Detective* series help enrich the stories told by Hong Kong filmmakers in general in recent years. The focus of their films is no longer just on how the Hong Kong Chinese are dealing with their lives after the Handover, but also on widening the public awareness and imagination regarding ethnic minorities who live among the Hong Kong Chinese.

The McDull Series

Among the existing scholarly investigations into contemporary Hong Kong Cinema, animation is probably one of the most under-researched areas. The relatively insignificant number of animation outputs from Hong Kong certainly does not help. Even if they are made, Hong Kong's local animations are often produced under the shadow of two dominant players in the field of world animation – Japanese animated films (especially those turned out by Miyazaki Hayao's Studio Ghibli) and the Walt Disney cartoons. Since the beginning of the new millennium, the Hong Kong screenscape has been marked by cartoons about McDull and his group of kindergarten friends.

In the animation, McDull's year of birth is given as 1995. He is a little pinky piglet with a brownish birthmark around his right eye and another on his forehead (reminiscent of Mikhail Gorbachev's forehead birthmark). McDull lives with his mother Mrs Mc (aka Tam Yuk-lin) in Tai Kok Tsui on the Kowloon side of Hong Kong. While Mrs Mc is a streetwise single parent, McDull is not very smart and does not do well in school. However, he is very kind and obedient to his mother. McDull goes to the neighbourhood Springfield Flowers Kindergarten that is run by the Principal and taught by Miss Chan. Like many big-screen Japanese animated figures, McDull has his origin in a Hong Kong local comic series, *McMug*, in which he is a supporting character. The eponymous McMug is McDull's distant cousin and a much smarter pinky piglet. The comic series was created by cartoonist Alice Mak and her colleague-turned-husband, author Brian Tse. It started coming out in the *Ming Pao Weekly* magazine in 1988. Whereas the cartoon figures are drawn in a simplistic, childlike style with a very light outline and pastel-tone watercolours against a minimalist background, the content of this comic series caters to an educated adult audience. Through the characters' witty conversations, spoken in Cantonese, and their satirical comments on the current affairs of Hong Kong, this delightful series is known for its reflection of authentic Hong Kong culture (Lau 2012).

Over the years, McDull has gained increasing popularity, stealing much of the limelight from his cousin McMug. McDull makes frequent appearances in various mass media and has been featured in six animated films since 2001. They are *My Life as McDull* (Toe Yuen, Hong Kong, 2001); *McDull, Prince de la Bun* (Toe Yuen, Hong Kong, 2004); *McDull, The Alumni* (Samson Chiu, Hong Kong, 2006); *McDull, Kung Fu Kindergarten* (Brian Tse, China/Hong Kong/Japan, 2009); *The Pork of Music* (Brian Tse, China/Hong Kong, 2012); and *McDull. Me & My Mum* (Brian Tse and Li Junmin, China/Hong Kong, 2014). These animations enjoyed mainstream theatrical release in Hong Kong (and also mainland Chinese theatrical release since the 2009 film), while all *McDull* films have been screened at various international film festivals around the world, such as Hong Kong, Moscow, Chicago, Tokyo, Paris, Hamburg, Singapore, Locarno, Annecy International Animated Film Festival and in Cannes Film Market. The *McDull* films are popular among Hong Kong and non-Hong Kong audiences for their charm and authenticity (Kraicer 2002; Elley 2002–3).

The *McDull* films are easily recognizable by their fragmented contents (except for the 2012 and 2014 episodes, each of which has a complete plot). There are usually no main threads spanning the entire film. The philosophical voice-over (by an adult version of McDull) hence becomes an important element, giving a sense of unity to each of the films and putting all the fragments in a wider perspective. At the same time, the untranslatable, colloquial and at times vulgar Cantonese language spoken in the voice-over and the film dialogues is a major characteristic of the *McDull* series (Elley 2004). The voices of *McDull's* main characters are performed by famous Hong Kong actors and actresses, including Sandra Ng as Mrs Mc (Ng is the partner of Peter Chan in real life), Anthony Wong as the Principal/waiter and Andy Lau as McDull's father. Another noticeable feature of the *McDull* series is the frequent use of real street scenes from Hong Kong as a background, highlighting the setting of the story. By means of 3-D imaging, hand-drawn 2-D cartoon figures often appear against a backdrop of recognizable Hong Kong streets to tell their own stories and the stories of Hong Kong (Paquet 2006). Film critic Shelly Kraicer (2002) compares *McDull* to Disney's cartoons: 'Disney's move is ideological: it falsifies history/reality to sanitize and give false comfort. *McDull*, on the other hand, captures something like "authenticity" via patently artificial means: it defamiliarizes, provoking thoughtful reengagement with the society it depicts'. In this context, it is thus not difficult to see that the creators of the *McDull* stories use McDull and other characters to represent different types of local residents of Hong Kong and how they think about their home city. The animated porcine hero is both an outsider to the human society of Hong Kong and also an absolute local, as evident during the finale of *My Life as McDull* when the grown-up McDull suddenly assumes a real human form.

In little McDull's eyes, Hong Kong always undergoes constant development and redevelopment. His neighbourhood in Tai Kok Tsui is cramped with old buildings waiting to be torn down by wealthy land developers in urban renewal projects. Although McDull tries very hard to learn different life-enhancing skills (such as 'bun snatching' in *My Life as McDull* and martial arts in *McDull, Kung Fu Kindergarten*) under Mrs Mc's great expectations, he is basically very content with what he has. As the little piglet says repeatedly in *McDull, Prince de la Bun*, he prefers to live in the present. McDull's attitude to life echoes those Hong Kong Chinese who are happy with what they have amid certain sociocultural constraints of the environment. His parents, however, see things differently. Mrs

Mc works very hard and considers various new ideas on how to earn money in order to prepare for an imagined better life in the future; she even buys a plot in a graveyard in Guangdong, China to prepare for her afterlife. Contrarily, McDull's father Mc Bing, who has long disappeared from their lives, wants to find his glorious past. He is only mentioned in a bedtime story, *the Prince of Bun*, told by Mrs Mc to McDull. Allegedly a lost prince, Mc Bing is a useless man and for years has stranded himself in a place that is not his home. His sudden disappearance (in an attempt to go and find his kingdom) symbolizes those diasporic Chinese who reside in Hong Kong but do not quite know where home really is. This is reinforced by a mix and match of nostalgic street scenes of 1960s Hong Kong, contemporary Hong Kong streets full of Filipino domestic helpers and the animated scene of Cantonese opera (a dying performing arts tradition in Hong Kong). While these characters understand that they might have Chinese roots (as is said of their distant ancestor, McFat, in *McDull, Kung Fu Kindergarten*), they do not have direct connections with mainland China. Tai Kok Tsui in Hong Kong is and remains their home. No matter how hard life is for them in Hong Kong, there is always hope; and love abounds.

Concluding Remarks

This chapter has reviewed different kinds of representations (and representatives) of Chineseness via the use of outsider characters in the New Hong Kong Cinema. Over the past thirty-plus years, it has by no means been a random decision to feature various non-Hong Kong Chinese personalities in film, whether they are Vietnamese refugees, mainland illegal immigrants, Chinese minorities in South East Asia or beloved animated figures. Very often the existence of these specific characters in Hong Kong-related Chinese-language films coincided with the most debated topics in the public domain in Hong Kong. Filmmakers could provide the audiences with opportunities to revisit these heated discussions in condensed and dramatized versions through the medium of film. They have thus made use of their roles as members of a cultural and creative labour force to experiment with the idea of being 'Chinese' today. Film viewers, especially the local audience in Hong Kong, could imagine themselves in similar situations to those of these sociopolitically foreign characters in a diegetic environment. The resulting empathy with the filmic characters was (and still is) likely to be useful for film viewers to deal with their own selves in real life in a transitional, historical time of Hong Kong. Nonetheless, as in other cinematic phenomena (e.g., the abundance of 'journeys' and 'journeying' in film) that I have discussed, these outsider characters are not quick solutions and direct answers to the Hong Kong Chinese's identity quest, not least because circumstances within and beyond the city have been changing drastically in the course of Hong Kong's political-historical transitions.

Ironically, although these non-Hong Kong Chinese personalities and their cinematic presentations could help Hong Kong filmmakers and film viewers alike to explore issues relevant to their identities in real life, their 'outsider' status has once again been reinforced. One may also argue that featuring these outsider characters on screen highlights the superiority-inferiority complex from which the Hong Kong Chinese have suffered on an ongoing basis, and which they must resolve in order to come to terms with their new identities in the new political-historical era. In the next chapter, I will further explore the Hongkongers' transitional identity complex in the cases where Hong Kong filmmakers attempt to inscribe themselves and their authorial vision more directly in film.

Notes

1. Relevant survey findings were drawn from the Chinese-language press release entitled 'The Identity and National Identification of Hong Kong People – Survey Findings' (dated November 2012). The press release was obtained by the author via personal email exchanges with the Centre for Communication and Public Opinion Survey at the Chinese University of Hong Kong in late December 2012. See also the Centre for Communication and Public Opinion Survey's website (English), www.com.cuhk.edu.hk/ccpos/en/tracking3.html (accessed 5 May 2015).
2. In Cantonese, the written form of 'Huaren' is read as *wa yan*.
3. Mandarin is by no means the lingua franca of ethnic Chinese. The mother tongue of most overseas Chinese, especially those settled in North America, is Cantonese. Oral communication between these Chinese communities and, for example, the Hong Kong Chinese, whose mother tongue is Cantonese, would more likely be conducted in the Cantonese language. In this scenario, Cantonese, not Mandarin, becomes the common language of different ethnic Chinese communities living outside mainland China.
4. There are three segments in *Three* (2002): *Going Home* (directed by Peter Chan, representing Hong Kong); *Memories* (directed by Kim Jee-woon, representing South Korea); *The Wheel* (directed by Nonzee Nimibutr, representing Thailand).

5. It is said on the 'Nationality and Ethnicity' online interactive chart of the 2011 Population Census of Hong Kong that, 'The ethnicity of a person is determined by self-identification. The classification of ethnicity is determined with reference to a combination of concepts such as cultural origins, nationality, colour and language. This practice is in line with the recommendations promulgated by the United Nations in 2008, and has taken into account the practices of other countries as well as local circumstances'.

6. In the Hong Kong context, 'leftist' is often used interchangeably with 'pro-Chinese Communist'. This is different from what the 'left' might mean in Europe or the United States.

7. Although they are controversial and always under public scrutiny, local Hong Kong newspaper reports have formed one of the main sources informing the Hong Kong general public of the problems that the mainland Chinese bring to the city, e.g., the illegal child migrants, the mainland Chinese prostitution, the birth tourism and anchor babies in Hong Kong (aka babies born in Hong Kong to mainland Chinese couples), the problem of the mainland Chinese's right of abode in Hong Kong, the issues of bulk purchase of baby milk powder in Hong Kong by the mainland Chinese, the quarrels on public transport between the Hong Kong Chinese and the mainland Chinese tourists, etc. (Yeung 2000; Life in the Shadows 2006; Mainland Girl 2012; Parallel Importers 2013; see also J. Liu 2012).

8. Fruit Chan did not release a film in 1999, but released two in 2000. They are *Little Cheung* and *Durian Durian*.

9. About ten more minutes of footage was added to make *Going Home* a feature film. The feature version is entitled *Three: Going Home*. It enjoyed separate yet limited release in 2002 in Hong Kong shortly after *Three* was theatrically released there (See Li C. 2012: 201).

10. The film was shot on location in the former Police Married Quarters, located on Hollywood Road on Hong Kong Island, Hong Kong.

11. There are three segments in *Three... Extremes* (2004): *Box* (directed by Miike Takashi, representing Japan); *Cut* (directed by Park Chan-wook, representing South Korea); *Dumplings* (directed by Fruit Chan, representing Hong Kong).

12. Film information: *The Eye* (Oxide and Danny Pang, Hong Kong/Singapore, 2002); *The Eye 2* (Oxide and Danny Pang, Hong Kong/Singapore, 2004); *The Eye 10* (aka *The Eye Infinity* and *The Eye 3*) (Oxide and Danny Pang, Hong Kong, 2005).

13. Source: We Pictures' official website, www.wepictures.com (accessed 5 May 2015).

CHAPTER THREE

Hong Kong Filmmakers
Authorial Vision, Self-Inscription and Social Underdogs

Since the late 1990s, the local Chinese mass media in Hong Kong have widely started to use the term 'collective memory' to give meanings to specific events, landmarks and personalities that have disappeared in the society. They connote the Hongkongers' remembrance of their recent past that has nothing to do with the 5,000 years of Chinese civilization history. The 'collective memory', then, allows the Hongkongers to change their perspective from worrying about the complicated nationality issues and sovereignty change, to focusing on their mutual experience over a period in history when Hong Kong society has been constructing its own identity and sociocultural sphere. Literally, the 'collective memory' of the Hongkongers is unique to them.

Just when the Hongkongers in general are inclined to pay attention to a disappearing past (Abbas 1997), so are many Hong Kong Chinese mainstream, commercial filmmakers exploring multiple subjects of interests in their films to revisualize that part of history solely belonging to the Hongkongers. Although suffering from financial constraints in film production, these filmmakers have developed their individual authorial vision, which I refer to as their concerns and preoccupations in life, and the stances they take to see/opine about their concerns with strong reference to their personal experiences. A mutual experience among these filmmakers is their displacement from places of birth. Many of them were born in nearby East and South East Asian regions, such as mainland China, and moved to Hong Kong at a very young age with their families. This background has led the filmmakers to develop a strong diasporic consciousness that has proven difficult to dissipate even in their adulthood.

This chapter discusses several representative filmmakers of the New Hong Kong Cinema and their authorial vision and concerns, and how they inscribe themselves in their films to convey their messages. They are Ann Hui, Johnnie To, Fruit Chan and the 'New Generation Directors' (the newest group of filmmakers in Hong Kong). No two Hong Kong filmmakers demonstrate completely identical preoccupations. Yet many do have the tendency of mirroring and

complementing each other's interests in life. I believe it is significant and necessary to understand their authorial concerns and what they care to talk about
before we can truly appreciate their choices of particular audiovisual styles and
cinematic elements in film. I commence this chapter with a section on the issue
of film authorship, illustrated by the profiles of the chosen filmmakers. Detailed
information on their personal backgrounds, career paths and representative
works is given as a prerequisite for understanding their approaches to films, filmmaking and life more generally. I am keen to find out how they represent, respectively, several generations of mainstream filmmakers in the local film industry
in Hong Kong. Some of them, like Hui and To, are well-established and highly
respected inside and outside the local film sector. Others, like Fruit Chan, built
their directorial careers at specific historical moments and then, after a few years
of prolific creativity, stopped all of a sudden to pursue their professions further
until their next chances to return to the field. The newest generation of filmmakers, like Clement Cheng and Derek Kwok, who previously worked in other capac-
ities in the local film industry, have only just started their directorial careers in
the last few years. They are at the crossroads of either making it or breaking it
in the continuously volatile environment of Hong Kong's film sector, amid the
ever-increasing influence of China's film industry and audience market on the
region. Above all, I seek to find in the works of these filmmakers any possible
reactions they may have had towards the changes of the larger sociopolitical
environment that have not been detected in previous critical studies on them.

Although these chosen filmmakers are at different stages of their careers, they
share common concerns about the dark side of contemporary Hong Kong society.
Interestingly, in recent years they display such concerns by featuring in their films
different kinds of social underdogs, which were not a favourite subject matter of
the previous generation of locally produced mainstream Hong Kong films. In order
to closely examine how these filmmakers approach the topic of social underdogs
as a way of inscribing themselves in film, in the second half of this chapter I critically study Ann Hui's *Ordinary Heroes* (Hong Kong, 1999), Johnnie To's *Sparrow*,
Fruit Chan's *Made in Hong Kong* and *Hollywood Hong Kong*, and Clement Cheng
and Derek Kwok's *Gallants* (Hong Kong, 2010). These new Hong Kong films may
sometimes be regarded as realist films, art-house films, or even semi-documenta-
ries, depending on the contexts in which they are discussed. Nonetheless, each of
them is widely considered by the local general audience in Hong Kong as providing
a record of the Hongkongers' 'collective memory' of a recent past.

Hong Kong Filmmakers: Who's Who?

I deliberately use the term 'filmmakers' instead of film directors or film auteurs to identify a group of Hong Kong-based mainstream, commercial filmmaking professionals. The reason for this choice of term is to acknowledge that these film practitioners excel in multitasking. Many filmmakers, especially the well-established ones, are not film directors alone. They may simultaneously work for their own or other peoples' films in the capacity of producer, main creative source, artistic director, cast recruiter, screenwriter, narrator, actor/actress, financier, marketer and distributor. Many of them exert a strong influence on the outcome of the films in which they are involved. The famous filmmakers are, of course, a brand name of their own. Film scholars Gina Marchetti and Tan See Kam (2007: 2) call them 'stars without specific studio affiliation' in the post-Shaw Brothers era. Many others are but employees on the staff of films. They have to follow the orders and final decisions of the senior management of the film projects; decisions are based on economic, and sometimes micro-political, considerations.

However, in view of their roles in the local, as well as in the East Asian regional, China-led film business, these filmmakers often find themselves struggling to survive professionally. They face fierce competition to fund their films and to please their audiences. In the post-CEPA era, in order to entertain the huge audience market on the mainland, many Hong Kong filmmakers reluctantly give up the defining local sensibilities and cultural content of Hong Kong films to act according to the rules of the game set by the mainland Chinese film industry, in areas such as the censorship of film scripts and final cuts, and the employment of specific cast members. Cultural studies scholars Mirana M. Szeto and Yun-chung Chen (2013) call the phenomenon 'mainlandization': 'all film production segments, from pre-production, production, post-production to distribution, increasingly take place in mainland China'.

The authors also note that in the post-Handover era, there is 'heightened awareness about the inter-local nature of injustice, exploitation and political repression in China and Hong Kong' (Szeto and Chen 2012: 116). Many Hong Kong local film viewers and informed South East Asian audiences are inclined to watch films with authentic depictions of Hong Kong. Those Hong Kong film-makers who act according to the standard of practice of the mainland Chinese film industry may run the risk of upsetting these Hong Kong and South East

Asian audiences. On the other hand, following the mainland Chinese film practice does not always lead to these Hong Kong filmmakers' success in their mainland endeavours (Szeto and Chen 2012: 116–17; Y-W. Chu 2013: 116–20). Filmmakers who would rather work in Hong Kong also suffer and are possibly in a worse professional situation, with pay cuts and little job opportunities locally (Szeto and Chen 2013). To carry on within the mainland Chinese-led filmmaking environment of East Asia, as well as in the larger, international filmmaking world where China (instead of Hong Kong) is becoming the more favoured film business partner from East Asia, it is imperative that Hong Kong filmmakers continue to carve a niche of their own.

Hong Kong filmmakers' situation remind us of those diasporic/exilic filmmakers from Third World and postcolonial countries (or the global South) now working and striving to survive among host film industries and cinematic practices chiefly in the West. According to diaspora and film scholar Hamid Naficy (2001: 10–17, 291), the accented filmmakers are liminal and interstitial figures not only in their physical locations but also in their cultural and social locations. Although many of these displaced filmmakers have primary goals of sustaining themselves politically and socioculturally in the West, the idea of exploring them as a part of the accented cinema is clearly applicable to discussing the directorship of those Hong Kong filmmakers working within the wider context of the New Hong Kong Cinema. Hong Kong filmmakers are arguably liminal and interstitial when situated in the interstices of the East Asian regional filmmaking environment. Their interstitiality often simultaneously yet unintentionally challenges the previously limited concept of (pan-)Chinese cinema in a globalized world (M. Berry 2005: 2, 10–16; Curtin 2007; Davis and Yeh 2008).

As proposed by Naficy (2001: 33–34), two of the qualities that establish the accentedness of filmmakers are their 'locatedness' and 'historicity'. Their displacement from places of origin and their '(dis)location as interstitial subjects within social formations and cinematic practices' (Naficy 2001: 34) define what they and their films are, and the very discussion of their authorship. Naficy's stance on how to treat the topic of film authorship in the accented cinema thus contrasts with and problematizes the treatments of authorship found in pre-structuralism (authors being 'outside and prior to the texts') and post-structuralism (authors being fictive and part of the texts, to be revealed only through spectating) (Naficy 2001: 33). Naficy observes that many accented filmmakers have inscribed themselves in film in multiple ways, spanning from pre-structuralist to post-structuralist, and engaging in the 'performance of the self' (Naficy 2001: 35). In these cases, spectators across cultures and within collective formations also play a part in interpreting the special features in the authorship of individual accented filmmakers (see more discussion of spectators in Chapter Four of this book). Applying Naficy's idea on the accented filmmakers' authorship to that of Hong Kong filmmakers working in the context of the New Hong Kong Cinema, we can find Hong Kong filmmakers' 'locatedness' being closely associated with their sociopolitical relations to the place Hong Kong, as well as to China and East Asia. In terms of 'historicity', these filmmakers utilize themselves and their films to give evidence to the happenings in Hong Kong in a particular historical (also an ongoing) period relevant to the Handover. Their 'locatedness' and 'historicity' on top of their interstitiality in the regional filmmaking environment shape their own inscription in film, which nonetheless may not be as easily detected as that of the archetypal accented filmmakers. One of the major obstacles to unearthing these Hong Kong filmmakers' self-inscription is the commercial nature of their films, which may be subject to the conditions predetermined by others (government policies, senior film executives, investors, film distributors, buyers, specific groups of target audiences, etc.). This leads to cases in which filmmakers' authorial concerns and vision are deeply buried within the seemingly run-of-the-mill film production. For this reason, I believe it is important to understand, in the first place, the specific biographical and professional conditions that have given rise to their authorship. Several representatives are chosen in the following discussion for this purpose.

Ann Hui

Dubbed by the U.K.-based *Sight & Sound* magazine in August 2012 as 'one of the most unjustly neglected of all contemporary filmmakers' (Clarke 2012: 50), Ann Hui may probably be an unknown figure in the United Kingdom, where she received her training as film practitioner. However, Hui is in fact one of the most successful and highly respected Hong Kong filmmakers. She became a famous film director in Hong Kong in the late 1970s and had already gained a firm foothold in Chinese-language cinemas by the time world-famous ethnic Chinese directors, such as Ang Lee and Zhang Yimou, started to make films. In discussions of contemporary Hong Kong films, Hui's name and her works is often a favourite topic among Chinese-language film admirers.

Born in 1947 in Manchuria, China, to a Chinese father and a Japanese mother, Hui moved south to Hong Kong with her family when she was only five. This move has had an obvious impact on how Hui sees herself: as a diasporic or even exilic person of Chinese descent who is at the same time a Chinese-language film director (see how she explores the issue of identities in her semi-autobiographical film *Song of the Exile* in Chapter One; see also Naficy 2001: 233–34; M. Berry 2005: 423–25, 431). Settled in Hong Kong, Hui received her formal education there and graduated with a master's degree in comparative literature from the University of Hong Kong. She later moved to London to study filmmaking and then returned to Hong Kong in the mid 1970s to commence her career in the screen industry – first as an assistant to the martial arts film guru King Hu and then directing programmes for local television stations for several years.

Over a directorial career of more than thirty years, Hui has so far made twenty-four fictional feature films (up until the end of 2014). Her directorial works have earned her numerous best director and best picture awards. Although repeatedly emphasizing that she is not interested in politics, earlier in her career Hui directed many television programmes based on current affairs and social issues, which often required her to research thoroughly on topics like drug addicts and Vietnamese refugees (M. Berry 2005: 427–28; E. Cheung, Marchetti and Tan S. 2011: 70). In 1979, she directed her first feature film *The Secret* (Hong Kong, 1979), loosely based on the true story of a murder case in Hong Kong. She soon became a mainstay of a group of young (on average, not older than thirty in the late 1970s and the early 1980s), non-united, Hong Kong-raised (if not born there), overseas-trained film directors, who had early directorial careers at local television stations. The local mass media dubbed them the Hong Kong New Wave (later they came to be referred to as the first New Wave, when the Second New Wave of Hong Kong directors such as Wong Kar-wai, Stanley Kwan, Eddie Fong and Ching Siu-tung attained their calibre (Teo 1997: 184)). They were willing to search for and construct a local Hong Kong identity through film, often benefiting from their film-making training obtained in the West (Cheuk 2008, 2012: 457–72).

Apart from approaching narratives that have social concerns, many of Hui's works show a humanist stance taken from a female perspective. Many are attentive to complicated interpersonal relationships (Po 2002). The prominent ones include *Starry is the Night* (Hong Kong, 1988); *Song of the Exile*; *Summer Snow* (Hong Kong, 1995); *The Stunt Woman* (Hong Kong, 1996); *Eighteen Springs* (China/Hong Kong, 1997); *July Rhapsody* (Hong Kong, 2002); *The Postmodern*

Life of My Aunt (China/Hong Kong, 2006); *The Way We Are* (Hong Kong, 2008); *Night and Fog*; and *All about Love* (Hong Kong, 2010). Hui is a rare gem in the male-dominated local film industry, as well as in world film production.

Hui is renowned for her versatility in using various film genres. She often employs conventions of such genres as melodrama, martial arts and horror, while finding ways to bring her personal touch to them. Her films are sometimes regarded as situated between the domains of art-house and commercial cinemas (E. Cheung, Marchetti and Tan S. 2011: 67–68). Szeto (2011: 51) comments that Hui is at the margin of Hong Kong mainstream cinema, satisfying both mainstream and critical/cultural anticipations (see also M. Berry 2005: 434).

Moreover, she was one of the first in her generation of Hong Kong filmmakers who started working regularly on cross-border projects in the Greater China region (encompassing Hong Kong, mainland China and Taiwan) in the late 1970s and the early 1980s, a time when each of these three different Chinese communities had its own film industry backed by particular political-economic ideologies. While working with small, local production companies in Hong Kong, Hui forged long-lasting partnerships with mainland Chinese and Taiwan filmmakers and investors (M. Berry 2005: 425, see also 42–44). Besides film directing, Hui frequently takes up other roles, such as film producer, planner, and at times actress, in her own or her peers' films. Her tactful relations and solid connections with both the mainland Chinese and the Taiwan film industries have allowed her to blend in with these cinematic systems relatively easily while consolidating her base in Hong Kong – a typical characteristic found among accented filmmakers (in Naficy's sense).

Hui is also known for her influence on newer generations of filmmakers. In recent years, she has been working with filmmakers like Stanley Kwan (considered part of the Hong Kong Second New Wave), Ivy Ho (a seasoned screenwriter who started making films in the 2000s), Vincent Chui and Yu Lik-wai (the latter has forged a close work relationship with the renowned Sixth Generation director Jia Zhangke from China).

Johnnie To

Johnnie To is another prolific and highly respected Hong Kong filmmaker that has continued to flourish in what has become, since the mid 1990s, a sluggish local film business. He was given official recognition as a major filmmaker as late as 1999 by the Hong Kong International Film Festival. But this belatedness seems to have been a blessing in disguise, as it made him even more outstanding at a time when other Hong Kong film directors from earlier generations were no longer directly involved in film directing (Teo 2007: 101).

To was born to a working class family in Hong Kong in 1955. He quit school after finishing third form of secondary school and became employed initially as a messenger at the local television station TVB at the age of seventeen. While at TVB, he enrolled in the company's full-time acting class, the same type that has bred important Hong Kong actors such as Chow Yun-fat, Andy Lau and Tony Leung Chiu-wai. In 1974 upon graduation, To was assigned to work as assistant director to several experienced directors, including Wong Tin-lam (aka Wang Tianlin), whom To worked with for the longest period (about two years). Wong was one of the most prominent film directors from the then closed Cathay Organisation (HK) (formerly Motion Picture & General Investment; in the 1950s and 1960s this company was the biggest competitor of the Shaw Brothers studio in Hong Kong). To learned much about directing from Wong, especially about shooting the martial arts genre (Teo 2007: 215–16).[1] In 1977, To was promoted to the position of director at TVB. In 1980 he released his debut feature film, *The Enigmatic Case* (Hong Kong, 1980), a martial arts film starring Damian Lau Chung-yan (a veteran television actor) and Cherie Chung (who in the 1980s became one of the most famous Hong Kong actresses). The film was generally regarded as a box-office and critical failure. To then returned to the television industry and remained there for another seven years.

Between 1986 and 1996, To explored different film genres, ranging from comedy, romance, melodrama, to cop-and-gangster, and occasionally enjoyed local box-office success. Some of his major works during that period include *All about Ah-Long* (Hong Kong, 1989), starring Chow Yun-fat as a single father who eventually dies in a motorbike race, and *Lifeline* (Hong Kong, 1997), a story about a group of firemen. Film scholar Stephen Teo (2007: 1) argues that To has utilized and transcended the limitations of film genres (in particular, of action films) to the extent of changing their very nature and the related industry. However, To's main concern in filmmaking is to explore human lives and the existences of people rather than to comply with genre requirements (Teo 2007: 219), even when he is under the pressure of commercial filmmaking conditions and the high expectations of the audience. Unlike Hui, who would not want to admit outright her films' political messages, To has been quite frank about this and has made harsh comments about the authorities (Teo 2007: 237).

In 1996, To and his former TVB colleague Wai Ka-fai formed a film production company, Milkyway Image. The company provides an excellent platform for To and Wai to make independent and quality films (Bordwell 2003; Teo 2007: 227). It allows To to focus on directing cop-and-gangster films or films having action as a major part. These works have brought him international fame. They include *Running out of Time* (Hong Kong, 1999); *The Mission*; *Fulltime Killer* (co-directed with Wai Ka-fai, Hong Kong, 2001); *PTU*; *Running on Karma* (co-directed with Wai Ka-fai, China/Hong Kong, 2003); *Breaking News* (China/Hong Kong, 2004); *Election*; *Election 2*; *Exiled*; *Life without Principle* (Hong Kong, 2011); *Drug War* (China/Hong Kong, 2012); and *Blind Detective* (China/Hong Kong, 2013). Most of these films focus on group morale, non-blood brotherhood and gangster activities, and were shot stylistically in accordance with To's own definition of action aesthetics, which he has been applying since the late 1990s. By the mid 2000s, To had acquired great international fame for his action films. His simple yet stylistic cinematic language conveys a strong sense of neo-noir rarely found in the oeuvres of other Hong Kong-based action filmmakers. To has become an icon of Hong Kong's cult action films.

Admittedly devoting much time to making action films, To does not confine himself to this genre alone. He is celebrated, especially in Hong Kong and its neighbouring audience markets, for his urban romantic comedies that explore city life, interpersonal relationships among young professional couples and existential situations in Hong Kong. Some of the box-office hits include *Needing You ...* (co-directed with Wai Ka-fai, Hong Kong, 2000); *Love on a Diet* (co-directed with Wai Ka-fai, Hong Kong/Japan, 2001); *My Left Eye Sees Ghosts* (co-directed with Wai Ka-fai, Hong Kong, 2002); *Turn Left, Turn Right* (co-directed with Wai Ka-fai, Hong Kong/Singapore, 2003); *Yesterday Once More* (Hong Kong, 2004); *Don't Go Breaking My Heart*; and *Romancing in Thin Air* (China/Hong Kong, 2012). Many of these films feature To's long-time actor-collaborators from the Hong Kong mainstream film industry, such as Andy Lau, Sammi Cheng, Sean Lau Ching-wan and Louis Koo. This fine balance between the action genre, non-action genres like romantic comedy, and other more personal and hard-to-classify film projects might in fact be due to To's astute commercial calculation in conducting his film business (Jost 2011: 43). Over the past twenty years these works have brought To serious financial returns and earned him multiple awards at important film events. They have also brought him attention at major international film festivals, including Venice, Berlin and Cannes (Jost 2011). Teo calls him an 'uneven auteur' (2007: 145–76).

With Milkyway, To has also increasingly taken up a kind of coach-cum-producer role for films made by other directors attached to his company, such as Wai Ka-fai, and the 'New Generation Directors' Yau Nai-hoi and Law Wing-cheong. Yau, who used to be a screenwriter for To's films, directed *Eye in the Sky* (Hong Kong, 2007). This film won him the Best New Director Award at the twenty-seventh edition of the Hong Kong Film Awards in 2008. Law directed *Punished* (Hong Kong, 2011). Both of these cop-and-gangster films display To's strong stylistic influence, signifying his ongoing contribution to the Hong Kong film industry.

Fruit Chan

Fruit Chan is an acclaimed Hong Kong, grass-roots, independent film director, who is famous for his small-budget films saturated with political messages. Similar to many other Hong Kong filmmakers, Fruit Chan had diasporic experience early on in his life. He was born in Guangdong, China, in 1959 and moved to Hong Kong with his parents at the age of five. For more than ten years Fruit Chan lived in Hong Kong's public housing, built by the local government to provide affordable homes for low-income families and new immigrants to the city.

After finishing secondary school, Fruit Chan enrolled in short filmmaking courses at the Hong Kong Film and Culture Centre set up by a group of New Wave film directors, including Tsui Hark, Ann Hui and Yim Ho (Gan 2005: 4–5; E. Cheung 2009: 4–5). They taught Fruit Chan filmmaking and brought him into the local film industry in 1980. Fruit Chan started with all sorts of odd jobs in film studios, but quickly moved up the professional ladder (M. Berry 2005: 461–62). He joined Century Film Company in 1982, and, later, Golden Harvest as assistant director. It was a position that he held for close to ten years and in which he excelled. During that time, he served many local film directors, such as Kirk Wong, Alfred Cheung, Jackie Chan and Sammo Hung.

In 1989, Fruit Chan was at the time the assistant director of Tony Au's *Au Revoir Mon Amour* (Hong Kong, 1991). The film had to be given a shooting break due to some major production problems. In order to retain the set, which was built on a piece of borrowed plot, during the shooting break Fruit Chan was asked to take it over to shoot a film without a finished script. The result was Fruit Chan's first feature *Finale in Blood* (Hong Kong, 1993), a romantic ghost story set in 1920s Hong Kong (M. Berry 2005: 463–66). The film was, however, shelved by Golden Harvest for three years before being given theatrical release. It did not do well in box offices but received positive critical reviews. Fruit Chan also made the comedy *Five Lonely Hearts* (Hong Kong, 1991), which did not enjoy any privileged publicity or reviews and ultimately sank into complete oblivion.

Hence, in terms of his years of active involvement in the Hong Kong film industry, Fruit Chan should be regarded as a contemporary of the Second New Wave. The Second New Wave refers to the rise of a group of Hong Kong film directors in the late 1980s. They followed in the footsteps of the first Hong Kong New Wave and received international recognition. Nevertheless, critics do not generally refer to Fruit Chan as part of this Second New Wave, most likely because he worked for a long period of time as assistant director (not director). Fruit Chan's long experience in the local commercial film production environment, however, stimulated his yearning for creative freedom not easily allowed in a commercial filmmaking setting. In 1996, he was given 40,000 feet of expiring film stock leftover from David Lai's *Heaven and Earth* (China/Hong Kong, 1994), produced by Andy Lau's Teamwork Motion Pictures, which was renamed Focus Group Holdings Limited in 2004. Fruit Chan continued to collect more unused film stock from other film companies (T. 1998: 56; M. Berry 2005: 466) and started planning his first independent production, *Made in Hong Kong*. Andy Lau agreed to be the film's executive producer. The whole production was completed with a crew of only five persons, no professional actors in the cast and a shoestring budget of HK$500,000 (£39,000 or U.S.$64,000), which Fruit Chan had managed to raise through his personal savings, and loans from family and friends. The film turned out to be an overnight success. It gave Fruit Chan the reputation of independent filmmaker without financial backup from large companies or investors, and registered his actions as one of the first bold attempts to fight against the commercialization of the local film industry. However, the concept of independent film production that arises as a result is rather confusing, for most Hong Kong films made since the last major studio Shaw Brothers stopped film production in 1986 can in effect be regarded as independent films. As in Fruit Chan's case, his independence refers mainly to his independent, small amount of film funding, while in practice he was still working within the established film business framework in Hong Kong. As film scholar Esther M.K. Cheung (2009: 9) rightly points out: 'his [Fruit Chan's] independent debut cannot be considered as totally separable from the mainstream because he did receive some resources from Andy Lau's Team Work'. Moreover, Fruit

Chan also utilized mainstream distribution and exhibition channels to reach out to his audience, thus undermining the purity of his independence (see also Veg 2014 note 7 for a political-oriented definition of independent films).

Fruit Chan openly admitted the political subtext of *Made in Hong Kong* (from the perspective of teenagers) in relation to the 1997 Handover, and other concomitant social changes and anxieties (E. Cheung 2009: 131–32). He made *The Longest Summer* from the perspective of middle-aged people, and *Little Cheung* from the perspective of young children. These three form the Handover Trilogy. After the Handover Trilogy, Fruit Chan moved on to his (incomplete) Prostitute Trilogy, which includes *Durian Durian* and *Hollywood Hong Kong*, to explore the relationship between China and Hong Kong after the political reunification. In making the latter two films, Fruit Chan also started to work with a larger crew and professional actors (see discussion on *Durian Durian* in Chapter Two).

Between 1997 and 2002, Fruit Chan released an independent film project every year except 1999. His last one during this period was *Public Toilet*, discussing the issue of life and death. The film's acceptance of South Korean and Japanese investments foretold the director's gradual return to commercial filmmaking. In 2004, Fruit Chan was employed by Peter Chan's Applause Pictures (the two Chans are unrelated) to direct *Dumplings* (as one segment of the pan-Asian *Three... Extremes*, and as a feature film). In 2009, Fruit Chan was involved in the making of *Chengdu, I Love You* (China, 2009), produced by the mainland Chinese company Zonbo Media. He was also employed to direct a Japanese-South African-U.S. horror film *Don't Look up* (2009). In 2013, Fruit Chan took part in a Hong Kong mainstream horror anthology *Tales from the Dark* (Part 1) (Hong Kong) to direct a half-hour segment *Jing Zhe*.[2] In 2014, Fruit Chan released the box-office success *The Midnight After* (Hong Kong), a mid-budget thriller that reflects the political deterioration and social sensibilities in Hong Kong.

The 'New Generation Directors'

Since the new millennium, a group of new film directors has begun to gain visibility in the Hong Kong film industry. They have been designated by the mass media and critics as the 'New Generation Directors' (L. Pang 2009: 84). Some critics call them 'the Hong Kong SAR New Wave' (Szeto and Chen 2012). I use the former term here to avoid confusion with the two previous New Waves of Hong Kong directors, who dominated Hong Kong's big screens from the 1970s to the early 1990s. Most of the 'New Generation Directors' released their first feature films in the 2000s. They have more diverse backgrounds in the film industry than their predecessors. Some of them used to work as screenwriters or assistant directors to established Hong Kong film directors. Some are actors-turned-directors. Others might be graduates of formal film and video production courses at local and foreign universities. The better-known names among them, in alphabetical order of their surnames, include Susie Au, Kenneth Bi, Cheang Pou-soi, Clement Cheng, Cheung King-wai, Tammy Cheung, Felix Chong, Roy Chow, Stephen Chow, Vincent Chui, Stephen Fung, Ivy Ho, Patrick Kong, Adrian Kwan, Derek Kwok, Carol Lai, Law Chi-leung, Law Wing-cheong, Lee Kung-lok, Heiward Mak, Mak Yan-yan, Edmond Pang Ho-cheung, Calvin Poon, Jessey Tsang Tsui-shan, Brian Tse, Adam Wong, Barbara Wong, Wong Ching-po, Daniel Wu, Yau Nai-hoi, Patrick Yau and Toe Yuen.

Many of these new Hong Kong filmmakers are much younger in age (between thirty and fifty), and greener in their professional experience, than the first and second Hong Kong New Waves. Although many of them were born and raised in Hong Kong, and have not undergone any life-changing, first-hand diasporic experience, their late arrival in the local film industry after the beginning of its long-term recession has provided them with another kind of interstitial, film-industry-relevant experience. On the one hand, they work in the deteriorating local film sector; on the other hand, just across the border is the towering China-led, regionalized filmmaking environment. Due to the difficult operational situation of Hong Kong filmmaking since the mid 1990s, these new film directors have often had to struggle much harder for their professional survival than did their predecessors, whose careers benefited from the prosperous socio-economic environment of Hong Kong in the 1980s and the early 1990s. Except for a few exceptions such as those named above, many 'New Generation Directors' only had the opportunity to make one or two films before quitting filmmaking completely. The film funding they are able to raise is usually small. It allows them to work only on locally oriented projects, catering to the local Hong Kong audience only with timely and locally relevant social-cultural-political-economic subjects. Just to be able to make films, these filmmakers are prepared to work in genres of all kinds, and on films of varying commercial or artistic natures. This might explain why, in order to make ends meet, many of these new directors often take up multiple jobs in addition to filmmaking. Film scholar Laikwan Pang attributes the current phenomenon of unemployment and underemployment in the Hong

Kong film industry to the competition from mainland China, with its 'cheaper production costs and cultural proximity with the target audiences' (2009: 83).

Those of the 'New Generation Directors' who have managed to sustain their careers have tried out ever-newer ways to preserve filmmaking opportunities. These methods might not have been needed or used at all by their predecessors already active during the time of the apex of Hong Kong's local film industry. For example, these new directors might resort to governmental help coming through film-related policies, funding (though limited), planning and activities under the auspices of the newly established Hong Kong Film Development Council (HKFDC). Aware of the film funding, marketing and distribution possibilities at various film festivals, the 'New Generation Directors' might try their luck and send their new films to première at these events before generally releasing the films in target audience markets (R. Cheung 2011c: 205–6).[3] Taking these actions has now become one of the most vital film business tools for the 'New Generation Directors' to survive.

In 2002, the Hong Kong Film Awards started to give recognition to new directors by giving out the Outstanding Young Director Awards. The first winner was Stephen Chow, a veteran comedian-turned-director, who was awarded for his international box-office hit *Shaolin Soccer*. The film also won the Best Picture Award in that same event. Two years later, in the event's twenty-third edition in 2004, the award was renamed as the Best New Director Award and went to Edmond Pang Ho-cheung for his *Men Suddenly in Black* (Hong Kong, 2003). The award is still in place to this day. In 2011, the Best Picture Award of the Hong Kong Film Awards went to *Gallants*, a locally produced film co-directed by two 'New Generation Directors', Clement Cheng and Derek Kwok. The film was Kwok's third directorial attempt since he started film directing in 2007, and was Cheng's debut work. Kwok had worked as screenwriter for Wilson Yip's action films *Skyline Cruisers* (Hong Kong, 2000) and *2002* (Hong Kong, 2001); romantic comedy *Dry Wood Fierce Fire* (Hong Kong, 2002); and urban romance *Leaving Me, Loving You* (Hong Kong, 2004). Cheng, who worked in various areas in the sphere of mass communications, is a friend of Kwok's. I will discuss this film in the next section, which is devoted to the authorial concerns and vision of the Hong Kong filmmakers in question.

Authorial Vision and Self-Inscription: Social Underdogs in New Hong Kong Films

By highlighting some of the most notable names of the New Hong Kong Cinema in the above section, I did not mean to single them out as auteurs from Hong Kong or to take an auteurist critical approach to reading their films. I am more interested in exploring their authorial vision and concerns. Studying these issues, I argue, serve as a prerequisite to understand the kinds of films that the directors focus on making, and the possible audiovisual styles they employ as devices to convey and contain messages about the place and people of Hong Kong.

Moreover, these chosen filmmakers serve here representational purposes with regard to particular periods in Hong Kong's mainstream film history. Given the collaborative nature of Hong Kong filmmaking practice (a prime example of this kind of practice in cinema), the names of famous filmmakers are only part of the brand ethos, which covers their filmmaking approaches, the groups of talent working with them and the specific stylistic traditions (similar to different schools of thought) that filmmakers follow. This last point is particularly intriguing, for it is not difficult to find a loose masters-and-protégés culture connecting earlier and newer generations of Hong Kong mainstream filmmakers, a point I have mentioned in the above section on their professional paths. Let me reiterate here as an example: Wong Tin-lam's expertise in shooting the martial arts genre has had a profound influence on Johnnie To's action films, which in turn affected how Yau Nai-hoi shot his cop-and-gangster film *Eye in the Sky*. The filmmaking approaches and filming styles that these Hong Kong filmmakers have shared cross-generationally are thus arguably products of collectivism and mutual influence, on top of the inevitable exchanges between Hong Kong films and other cinemas over the decades in a world of economic globalism (Marchetti and Tan S. 2007). Interestingly, such a collective development of work approach reflects, to a large extent, the Chinese people's underlying Confucian emphasis on the well-being of the group (rather than of the individual) as most important for the attainment of social harmony.

In detecting their shared concerns for their base in Hong Kong and the intergenerational influences among different Hong Kong filmmakers, I find a recent phenomenon in the New Hong Kong Cinema that is worth discussing: different Hong Kong mainstream filmmakers have featured social underdogs' fictional presence in one or a few films that may or may not be found in most other films in their individual oeuvres. In real life these underprivileged people live at the lowest socio-economic stratum of Hong Kong society. They have been struggling against the backdrop of the city's economic prosperity. They are true Hongkongers and insiders of Hong Kong, as opposed to the outsider figures discussed in Chapter Two. I argue that the social underdog serves as an indispensible diegetic element for different generations of Hong Kong filmmakers to inscribe themselves, albeit problematically, in their films in order to carry out the 'performance of the self' in the transitional period of Hong Kong and the Hong Kong film industry in recent years (Naficy 2001: 35, 291). Filmmakers' resorting to the on-screen visibility of the underprivileged Hongkongers and the stylistic methods employed to represent them stands in contrast to, and serves as a 'disenchantment' of, the glossy and glamorous image that the SAR government has continuously and systematically strived to promote for the city when it is already in a state of loss (see Y-W. Chu 2013). In addition, these diegetic characters are in strong contrast with the mediated images of Hong Kong to be found in 1980s Hong Kong mainstream films, which tend to show the glamorous side of the city.

Ann Hui and *Ordinary Heroes*

Hui has often displayed a humanist stance in her twenty-four feature films made in the past thirty-plus years. *Ordinary Heroes* is her only feature film in which she includes a self-reflexive cameo and allows her own existential stance to resonate closely with the characters. In *Ordinary Heroes* Hui intends to reflect the situation in Hong Kong after the Tiananmen Square Massacre in June 1989 up until 1997 arrived (S. Ho 1999: 18). The film's Chinese title, *Qian Yan Wan Yu*, literally means 'thousands of millions of words'. It has a direct reference to a song of the same name by the late Taiwanese popular singer Teresa Teng. The reference also strongly alludes to the intricate relations between China and Hong Kong, as Teng's song was one of the first to enter the mainland via Hong Kong after the start of economic reform in China in 1978 (see also V. Lee 2009: 63).[4]

The film tells the story of a group of Hong Kong social activists and their intertwining personal relationships against the backdrop of the history of social activism in Hong Kong over a period of time from the 1970s until the Tiananmen Square Massacre in 1989, which shocked the world. Although containing re-enactments of real incidents and social protests, the film is not a genuine political film, nor was it explicitly intended as such (Li C. 1999: 20; Long 2003: 136–37; E. Cheung, Marchetti and Tan S. 2011: 68; Hui 2012a: 88). There are four main characters: Yau (Tse Kwan-ho), a student activist-turned-politician; Sow (Rachel Lee), an orphan girl from a fishing family; the marginalized local youth Tung (Lee Kang-sheng); and an Italian priest Father Kam (Anthony Wong), who is an adherent of Maoist principles. They are depicted as unlikely activists who join Hong Kong's social movements for their separate, personal reasons (V. Lee 2009: 60). Yau once condescendingly hoped to help the underprivileged, but eventually turns into a power-hungry politician; Sow joins his camp because she is in love with him. She later becomes Yau's extra-marital lover after he has married another woman. Tung benefits from Father Kam's missionary work and care for the poor. He later follows Father Kam to join in street protests. Tung secretly falls in love with Sow and becomes her main carer after she is injured in a car accident: the accident occurs after Yau has raped her in a fit of violent emotion provoked by the Tiananmen Square Massacre. These characters can be understood as representatives of various groups of social underdogs that usually remain invisible in the public domain, since the lives they lead marginalize them from the rest of the society.

Their stories are unveiled in three different plot segments entitled respectively 'To Forget', '10 Years of Revolution' and 'Not to Forget'. The film is punctuated by episodes showing a street theatre called 'The Story of Ng Chun-yin' (played most of the time solely by the leftist theatrical performer Gus Mok). The performance depicts the life of a legendary Hong Kong leftist social activist and his ultimate failure. Although this street theatre seems to have no connection at all to the main story, the theatrical dialogues in it in fact add extra dimensions to the film, enabling the audience to understand the background of Hong Kong's history of social movements. In addition, the theatrical dialogues also hint at the main characters' disappointments in life.

Hui has commented succinctly that *Ordinary Heroes* was a risky project (Hui 2012a: 88). This estimate is understandable in the context of the commercial filmmaking environment in a city where political activism or anything remotely related to politics does not guarantee a good box-office income. Financing the film proved very difficult and it enjoyed only limited theatrical release, probably because its topic was unconventional for Hong Kong mainstream cinematic practice. It was premièred at the forty-ninth edition of the Berlin International Film Festival in February 1999 and was chosen as the opening film of the twenty-third edition of the Hong Kong International Film Festival, also in 1999. Unlike Hui's other films, which went to different parts of the world, *Ordinary Heroes* was generally released only in Hong Kong, Japan, Singapore and Taiwan.

Hui's self-claimed emphasis on existentialism rather than on political stances might easily become a source of other risks that the director did not intend, such as unconsciously confining the social underdogs to circumstances in which they are hopelessly stuck. This would counteract Hui's good intentions in giving filmic visibility to these neglected groups (S. Ho 1999: 18). On the other hand, the film demonstrates indirectly the director's revisit to a bygone historical era that defined the best part of her youth and her directorial success (Hui 1999: 15, 2012a: 88; Po 2002: 121–23).

This is most evident in a sequence in which the director plays the role of an unnamed television documentarist interviewing the characters (a role that Hui used to perform in real life when she worked at the local television stations). In this sequence, Yau is seen working on a campaign that has its real-life roots in the sociopolitical incident of the illegal resident 'boat brides' – mainland Chinese women who married Hong Kong men (usually fishermen) but were not granted the same right of abode as their husbands and their Hong Kong-born children. Yau has by now moved successfully into the political mainstream and become a full-time politician. Hui, the diegetic television documentarist, is given the permission to film at Yau's office on the ground floor of a public housing estate (shot on location in a real dilapidated public housing estate). This sequence consists of Hui's off-screen interviewing and on-screen grainy television footage of Yau and Father Kam (in close-ups) giving standard answers. With televised interview footage added to the normal screen frame, these characters are given an initial double on-screen visibility to show clearly their facial expressions and tone of speech. But all this unobtrusively reveals some deeper political agendas. We no longer see the seemingly innocent social activists who are unconditionally willing to sacrifice everything to help the underprivileged. Instead, the activists appear either as cunning politician (in the case of Yau) or as overly idealistic protestor (in the case of Father Kam) who are unaware how naive they actually are. This testifies to Hui's own scepticism about politics, as she comments:

> I understand that people participating in politics in 1960s and 1970s Hong Kong actually only participated in it indirectly ... because there was no such ideology as democracy [in Hong Kong] back then. Hence, those who wished to

take part in politics were meant to fail. To them, revolution was only a dream
... Those so-called political campaigners in Hong Kong collapsed at once when
they were intimidated by actual politics, due to their naivety and ignorance
about politics. (An Interview with Ann Hui 1999: 28; my translation)

While Hui scrutinizes the real motives and moral integrity of these fictional-
ized social campaigners whose presence in the film might overshadow some
quieter, more ordinary heroes in society, her role as the unnamed documentarist
offers us clues to evaluate the function of the mass media as social watchdogs.
The most recent sociopolitical conflicts in the 2010s between various ethnic
Chinese communities in Hong Kong and mainland China, mostly televised and
mediated by the mass media, could be read as real-life footnotes to Hui's cameo.

This cameo of Hui is one more piece of filmic evidence confirming the
similarities between Hong Kong filmmakers and the accented filmmakers, who
frequently use self-inscription in their films. Naficy argues that 'self-reflexive
techniques distance the audience from the film, undermining full identification
with the diegesis and with its characters' (Naficy 2001: 276). As we watch the
interactions between Hui and the characters in non-stylized medium shots completely stripped of ornate mise en scène, the camera reminds us of Hui once
working as a television programme director whose duties were to expose social
injustice through her camera. Those were the years when she started to gain fame
as a director with a good conscience, and the years when Hong Kong also started
to enjoy a positive public image globally. However, in this particular sequence in
the film, Hui's camera seems like a silent, helpless observer, re-evaluating how
the mass media work with, and for, politicians and activists alike to unconsciously
marginalize those who are forever at the bottom strata of the society. As an intellectual, Hui's self-inscription and self-rediscovery appear as a humble yet excru-
ciating experience rather than as relaxing nostalgia about her career's golden past:
Hui looks tired as she squats right outside Yau's office, chatting with the fictional
characters, who stand around her in the diegetic shooting break (in full shot).

Johnnie To and *Sparrow*

While Hui's cameo belies her supposed sympathy for these ordinary heroes and
fond memory of an innocent past, To's *Sparrow* renders a more light-hearted

version of a Hong Kong filmmaker's personal record of the changes that have taken place in Hong Kong society. The film was shot on and off for three years, during which To was also working on other projects. It was released initially through the film festival route in 2008, going to the Berlin International Film Festival and the Barcelona Asian Film Festival before it was screened on its home turf (Elley 2008: 29).

Sparrow is set in present-day Hong Kong. Its main characters are four pick-pockets, who usually work as a group led by Kei (Simon Yam). They operate mostly in the old neighbourhoods of the Wanchai and Causeway Bay districts on the island side of Hong Kong. They live separately in old residential buildings and usually ride on bicycles instead of in cars. When they are not busy thieving, they like to dine in the neighbourhood's old-fashioned tea restaurants. Although they are thieves, they are generally good-natured guys and stick to their own princi-ples in stealing. For example, they take people's money, but never physically hurt those they steal from. They are also on good terms with their neighbours. They seem to represent something that is associated with an immediate past and is now rarely found in hectic big cities. In fact, the film's Chinese title *Man Jeuk* (in Cantonese pronunciation, or *Wen Que* in Mandarin) in local Cantonese slang means 'pickpockets'. The term is more popular among working-class, middle-aged to elderly groups than among the younger generations. The Chinese title thus additionally gives a nostalgic feel to the whole film.

The calm life of this group of pickpockets is soon disturbed by a sparrow that flies into Kei's flat: everyone in the group considers this a bad omen. Before long, they are separately approached by a mysterious, beautiful, Mandarin-speaking, mainland Chinese girl (Kelly Lin) for their help.[5] This is because her rich 'sugar daddy' Mr Fu (Lo Hoi-pang) has kept her passport away from her in order to stop her from going to join her true love, and so she asks the group of thieves to steal it from Mr Fu for her. Mr Fu is a rich merchant, but he was once a pick-pocket himself. The girl's problem soon leads to a clash between two groups of pickpockets – Kei's and Fu's – who, on a rainy night, fight it out for the girl's mainland Chinese passport. Kei's group wins and Fu keeps his promise to release the passport and the girl.

Compared with To's other signature action or urban romance films, *Sparrow* seems to have characteristics from both genres while transcending the genre boundaries. Although this is a story about thieves and a femme fatale-like figure, the film does not offer many action scenes or gunfights. The main thief characters are all attracted to the girl, but there is no exciting romance between them. The feelings are confined to the platonic level. This makes the film one of To's very few commercial films that cannot easily be fitted into any existing genre. Aside from his commercial decision, To openly and specifically declares that he employs the film to document a specific time and place, and to comment on the disappearing cityscape of Hong Kong (10th Osian's-Cinefan Festival 2008).[6]

This seems to be particularly true, considering the fact that the director shot major parts of this film in old buildings and alleyways in Wanchai, Sheung Wan and Central districts in Hong Kong. As To comments, Hong Kong has indeed developed rapidly, but certain places and landmarks of the city are important to be preserved as representatives of collective memories of the community. Unfortunately, the local government has been incompetent in carrying out the necessary local heritage preservation. To says that through *Sparrow* he wants to record some parts of the history of Hong Kong on film before all the period elements (such as neighbourhood shops, streetscapes and corners, buildings and alleyways) completely disappear, and are replaced by newer buildings and other kinds of city constructions.[7] His personal mission of capturing the disappearing present is precisely embraced by the character Kei, who happens to be an avid amateur photographer like To himself (Cheng T. 2014). Kei likes taking photos with his vintage Rollieflex twin-lens reflex camera, and develops the negatives himself in a darkroom. In the scene where he is taking photos in the neighbourhood, the taken shots are shown directly on screen as black-and-white photos one after another in a still-shots slide show. There are photos of: (1) a smiling elderly man, (2) overhanging shop signs of different Chinese herbal shops in Sheung Wan on Hong Kong Island, (3) quiet park amenities right next to residential buildings, (4) workers taking care of recycled cardboards, (5) elderly working-class people sitting and chatting in small parks, and so on. Shot from a slightly high angle (except for the one with overhanging shop signs) to indicate Kei's riding on his bicycle, the subject inside each on-screen 'photo'/frame is in a well-balanced position. It blends neatly with the rest of the mise en scène to project a relaxed and harmonious atmosphere. Within each frame, we do not see any jarring props, costumes, make-up or lighting. The frames simply capture what ordinary citizens can see daily in these serene parts of the city during the day. They look so natural that we would mistake them for stand-alone, timeless postcard photos. Although these black-and-white shots do not seem relevant to the main story about pickpockets, in terms of the look and feel they go perfectly well with the rest of the (coloured) film, which is, among other things, a moving picture album that keeps certain images unique to Hong Kong. More black-and-white photos of different street scenes in Hong Kong are displayed alongside the ending credits of the film.

To's intention to authentically preserve the cityscape of Hong Kong on screen is, however, challenged by the film's finale, which shows a razor blade fight between Kei's group and Fu's group in slow motion under a blanket of black umbrellas. This sequence is stylishly rendered in a way unmatched by other parts of the film. Inspired by *The Umbrellas of Cherbourg* (Jacques Demy, France/West Germany, 1964), it reveals that the director's original plan was to make this film a musical.[8] The encounter takes place in the districts of Sheung Wan and Central (on location shooting). It starts with Kei carrying the girl's passport in heavy rain, paying attention not to lose it to the pickpockets on Fu's side. As the fight begins, the slow motion of breathtaking human movements and the effective use of chiaroscuro cross-cutting, with claustrophobic close-ups of slow splashes of raindrops displaying all the determining moments of this duel, render the finale an exquisite neo-noir episode. As film music scholar Charles Kronengold (2013: 278) notes, 'In keeping with To's group-oriented narrative strategies, this sequence projects rhythmic structures based on *one* guy doing an action, then *another* guy, then another, then another. And every character is shown at least once in close-up with a *changing* expression that can read as purposefulness or thoughtfulness' (italics in original). The slow motion here then offers one more level for us to appreciate To's static shots used for freezing and slowing down the fast moves typical for action scenes. According to the director, the static shots allow audiences to cultivate the sense of movement in their imagination (Teo 2007: 234). It shows To's distinctive action aesthetics, which had been evolving over an entire decade before this film. Without filling the screen with gunfights and gory scenes, To thus presents us with a graceful duel between Kei's and Fu's pickpockets that is rich in rhythms. With more and more umbrellas and extra pickpockets joining in this fight in *Sparrow*, the director turns Sheung Wan into a theatre-like stage upon which the pickpocket characters perform something not very different from a beautifully choreographed umbrella dance in the rain. Their actions are accompanied non-diegetically by the French composers' original cabaret music, which further enhances the stage-like feel. This sequence is probably one of To's most elegant treatments of action in a non-blood brotherhood film since *The Mission* (1999).

However, precisely because the director separates this sequence as a stand-alone stage-like act, all the pickpockets suddenly shed their social underdog status and don the limelight that only superstars would receive on stage. The thin line that, until this point in the film, separated superstars from social underdogs is now completely effaced; and the amazed audience is admiring the actors' splendid performance rather than thinking about what they stand for as characters. The rendition, which is supposed to feature the virtuoso techniques of pickpockets, then undermines and confuses the director's purpose of spotlighting these underprivileged personalities and the disappearing present of Hong Kong.

Fruit Chan and His '*Hong Kong*' Films

While Hui's and To's films might raise the question as to the effectiveness of the directors' self-inscription in film, Fruit Chan seems to have offered a more authentic version of social underdogs in his award-winning independent film production *Made in Hong Kong*. Spending about five years in preparation and working with only five crew members around a shoestring budget of half a million Hong Kong dollars, Fruit Chan completed the shooting within four months (T. 1998: 54–57; M. Berry 2005: 466; Gan 2005: 5).[9] All the major roles are played by non-professional actors and actresses whom the director discovered on the streets. This is a major point that distinguishes this social underdog film from those of Hui and To. The choice of a non-professional cast certainly avoids the potential drawbacks of hiring popular professional actors who might show too much of their star personas instead of highlighting the marginality of the socially underprivileged. *Made in Hong Kong* was shown at the 1999 Hong Kong International Film Festival after being denied an entry early on (E. Cheung 2009: 3). Fruit Chan went on to release the film theatrically in October 1997 through his personal network in the Hong Kong mainstream film industry. The general release schedule chosen for the film sharpened its political allusion to the Handover (Richards 1999: 34; Lok 2002: 140; E. Cheung 2009: 131). Shu Kei, veteran film critic and film distributor, has been given the credit of helping Fruit Chan to distribute the film (M. Berry 2005: 466; E. Cheung 2009: 3).

Set in contemporary Hong Kong in the pre-Handover period, *Made in Hong Kong* tells the story of four marginalized Hong Kong adolescents who live in public housing and are nowhere close to heroes. Moon (Sam Lee) is the triad society member among the four but he works for bosses on petty jobs only, such as debts collection. He appoints himself as protector to the intellectually disabled Sylvester (Wenders Li). Moon meets Ping (Neiky Yim) while trying to collect debts from the latter's mother. The girl later reveals that she has terminal kidney disease. The three teenagers all come from dysfunctional families (featured by the absence of their fathers), and due to their similar backgrounds they become good friends. One day, Sylvester picks up two bloodstained suicide letters left by Susan (Amy Tam), a high-school girl who has killed herself because of a failed romance with her school teacher. The three then set themselves the mission to deliver the two suicide letters to the addressees: the teacher and Susan's parents. Moon is constantly imagining and dreaming about how Susan committed suicide. The director shows Moon's obsession by repeatedly screening the moments before, during and after Susan jumps off a tall building, and thereby turns her into the fourth major character. In the finale, Moon reveals that he and his two friends have already died for various separate reasons, and that the whole story has in fact been narrated and commented on by Moon in his afterlife voice-over.

In giving these deprived youths the necessary visibility, Fruit Chan not only allows their *voices* to be heard (the characters take turns to read out the suicide letters in voice-overs at the finale), but also identifies with them by pondering over his own situation of a helpless Hong Kong citizen living under broader political circumstances, a citizen who might not welcome much the political reunification of Hong Kong and China (E. Cheung 2009: 131–32). Such an identification with the characters does not come easily, as there are no proper communication channels that these youngsters can and are willing to use. Eventually, the director chooses the suicide letters and the quiet images of dysfunctional television sets (either turned off or screens filled with flickers of 'snow'), which both bridge and emphasize the gaps between individuals (Naficy 2001: 106; W. Cheung 2007). Besides these two upsetting aesthetic icons, this film is full of other visual elements that indicate its bleakness: claustrophobic indoor scenes, various fences and bars blocking the faces of the protagonists from the film audience's view and at times blocking the characters' view as well, dim and faded colouring suggesting a realist setting in a grass-roots community, and, of course, the hopelessly disheartened facial expressions that every character carries around (see also E. Cheung (2009: 105–7) for Fruit Chan's 'ghostly chronotopes').

From the angle of political symbolism, we can see that the film aesthetics might mirror the director's despair and distrust, and that of many of his fellow Hongkongers, regarding a future that is deemed to be China-oriented. Asian studies scholar Shu-mei Shih (2007: 149) reads the allegory of this film as a 'guerilla tactic' to appropriate, confiscate and usurp meanings of Hong Kong from the control of both the British colonialists and the Chinese nationalists. The negative feelings are verbalized at the end of the film by a surreal propaganda broadcast coming from a Chinese communist radio station. From the angle of film production, on the other hand, I tend to believe that the evident toning down of stylized film aesthetics reflects Fruit Chan's thrifty mode of filmmaking. The director's self-declared interstitial position at the margin of Hong Kong's mainstream film industry, then, aligns him with the accented filmmakers from Third World and other postcolonial territories who attempt to survive politically and professionally in the West. Yet, Fruit Chan's interstitial position is not without a certain degree of self-contradiction, as he is fully aware of his necessary reliance on the setup of Hong Kong mainstream film financing, production, distribution and exhibition (M. Berry 2005: 472), even when working in the mode of 'independent' filmmaking. Seen from this perspective, Fruit Chan's turning against the commercialism of the Hong Kong film industry can be read as a way of promoting his film, rather than as a real declaration of war against his 'enemies' in the mainstream: in fact, he has never actually left the local mainstream film industry (Fong 1999: 52; Ye 2000: 23; M. Berry 2005: 467). Likewise, his visual style can be understood as part of his film publicity exercise. Fruit Chan's trumpeted independence did indeed make the film an instant talk of the town, and among international film critics (Fore 1999: 7; Rayns 1999: 47–48; Reynaud 1999: 8).

Although *Made in Hong Kong*'s seemingly unconventional mode of production has always been a much commented feature, the film does play around generic conventions and aesthetic elements that belong to the typical gangster and juvenile delinquent Hong Kong films of the 1990s.[10] Fruit Chan adds his mockery of the naive glorification of gangster heroism and makes *Made in Hong Kong* stand out among these popular gangster films (How Does *Made in Hong Kong* Produce the Legend of Independents 1997: 47; E. Cheung 2009: 135). Esther M.K. Cheung (2009: 7, 18) calls *Made in Hong Kong* a genre piece of an impure kind. Others from the 'New Generation Directors' tread in Fruit Chan's footsteps to make fun of the once-popular gangster films. For example, in 2010 the screenwriter-turned-film director Felix Chong made *Once a Gangster* (Hong

Kong, 2010), an anti-gangster comedy mocking its characters, who have grown from being the twenty-something triad society big brothers into middle-aged men. The characters are disillusioned with their heroic deeds in the past and are concerned now with the reality amid the Global Financial Crisis and globalized economic restructuring. The comic effects are highlighted by the stars Ekin Cheng and Jordan Chan, who used to play the main characters in the *Young and Dangerous* series. Apart from the gangster genre, *Made in Hong Kong* also explores the problem of growing up, and of life and death (E. Cheung 2009: 143). Esther M.K. Cheung associates the film with the ghost genre due to its recurrent theme of death and the main character's afterlife voice-over.

In 2001, Fruit Chan made the second instalment of his Prostitute Trilogy, *Hollywood Hong Kong*, which is the second of his independent films named after Hong Kong (E. Cheung 2009: 136). Like *Made in Hong Kong*, *Hollywood Hong Kong* was also created on a shoestring budget of HK$500,000 (£39,000 or U.S.$64,000), self-funded by Fruit Chan. Unlike the former film, *Hollywood Hong Kong* did not bring profit and was a financial loss to the director (of about HK$33,000, i.e., £2,600 or U.S.$4,000, in Hong Kong's box offices), as it did not enjoy wide release even in Hong Kong (E. Cheung 2009: 148). The film was produced by Fruit Chan's Nicetop Independent Limited, together with Capitol Films (U.K.), Golden Network (Hong Kong), Hakuhodo (Japan), Media Suits (Japan) and Movement Pictures (unknown country).

The title of *Hollywood Hong Kong* suggests the film is a bookend closing the period of Fruit Chan's self-proclaimed filmmaking independence working on the subject matter of 'Hong Kong'. It tells the story of a Hong Kong local family living in a shanty town Tai Hom Village and their relationships with a mainland Chinese prostitute. The family consists of a fat father Mr Chu (Glen Chin),[11] a fat teenage elder son (Ho Sai-man) and a fat younger son of primary-school age (Leung Sze-ping). The mother is absent, a feature that resonates with the absent fathers in *Made in Hong Kong* (although in the film there is a stand-in mother figure – a female pig as their house pet). All three obese males and their teenage neighbour Wong Chi-keung (Wong You-nam), who is a skinny, self-confessed gangster, are attracted to the mysterious femme fatale-type mainland Chinese prostitute Tong Tong (aka Hung Hung; played by Zhou Xun). Tong Tong turns out to be a con artist and cheats these men (except the young fat boy) out of huge sums of money. Before the men try to avenge themselves on Tong Tong, she manages to escape out of Hong Kong and goes to the real Hollywood.

As far as the cast is concerned, the uniqueness of *Hollywood Hong Kong* among Fruit Chan's other independent films is his employment of two well-established, professional actors. The fat father Mr Chu is played by Glen Chin, an acclaimed Chinese-American actor working in Hollywood. Zhou Xun, playing the female lead, is one of the most famous award-winning mainland Chinese actresses. She frequently stars in China-Hong Kong mainstream co-productions, such as *Temptress Moon* (Chen Kaige, 1996); *Perhaps Love; Painted Skin* (Gordon Chan, 2008) and *Flying Swords of Dragon Gate* (Tsui Hark, 2011). Zhou was certainly at the peak of her career when she was cast as the female lead in *Hollywood Hong Kong*. Although she toned down her star qualities to play the role of a mainland Chinese prostitute who speaks Cantonese with a strong mainland accent, her presence in *Hollywood Hong Kong* did not help much to improve the film's box-office earnings. This specific cast of professional actors with non-professional actors reflects Fruit Chan's own oscillation between independent film production and mainstream film production.

In the film, we also find Fruit Chan's subtle comments on his fellow Hongkongers' sociopolitical situations, haunted by Hong Kong's rapid redevelopment and China's economic rise in the 2000s. While Tong Tong is trying to earn enough money to go (for unknown reasons) to the real Hollywood, the eventual move of the Chus (the family of fat men) only comes along as a consequence of the local government's redevelopment plan to pull down the whole Tai Hom Village. This village was the oldest of its kind in Hong Kong (Long 2003: 148–49; M. Berry 2005: 477) and was located right across the road from the newly built, luxurious, high-rise residential complex Plaza Hollywood before being demolished. The village as portrayed in the film offers yet another dimension for the director to express himself on the difference between the rich and the poor, the mainstream and the marginalized, the privileged and the underprivileged, the good and the bad, the old and the new, Hong Kong and China, and the Hong Kong film industry versus Hollywood (Chang 2002: 86–88; P. Feng 2011: 253). However, after having worked for a few years as Hong Kong's independent filmmaker, in *Hollywood Hong Kong* Fruit Chan seems to be looking for a way out of the awkward in-between position among these binary sets. The film conveys a less emotionally burdened sociopolitical message than the one we get in *Made in Hong Kong* (How Come There's a Hollywood in Hong Kong? 2002: 41). Instead of focusing on stars, gangsters or ghosts, Fruit Chan highlights the black humour in *Hollywood Hong Kong* by means of a stylized surreal touch: each of the male characters fantasizes in his own way about having an intimate relationship with Tong Tong (Between Human and Pig 2002: 96).

In addition, there is an abundant use of symbolism in colours and props. For example, the colour red is used throughout the film to symbolize eroticism as well as to indicate the dangers menacing these men when they confront the femme fatale (who, in turn, represents mainland China). The obsessive use of the Internet by the teenage fat boy and his thin neighbour seems to have widened their so-called online social circle, but has in fact only heightened the boys' wishful thinking about moving out of their current stifling situation in the shanty town (W. Cheung 2007: 281). The symbolism in Fruit Chan's realist-cum-surrealist film, then, does have the effect of enhancing the cinematic visibility of Hong Kong social underdogs and increasing social awareness regarding the local government's violent demolishment of buildings that are part of Hong Kong's history (represented here by the very existence of Tai Hom Village). Whether Fruit Chan has effectively aroused greater public interest in these social under-dogs and rescued them from their current situation in Hong Kong's poorest corner is another matter, given the film's limited theatrical release and poor box-office performance. With the benefit of hindsight of Fruit Chan's subse-quent career development outside Hong Kong, we can read the ending of the film as suggesting an alternative solution to the characters' problems (as well as his fellow Hongkongers' China-related problems): going away – admittedly an implied theme in Fruit Chan's works since *Made in Hong Kong* (Y-W. Chu 2013: 99). Going away might not reflect an entirely negative attitude. When the people have learned a lesson from their past experience, it is time to let go and move on to find a new path (Shin and K. Lam 2003: 90).

The 'New Generation Directors' and *Gallants*

Fruit Chan's record of a forgotten corner of Hong Kong in *Hollywood Hong Kong* is echoed by another film, *Gallants*. Both films find their own ways to connect with an immediate past of the city. While *Hollywood Hong Kong* discloses the history of the housing problems of Hong Kong's grass-roots community, *Gallants* talks about the Hongkongers' interests in learning kung fu in the past. *Gallants*, in particular, also conveys a more universal theme of a positive attitude to life. The film was made in 2010 by two of Hong Kong's newest generation filmmakers,

Clement Cheng and Derek Kwok, and was shot over a shooting period of only eighteen days (Ambroisine 2010). In fact, *Gallants* was originally conceived as a story not about kung fu but about a music band (Ambroisine 2010). In order to sell the idea to potential investors, the two directors repackaged the film into the present kung fu comedy. It was produced by veteran actor Gordon Lam and co-produced by Andy Lau's Focus Films, Sil-Metropole Organisation, Beijing Polybona Film, and Zhejiang Bona Film and TV Production. The film's world première took place at the thirtieth edition of the Hong Kong International Film Festival in March 2010, and was screened at other major international film festivals such as Udine Far East Film, Fantasia, Fantastic Fest, Vancouver, Sitges, Tokyo and Berlin Fantasy Filmfest (Ambroisine 2011). It was the third highest grossing film at its opening weekend in Hong Kong and received critical acclaim.[12] It won the Best Film Award at the thirtieth edition of the Hong Kong Film Awards in 2011.

Gallants is mainly set in the present-day Hong Kong, where the city is dominated by wealthy land developers who ignore the old traditions connected with places and people. The film starts with references to some grainy visuals of old sepia photos that capture moments of truth of boxing championships and kung fu fights in the 1960s and the 1970s. It is narrated by Tam Ping-man (a veteran actor/broadcaster whose voice is often associated with the golden period of Hong Kong radio broadcasting in the 1960s) to bring in the idea of 'survival of the fittest'. Fast-forwarding to the 2000s, we see how the physically meek and fragile Cheung (Wong You-nam) has performed badly in an office environment. As a result, he is seconded by his land developer boss to do a disgusting job – go to the New Territories to claim the properties for his client's redevelopment project. Cheung first meets Tiger (Bruce Leung Siu-lung) in the village where the properties are located, when Tiger saves Cheung from being beaten up by the local gang. Then Cheung meets Dragon (Chen Kuan-tai) at a dilapidated tea restaurant. The place used to be a kung fu training school run by Master Law (Teddy Robin Kwan) and is now operated as a local tea restaurant by his loyal pupils Dragon and Tiger, so that they can at least keep the rented property site for their master. It is revealed that during a kung fu competition thirty years ago, Master Law suffered a stroke and has been in a coma ever since. The two pupils, now in their sixties, are still waiting for their master to wake up. At the very beginning, Cheung is hoping to learn kung fu from Tiger, but later he is deeply moved by Dragon and Tiger's loyalty to their master; he decides to defy his client's plan and instead help Dragon and Tiger fulfil the last wish of the temporarily awake Master Law – to have a good fight again in the boxing ring. Master Law passes away eventually while sleeping, and the pupils insist on participating in a kung fu challenge with their opponent, the clan of Master Pong, who runs a modernized martial arts club. Although the fight ends with no winner or loser, Master Law's pupils complete the fight gracefully. They live up to their master's expectations of perseverance, integrity, respect for traditional kung fu principles and keeping a positive outlook on life.

Featuring a collapsed kung fu school, *Gallants* inherits and pays tribute to the traditions of Hong Kong kung fu comedies that were the mainstay of mainstream Hong Kong cinema in the late 1970s. Some famous Hong Kong films of that time include *Snake in the Eagle's Shadow* and *Drunken Master*, both directed by Yuen Woo-ping in 1978 and starring Jackie Chan. *Gallants'* Chinese title, *Da Lui Toi* (in Cantonese) or *Da Lei Tai* (in Mandarin) literally means 'fighting in a boxing ring' and is the same as that of Kirk Wong's *Health Warning*, which is a 1983 Hong Kong sci-fi kung fu film. At the same time, and perhaps more importantly, the directors of *Gallants* bring in their new vision in revisiting the kung fu film genre, which includes the use of a specific cast and other stylistic elements.

The cast of *Gallants* includes some very popular actors of the Hong Kong film industry of the 1960s and 1970s. Teddy Robin Kwan, playing Master Law, is a veteran film director and actor (he was the singer and guitarist of an extremely popular band Teddy Robin and the Playboys in 1960s Hong Kong). Siu Yam-yam (aka Susan Siu), playing Master Law's girlfriend Fun, was a sex symbol in the Hong Kong film industry in the 1970s and early 1980s. The other main actors in *Gallants*, including Chen Kuan-tai as the elder pupil Dragon, Bruce Leung Siu-lung as the younger pupil Tiger, Lo Meng as Jade Kirin, and Michael Chan Wai-man as Master Pong, were once the icons of Hong Kong kung fu/action films. In their heydays they were closely associated with the Shaw Brothers studio. But at their present ages, they are no longer the most sought-after in the local film industry. In working with these senior action actors, who are now underdogs in the local film sector where only the fittest survive, the film directors learn from these men's principles in kung fu and in life, and re-channel these virtues into their own situation of directorship in a volatile filmmaking environment in the early twenty-first century (Ambroisine 2010). The senior cast is accompanied by a group of younger actors, who suggest not only a revitalization of the old-school kung fu group but also a continuation of an uncompromising attitude and belief in life.

The film directors also effectively project their childhood memory of kung fu films in *Gallants* without using overtly stylized visuals to do so. Mise en scène, costume and make-up, and lighting, are employed and changed following the needs of the plot progression to give natural visual effects. For example, Tiger's lame leg and the knuckle calluses on one of his hands are highlighted in close-up shots before his face appears in front of the audience. The visuals work to show that Tiger is well-trained in kung fu but has probably been injured. Medium shots and medium close-ups are used interchangeably with rapid cuts and occasional slow motion during fights to demonstrate the beauty of the kung fu masters' bodily movements. A blue hue under dim lighting in the last fight scene solidifies the seriousness of the fight and what it represents about life and human virtues. There are no complicated computer effects for enhancing the action scenes. Every punch and kick is forceful and filled with strong kinetic energy, reminding the audience of the beauty of actions that were once abundant in the kung fu film genre in the 1970s. Moreover, the film's Cantonese dialogues and nostalgic song lyrics are often witty and full of wisdom. Even the seemingly old-fashioned characters and their emotions, and the way they are filmed, generate in the audience a feeling of the good old days. Everything looks so down to earth, turning the film into an on-screen album of these disappearing kung fu styles and characters. Consciously or not, the two directors have made an important imprint on the continuous development of Hong Kong's kung fu films and cinematic practice in general. They have demonstrated the high degree of flexibility of Hong Kong Cinema in responding to the latest developments in world cinemas.

Concluding Remarks

This chapter has focused on individual Hong Kong filmmakers' authorial vision and how different film directors inscribe themselves and their views in film. The directors discussed have benefited from, and utilized, their own personal backgrounds and professional training to build up their careers locally. They show us how different generations of Hong Kong film professionals have made use of their strengths and their own limitations to open a path and develop a cinematic practice of their own. Established film directors under discussion, such as Hui, are the first generation of Hong Kong filmmakers to start making films genuinely for and about Hong Kong society. They were later joined by newer film directors (such as To and Fruit Chan) and, more recently, by the 'New Generation Directors', in the search for and building of local identities through film. Unlike their Hong Kong filmmaking predecessors in the 1950s and the 1960s, who were heavily influenced by a strong desire to return to their homeland in China one day (a typical wish of diasporic people), most of the Hong Kong film directors working in the local film industry after the 1970s have chosen to free themselves of this emotional and cultural constraint. For them, Hong Kong has become the place where their roots are. In featuring social underdogs and inscribing themselves in their films in various ways, including reflexive cameo, on-screen photos of ordinary people and their way of life, different props and re-enactment of traditional genre, these filmmakers have contributed to revisualizing the 'collective memory' of the Hongkongers.

In the next two chapters, I will move above this local perspective to see how the New Hong Kong Cinema fares on a broader, regional level as an integral part of the continuous restructuring of East Asia's film industries. Understanding the New Hong Kong Cinema from a broader East Asian regional perspective helps us expand our knowledge of this cinematic practice, which reflects multiple transitions in the society. I will start with the receiving end of Hong Kong-related Chinese-language films – their Sinitic-speaking/writing, ethnic Chinese audiences in the region – and probe their actual interpretations of these films.

Notes

1. Probably as a way of repaying his mentor, To often recruited Wong to play respected figures in his films. One notable role is that of Uncle Teng in *Election*. Wong passed away in 2010 at the age of eighty-three.
2. Information on the segments of *Tales from the Dark* (Part 1): *A Word in the Palm* (directed by Lee Chi-ngai), *Jing Zhe* (directed by Fruit Chan) and *Stolen Goods* (directed by Simon Yam).
3. Personal interview with Li Cheuk-to, Artistic Director of the Hong Kong International Film Festival (HKIFF), conducted by the author in Hong Kong on 7 July 2010 (within the context of the 'Dynamics of World Cinema' project at the University of St Andrews).
4. Similarly, the Chinese title *Tian Mi Mi* (literally meaning sweetie) of Peter Chan's *Comrades, Almost a Love Story* has a reference to Teresa Teng's other famous song, *Tian Mi Mi*.

5. In *Sparrow* (DVD) (Hong Kong version, bonus track), Johnnie To mentions that this mysterious mainland Chinese girl represents new immigrants in Hong Kong hailing from China.

6. Source: interview with Johnnie To in *Sparrow* (DVD) (Hong Kong version, bonus track).

7. Source: interview with Johnnie To in *Sparrow* (DVD) (Hong Kong version, bonus track).

8. Source: interview with Johnnie To in *Sparrow* (DVD) (Hong Kong version, bonus track).

9. In Susanna T.'s interview with Fruit Chan, the shooting period of four months is mentioned in the Chinese version of the interview transcript. No such mention is found in the English version.

10. Some famous Hong Kong gangster films made in the 1990s include the *Young and Dangerous* series. See note 12 in Chapter One.

11. When read in the Cantonese language, the surname Chu is a homonym of 'pig'. Locals in Hong Kong often associate pigs with dirt, laziness and shabbiness.

12. Source: Box Office Mojo, www.boxofficemojo.com (accessed 5 May 2015).

CHAPTER FOUR

Ethnic Chinese Film Audiences
The *Red Cliff* Experience in East and South East Asia

Different Hong Kong-raised or Hong Kong-based ethnic Chinese mainstream film directors may employ various cinematic devices to deliver their authorial vision, and their concerns about the changes in Hong Kong's sociopolitical environment and the Hongkongers' social-cultural-political status under the influences of the Handover. Generally, commercial film professionals are inclined to refer to box-office statistics to determine whether a film is successful or not (see, for example, Chan C. 2000; Shackleton 2012b; see also the 'audience-as-market' paradigm in Ang 1991: 26–32; McQuail 1994: 288–89). On the other hand, film audiences are often treated (or thought to be) in a passive position to be impacted by the films they watch. If audience comments are available, they are likely to be filtered by the organizers of audience survey, or be exploited as free marketing tools for the films in question.

With the affordability, accessibility and, indeed, trendiness of advanced technology in the form of cheap or free Wi-Fi facilities, increasingly light laptops, inexpensive mobile devices and countless instant messaging apps, film audience comments unofficially circulating through different social networking media should not be overlooked. Cases when film audiences were the proactive, driving force of certain films' production and distribution have already aroused intense discussions among different national and transnational film industries.[1] Questions also arise as to how, when, why, to whom, by whom these audience comments were made, what they were about, and what the impacts of the comments were on the film viewers themselves and on others. As for the New Hong Kong Cinema, audiences are important not only because they contribute to the box-office income that sustains the operation of the film industry. Their spectatorship (with which Hong Kong-related Chinese-language films are watched, listened to, read, written about, translated and reinterpreted across national boundaries) contributes a great extent to the New Hong Kong Cinema's interstitiality – in ways similar to how the archetypal accented films and the filmmakers' authorial vision are appreciated by their spectators (Naficy 2001: 4). For this reason, there is an urgent need for systematic and in-depth investigations into empirical audience comments on Hong Kong-related Chinese-language films, which box-office figures or professional film critics could not inform. However, there are no noticeable, systematically organized, independent, non-marketing related and consistent channels to allow film audiences of the New Hong Kong Cinema to register their views, not to mention that there are no such channels specifically at the disposal of ethnic Chinese film viewers. Even rarer are those platforms dedicated to individual films for similar purposes.

To address the above issue, in this chapter I trace the *actual* viewing experience and reception of ethnic Chinese film audiences of the New Hong Kong Cinema. Their spectatorship, I argue, helps negotiate and articulate the cinema's state of transitions and interstitiality in recent years. I am particularly interested in researching those traditional audiences of Hong Kong Cinema found among ethnic Chinese communities in East and South East Asia – those called overseas Chinese or diasporic Chinese in Hong Kong, Indonesia, Malaysia, Singapore, Taiwan and Thailand (Hau 2012), in addition to the cinema's mainland Chinese audience. I first review the existing studies on fans and film audiences. I point out the lack of studies on non-Euro-American and non-white film audiences. Establishing this lack in the field of Chinese-language film studies, and in audience and fan studies, is imperative with respect to my own audience surveys: I was prompted to conduct them when I could not find any information about scholarly reception studies on ethnic Chinese film audiences. I then detail the context, aims, methodology and data analysis of a series of original fan-audience online surveys regarding the Chinese-language mega blockbuster *Red Cliff* (2008 and 2009) (as a representative of the New Hong Kong Cinema), together with a follow-up study, which I undertook independently (see R. Cheung 2011b).[2] My empirical findings delineate a dynamic picture of how different ethnic Chinese film audiences in East/South East Asia received this film. Those diasporic Chinese viewing communities in the region magnified the problematic Chineseness and diaspora-related aspects of *Red Cliff*, which did not seem to have been acknowledged by the initial authorial vision of the film's director John Woo. Besides their distinct fandom, diasporic Chinese audiences of the New Hong Kong Cinema living in the region and under my study testified to a reality of diaspora practice with their diasporic reading of *Red Cliff*: the mentality of 'diaspora' has an expiry date (Shih 2011: 713–14, 717). Many of them come from the second (or later) generation of ethnic Chinese settling in their present territories of residence. Unlike their grandparents or parents, they see themselves and live their lives more as 'locals' than as 'immigrants' in where they are. Their spectatorial responses to *Red Cliff*, which were based on their extra-filmic experience, demonstrated the subtlety and complexity of the diasporic Chinese's mentalities and multiple attitudes to 'China' and 'Chinese history'. They added new dimensions to the interstitiality and liminality of the New Hong Kong Cinema.

Hong Kong-Related Chinese-Language Films: Audience Reception

In the considerations of accented cinema by diaspora and film scholar Hamid Naficy (2001: 23), not only the filmmakers' but also the audiences' deterritorial-ized locations conduce to the accentedness of the films. Similar to the accented filmmakers who, according to Naficy, are not only textual structures or fictional figures in film but also empirical subjects, the audiences of accented films are also real and actual. The ways these audiences watch, listen to, read, translate and write about the films 'are part of the spectatorial activities and competen-cies that are needed for appreciating the works of these [accented] filmmak-ers' (Naficy 2001: 4; see also 25, 124–25). The audiences bring with them their own experience of dislocations and displacements, and hence corresponding demands for and expectations of certain 'authentic' and corrective representa-tions, to consume the films that reflect the accented filmmakers' own diasporic existence (Naficy 2001: 6). As Naficy (2001: 35) remarks about the accented filmmakers' mode of production and authorship, 'The interpretation of these [authorial] signatures and accents depends on the spectators, who are them-selves often situated astride cultures and within collective formations. Hence, the figures they cut in their spectating of the accented filmmakers as authors are nuanced by their own extratextual tensions of difference and identity'. The accented filmmakers in turn use different cinematic devices to appeal to and address directly the target audiences' sense of morality and justice, providing alternative discourses to official records (Naficy 2001: 114–15).

Here we can see that the accented filmmakers and their films' audiences are complementary. They rely on each other's sensitivity, recognition and acknowl-edgement to keep each other going and to sustain the qualities of the accented cinema (Naficy 2001: 68–70). Applying this insight to the reception of the New

Hong Kong Cinema, I believe a thorough understanding of how different audiences watch, interpret, talk and write about these Hong Kong-related Chinese-language films is necessary for us to critically examine the New Hong Kong Cinema. I am particularly interested to unearth the information among Hong Kong Cinema's traditional target audiences, i.e., the Chinese communities in domestic and overseas markets in East and South East Asia. As Asian studies scholar Caroline S. Hau (2012) notes, 'In the early postwar era, the production of Hong Kong films relied heavily on financing by overseas Chinese and pre-selling to distributors in Southeast Asia'; and in the Cold War period, 'Taiwan emerged as the Hong Kong film industry's main market and a leading source of non-Hong Kong financing' (see also G. Leung and J. Chan 1997; Chan C. 2000; Li C. 2000: 13). In the following, I will first take a look at the essentials of audience and reception studies before I move on to discuss my own research on the ethnic Chinese audiences of the New Hong Kong Cinema.

Audiences and Fans (Anglo-Saxon Concepts)

To understand film reception from the audience's angle, the first question we should ask ourselves is 'what *exactly* is an audience?' The answer to this seemingly lucid question may reveal the background of different individuals and the prevailing ideological concerns of a given historical period. To professionals working in cultural and mass media industries, audiences have long been regarded as the submissive, vulnerable receiving end of a finished cultural product, if they have not been objectified and quantified in terms of the ratings in the television industry or the box-office earnings in the film business, for example. Media academics have also historically tended 'to treat media audiences as passive and controlled' (Lewis 1992: 1). Their attitude often reveals a 'tendency to privilege aesthetic superiority in programming', their 'reluctance to support consumerism' and their 'belief in media industry manipulation' (Lewis 1992: 1). Cultural theorist Ien Ang, for instance, in *Desperately Seeking the Audience* (1991) characterizes the media (television) industry dominance over the audience and the lack of understanding of the audience in the message production/reception environment as 'colonized by ... the institutional point of view' (Ang 1991: 2). She argues that this dominance has also influenced the ways academic audience research is conducted (Ang 1991: 10–11; Hall 1993: 100).

In relation to film, the cinema audiences are 'people who assemble to watch films in cinemas and other venues, both public and private; and also those who consume films via alternative platforms such as video, DVD, home cinema, and television' (Kuhn and Westwell 2012: 21). The concept of 'audience' here points to empirical viewers who nonetheless remain as rather passive entities along the circuit of message (or media contents) production, circulation and reception. They are not sufficiently understood by media text producers and the authorities. What examinations there are of film audiences' viewing experience and context tend to be conducted from the perspective of the survey organizers for perpetuating the purposes of the government, the film industry, marketing companies and journalists alike (Ang 1991; Austin 2002: 24–25). Scholarly research on the empirical film audience is still a minor area within the field of audience studies and the larger field of film studies (Barker with Austin 2000: 8–31, 48–49; Austin 2002: 1, 11–42).

The actual experience of everyday audiences seems an even more marginalized topic in the scholarly research of Hong Kong-related Chinese-language films. In many existing academic studies, these films are primarily read with regard to their aesthetic merits, literary qualities, cultural-historical implications, philosophical inspirations, psychoanalytical revelations, political-economic or even business concerns, while there are not many noticeable studies on Chinese-language films' audience reception, not to mention Chinese-speaking audiences in particular.[3] This certainly leaves our efforts to explore Chinese-language cinemas incomplete, especially considering that Chinese-language films have a history almost as long as the history of the motion picture itself.[4] If we agree with film scholar Thomas Austin's opinion that 'film viewers are productive agents in the creation of meaning, pleasure and use' (Austin 2002: 2) within an intertwining nexus that also includes film text and corresponding contexts, then film audiences and their empirical functions in the whole film production/distribution/exhibition setup in relation to Chinese-language films are too important to be treated on a level second to film texts, directorial styles or production context.

Among different types of film audience activities, the most visible are those of fans.[5] Despite the 'fan' to be possibly found in all of us, the label 'fans' is often negatively associated with those enthusiastic, extremely devoted yet brainless radical audiences of mediated texts, such as films, television programmes, literary works, or celebrated film stars/directors/singers, etc. 'Fans' have only started to receive close readings in the Anglo-Saxon academic setting since the early 1990s in the vein of cultural studies practised by media scholars such as

John Fiske (1992) and Henry Jenkins (1992a) (see also J. Gray, Sandvoss and Harrington 2007: 1–16). Although fans have thus been given the serious attention they have long deserved, early investigations of fan studies preserved the stereotypical images of their subject: that the 'fans' are 'abnormal' social constructs, fanatic, non-legitimate, socioculturally deprived,[6] anti-institutional, and people with issues related to their class, gender and age (Fiske 1992: 30).[7] Jenkins, who was Fiske's mentee, developed the concept of 'fandom' along these lines in the early 1990s, although he held a different take on the term:

> When my mentor, John Fiske (1992), said he was a 'fan', he meant simply that he liked a particular program, but when I said I was a fan, I was claiming membership in a particular subculture. Meaning-making in Fiske was often individualized, whereas in my work, meaning-making is often deeply social. (Jenkins 2013: kindle loc 200)

In his early fan-related works, Jenkins dissected 'fandom' into four levels: (1) fans have a distinct mode of reception in the form of socioculturally informed, ongoing, active meaning-production (Jenkins 1992a: 209–10, 1992b, 2013: kindle loc 395, p. 3 and p. 45), (2) fans are specific interpretative communities with their own 'reading protocols and structures of meaning' (Jenkins 1992a: 210–11), (3) fans are involved in their own creative and artistic productions, called 'textual poaching', for which they use materials from original mediated texts (Jenkins 1992a: 211–13, 2013: kindle loc 328, p. 23), (4) fans form their own communities, which are different from the ones they live in in the real world (Jenkins 1992a: 213).

While Fiske and Jenkins were instrumental in introducing fan studies to Anglo-Saxon academia, they only discussed the kind of fans who fit in the dominant ideological framework of self and 'other'.[8] Germinal fan investigations did not explore fans who keep their fandom to themselves and do not label themselves as such, fans who only love one single film or one single literary classic for a certain while, or fans who behave in their everyday lives no differently than non-fans (see also J. Gray, Sandvoss and Harrington 2007: 1–4). In many research works following these first studies, 'fans' as a collective noun remains a specific label for enthusiastic audiences/readers/followers/collectors of fandom objects, while fans' regular identities, professions, other interests and hobbies, family backgrounds, ethnic origins, educational characteristics, language skills, religions, political stances and the potential changes to any of these traits are largely taken for granted or hidden in the research assumptions. 'Fans' are by and large scrutinized as a singled-out subsection of a society, which seems not to have any direct effect and affect in relation to its surroundings (for example, wars, natural disasters, job market decline, Global Financial Crisis, etc.). How the various fans might *actually* be affected by, and respond to, the vicissitudes in micro and macro milieus (economic, political, environmental and so forth) has only recently started to draw the attention of academic researchers (see Austin 2002; Hills 2002; Chin 2007; Napier 2007; Larsen and Zubernis 2012; Jenkins, Ford and Green 2013; among others).

Above all, there is the problem of a lack of studies on non-white fans and fandom, and how ethnic-historical-cultural-geopolitical-specific factors might have influence on non-white fans in their particular thinking and behaviours as fans, and in other areas of their everyday lives. Although a small body of works on non-white fans and fandom is gradually starting to grow, the problem is that they attract insufficient academic attention – a problem recognized, in passing, as early as 1992 by Fiske and which remains unresolved to this day (Harrington and Bielby 2007; Y. Chow and de Kloet 2008; Chin and Hitchcock Morimoto 2013 (in particular endnote 5); see also Ciecko and H. Lee 2007; Punathambekar 2007). This lack indirectly mirrors the bias still often found in the Euro-American-centric conceptual and methodological approaches to audience studies (and film studies in general).

In spite of the above context of audience and fan studies, fans' constantly changing fandom, their relationships with different media texts and with these texts' official producers, and their interpersonal relationships within and beyond their own fan communities give us a promising entry point to understanding the supposedly passive audiences and their empirical reception of contemporary Hong Kong-related Chinese-language films. Some of the most obvious viewing communities of these films are the ethnic Chinese audiences living in East and South East Asia (Hau 2012). Regrettably, more than twenty years have passed since the first waves of fan studies in academia and there is still a lack of systematic, qualitative investigations of non-Anglophone fans and their reception of film texts (Jenkins 2013: kindle loc 677–83). The lack of empirical qualitative information on film reception of ethnic Chinese audiences in Chinese-language film studies, and in audience and fan studies, hence inspired me to conduct a series of online surveys with the aim of finding out about actual reception among ethnic Chinese audiences of the New Hong Kong Cinema. The complete version of the Chinese-language mega blockbuster *Red Cliff* as a representative of this cinema was chosen to be the anchorage of my research, due to the film's heavily promoted East and South East Asian reach.

Red Cliff, History and John Woo

Officially, *Red Cliff* has multiple places of origin: China, Hong Kong, Japan, South Korea, Taiwan and the United States. It was a co-production project funded entirely by four East Asian film equity investors from China, Japan, South Korea and Taiwan respectively (Frater 2008; M. Lee 2008; Thompson 2008). They were China Film Group Corporation (China), Showbox Entertainment (South Korea), CMC Entertainment (Taiwan) and Avex Entertainment (Japan). Their investments were matched against a bank loan taken out by the film's producer Terence Chang (Thompson 2008). With a budget of U.S.$80 million (£49 million), *Red Cliff* is thus, by far, one of the most expensively produced Chinese-language films catering to mainstream audiences. Most of the other Chinese-language blockbusters are known to have had budgets below U.S.$50 million (£31 million) (see Table A.1 in the Appendix for a summary of the budgets of Chinese-language blockbusters produced between 2000 and 2010, a period during which China started to turn out its own blockbusters).[9] In mainland Chinese publicity terms, blockbusters are referred to as *dapian* (literally meaning big films), which are 'costume pictures with martial arts, big budget, big stars, big directors, big special effects and backing from the authorities' (Yeh 2010: 193). According to film scholar Darrell William Davis (2010: 125), Chinese-language blockbusters 'enjoy around 80 per cent of the annual domestic box office revenue'.

 Red Cliff was generally released for its target audience markets in East and South East Asia, including China, Hong Kong, Indonesia, Japan, Malaysia, Singapore, South Korea, Taiwan and Thailand on dates that coincided with two separate, monumental Chinese cultural events. Part I opened in these markets in July 2008 (except in Japan where it opened in November 2008), a time near to the Beijing Olympics held in August 2008. Part II opened in the same geographical region in January 2009, close to the time of the Chinese New Year holidays that year (in Japan it was generally released in April 2009). Both releases were backed by a blanket of strategic film marketing efforts across the whole region. Part I runs for 146 minutes; and Part II for 142 minutes. The film was the box-office champion at its opening weekend in most of its target markets, indicating that the film would likely recoup most of its investments from East and South East Asia (M. Lee 2008).[10] The two instalments of *Red Cliff* were compressed into a single, 148-minute version with minimized back story for release outside Asia in 2009. According to the director John Woo, some major scenes were deliberately trimmed to produce this condensed version for audiences not well versed in the history of the Three Kingdoms re-presented in the film (Bunch 2009; Chow C. 2009; Solomons 2009).

Red Cliff depicts historical incidents and separate battles that led up to the famous Battle of Red Cliffs (aka the Battle of *Chi Bi*), which took place in the winter of AD 208–9 during the Han Dynasty in Imperial China. The film starts in the period when China was practically a divided country nominally under the rule of the political figurehead Emperor Xian, the last emperor of the Han Dynasty. The actual rule was in the hands of warlords who had absolute power over their respective territories. In the plot, the most powerful warlord, Cao Cao (Zhang Fengyi), has newly united the northern frontier and has been appointed chancellor. He asks the emperor for support in order to wage more wars in the south on individual warlords and to reunite the country. In effect, Cao has taken over all the imperial power and is controlling an army of as many as 800,000 soldiers. While marching south, Cao's army meets the allied forces of two warlords, Liu Bei (a distant cousin of Emperor Xian; played by You Yong) and Sun Quan (Chang Chen). The two opposing factions fight with each other in the Battle of Red Cliffs (the place of the battle is believed to be located on the south bank of the Yangtze River, somewhere between the present-day cities of Wuhan and Yueyang). The film ends with Cao, who is badly defeated, being forced to retreat back to the north.

The Battle of Red Cliffs and the subsequent period of the Three Kingdoms are of great importance from a historical perspective. Historians believe that the Battle of Red Cliffs decisively changed the course of Chinese history as it made each of the three warlords aware that they lacked the military power to gain complete control single-handedly over the whole country. Cao was frustrated and had to confine his control to the north of the Yangtze River, whereas the allied forces of Liu and Sun secured control over their respective lands to the south of the Yangtze River. The battle thus directly led to a situation in which the three camps divided China into a tripartite territory and started the historical period of the Three Kingdoms (AD 220–80), one of the most infamous periods of disunity in China's history. However, since the official and unofficial records for that period of Chinese history vary, what its valid sources are remains debatable. The *Records of the Three Kingdoms* (aka *Sanguo Zhi* or三國志) written by Chen Shou in the fourth century is believed to be the authoritative record covering the history of Red Cliffs and the Three Kingdoms. Yet, the related events and people were dramatized and made popular by the classic work of Chinese literature *Romance of the Three Kingdoms* (aka *Sanguo Yanyi* or三國演義) written by Luo Guanzhong in the fourteenth century. Folklore traditions, myths, classical art and popular cultural forms (such as stage operas, poems, Chinese paintings, films, television series and computer games) related to the stories of the Three Kingdoms and the personalities involved were adapted mainly from these two works, especially the *Romance of the Three Kingdoms*. In recent times the Three Kingdoms stories are often included in the school curriculum in Chinese communities. In short, the tales of the Battle of Red Cliffs and the Three Kingdoms have for centuries been household stories among Chinese people living around the world as well as among nationals of other countries (for example, Japanese and Koreans) who have been exposed to Chinese history and culture.

The screen interpretation and representation of the Battle of Red Cliffs by Woo offers one of the numerous glimpses of how people in our time may think of and imagine the distant past. It also indirectly displays Woo's worldview, biographical background and his earlier filmmaking career. Similar to many Hong Kong film directors I discuss in other chapters of this book, mainland China-born Woo has a diasporic background. He moved to Hong Kong at the age of five with his family, who then lived in the slum area in Hong Kong for a number of years. Woo was lucky to be sponsored by an American family to go to a local Catholic school, where he received his education and was inspired by the Christian religion. Starting from 1969, Woo worked in the local film industry in Hong Kong as an assistant. His work at the Shaw Brothers studio and his assistantship to action cinema master Chang Cheh (aka Zhang Che) would have a lasting influence on Woo's subsequent directorship. By the mid 1980s, Woo had become a film director for Golden Harvest studio and made several comedies. But his early films did not do well in local box offices. The initial failure caused him to go to Taiwan in the early 1980s to work as a director; this was a kind of self-exile from the booming Hong Kong film industry. In 1986 he had the opportunity to return to Hong Kong to direct *A Better Tomorrow*, the film that would soon become one of the classics of contemporary Hong Kong Cinema. The filmmaker's success in the late 1980s in Hong Kong attracted the interest of Hollywood, and in 1993 Woo got a contract to work there. This coincided with the period when, in connection with the approaching Handover in 1997, the Hongkongers were generally considering whether to migrate or stay behind. Woo took up the Hollywood job and stayed in the United States until 2008. He did not have an incredibly successful career there, and *Red Cliff* marked Woo's major comeback to Asia and his decision to make films on his home turf again. Contrary to his Hollywood experience, which often involved levels of discussions with film producers and investors before decisions could be made, Woo has enjoyed much greater directorial control in his Asia-made films (Renowned Director 2005; Li L. and Chen X. 2008).

Red Cliff, as Woo confirms in media interviews, carries his own personal romanticization of historical incidents that are factually based on the official *Records of Three Kingdoms* (Chow C. 2009; John Woo 2009).[11] Important personalities in history are introduced on screen with little information about their names and backgrounds. The result is that the film relies heavily on the history knowledge of the viewers in order for the story to be understood; those who are not familiar with that part of Chinese history can easily lose track at certain points in the film. In detailing the interpersonal relationships of these historical characters, Woo inscribes in them his other favourite themes, such as social collectivism, male bonding, courage and bravery, and anti-war idealization. Above all, the film conveys a strong urge for national unity similar to what the rulers of China would have been eager to achieve at all costs, leaving no space for thinking otherwise. Moreover, the evocation of Chinese national pride and nationalistic ideals in the film ignores different choices of lives people would hope to pursue, and the complex history of China/Chinese civilization (characterized by wars, colonization and the succession of different ruling dynasties and races of people – Hans, Mongols, Manchus). This is particularly problematic when we consider historian Robert A. Rosenstone's argument (2006: 39) about history and historical films that '[t]hey are what help to create in us the feeling that we are not just viewing history, but actually living through events in the past, experiencing (or so we think, at least momentarily) what others felt in times of war, revolution, and social, cultural, and political change'. In Woo's interpretation of history presented in *Red Cliff*, Liu and Sun represent the good guys who unite together to fight for a righteous cause. The good guys finally defeat Cao and his army, the bad guys, and their ambition to bring further turmoil to the country. This seemingly politically correct interpretation of past events in fact brings forth a perpetuation of that version of history having been passed down by the winners and dominators, who themselves had to kill and stifle the voices of their opponents barbarically to become the winners. Who then were good and bad?

The diegetic call for Chinese national unification and unity in *Red Cliff* can also be found on a non-diegetic level via its cast, whose members come from different territories in East Asia. Regardless of where the actors and actresses are originally from, they all play Chinese nationals in the film, dress in Chinese period costumes and are dubbed over as speaking 'perfect' Mandarin Chinese. This linguistic treatment is different from what Ang Lee does in *Crouching Tiger, Hidden Dragon*, in which the director preserves the different accents actors speak within the film and reattaches himself to a 'China' he actually has never known from his diasporic perspective (Klein 2004: 25). As Asian studies scholar Shu-mei Shih (2007: 2) remarks on the accents with which the actors speak in *Crouching Tiger, Hidden Dragon*, 'the accents break down the idea that the characters live in a coherent universe'.

Instead of representing effectively a national wholeness, *Red Cliff*'s star-laden cast ironically aggravates the Sinocentric problem coming through the film. The places of origin of individual actors and actresses in the context of working on this film induce informed audiences to draw parallels between the restaged battle and the present-day situation in East Asia, as well as to speculate on deeper geopolitical implications beyond the diegetic scenarios. To be exact, multiple award-winner Tony Leung Chiu-wai from Hong Kong and Kaneshiro Takeshi from Taiwan (he was born to a Japanese father and a Taiwanese mother) play the two male leads, Zhou Yu and Zhuge Liang respectively. While Zhou is the viceroy of Sun's camp, Zhuge is the strategist working for Liu. Both Zhou and Zhuge (the righteous, good guys) work together trying to fight off the invasion of Cao's camp (the arrogant, bad guys). Cao, on the other hand, is played by renowned mainland Chinese actor Zhang Fengyi. These three major roles are supported by a constellation of East Asian film stars who were already very famous before acting in *Red Cliff*. For example, Sun Quan is played by Chang Chen (Taiwan). Sun's sister is played by Vicki Zhao (aka Zhao Wei), who is from China. She is one of the two main female characters in the film, the other being Xiaoqiao, played by Lin Chiling (a model-turned-actress from Taiwan). While

Hu Jun (China) plays Zhao Yun (military general on Liu's side), Nakamura Shido (Japan) plays Gan Xing (military general on Sun's side). What we are prompted to see here, then, is more than just the interaction of the stars in the film. It inevitably also involves associations with the often difficult international relations among the places of origin of the stars.

Empirical Audience Research among Ethnic Chinese

Before I detail my independent study on the audience reception of *Red Cliff*, I should say that my initial interest in researching audiences was a by-product of my contribution to *The Epic Film in World Culture* (Burgoyne 2011). The idea of studying Chinese-language epic film audiences came along after I had watched the full two-diptych version of *Red Cliff* (in its Hong Kong-version DVD format), and had had mixed feelings about it, before the film was generally released outside Asia. As a film researcher, I was impressed by Woo's stylistic achievement and technical competence in this Sinitic epic film. But as an ethnic Chinese film viewer who has a different understanding of 'Chinese' identities, I was not (and still am not) convinced by Woo's simplistic interpretation and urging for a national unity through his approach to romanticizing the debatable historical incidents and personalities in the film. The way that Woo conceals the disunity of the places of origin of the cast by means of giving them a unified 'Chinese' look in their costume and spoken language (speaking 'perfect' Mandarin Chinese without an accent) reminds me of the cultural Sinocentrism and the concomitant feeling of national superiority. This kind of cultural/national essentialism has been notoriously a top-down practice, encouraged by the Chinese authorities and perpetuated by those who fail to see the danger in such an ideology in a period when China is expanding its hard and soft power worldwide (see, for example, R. Chow 1993; Ang 1998, 2001; Chua B. 2012; Jacques 2012). My mixed feelings for this box-office winner thus prompted me to explore the viewing experience of other ethnic Chinese spectators of the film (complete, two-part version), especially those not living in mainland China and having their own ideas of what 'China', 'Chinese' and 'Chineseness' might mean. As I mentioned earlier, there were in fact no such qualitative film audience investigations available in the field of Chinese-language film studies, and in audience and fan studies. This discovery inspired me to conduct one myself, via a series of online audience surveys (see R. Cheung 2011b). My online investigations proved very useful for obtaining first-hand audience reception data that would have been expensive and time-consuming to gather through conventional focus group discussions or in-depth personal interviews. I will now discuss my methods of gathering these audience opinions.

Methodology: Online Surveys 2009 and 2013

My investigations followed the tradition of cultural studies. The main aims were: (1) to uncover ethnic Chinese's spectatorial responses to *Red Cliff* (complete, two-part version) that might or might not have been influenced by the audiences' own historical awareness and diasporic consciousness, (2) to discover whether such spectatorial responses were equal to or differed from Woo's directorial vision in restaging a past of 'China', and (3) how the audiences might contemplate the future as a result of watching this film. Spectatorial responses to the condensed version of *Red Cliff* were not considered, as this shortened version has left out important parts of the restaged history. The first round of studies was conducted in 2009, and the follow-up was in 2013.

First Surveys, 2009

During two randomly chosen months, March and August of 2009, I designed and conducted a series of online studies on major social networking websites and fansites. My investigations were based on online participant observation, and on content and linguistic analysis of fan-authored messages posted on these websites in the first year after the general release of *Red Cliff* (Part I) in East and South East Asia. My research had two levels. The focus at the first level was the film itself. It included finding out audience comments on the film's official websites.[12] Among them, only the China and the U.S. sites had sections for audiences' comments, which were 'shared' externally from other online forums. Whereas the one on the China site linked to blogs hosted by sina.com.cn, *Red Cliff*'s U.S. site was linked to Facebook pages that were dedicated to the film. I also did similar investigations to dig out online comments and discussions on *Red Cliff* on five of the world's most popular social networking websites at that time – Facebook, MySpace, Twitter, Friendster and Bebo (see Table A.2 in the Appendix for the accumulated statistics up until 24 August 2009).

I conducted the online surveys through my personal registration as a member of these social networking media. Owing to my language capacity, I considered only audience comments and discussions written in English and Chinese (simplified and traditional scripts) at this initial stage of investigations. Besides English, I am fluent in Cantonese and Mandarin Chinese, and can read and write equally well in traditional and in simplified Chinese scripts. These language skills enabled me to distinguish the nuances in the writings of Sinitic speakers/writers in particular from mainland China, Hong Kong and Taiwan respectively, who write with words, tones, grammar and syntax unique to their own respective geopolitical territories. While traditional Chinese characters are used by Sinitic writers in Hong Kong, Macau, Taiwan and among older generations of Chinese immigrants in the West, simplified Chinese characters are officially used in the PRC and Singapore, as well as among Sinitic writers in Malaysia. Shih uses the term 'Sinophone' to align the Chinese linguistic heterogeneities and multiplicities that occur in various degrees across Sinitic-speaking ethnic Chinese communities settled in East and South East Asia as well as along the Pacific Rim (Shih 2007: 7). According to Shih (2007: 4), 'Sinophone' depicts 'a network of places of cultural production outside China and on the margins of China and Chineseness, where a historical process of heterogenizing and localizing of continental Chinese culture has been taking place for several centuries'. Shih's idea thus echoes Ang's argument (1998: 225) that there are 'many different Chinese identities, not one'. Language in the case of Sinophone regions is not related so much to the ethnic-cultural origins of people as to these people's everyday encounters in their present places of residence (for example, consider the difference in the use of written/spoken Chinese languages between those ethnic Chinese living in Hong Kong and Taiwan). 'Sinophone' is thus place-specific. It refers to multiplicity not only in verbal but also in script forms (Shih 2011: 715). Most importantly, the concept of 'Sinophone' refuses the hegemonic call of Chineseness that has its political roots in a hollow Sinocentrism. 'Sinophone' sets an 'expiration date' for those in diaspora to become *locals* in their host countries (Shih 2011: 713–14, 717).

To keep my research manageable, this initial stage of online investigations served to filter out non-essential online audience messages that were not what I set out to look for. In particular, the findings from the five popular social networking media were far from inspiring. Some of these media, for example Twitter, having strict word limits for posts, only displayed very brief written messages from *Red Cliff*'s audiences. They could not reveal much of these audiences' thoughts. As many of these messages were written in non-Sinitic languages such as English, they did not tell easily the ethnic-cultural-geopolitical origins of the post writers. They also did not tell clearly whether the claimed locations of the post writers were real and whether these post writers had watched the complete version of *Red Cliff* (which was only shown in designated markets in East/South East Asia).

I discovered long blog posts written solely in simplified Chinese characters on the film's official website in China. The way in which these posts were written suggested the mainland origin of the writers. In terms of content, most of these audience comments were positive (indicating to a certain extent the film marketing efforts behind the so-called interactive forum). They focused primarily on the spectacular battle scenes that feature tens of thousands of soldiers in military formations. This discovery was in striking contrast with those mainland Chinese media reports that stressed dissatisfaction of the film among its mainland Chinese audience. According to these media reports, film viewers in China thought that *Red Cliff* deviated noticeably from the supposedly 'true' history. The characterization of famous historical personalities on screen also raised an issue as to how thorough Woo's understanding of Chinese history was (Li L. and Chen X. 2008; John Woo 2009). If the mainland Chinese audience dislikes *Red Cliff* mainly for its 'unfaithfulness' to the 'history' that the audience is familiar with, how would different opinions among diasporic Chinese audiences attest to the effects of their diasporic experience and to the impacts of the 'historical process of heterogenizing and localizing of continental Chinese culture' on them (Shih 2007: 4)?

This brings us to the second level of my research, which revolved around the fans and their fandom dedicated to Kaneshiro Takeshi, one of *Red Cliff*'s male leads. As Chin (2007: 215) mentions, fandom in East Asia is practised differently than in the West. Rather than focusing their energies on a particular film text or characters in films or television programmes, fans in East Asia are 'idol-driven'. East Asian fans enjoy building up imagined 'intimacy' with their star idols (Yano 2004: 44; see also the concept of the 'imagined communities' in Anderson (1983)). By default, they will be the first to see the films, television programmes and commercials in which their idols are involved, and will buy the music albums that their idols turn out.[13] These fans demonstrate profound knowledge of their idols' likes, dislikes and the mundane details of their lives, and often show this knowledge off to their fellow fans. Instead of displaying grass-roots resistance to the media texts produced through official channels (Fiske 1992), fans in East Asia show dedication and 100 per cent support for their idols and their idols' activities. Among these fandom efforts, online fansites are often mounted to give the fans a place to express their love for their idols, to discuss their idols' works in detail, to interact with each other and build communion over the love they share for the same stars.

My choice of Kaneshiro as the centre point of the second level of my research owed much to his being an interesting figure. Unlike other major actors/ actresses in *Red Cliff*, Kaneshiro has an ambiguous ethnic-cultural background. He was born in 1973 in Taipei, Taiwan to a Taiwanese mother and a Japanese father. Whereas Kaneshiro was raised, educated and later started his entertainment career in Taiwan, which the star often declares publicly to be his real home, he is officially a Japanese citizen. His Japanese nationality, however, made him ineligible for the competition of the Outstanding Taiwanese Filmmaker of the Year Award in the forty-fifth edition of the Golden Horse Awards (the Taiwan equivalent of the Oscars') in December 2008 (M. Lim 2008). On the other hand, the handsome Kaneshiro has good command of Cantonese, English, Japanese, Mandarin and Taiwanese, and is welcomed by fans from different territories in East Asia. These fans find it easy to build a close ethnic-cultural connection with the star.

In order to understand what Kaneshiro's fans thought about his role in *Red Cliff* and about the film, and in a further attempt to find out different opinions of diasporic Chinese audiences on the film, I examined the fan pages and member groups dedicated to Kaneshiro on Facebook, MySpace, Twitter, Friendster and Bebo (see statistics in Table A.3 in the Appendix). Again, the brevity of the messages and the dubiety of the ethnic-cultural-geopolitical origins of the post writers on these online media made the found audience comments not ideal vehicles for understanding the views of diasporic Chinese audiences on Kaneshiro's role in *Red Cliff* and on the film itself. I also investigated nine of Kaneshiro's fansites. The Chinese-language fansite with the URL www.takeshikaneshiro.net stood out from among the rest as carrying the useful information I was looking for, for further audience reception analysis. It was an extremely well-organized fansite, built and managed by a Hong Kong-based fan-cum-administrator. The interactive forum on this fansite allowed registered visitors (other fans of Kaneshiro) to communicate to each other freely, mainly in Chinese (simplified and traditional scripts) and, to a much lesser extent, in English. Through this online forum, Kaneshiro's fans posted their comments on the star and all kinds of activities the star was involved with. Between 11 October 2006 (when the first message was posted on the interactive forum on this fansite) and 26 August 2013, there were fifty-six threads (aka topics) of comments (each thread with an original post and numerous replies) about the fan-audiences' viewing experience of *Red Cliff*, out of a total of 321 topics regarding Kaneshiro's various professional activities. The language use on this site and the post contents confirmed the ethnic-cultural-geopolitical origins of the post writers, who claimed to reside in East and South East Asian territories and mentioned watching the two-part version of *Red Cliff*. This fansite thus became a useful information source for exploring insightful diasporic Chinese fan-audience opinions on *Red Cliff*.

Follow-up Survey, 2013

In August 2013, exactly four years after my first online surveys on *Red Cliff*'s audiences, and a time that marked the fifth anniversary of the general release of *Red Cliff* (Part I) in East and South East Asia, I conducted a second online study to follow the first one up. The film had by then already been widely available on DVD, Blu-ray Disc; through television reruns; legal or illegal online streaming platforms and so on. Instead of using the film's official China website as a springboard for my follow-up research, I conducted content analysis on Sina Weibo and Tencent Weibo, the two most popular China-based microblogging spaces in most recent years (when written in Chinese script, *weibo* is 微博; the two words form the Chinese term for microblog). They are subscribed to mainly by mainland China-based users. Sina Weibo was launched in August 2009 and quickly became the market leader in China. Members of Sina Weibo use the platform as a hybrid version of Facebook and Twitter. Tencent Weibo (beta version) was launched in April 2010. Tencent QQ, the umbrella portal of Tencent Weibo, covers even more online aspects for users to choose from, ranging from a Facebook-like profile page, tweet-like weibo posts, to gaming and shopping conveniences. My research on these two new virtual platforms was implemented from 23 to 24 August 2013. I made use of the respective search engines on these two microblogging platforms to search for posts that were concerned with *Red Cliff* (see statistics in Table A.4 in the Appendix). The posts I found had a similar format and word limit to that of a tweet on Twitter. Those I closely examined had been published between 31 March 2010 and 24 August 2013.[14] I then juxtaposed the results with the fan-authored opinions on *Red Cliff* at www.takeshikaneshiro.net, which I revisited on 26 August 2013. Posts on this fansite related to *Red Cliff* or Kaneshiro's role in the film had not been updated since my first online surveys in 2009.

Methodology Strengths and Limitations

My independence in undertaking these online surveys gave me freedom to stay away from any possible pre-existing institutional bias and agendas. Also, the online survey methods that I employed were more cost and time effective than other conventional qualitative research methods. They allowed me to have complete control over what I was studying and the choice of time at which I conducted the investigations, as long as I had access to the online forums. However, my independence as a lone researcher also meant that I was inevitably subject to constraints in terms of human and financial resources for carrying out more comprehensive research on the topic. Given the parameters of the online environment, my investigations were unable to draw opinions from *Red Cliff*'s audiences that were financially disadvantaged, technically less competent, or simply did not use online platforms to express their views publicly. In addition, although online forums allow participants to share their opinions in a supposedly 'participatory culture' in which 'fans and other consumers are invited to actively participate in the creation and circulation of new content' (Jenkins 2008: 331), as individual users of these Internet platforms we can never know how many individual messages have actually been published, accessed and archived by organizers of the forums. This is because most of these online forums are empowered by large corporations that have their own corporate agendas (Jenkins 2006: 157, 2013: loc 136, pp. 1–2). China-based forums offer us examples of such corporate self-censorship (if not politically required state censorship) of grass-roots interventions exercised online. Furthermore, due to the problem of verifying the Chinese and diasporic status of the post writers if they wrote only in English or other non-Chinese languages on online platforms, their comments, even if insightful, were filtered out at the early stage of the 2009 surveys to avoid misrepresentations of diasporic Chinese comments on the film. This inevitably reduced the pool of useful online audience comments for my further analysis, which I will turn to in the next section.

Understanding Ethnic Chinese Audiences

Notwithstanding these methodological constraints, my two rounds of online surveys in 2009 and 2013 respectively showed that there were indeed differences between Woo's directorial intent, and the empirical reception and interpretation by *Red Cliff*'s target Chinese audiences in the region. As the two rounds of online surveys yielded similar results about the distinct use of film text by the film's mainland Chinese audience and East/South East Asia regional fan-audiences respectively, they also indicated discrete fandom of declared fans of certain (mediated) texts and stars. Firstly, the age, class and gender of the fan-audiences under discussion did not appear to have an overarching influence on their fannish activities, in contrast with what Fiske emphasizes (1992: 32–33). These audiences might read against the grain of *Red Cliff*, but they were not ready to do anything antisocial, anti-institutional or readily artistic (again, as opposed to what Fiske (1992) and Jenkins (1992a) discussed about the U.S.-based fans). Secondly, in the case of declared fans of Kaneshiro, their online sharing and support for the star displayed the distinctive fandom of 'intimacy' in the East/South East Asian context (as identified by Yano (2004), and Y. Chow and de Kloet (2008)). Thirdly, many of those audiences I surveyed conformed to, and confirmed, the dominant ideology and their identification as ethnic-cultural Chinese people regardless of their places of residence. Whether based in mainland China or in Sinophone regions along the Pacific Rim, these audiences were eager to apply their cultural-historical knowledge to judge *Red Cliff* on (re) presenting Chinese history and historical personalities. As far as Sinophone fan-audiences living in East/South East Asia are concerned, they also displayed prominently their acceptance of multiplicities in Chinese languages and their negotiations of their ethnic-cultural identities as Chinese descendants not living in the geographical mainland of China. This helped turn them into cultural-historical agents to make sense of a bygone past while living an empirical present.

Accordingly, how much these audiences in various locations differed from each other can be detected in two key areas: their practice of fandom and spectatorship in East/South East Asia, and the intellectualization of their ethnic-cultural existential conditions (Safran 1991: 87). The discussion of these two key areas below is supported by extracts from microblogger posts and fan-authored online messages posted under the post writers' public screen names, when available.[15] No information as to the real personal identity of any individual microblogger or fan is available. The time and place of postings are given as they were shown on the public online platforms. The online messages were originally written in either traditional or simplified Chinese characters and are translated here by me.

Practice of Fandom and Spectatorship in East/South East Asia

Whereas in the West we can easily find long-running television programmes (e.g., *Star Trek*, *Doctor Who* or *X-Files*) gathering a large group of fans over time, audiences in East Asia do not demonstrate the same degree of attachment to their favourite film or television texts. Rather, they would choose to be fans or simply defenders of traditional literary works, star idols, film directors, etc. In fact, their impressions of a film seem to quickly fade away with time, no matter whether they loved it or not at the beginning. Compare the following two sets of negative comments on *Red Cliff* that I found in my 2009 and 2013 online surveys respectively:

(*Comments found in 2009 from* Red Cliff's *official website for its China-based audience market*):

'Yihua' (posted 7 January 2009, 19:53): ... *Like other Chinese costume block-busters,* Red Cliff, *whether Part I or Part II, are earning heaps of renminbi from its viewers in China amid waves of audience disapproval. Viewers are not happy with the film narrative, characters' lines, and the role of Xiaoqiao played by Lin Chiling.*

'Jiang Xiaoyu' (posted 16 January 2009, 13:20) [in a mocking manner]: ... *The quality of this no-good film is really bad ... many well-known historical scenes are badly treated ... many lines are laughable and do not make any sense. They do not match with what was there in history ...*

Examples of medium-length to quite long harsh criticisms written in simplified Chinese characters by the mainland Chinese audience abounded on the film's official China website, albeit there were fewer of these than the positive messages on the same site. My excerpts here highlight some of the major concerns the mainland Chinese viewers had with the diegetic environment of the film when it was newly released. These mainland viewers found faults in character presentation, anachronisms in conversation style and lifestyle, and so on. These harsh comments continued to find their way onto the newest microblogging platforms, like Sina Weibo and Tencent Weibo, in the 2013 China-based cyber environment:

'Jiangnan Zhaojin' (posted 14 March 2013, 13:00): Many people thought that
Red Cliff was not good. John Woo was sworn at. Kaneshiro Takeshi speaks
funnily in his role as Zhuge Liang. What's wrong with the scriptwriter?

These challenges were primarily made by the mainland Chinese film viewers
who thought they were familiar with the folk stories and myths about the Battle
of Red Cliffs and the Three Kingdoms. The details of the stories they turned to
had come through grass-roots circulation over the centuries and had been part
of the modern-day school curriculum for Chinese history and classical literature.
Apparently acting as the defenders of the 'most genuine' version of history they
knew about, the mainland *Red Cliff* viewers became offensive in criticizing Woo's
romanticized adaptation of the historical past in film. Other post writers I found
on these China-based online platforms used wordings such as 'insults to the
nation', 'destroying our history', 'pleasing the West only' to condemn Woo and
Red Cliff for not being 'Chinese' enough. For instance:

'Yihua' (posted 7 January 2009, 19:53): ... John Woo's battle spectacles in the
film are ok. After all, he made himself famous in the West by his unique vio-
lence aesthetics ... Woo makes this blockbuster based on the Western way of
thinking. No wonder the mainland Chinese audience finds it hard to accept ...

'Friend of Sina.com' (posted 5 April 2009, 22:34): Red Cliff has insulted the
traditional culture of China. It distorts our history in front of foreigners. It is a
classic example of forgetting about the past.

'Wangzun' (posted 9 January 2009, 13:45): What a detrimental adaptation
from the Records of the Three Kingdoms *and the* Romance of the Three
Kingdoms! *The wisdom of the Ancient Chinese classics is destroyed. Blame*
commercial blockbusters! ... If the characters were played by Westerners, and
the setting became what it looked like in Ancient Greece or even the Medieval
period in Europe, it would make more sense. I think Red Cliff is basically a film
made for Western audience ...

What these post writers highlighted was their anger at a Chinese-language
blockbuster that violated the ethos of the so-called Chinese cultural essence.
Their implicit statement was that film adaptations of Chinese history or classic

literature needed to be faithful to the original. Otherwise, the film would be 'laughable', 'disrespectful' and essentially 'non-Chinese'. While dismissing *Red Cliff* as a film not for Chinese people, these viewers expressed between the lines their unyielding stance regarding Chinese history and their entrenched cultural-essentialist conformity to Sinocentrism, which they had embodied and further confirmed.

The anger thrown at *Red Cliff* by the film's mainland Chinese viewers seemed to calm down after a few years. Microbloggers on Sina Weibo and Tencent Weibo on the whole were reluctant to live with the fact that Woo had made a Chinese historical epic that had gone 'wrong' in its treatment of history. But as time went by, they were more eager to embrace a wider international outlook, and to talk about the global film business and how Chinese blockbusters might be able to fit in it. For example:

'Zhou Yundong' (posted 11 March 2013, 17:18): ... The market scale is not mature enough for Chinese epic blockbusters that cost more than US$1 billion [£61,000]. Whereas Hero *is a martial arts epic,* Red Cliff *is weird and uncategorized ...*

'Xige' (posted 2 December 2012, 13:55): There are more and more Chinese blockbusters like Red Cliff, The Flowers of War, Back to 1942 *and* The Last Supper *that employ 'history' as their topic.*[16] *Experts disapprove of this phenomenon, believing that Chinese films are giving up their pursuit of artistic ideals ...*

'Fan' (posted 10 October 2012, 16:37): ... Chinese people are too proud of themselves + Chinese filmmakers lack international influence – it is not surprising to see Red Cliff *not being received well globally ...*

In each of the above cases, none of the writers said explicitly whether they were or were not fans of specific film texts, stars or directors. If East Asian fans are avid admirers of stars, hoping to build imagined 'intimacy' with their objects of adoration, the mainland Chinese film viewers of *Red Cliff* (or any Chinese-language historical epic film for that matter) could also fit the bill for becoming a type of fan. However, their fandom did not build for the film but for what they were defending – a dead past of Chinese history, which, according to them, must not be questioned, surpassed or revisited from today's perspective.

In contrast, the fan-audiences of Kaneshiro that were based in China or in neighbouring territories did not bother to pay too much attention to the film's departure from 'real' history. Their focus was ultimately on their idol in the film. Consider these examples:

'HoneyChou-Destiny' (posted 8 August 2013, 06:55): The flaws in Red Cliff *do not just include the horse that is called Meng Meng. They should also include the role of Zhuge Liang who always makes funny remarks.*

'Jinger' (posted 11 July 2008, 10:09): ... The battle scenes in Red Cliff *are really spectacular. Costumes and props are beautifully made, matching with history ... Takeshi is gorgeous in the film. Dressed in white robe, Takeshi looks so fine. His way of conversing is excellent. Every word is pronounced so well. I can tell that he must have been working hard on it ...*

'Jinger' (posted 10 January 2009, 19:00): The most exciting sequence is the one that portrays Zhuge using straw boats and scarecrows to snatch arrows from the Cao camp. This story is so famous in history ... Takeshi is so great in that scene. He strongly resembles the Zhuge in the minds of readers of the Romance of the Three Kingdoms *...*

'amy' (posted 11 July 2008, 22:31) [claimed place of origin: Hong Kong]: ... The character [Xiaoqiao, a little-known figure in history] played by Lin Chiling cannot be cut out ... because it is mentioned in the film that Cao wages the war because of her ...

While 'HoneyChou-Destiny' was a microblogger on China-based Sina Weibo and did not declare any particular fandom on his/her post, 'Jinger' was a self-declared female member at www.takeshikaneshiro.net and a devoted fan of the star. The writing style these bloggers used in their posts suggested that they hailed from China. 'HoneyChou-Destiny' displayed the typical mainland Chinese dislike of the film. 'Jinger', on the other hand, did not criticize Woo. In fact, this fan made a great effort to praise the film in which her idol plays a key role. The fan-audience's love for the Japanese-Taiwanese star thus overshadowed history issues. This feeling aligned 'Jinger' closer to 'amy' (another declared Kaneshiro fan active on the same fansite), who hailed from Hong Kong and probably had

had a different cultural upbringing under British colonial rule than 'Jinger's' fellow mainland Chinese viewers of the film. Both 'Jinger' and 'amy' were more eager to appreciate Woo's way of representing renowned historical figures from a completely new angle, even when this might conflict with common knowledge about them.

In addition, 'Jinger' also demonstrated an East Asian style of fandom by attempting to build 'intimacy' with her idol. This was revealed via her addressing Kaneshiro on a first name basis, which is quite an unusual manner in the East Asian social milieu, unless both the addressor and addressee are well acquainted. Saluting someone by his/her surname is a more acceptable form of social etiquette in East Asia, where, rather than just 'Takeshi', it would be more usual to address the star as 'Mr Kaneshiro',[17] as in the following example from the post of another Kaneshiro fan on the same fansite:

> 'A-Guan' (posted 13 July 2008, 13:42): I like watching Red Cliff but the voice-dubbing is horrible. I can't hear Mr Kaneshiro's deep voice in the film. I need to calm down. [Note: in real life, Kaneshiro has a strong Taiwanese accent. He has been dubbed over in Red Cliff to sound like he is speaking the so-called standard Mandarin Chinese.]

Intellectualization of Ethnic-Cultural Existential Conditions

Intervention and Language Use

When expressing various emotions related to Red Cliff, the fans of Kaneshiro in particular and the film's audiences in general adopted a more restrained way of intervention on these online platforms than the period film fans in an Anglophone setting would have done (Monk 2011: 452–53). Fan fictions, fan arts, fan-generated music or fan videos, if any such were at all created for Red Cliff by fan-audiences, were not as easily found as online comments and discussions in written text form. One of the main reasons for this could be that there had not been any noticeable fan base for Red Cliff in the Sinitic-speaking/writing world, although I would not rule out the possibility that there might be some individual fans of the film out there. Nor were there any declared non-fans or anti-fans of the film. These written web posts thus became a major source of information for us, whereby we could delve deeper into the backgrounds of fan-audiences. They represented the 'audience-as-text' (Hills 2002: 177), an extension of the film through the actual viewing experience of fan-audiences, together with their activities afterwards, that amounted to the self-representation and self-performance of people in these web posts.

Nonetheless, access to interactive online platforms is not as much of a problem in the case of Anglophone fans as it has been in China, where the government has banned some of the world's most popular social networking media, including Facebook and YouTube. This might be one of the main factors that led to the launch of Renren (a Chinese version of Facebook) in 2005 and Youku (a Chinese version of YouTube) in 2006. The use of these new China-based online platforms by the mainland Chinese has been closely watched by the Chinese government, and is also under the self-censorship of the service providers. At the time when I conducted my audience survey, the mainland Chinese residents needed to submit their identification details when they registered as users of Tencent's online platforms. These personal details would then be passed directly via Tencent Weibo's registration page onto the Chinese authorities' authorized websites for further processing.[18] As a result, many microbloggers were often found paying extra attention in wording their comments on *Red Cliff* (the film was sponsored by the government-endorsed China Film Group Corporation), to the extent that the posts sometimes read awkwardly. There were some apparently self-contradicting comments written by the mainland Chinese post writers, such as this one:

'Bixue Danxin' (posted 1 March 2012, 21:59): Red Cliff *is really a rubbish film. But then several scenes have been restaged successfully the truth of history.*

In the context of 'audience-as-text' and the fan-audience web comments being an online extension of *Red Cliff*, the interactive forum on the Hong Kong-based fansite at www.takeshikaneshiro.net offered us thought-provoking insights. The fan-audience posts found there enabled us to study the writers' intellectualization of their existential situations as mainland or diasporic Chinese people. Also, the fans' continuous negotiations of their own ethnic-cultural identifications let us appreciate once again the transition aspect of the New Hong Kong Cinema through its audiences. One of the ways these fan-audiences made their continuous identity negotiations was through written Chinese web messages on the fansite. See the following sets of online exchanges between the Shanghai-based fan 'Jinger' and two of her fellow fans:

'Jinger' (posted 14 July 2008, 14:08) ['Jinger' quoting 'amy' in the first few lines before she mentioned about her own idea of the restaged war in Red Cliff] 'amy': 'The character played by Lin Chiling cannot be cut out ... because it is mentioned in the film that Cao wages the war because of her. But the sex scenes are really not necessary ... (When I saw the film, I felt like I was watching 300).'[19]

The director invented all the extra stuff in the film. When men waged wars, they were motivated by their ambitions and greed for power. Once they became emperors, they could have as many beautiful women as they wanted. Claiming to fight a war because of a woman is really a bad excuse. This point has caused some complaints from among Cao Cao's fans ...

* * *

'Jinger' (posted 14 July 2008, 13:44): ... Last Friday I went to see Red Cliff again, at least this time I did not laugh because I was already fully prepared psychologically for those laughable scenes. The first time I saw the film, it was for its narrative. This time I studied more details in the film ...

'A-Pei' (posted 14 July 2008, 22:19) [claimed place of origin: Malaysia]: Jinger has seen it for three times [sic], bravo! This Thursday, Malaysia, general release all over the country.

On the surface, the fans voiced their comments in these posts in written Chinese and they seemed to understand each other perfectly well.[20] The first set above contained two different opinions regarding the character Xiaoqiao and the dubious part she plays among other more important historical personalities in the narrative – for Xiaoqiao is actually a little-known figure in history. The second set was basically a showing off of how quickly the fans had gone to see the film and support their idol Kaneshiro. Note that 'Jinger' did not have a published place of origin in her screen information. She only told her fellow fans that she was based in Shanghai in some of her posts, whereas 'amy' in her earlier post had a screen place of origin marked as 'Hong Kong'. 'A-Pei's' screen place of origin was Malaysia. In effect, some nuances in their linguistic usage, which are lost in English translation, confirmed their social-cultural-geopolitical origins and their mutual respect for each other on this egalitarian platform.

'Jinger's' posts were especially interesting. She published all her posts in traditional Chinese characters but wrote them in a tone that prevails in the writing style of the mainland Chinese. It was not clear why a mainland Chinese fan would be using traditional Chinese script on an online forum that can support both traditional and simplified Chinese language interfaces. It could have been a way for 'Jinger' to show rapport for her fellow fans who wrote principally in traditional Chinese script, but there could be a number of other reasons. Even more fascinating was 'Jinger's' complete understanding of an earlier post by Hong Kong-based 'amy', and her sensible answer to 'amy's' post. 'amy' wrote in traditional Chinese script and in a Hong Kong Cantonese style that could be regarded as colloquial by speakers and writers of the 'standard' (Han) Chinese language used in China and Taiwan. As Cantonese speakers/writers use a mixture of Cantonese, English and Chinglish (which is itself a mixture of Chinese and English that originated during more than 150 years of British colonial rule over the territory), 'standard' Chinese speakers/writers would find it hard to understand what 'amy' meant. Yet, China-based 'Jinger' had no problem understanding 'amy' in this Internet conversation. This fact is in contradiction with cultural and media studies scholars Yiu Fai Chow and Jeroen de Kloet's argument (2008) in their study of the respective Hong Kong-based fans of a Hong Kong star and the Netherlands-based fans of a Dutch star. The authors argue that the Cantonese way of speaking/writing is a way for the Hongkongers to 'mark out [their] own virtual territory' and to deny access to non-Hong Kong Cantonese users, such as those from China and Taiwan. On the other hand, as in the second example above, 'A-Pei' from Malaysia, who wrote in simplified Chinese characters, also had no problem understanding the traditional Chinese characters in 'Jinger's' post.[21]

Their online written exchanges thus displayed an interesting and inclusive Sinophone virtual zone on this fansite, in which speaking and writing the hegemonic 'standard' Chinese was not of top priority as long as fans understood each other. In this way, participants in this Sinophone virtual zone, which involved users writing in various Chinese languages and therefore included the mainland Chinese residents outside Shih's Sinophone network (Shih 2007: 4), unintentionally subverted the cultural and national uniformity urged by Woo in *Red Cliff*. Fan-audiences' Sinophonic dissonance in real life was harmonized and smoothed over in this virtual enclave by the fans' unwavering love for their idol. Such amicable communications had nothing to do with Woo's wishful thinking when the director created a filmic, all-in-one, uniform 'China' in *Red Cliff* – the kind of 'China' that would be welcomed by the Chinese authorities.

Yet, one may also argue that, precisely because this Sinophone virtual zone was inclusive, it was also inevitably exclusive and inaccessible to non-Chinese speakers/writers, thus engendering Sinolinguistic-centric effects in a non-Sino-centric context. This then attests to Fiske's argument that '[f]ans discriminate fiercely: the boundaries between what falls within their fandom and what does not are sharply drawn' (Fiske 1992: 34). This fansite was primarily created by a Sinitic-writing Kaneshiro fan for a group of fellow Sinitic-writing fans of the same star. Although there was no clear declaration of official language used on this fansite, the posts, shared contents and news items appearing there were almost entirely written in Chinese characters, traditional or simplified. The only exceptions were four threads of thematic posts that carried excerpts of Kaneshiro-related articles about his role in *Red Cliff*, published originally in the English-language press. Not surprisingly, these four threads of posts attracted far fewer replies to the topic starter's original post in each thread.

Existential Conditions

Having said that, the multiplicity and heterogeneity of these fan-audiences were not so much manifested by the encoding and decoding in and among different Sinitic languages as they were by the fan-audiences' awareness of their own existential conditions, especially in the case of the diasporic Chinese audiences born and/or raised outside mainland China. This specific awareness was crystallized in the differing attitudes displayed by fan-audiences regarding Chinese history on film and films on Chinese history (Rosenstone 2006: 39), thus creating intra-zonal dynamics in this Internet Sinophone enclave. The following string of online chats demonstrates this point. It was generated after a China-based Kaneshiro fan, 'Beijing Cat', had shared a sarcastic, negative film review of *Red Cliff*, originally posted somewhere else:

'sara' (posted 16 July 2008, 18:28) [replying to 'Beijing Cat's' shared review]: *I haven't seen the film. This film review seems to suggest that* Red Cliff *is a summer vacation comedy.*

'Beijing Cat' (posted 16 July 2008, 22:13) [claimed place of origin: Beijing] [replying to 'sara's' post above]: *Depends. The reviewer no doubt understood the scriptwriter's intention – just see* Red Cliff *as if you were watching* Pirates of the Caribbean[22]...

'sara' (posted 29 July 2008, 16:44): ... *It depends on what you expect to see in* Red Cliff. *If you anticipate watching a real history on screen, you will be disappointed ... Although the lines delivered in* Red Cliff *sound contemporary, I didn't find them laughable. I watched the film at around noon on a Tuesday on Hong Kong Island. The cinema was 90 per cent full that day. All spectators took the film very seriously and didn't laugh at its historical inaccuracies ... I really don't understand why the audience on the mainland complain so much about this film.*

'Floating Cloud' (posted 30 July 2008, 02:22) [replying to 'sara's' post immediately above]: ... *I agree with sara ... On the sources of this film, director Woo said many times in media interviews that he had collected information from legitimate, historical texts as well as anecdotes and fictions in order to re-create a group of personalities from the period of the Three Kingdoms. Woo is very creative in re-interpreting the stories of that historical period. Now we see all the good guys from the angle of Liu and regard the others, such as Cao, as bad guys. How about if we stand in the position of Cao, will it make any difference to our understanding of these historical figures? ...*

From the publication times and dates of 'sara's' two posts, we can identify a change of stance in her reading of the film. She was initially introduced to *Red Cliff* by her mainland counterpart 'Beijing Cat', who, like many mainlanders, judged the film against the accepted wisdom of 'real' history. What the mainland audience thought of as 'real', however, had not been examined by them closely. To those mainland viewers who disapproved of the film, the version of 'real' history came as part of the package of the Sinocentric hegemony imposed on them without their realizing the 'cultural violence' (R. Chow 1993: 26) and danger of cultural essentialism it involves. This Chinese hegemony, however, faced a direct challenge in this Sinophone virtual zone at www.takeshikaneshiro.net, where overseas or diasporic Chinese could openly express different understandings of the concepts of 'Chinese', 'Chineseness', 'China' and 'Chinese history'. As Shih powerfully argues:

> *... Sinophone articulations ... contain an anticolonial intent against Chinese hegemony. The Sinophone is a place-based, everyday practice and experience, and thus it is a historical formation that constantly undergoes transformation reflecting local needs and conditions. It can be a site of both a longing for and a rejection of various constructions of Chineseness; it can be a site of both nationalism of the long-distance kind, anti-China politics, or even nonrelation with China, whether real or imaginary. (Shih 2007: 30)*

'sara's' insights in her second post above, dated 29 July 2008, exemplified her empirical use of the Sinophone site to express her ideas in Hong Kong-style Chinese writing (all written in traditional Chinese characters), while she unintentionally assumed a role of a historical agent having a function to reinterpret and re-appreciate that part of Chinese history in her own way. Her possible British colonial and ideological upbringing, and her local existential experience in Hong Kong, had certainly led her to have a degree of appreciation for the film unlike that of other *Red Cliff* audiences. 'sara's' post was agreed with by 'Floating Cloud', another Kaneshiro fan on this fansite, who did not say where he/she was from but whose writing style strongly suggested a Sinitic Taiwanese background. In publishing these two posts, both these diasporic fans showed a clear sign of re-mediating the historical past in their unique ways without any fear of, or submission to, the pressure of the Chinese hegemonic 'other'. They raised questions in their posts in hopes of furthering their understanding of the received knowledge of the Chinese historical past, which in turn would reflect/affect their present selves and attitudes towards the future.

Of course, the intrinsic functions of the Sinophone virtual site were such that I could easily find other kinds of discussions having nothing to do with the topic of history. For example:

> *'A-Pei' (posted 18 July 2008, 03:00) [claimed place of origin: Malaysia]: ... Why is there censorship here? Why can't we watch the scene where Zhuge delivered the cow [sic: horse] of a calf? ... The Malaysian government just censors whatever is important in the film. The DVDs released here will also be like this. I am angry. I will get the Taiwan version of the film's DVD ...*

* * *

'sara' (posted 3 November 2008, 17:25): A poll in Japan shows that Takeshi's Zhuge Liang is the most popular role in Red Cliff. Takeshi wins the hearts of the Japanese people easily because he is of Japanese background. He is also attached to Taiwan but he was disqualified from competing in the Golden Horse Awards ... Boo ... Taiwan has broken Takeshi's heart.

'A-Guan' (posted 3 November 2008, 17:52): Mind you! The Golden Horse Awards ceremony is different from the place Taiwan. I believe Mr Kaneshiro still loves Taiwan very much, as Taiwan is his home ... but I really don't understand why he is not there at the event ...

* * *

'Never-ending Kingdom' (posted 23 October 2008, 17:59) [claimed place of origin: Taiwan]: ... Don't you think that there are some hideous romantic attractions among Zhuge, Sun Quan, Zou Yu and Sun's younger sister?

'Bububei' (posted 22 October 2008, 23:27): ... in the scene where Zhuge and Zhou play the musical instruments together, I can smell some unnamed attraction between the two men in the air ...

Among the threads of posts by Kaneshiro's fan-audiences about their viewing experience of Red Cliff, 'A-Pei' from Malaysia groaned about the issue of the Malaysian government censorship, which had truncated her experience of watching a supposedly complete film. What is predominantly interesting in her post here is her remark that she planned to buy the Taiwan version of the film's DVD and not the version released in Hong Kong or Japan. Arguably, 'A-Pei's' remarks revealed a common belief among diasporic Chinese communities that the Republic of China in Taiwan, and not the PRC, had been the more capable preserver of the authentic Chinese cultural heritage (Shih 2007: 4). 'China' in 'A-Pei's' case was evidently not equal to the polity on the mainland.

Through their concerns about Kaneshiro's disqualification from the Golden Horse Awards competition, Hong Kong-based 'sara' and another Kaneshiro fan, 'A-Guan', demonstrated their China-less 'diasporic consciousness' and the effects of their existential conditions on their thinking and viewpoints. 'A-Guan' did not disclose his/her place of origin. It could not tell clearly from this fan's posts where he/she was from because in different posts he/she wrote in the styles of Cantonese and Mandarin Chinese, and in traditional Chinese characters. Yet, the content of this particular post suggested that the fan had a special attachment to Taiwan. The writer of the post highlighted that Kaneshiro's home being Taiwan was what enabled the fan to build his/her imagined 'intimacy' with the star. In their exchanges, 'sara' and 'A-Guan' only mentioned Kaneshiro's Japanese and Taiwanese background, making no reference at all to the star's Chinese roots. Thus, their conversations served to illustrate the innate subversion of the hegemonic Chineseness concept taking place on this Sinitic Internet platform and, apparently more important to them, their positive attitude towards negotiating a justifiable, diasporic present-day existence of their own. In the last set of exchanges above, 'Never-ending Kingdom' (claiming to be from Taiwan) and 'Bububei' (showing no clear place of origin in the post but writing in a way that was close to the Sinitic Taiwanese style) offered yet another topic unrelated to history. They read against the grain and detected the homosexual atmosphere in the film, a theme not openly intended by Woo in his films but widely acceptable in today's globalized world (see, for example, Woo's interview in the film's Hong Kong-version DVD bonus track, as compared to scholarly discussions of Woo's film masculinity and possible homosexuality concerns (Stringer 1997)).

Concluding Remarks

In this chapter I have examined New Hong Kong Cinema's interstitiality from the perspective of film audiences. How the viewers in Hong Kong Cinema's traditional East and South East Asian markets consumed new Hong Kong-related Chinese-language films provides us with an angle to interrogate the effects of transitions on Hong Kong and its local film industry in recent years. These audiences and their spectatorial responses thus serve as another piece of evidence to justify and identify the New Hong Kong Cinema as a Cinema of Transitions.

My interests in finding out how ethnic Chinese audiences responded to Hong Kong-related Chinese-language films grew out of my dissatisfaction with the way *Red Cliff* urges national unity, the representation of which would likely encourage Sinocentric ideology. After discovering a lack of previous empirical surveys on relevant Chinese audience reception in the academic fields of Chinese-language film studies, and audience and fan studies, I undertook an independent audience research to accomplish this task. My investigations consisted of two rounds of online surveys. They helped generate provocative information on the empirical reception of *Red Cliff* (as a representative of the New Hong Kong Cinema), especially among its Sinitic-speaking/writing ethnic Chinese audiences in East and South East Asia. Both arrived at similar results and revealed diverse audience opinions on Woo's treatments of the concepts of 'China', 'Chinese', 'Chineseness' and 'Chinese history' via the film.

In contrast to investigations in the field of fan studies, many of which are still Euro-American-centric and which often take for granted the language skills and the sense of history among their research targets, in my online surveys, written language skills and knowledge of Chinese history were identified as the two most prominent requirements for the Sinitic diasporic Chinese audiences to be able to participate effectively in their online written discussions on *Red Cliff* (Jenkins 2013: kindle loc 677). In the case of Kaneshiro fans, these two important elements helped the fan-audiences to share with one another their experience of watching *Red Cliff* in an exclusive Sinophone enclave in the cyber world. The space there allowed them to continuously negotiate their deterritorialized and hybridized versions of Chineseness in their positions as members of different segments of the Chinese diaspora. Their spectatorial responses to *Red Cliff* showed that they had been immersed in different degrees of heterogenization and localization of Chinese cultures in their present places of residence. Through their online discussions, they became historical agents to help reinterpret and advance the understanding of Chinese civilization and history from various viewpoints. These fan-audiences' own existential conditions and interstitiality, then, function as an extension of the New Hong Kong Cinema to consolidate and reflect the latter's state of transitions and interstitiality. In the next and final chapter of this book, I will scrutinize further the transitions of the New Hong Kong Cinema by situating it in the middle of continuous changes in the macro political-economic environment in East Asia – changes that have governed the most recent developments of the film industries and film business activities in the region.

Notes

1. One of the most widely known cases is *Snakes on a Plane* (David R. Ellis, United States, 2006). The producers added new scenes to the film after fans heatedly discussed it on the Internet during the production stage. In China, a recently released

romance comedy *Tiny Times 1.0* (Guo Jingming, China, 2013) made headlines not only because it earned huge box-office takings in its first several weeks of release in late June 2013, but also because its millions of China-based fans openly defended on the Internet the so-called corrupt, hedonic ideology prevailing in the film (China is still notorious for its strict online censorship) (At the Box Office 2013; Tsui 2013).

2. My 'independence' here means that I did not receive institutional funding or research support of any kind for undertaking the online surveys. The only resources I used in conducting the studies were my spare time and the already paid for home broadband facilities.

3. Since the 1980s, there have been a number of widely recognized and quoted monographs, anthologies and journal articles on Chinese-language cinemas. In chronological order of their publication dates, they are Chris Berry's *Perspectives on Chinese Cinema* (1985, reprinted in 1991 and 2003); John Lent's *The Asian Film Industry* (1990); the study by Nick Browne et al. *New Chinese Cinemas: Forms, Identities, Politics* (1994); Rey Chow's *Primitive Passions: Visuality, Sexuality, Ethnography, and Contemporary Chinese Cinema* (1995); Sheldon H. Lu's *Transnational Chinese Cinemas: Identity, Nationhood, Gender* (1997); Stephen Teo's *Hong Kong Cinema: The Extra Dimensions* (1997); David Bordwell's *Planet Hong Kong: Popular Cinema and the Art of Entertainment* (2000); Poshek Fu and David Desser's *The Cinema of Hong Kong: History, Arts, Identity* (2000); Esther C.M. Yau's *At Full Speed: Hong Kong Cinema in a Borderless World* (2001); Yingjin Zhang's *Screening China: Critical Interventions, Cinematic Reconfigurations, and the Transnational Imaginary in Contemporary Chinese Cinema* (2002); Sheldon H. Lu and Emilie Yueh-yu Yeh's *Chinese-language Film: Historiography, Poetics, Politics* (2005); Chris Berry and Mary Farquhar's *China on Screen: Cinema and Nation* (2006); Gina Marchetti's *From Tian'anmen to Times Square: Transnational China and the Chinese Diaspora on Global Screens, 1989–1997* (2006); Michael Curtin's *Playing to the World's Biggest Audience: The Globalization of Chinese Film and TV* (2007); Darrell William Davis and Emilie Yueh-yu Yeh's *East Asian Screen Industries* (2008); and the study by Tan See-Kam, Peter X. Feng and Gina Marchetti *Chinese Connections: Critical Perspectives on Film, Identity and Diaspora* (2009) among others. While many of these studies do not focus only on Hong Kong Cinema but also on other Chinese-language cinemas, such as those of mainland China and Taiwan, all of them prominently cover examinations of Hong Kong films. Nonetheless, the actual viewing experience of average audiences (not opinion leaders such as professional film critics and academic film researchers) of Hong Kong-related Chinese-language films is rarely discussed explicitly and analysed thoroughly in the existing studies (see, for example, S. Yu 2010: 135–51; see also Y. Zhang 2002: 43–113).

4. China-based film audiences are believed to have existed before Chinese-language films were ever made. As early as the 1890s, newspaper advertisements in Hong Kong (dated 18 January 1896) and Shanghai (dated 10 August 1896) respectively promoted screenings of films from the West. There is no record indicating what these

films were and who made them. While the Lumière Brothers, who were the earliest filmmakers in history, took their first films (made in 1895) to travel around the world in 1896, there is no written record showing that they included China or Hong Kong among their destinations (L. Pang 2006b: 67–68).

5. I use the term 'fans' here in a generic way to depict avid viewers/recipients/readers of certain mediated texts.

6. On this assumption, my mother, who is a Hong Kong native, now in her seventies and enjoying her relaxed retirement life in Hong Kong, would certainly protest bitterly against it, given the fact that she has been an avid fan of Cantonese opera in Hong Kong for decades. Once considered a grass-roots entertainment in postwar Hong Kong, Cantonese opera has gained a much improved social status in recent years in the south of China. However, most members of the audience of this Chinese traditional art form nowadays come from the elderly age group. Apart from Cantonese opera, I am also thinking about the affluent middle-class fans of Bruce Springsteen in order to challenge Fiske's argument on fandom (see also Cavicchi 1998).

7. The concern with fandom and gender is one of the most popular topics in fan studies. It has been revisited over the last two decades in numerous investigations on fans (see recent ones such as Busse 2009, 2013; Coppa 2009; De Kosnik 2009; Hellekson 2009; Lothian 2009; Russo 2009).

8. The introduction of fan studies into Western mainstream academia was not a straightforward one. Fan studies scholar Matt Hills opens his book *Fan Cultures* (2002) with critiques of the dubious status and stances of the earlier generation of fan studies scholars. In discussing Jenkins' *Textual Poachers*, Hills challenges Jenkins' stance as using fandom institutionally and politically as a tool to fit prevailing 'academic institutional spaces and agendas' (Hills 2002: 10). Hills' discussion thus unveils yet another layer of power struggles surrounding the topics of 'fans' and 'fandom'.

9. According to the Motion Picture Association of America (MPAA) in the United States, the average cost of producing and marketing a (Hollywood) studio film in 2007 was U.S.$106.6 million (£64.3 million). Since 2008, MPAA has stopped reporting filmmaking budget figures due to the fact that the 'increasingly complex nature of film financing and distribution made it difficult to obtain reliable data' (Verrier 2009).

10. The box-office data of individual target markets for *Red Cliff* in East and South East Asia were obtained from Box Office Mojo, www.boxofficemojo.com (accessed 5 May 2015).

11. Source: interview with John Woo in *Red Cliff* (DVD) (Hong Kong version, bonus track).

12. There were six official websites built for promoting *Red Cliff* to the respective audiences in China, Hong Kong, Japan, South Korea, Taiwan and the United States. These coincide with the territories where the film's equity investors and production companies are based.

13. It is worth noting that, unlike stars in the Western context having the tendency to concentrate on only one or a few areas of the entertainment business, stars in East Asia are often multitasking and appear to excel in numerous areas of show business simultaneously. They act in film and television programmes, and perform as pop singers, alongside other kinds of show business campaigns online and offline.

14. There were streams of posts about *Red Cliff* published in the first few months of 2013, partially triggered by Woo's resuming filmmaking for the first time after making *Red Cliff* – his long absence was due to health reasons. In July 2013, Woo was reported by mass media to be making his latest film entitled *The Crossing*, in which the director again features Kaneshiro as one of the male leads (Frater 2013b). The film is available in two parts. *The Crossing: Part 1* (China/Hong Kong, 2014) was theatrically released in China, Hong Kong, Singapore, Taiwan and Vietnam in December 2014. *The Crossing: Part 2* (China/Hong Kong, 2015) is scheduled for general release in the summer of 2015 (latest information at the time of writing).

15. These public screen names are given here as they appeared on screen if they had anglicized names or if their Chinese names could be translated literally into English. Those Chinese screen names that could not be translated literally are Romanized here in pinyin format.

16. Film Information: *The Flowers of War* (Zhang Yimou, China/Hong Kong, 2011); *Back to 1942* (Feng Xiaogang, China, 2012); *The Last Supper* (Lu Chuan, China, 2012).

17. In Japanese, the salutation would be 'Kaneshiro *san*'; in Mandarin Chinese it would be 'Kaneshiro *xian sheng*', and 'Kaneshiro *sin saan*' in Cantonese.

18. The information regarding the processing of the users' personal details was obtained from reg.t.qq.com/certification.php (accessed 24 August 2013). The registration instructions of concern were written in simplified Chinese characters.

19. Film information: *300* (Zack Snyder, United States, 2007).

20. The following are the originals of these translated fansite conversations:

靜兒 (發表於2008-7-14 14:08): amy: '林志玲呢個角色唔可以唔要 … 因為戲中提及曹操係因為她才會攻打劉備軍 … 不過場床戲真係有d多餘 … (睇既時候, 我覺得有d似戰郎300既感覺)'
那都是導演杜撰的啦, 男人發動戰爭通常都是爲了權利和野心, 只要能當上皇帝那天下所有的美女不都是他的, 怎麼可能爲了小喬出兵, 這點也引起曹操粉絲的不滿。

* * *

靜兒 (發表於2008-7-14 13:44): … 周五又去看了遍《赤壁》, 覺得比第一遍好多了, 起碼沒那麼笑了, 因爲有心理准備知道哪些地方會笑場。第一遍看劇情, 第二遍就看一些細節了 …
阿佩 (發表於2008-7-14 22:19): 静儿看了3遍了, 厉害! 星期四, 马来西亚, 全马上映 …

21. If the text is originally written in a style prevailing in the 'standard' Chinese, speakers of any Sinitic languages can understand the text easily by using convenient language

software products online or offline to convert the script from traditional to simplified Chinese characters, and vice versa, to suit their needs. But if the text is originally written in a style prevailing in spoken Cantonese, non-Cantonese speakers may not understand it easily even after a simple script conversion, because of the more complicated syntax and tone of the Cantonese language.

22. This comparison between *Red Cliff* and *Pirates of the Caribbean* is meant to be a derogatory remark to reject *Red Cliff*'s specific treatment of the historical subject matter. *Pirates of the Caribbean* is an adventure fantasy comedy series produced by Walt Disney Pictures, and originally released in a trilogy: *Pirates of the Caribbean: The Curse of the Black Pearl* (Gore Verbinski, United States, 2003); *Pirates of the Caribbean: Dead Man's Chest* (Gore Verbinski, United States, 2006); and *Pirates of the Caribbean: At World's End* (Gore Verbinski, United States, 2007). A sequel of the *Pirates* series, *Pirates of the Caribbean: On Stranger Tides* (Rob Marshall, United States, 2011) came out some time after 'Beijing Cat' had made this remark about the series. Another new sequel, entitled *Pirates of the Caribbean: Dead Men Tell No Tales* (Joachim Rønning and Espen Sandberg, United States, 2017) is scheduled for general release in 2017 (latest information at the time of writing).

CHAPTER FIVE

Film Policies and Transitional Politics
The Newest East Asian Film Business Network

In the previous chapters we focused our attention on new Hong Kong-related Chinese-language films, what they tell about the people and the society they represent, the vision of these films' directors and the ethnic Chinese audiences who watch and interpret these films. Being aware of these various aspects of the New Hong Kong Cinema allows us to appreciate the transitions and interstitiality embodied in this cinematic practice. But these different aspects may be perceived as piecemeal concerns if we do not also take into account the conditions of the surrounding geopolitical-economic environments. East Asia is one such environment in which Hong Kong and its cinema occupy a distinct position economically, politically and culturally.

If the accented filmmakers and their films are interstitial because they thrive by working both astride and in the cracks of social formations and cinematic practices (Naficy 2001: 4, 46–47), by adapting and extending this logic we can likewise locate the New Hong Kong Cinema's interstitiality astride and within the interstices of an East Asian film arena in its latest phase of development in the post-Asian Financial Crisis era. In this supranational sphere, we see synergies, connections, integration, extension, overlaps, as well as competition and disintegration among the operating filmmaking countries/territories, most notably China, Hong Kong, Japan, South Korea and Taiwan. Participants (i.e., individual film industries) in this regional arena engage in cross-border film business activities (ranging from film financing, film production, idea/talent/technique exchanges, to post-theatrical screening activities) that are motivated by causes beyond purely national, cultural and artistic ones. This sphere of film activities is highly unstable and by no means a level playing field, complicated further by the participation (through collaborating and competing with individual East Asian filmmaking territories) of Hollywood and other non-Asian (trans)national cinematic practices. The main purpose of this chapter is to understand how the New Hong Kong Cinema operates in East Asia liminally and interstitially, especially astride and within the metaphorical interstices left open or covered up by the workings of individual filmmaking systems in the region.

My discussion centres on film policies and film business politics among the major players in contemporary East Asia – Hong Kong being one of them. This chapter starts with a bird's-eye view of the most recent situations within the East Asian film business environment, which I call the 'newest East Asian film business network'. It is the 'newest', given the long history of film-related activities carried out among individual territories in this region. In order to discern how this network works and what kinds of intertwining relationships are in existence among major filmmaking territories in the region, I identify six cities – the nodes – where East Asian film businesses tend to concentrate. Based on their levels of importance, I call five of them (Beijing, Busan, Hong Kong, Shanghai and Tokyo) the main nodes, and Taipei the sub-node. For each of these nodes, I take a brief retrospect of its past governmental film-related policies and actions, before investigating the latest national/subregional film policies that support the city's film business architecture and workings. Comprehending the setup of individual nodes and their combined situations is necessary, as it allows me to situate the New Hong Kong Cinema within the unofficial nexus that these cinematic hubs have created. It also enables me to analyse the effectiveness of the supportive film policy in Hong Kong, which has only started to exist since 1997.[1] As it turns out, Hong Kong and the other cinematic nodes in the newest East Asian film business nexus thrive by keeping a close watch on each other's endeavours and countering the power imbalance among themselves in their complicated, multilayered, multidirectional, interweaving relationships.

Mapping the Newest East Asian Film Business Network: Several Issues

The New Hong Kong Cinema is by no means an 'island'. Its connections with other cinematic traditions and practices in the world are noted by different studies that may or may not revolve around 'Hong Kong' itself (for example, see Morris, S. Li and S. Chan 2005; Marchetti and Tan S. 2007; Ahn 2009: 84–85). Although Hong Kong has a prominent position in East Asia's actual and imagined communities, Hong Kong Cinema's functions and operations within East Asia's cinema-scape (to borrow theorist of globalization studies Arjun Appadurai's '-scapes' concept (1990, 1996)) has only started to attract researchers' attention recently in studies that are primarily concerned with East Asian cultural industries/exchanges (see, for example, Curtin 2007; Davis and Yeh 2008; Chua

B. 2012). There is certainly still a lot waiting to be discovered with regard to the New Hong Kong Cinema's most recent engagement in its immediate geo-cultural-economic-political vicinity – that is, East Asia in the post-Asian Financial Crisis period. As a prerequisite for carrying out the scrutiny related to the New Hong Kong Cinema in East Asia, in the following I will first put forward various interrelated issues that affect East Asia's regional film activities before I move on to discuss the particulars of each major player in the region.

Film Business

Film business comprises the commercial activities and economic architecture of the film sector (Squire 2006). It refers to the economic value of films, gained by passing through a value chain in the process of production/co-production, distribution, exhibition and consumption. In his book *The International Film Business* (2010), film business executive and commentator Angus Finney puts forward a film value chain model for independent film business that consists of the following components: consumer (end-users or audience of film); exploitation (through various exhibition channels such as theatrical release, DVD sales/rental and other long tail opportunities); distributor (e.g., international sales agents and film marketers, who receive a commission in return for their work); shoot/post (actual film production and people involved); financing (e.g., funds, funding providers, insurance); and development (related to the process of developing a film concept and hiring/developing talent) (Finney 2010: 11). These elements are interlinked. Each of them helps add economic value to a film as a commercial product ready to be transacted.

Money is always one of the key aspects of film business, whether we are talking about film financing, film investment capital, cost of production/distribution/marketing, sales volume or profit margins. Film business executives are, by default, concerned with profit-making, ticket sales and presence at important film marketplaces. They engage with other film buyers/sellers in the trade of films. Audiences are generally regarded as the end-users of the film product: they pay a certain sum of money to see the film, and they are thus the 'market' to be developed by film executives/distributors/exhibitors. In the Internet age, the audiences may take up other roles, such as investors through crowdfunding, and volunteer/unpaid film marketers through their online word-of-mouth recommendations. Seen in this context, a country/territory that has a film industry does not necessarily have robust film business activities (for example, the PRC before its economic reform in 1978 had a film industry but no noticeable film business activities), whereas a country/territory that is involved in film business activities will most likely have already developed some sort of film industry of its own.

Film Policies

Film business activities across national borders can only become possible with suitable sets of film-related policies that the governments of the trading countries implement. Depending on the contexts and the kinds of governments involved, not all the policies turn out to be beneficial to the cross-border film business. Film policy expert Albert Moran (1996) classifies two main models of film policies often used in Europe since the First World War (see also Guback 1969). They are protective and supportive measures (Moran 1996: 7). Protective barriers may include screen quotas, quotas on the number of imported films, censorship of, and tariffs levied on, imported films. The protective measures have had variants in other parts of the world at different times. Post-WTO China, for example, has imposed a restrictive policy with regard to imported films, allowing only thirty-four foreign films (mostly from the United States) per year to enter the mainland Chinese audience market on revenue-sharing terms. By the standards of the PRC, this already represents a relaxation, as before February 2012 China allowed the importation of only twenty foreign films per year. In addition, these foreign films have to be distributed within China by the state-owned film distributors China Film Group Corporation (CFGC) and Huaxia Film Distribution (China Agrees 2012; SIFF Debates 2012). The regular blackout periods in China are a part of the protective measures. During those periods, only mainland Chinese films can enjoy general release in China. This effectively allows mainland Chinese films to maximize their box-office takings in the domestic market.

The supportive and promotional film policies that Moran identifies may include a government's financial assistance to its domestic film production, active participation in the sectors of film production and distribution at home and abroad, as well as the conclusion of international treaties to stimulate cross-border co-productions. This has resulted in many multilateral film industry activities and networks (Elsaesser [2005] 2005: 120). Film scholars Darrell William Davis and Emilie Yueh-yu Yeh (2008: 9–37) chart the film policies, Hollywood influence and transnational cultural flows among East Asian cinemas. The South

Korean film industry in the late 1990s benefited from both the deregulations and heavy government support. The changes to South Korea's film industry ultimately triggered neighbours such as China to follow suit. Supportive film policies may not just be the means of improving a territory's GDP. For many countries, especially those newly independent nation-states or territories striving for independence, this type of film policy has been used as a nation-building tool of the state apparatus. The New Scottish Cinema shows a prime example of this type of film policy having been put in place (Petrie 2000: 153–69).

Besides protection and support, there are two other film policy models. One is to exercise film censorship and control with respect to a country/territory; the other is the laissez-faire model, in which domestic film industry is left to survive without much interference from the government (Kim H-j. Circa 2006). As we shall see below, different governments in East Asia may change from implementing one film policy model to another during different periods of the countries' film industry development. At times this might come in response to the changes in the larger political-economic environment; at other times it might occur as an initiative of the authorities to open up new film industry and business trends. Combinations of different film policy models might also be in use for a certain period of time.

Soft Power Competition and Network

The latest development, as we know it, in the film business landscape of East Asia originated around about 1997 – the year of Hong Kong's sovereignty handover, which I have widely discussed in this book. For the whole of East Asia, the year 1997 was a year of pain, as it marked the onset of the Asian Financial Crisis, which attacked almost all the economies in the region and shifted the economic and power relations of several major regional players – namely, China, Japan and South Korea thereafter. These major East Asian powers are neighbours and share Confucianism as their common philosophical belief. Yet, they have also been fierce competitors in areas such as economics, politics, the military and culture. Sociologist Chua Beng Huat (2012) sheds light on their relationship in the cultural production sector by evoking the concept of 'soft power' proposed by political scientist Joseph S. Nye, Jr. (2004) to investigate their export and import of popular cultural products (e.g., films, television drama series, songs and stars) to and from one another. At its core, 'soft power' refers to a country's ability to affect the views in other countries/territories/peoples by using cultural devices, not coercion (Chua 2012: 7, 120). According to Chua's elucidation (2012: 121):

> To achieve soft power, the exported pop culture must be able to shift its audi-
> ence's perceptions, preferences, interpretative frameworks and emotions, i.e.,
> a set of cognitive processes, towards a generally positive disposition and
> attraction to the exporting country, which is the applicant of soft power.

Chua remarks that these regional powers are in 'soft power competition', which is combined with various forms of mutual collaboration and amicability, as well as animosity at times (Chua 2012: 7–8). His study illuminates our understanding of how the East Asian triumvirate has been involved in laying out the fabric of the regional film network in contemporary period.

However, we should not forget that such a relationship in the cultural sector of major nations in East Asia reflects a phenomenon that dates back to the early twentieth century. Filmmaking was one of the main areas that witnessed the start of the soft power relationship in the region long before the concept of 'soft power' was invented. Japanese studies scholar Yau Shuk-ting, Kinnia (2010) has tracked the filmmaking collaborations between Japan and colonial Hong Kong from the 1930s to the 1970s, noting that there was a film network in Asia initiated by Japan during the wartime period in the 1930s. This network, which Chinese film companies joined for various reasons, is a blueprint for the present-day East Asian cinematic grid (Yau S. 2010: xviii–xxi). We can find exchanges of ideas, personnel, money, techniques and so on among participants in this network. The prominence of Japan in this sphere of activities continued after the Second World War via individual filmmakers' personal business networks, pushed forward in the 1950s and the 1960s by Shaw Brothers (HK) Limited founded in Hong Kong in 1958 by the sixth Shaw brother Run Run (1907–2014). He hired many Japanese film industry practitioners to go to Hong Kong and help improve the postwar Hong Kong Cinema in areas like film directing, lighting and visual effects (Yau S. 2010: xxii; see also S. Chung 2003, 2011). In fact, Shaw Brothers can be seen as a continuation of Tianyi (aka Unique) Film Productions, founded in Shanghai by the eldest Shaw brother, Runje (1896–1975). As early as the 1920s, Runje sent his third brother Runme (1901–85) and Run Run to go to South East Asia (Singapore and Malaysia primarily) to build up the Shaws' film distribution and exhibition network. Apart from the Shaws, Daiei Studio's Nagata Masaichi initiated the South Asian Motion Pictures Producers Association (established in 1953) and its annual event, the Southeast Asian Film Festival in 1954 (Yau S. 2010: xxi; S. Lee 2011: 242).[2] Run Run Shaw served as the co-founder of this film event. Mainly a film publicity exercise for films made by the biggest studios in the East/South East Asian region at that time, this was the first film festival in East Asia (R. Cheung 2011c: 203–4).[3] Meanwhile, there were more exchanges going on between film industry practitioners from Taiwan and Hong Kong. Filmmakers in Hong Kong at that time mostly hailed from pre-war Shanghai. Besides studio owners Runme and Run Run Shaw, some important Chinese-language film directors, like Li Han-hsiang and King Hu, worked in both Hong Kong and Taiwan at different stages of their careers.

Due to regulations and deregulations, and the rise of other cinemas in the region, from the 1970s onwards the prominence of personal film business networks has given way to a distinct establishment of bridgeheads in six strategic nodal points of film business in the region (Yau S. 2010: xxii). I further identify, in alphabetical order, Beijing, Busan, Hong Kong, Shanghai and Tokyo as the five main nodes, and Taipei as a sub-node. Since 1997, each of the main nodes has continuously been actively involved in film production, distribution and exhibition, and, even more proactively, engaged in organizing and developing global-scale film marketplaces held every year in these cities as major film business platforms. The volumes of film business, film production and co-production, distribution and exhibition taking place in and beyond the East Asian geopolitical region help define the gridlines of this network of cities. As engaging in the film business rather than concentrating purely on film industrialization in East Asia has taken on new meanings (Fu 2003; Hu 2003; Zhang Z. 2005; Yau S. 2010; S. Chung 2011; Sugawara 2011), I call this most recent network the 'newest East Asian film business network'.

Nodes and Media Capitals

What makes the most recent East Asian film business network distinct, I argue, is that instead of taking individual nation-states as units of concern, the newest round of industry and business restructuring in film in East Asia is built upon the connections and disjuncture between the identified six major filmmaking cities. Their relationships can be understood both from a historical and a present-day perspective, for it is important to remember that parallel film business networks involving similar cities and territories (e.g., Shanghai and Japan) had already been formed in East Asia before the Second World War (Sugawara 2011: 117). Hence, I opt to see these major East Asian film cities as the current connection points in this constantly mutating, transitional, semi-supranational, regional network saturated with local traits. My approach is thus different from theoretical frameworks, such as 'translocal' (Y. Zhang 2011: ix; Greiner and Sakdapolrak 2013), 'translingual' (S. Lim 2011: 17–22), 'intra-regional', 'inter-regional' (V. Lee 2011a: 1) and 'transnational', which can be employed to examine the spatial spread of this film business network.

There is no doubt that the six metropolitans found in this network have supported most of the film business activities of their respective countries or territories in the late twentieth to the early twenty-first century. They are in turn buttressed by their own clusters of talent, capital, film industry systems, demographic profiles (including residents and visitors), geopolitical infrastructures and the special backing of domestic governments. Not all of them, for example Busan, are or can be comparable to 'global cities' in the sense referred to by sociologist Saskia Sassen – cities that have turned from national industrial centres into major global providers of 'highly specialized services and financial goods' (Sassen 2001: 5). However, each of these metropolitans that I have chosen to highlight does have its own tradition of filmmaking. Each has its own uniqueness and superior interconnectedness that have enabled it to become prominent in the latest regional film business network, which, in turn, is part of the world political-economic system. Since film markets attached to the international-scale film festivals are held annually in these cities, they are the most popular stops for any film executive who works and travels along the film festival/film market circuit in that region. Moreover, these metropolitans are interdependent in that each rivals and works with the others through film deals and ideas/personnel/techniques/money interchange to gain the limelight, diming the advantages Hong Kong once enjoyed exclusively as the 'Eastern Hollywood'. At the same time, they are trying to protect their own film activities from other nodes in the network, other neighbouring cities or provinces, as well as from the biggest player in the global film business, Hollywood, while developing themselves so they might one day become some of the biggest players in the field, if not the single biggest. Discerning their correlations from historical, cultural and political-economic perspectives, we can also single out a Greater China subregional network formed by Beijing, Hong Kong, Shanghai and Taipei. In this view, the relationships of these cinematic nodes show the newest regional film business network as ever more complex, unbalanced, unstable and, at times, messier than it ever was in any previous periods.

It is important to note that by highlighting these cinematic nodes in the East Asian region in contemporary period, I do not mean they are constant stars; nor do I intend to marginalize other cities in the region that are in the process of building their burgeoning film industries and film trade activities. I have written elsewhere that 'Asia' as a concept and a geopolitical region is continuously being revisited and re-created (R. Cheung 2011a: 42–43). There are cities, such as Ho Chi Minh City (Vietnam), Manila (the Philippines), Pyongyang (North Korea) and Vladivostok (Russia), in East Asia bordering North East or South East Asia respectively that might one day become some of the brightest nodes in the future East Asian film business network. I should also note that Singapore is considered by some researchers to be part of the current East Asian film/cultural zone (V. Lee 2011b: 235–48; Chua B. 2012). Singapore has traditionally played the role of film consumer, and more recently film co-investor and co-producer, in the geopolitical East/South East Asian region. Its role as film business initiator and facilitator, however, remains ambiguous. This was made evident by the launch of ScreenSingapore (in 2011), which is neither a film festival nor a film market but some sort of 'hybrid cinema event' featuring film launches and seminars (Noh 2011a, 2012a). Therefore, I do not include it in the discussion of the latest East Asian film business network, but do not rule out the possibility of it becoming part of the network in future rounds of East Asian film business realignment.

Media scholar Michael Keane (2006) analyses the media capacity in contemporary East Asia by examining the situations of major media production cities within the framework of Asia itself. Keane (2006: 842–48) identifies that East Asia has emulated the advancement of the West mainly in five ways. The first way is through deterritorialization, or the adoption of a 'world factory model' (referring to their role of being used by advanced Western countries as low-cost outsourcing locations for production). The second is 'mimetic isomorphism', a term especially used in relation to small-sized cultural production companies and the way they imitate, or clone, the successful ways of others. The third method is by means of the transfer of cultural technology. Through joint ventures or franchising, local media companies in East Asia learn from international companies in the areas of talent training, employment and infrastructure investments. This knowledge will eventually help the local companies develop their own media industries. The fourth way is by creating niche markets and using multiple channels of innovation, production and distribution. The fifth method is via building culture/industry and creative clustering in designated localities (usually important cites) that are termed 'media capitals'.

I would like to expand on the concept of 'media capital' a bit more at this juncture, as it helps to understand the reasoning behind my choice of the six cinematic nodes in the newest East Asian film business network. The concept of 'media capital', as communications scholar Michael Curtin (2003) posits, was initially inspired by the cross-border, transnational flows of television programming from particular cities. Curtin refers to these cities (e.g., Bombay, Cairo and Hong Kong) as 'media capitals'. They are usually the 'centers for the finance, production, and distribution of television programs', 'centers of media activity that have specific logics of their own; ones that do not necessarily correspond to the geography, interests or policies of particular nation-states' (Curtin 2003: 203). These cities can be understood as being 'positioned at the intersection of complex patterns of economic, social and cultural flows' (Curtin 2003: 204). Importantly, their development 'hinges on their ability to register and articulate the social experiences of their audiences' (Curtin 2003: 205). A media capital is a 'nexus or switching point, rather than a container' (Curtin 2003: 204). In this sense, 'media capital' is also a relational concept, requiring these particular cities to be examined with regard to the operations of other, perhaps less prominent, cities nearby (Curtin 2003: 205).

Incorporating Curtin's 'media capital' concept, Keane's model allows us to understand the major characteristics of the six film nodal points in present-day East Asia. While we may still find traits of the first two ways of achieving success in Keane's proposition present in these cities, it is the latter three ways in his idea that chiefly characterize these nodes in the latest East Asian film business realignment. However, what is not coming to the fore in Keane's discussion, but in reality is becoming an increasingly acute issue, is the power imbalance *within* a fragmented East Asia (in the political and cultural sense), which shows through the implementation of national policies for the support of individual film industries and business. I argue that, in order to appreciate how things work within and beyond the newest East Asian film business network, this power imbalance should not be ignored. It needs to be understood as the backbone and the pre-requisite of how film business can be conducted at both the city and national levels. I will highlight below what Beijing, Busan, Shanghai, Taipei and Tokyo have that justifies their being considered the nodal points in this most recent film business network in East Asia. My emphasis is placed on each city's correspond- ing national governmental policies in promoting film industry development at a local level. These operations found at the local/city level congruously point towards the advancement of their national film and other creative industries, and the related supranational activities individual countries are involved in. This will be followed by a separate section on what Hong Kong has done since 1997 with regard to its supportive film policy.

East Asian Film Business: Main and Sub-Nodes

To delineate the involvement of the identified nodes in the newest East Asian film business network, for each of them in this section I give information of early film activity engagement. This will be juxtaposed by the node's present situ- ations, which reflect the corresponding national/subregional film policies and relevant film industry arrangements.

China: Beijing (Main Node)

Beijing's involvement in the early Chinese film industry was far from certain (Y. Zhang 2002: 157; Hu 2003). Apart from some extant information on the first China-made film, *The Battle of Dingjunshan* (aka *Conquering Jun Mountain*) by Ren Jingfeng via Fengtai Photography Shop (Beijing) in 1905, there is a lack of archival material to show any film production and exhibition activities in Beijing between 1906 and 1920 (Teo 1997: 3; Y. Zhang 2002: 157; S. Chung 2011: 154; Feng X. 2011: 142). Gliding through time to the twenty-first century, nonetheless, we have strong reasons to secure Beijing's nodal position in East Asia's cinema-scape and film business network on three fronts: talent, political power and money.

Talent

If Beijing was the birthplace of the first Chinese film, the Beijing Film Academy (BFA) and the Central Academy of Drama (CAD) are the 'hatcheries' of cel- ebrated members of China's film talent. Both state-run higher education institu- tions were established in 1950 to offer university degree courses in film-related areas. Over the years, the BFA has produced internationally renowned gradu- ates, including Zhang Yimou and Chen Kaige of the Fifth-Generation directors;

Jia Zhangke and Wang Xiaoshuai of the Sixth-Generation directors; and important actors/actresses such as Vicki Zhao (aka Zhao Wei) and Huang Xiaoming. The CAD specializes in professional training in drama and visual arts, and has graduates such as Gong Li and Zhang Ziyi. Each year, the two institutions together provide the quickly expanding mainland Chinese film industry with a large pool of talent, who in turn attracts film labourers from other places to work in Beijing. As Curtin argues, migration (and thereafter agglomeration) of creative labour is one of the principles for regarding a place as a media capital (Curtin 2003, 2007: 14–19, 23). In Beijing's case, the clustering of film talent in the city definitely makes it a well-positioned film business node in East Asia.

Political Power and Money

Besides film talent, Beijing as the current seat of China's highest authorities gives the city a distinguished advantage to exert political-economic influence on the East Asian regional film sector, following the country's WTO accession in 2001. Not only do serious film investments accumulate in Beijing, the biggest Chinese film companies and institutions (whether state-owned or privately run) are based there. By 2011 they accounted for more than 70 per cent of China's film industry (S-I. Yu 2011a). Among them is the newest international film festival in the region, the state-run Beijing International Film Festival (BJIFF) and its affiliated Beijing Film Market (BFM) (both established in 2011).[4] These Beijing-based organizations draw major international film companies to the city to build their China offices so as to work closely with their Chinese partners to explore the vast Chinese audience market. Among them, we see the prominence of CFGC in China's highly regulated mediascape.

The Chinese authorities founded CFGC in February 1999 on the eve of China's accession to the WTO, by merging the former China Film Corporation,[5] Beijing Film Studio and six other formerly separate film-related government units. CFGC has direct support from the State Administration of Press, Publication, Radio, Film and Television (SAPPRFT; formerly the State Administration of Radio, Film and Television (SARFT)), which is the country's highest government arm supervising relevant industries.[6] Through CFGC, which operates with a vertical integration business model, the Chinese government can actively engage in film production, Sino-foreign co-productions,[7] film distribution and exhibition, and film import and export (A Description of China's Film Industry 2007; Han Sanping: Biography 2009). With a total asset value of more than RMB2.8

billion (£283 million or U.S.$461 million), CFGC produces annually more than thirty feature films, some 400 television series and over 100 television films (Yeh and Davis 2008: 42).[8] During the period from 2010 to 2012, CFGC's domestic film distribution accounted for a 34 per cent market share, while foreign films it distributed enjoyed 47 per cent of the total Chinese market box-office earnings (Liu Y. 2012). China's state-run National Film Capital further boosts CFGC's financial muscle (China's NFC 2012). Yeh and Davis (2008: 38–44) argue that those supposedly commercial mega enterprises like CFGC in effect allow the Chinese authorities to secure strong profits from the market while continuing their control over propaganda organs – now from a backstage position. Termed 'film marketization' for rejuvenating the Chinese film industry, the practice actually heightens 're-nationalization' and 'hyper-nationalization'. The authors believe that in engaging in such a practice the Chinese state can avoid the risks involved in a real market economy (China Becomes 2002; Meng 2014). On the ideological/cultural/political level, CFGC can be considered as extending China's influences across East Asia through heavy involvement in pan-East Asian (especially Chinese-speaking) co-produced mega blockbusters.[9]

China: Shanghai (Main Node)

Journalist and historian Martin Jacques (2012: 252–58) points out that because of China's huge territory and population its central authorities de facto run the country like a federal system lest the state face governance difficulties. This may explain why nowadays in mainland China there are two film business centres located closely together. In the north-east lies Beijing; in the mid east there is Shanghai. Both are municipalities under the direct control of the central government.[10] They are competitors and also sister cities in China, and in the East Asian film business circle.

Shanghai's importance as a city began more than a century ago (Xiong 1996: 101–2). It is where the first film was shown in China (in 1896) (Hu 2003: 198–99),[11] where the first film production studio was established (in 1909)[12] and where the first talkie was made.[13] By the mid 1920s, the early Chinese film industry had been fully formed with numerous new studios emerging every year, and was dominated by privately run, commercialized enterprises (Zhang Z. 2005: xiii, xviii; Sugawara 2011: 97–98). The establishment of the joint venture United Film Exchange (aka Liuhe Film Company) in June 1926 by leading film companies[14] in Shanghai would soon bring the business mode of vertically integrating film production, distribution and exhibition to maturity (S. Chung 2011: 157–58; Sugawara 2011: 104–15). Their films in various genres enriched the local and overseas markets (particularly in East/South East Asia), while facing fierce competition from films imported from the West (Sugawara 2011: 103).[15] Shanghai's early filmmaking sector reached its peak during the 1930s and 1940s, accommodating more than 150 film production companies and producing more than 100 films annually (Zhang Z. 2005: xiv; Yao 2013). But the bombing raids carried out by Japan on 28 January 1932 and, subsequently, Shanghai's fall to the Japanese invaders in the Battle of Shanghai in 1937 badly damaged Shanghai's film industrial infrastructure, literally bringing the early Shanghai film industry to a halt. Filmmakers soon moved their business to Hong Kong or abroad, leading to the multiple trajectories of Chinese-language cinemas in the postwar period (Zhang Z. 2005: xiv; Yao 2013).

In the twenty-first century, the move of China restructuring and consolidating its large, overly bureaucratic state-owned enterprises gave rise to the present form of Shanghai Film Group (SFG), which has been instrumental in shaping Shanghai's participation in the newest East Asian film business network. As the second largest state-owned film group in China after Beijing's CFGC, SFG houses a bundle of formerly separate film-related companies, bringing Shanghai's film production, talent management, post-production and distribution efforts all under one roof (Who to Know in China 2011).[16] Although this corporate restructuring may lead to the problem of monopolization, the consolidation extends SFG's international expansion via co-production and co-financing, and enlarges its profitable exhibition networks (Goodridge 2003; Shackleton 2005a, 2006a, 2012a; Noh 2006; SFG 2010; Disney 2012).[17] It signifies Shanghai's readiness to take part in the current dramatic changes in China's and East Asia's film business landscapes.

Another important constituent of Shanghai's film industry in the present era is the Shanghai International Film Festival (SIFF),[18] which houses an affiliated film market, the SIFF Market (Jones 2007).[19] The SIFF was inaugurated in 1993, and in 1994 it obtained an A-category accreditation as one of the 'Competitive Feature Film Festivals' by the International Federation of Film Producers Associations (FIAPF). It is the only China-based festival in the same category as major festivals such as those of Berlin, Cannes and Venice. The SIFF (with its film market) is now the major platform from which news of important film deals and international partnerships of the Chinese film industry are often announced (Shackleton 2006a, 2006b; CJ 2010; SFG 2010).

Japan: Tokyo (Main Node)

Japan's capital, Tokyo, is the major location of the country's film and video production (Sugaya 2004: 7). It is the home of the headquarters of Japan's major film studios Kadokawa, Nikkatsu, Shochiku, Toei and Toho. These studios have forged close ties with Japan's public broadcaster Japan Broadcasting Corporation (NHK) and key commercial television stations based in Tokyo. These major players in Japan's film sector operate according to the principles of market competition, and without the government's direct administration and support. The city also houses the Tokyo International Film Festival (TIFF). The festival has been running since 1985 and is an 'A list', FIAPF-accredited competitive feature film festival.[20] Its affiliated multi-content market, TIFFCOM (launched in 2004),[21] is reputed among international film executives to be another important film trade event in East Asia.

The first Japanese film is believed to have been made before 1900 (Sharp and Arnold 2002; Miller 2011). After the Second World War the Japanese government essentially adopted a laissez-faire approach to formulating film-related policies, despite separate initiatives such as the restrictions on exporting Japanese Yen (1950s) and the Japan Arts Fund's subsidizing of certain film projects (1990s), which were employed to assist the Japanese film industry when it was not performing well (Gerow 2006). This reflects a general unenthusiastic attitude of the Japanese government at the time towards film, which was not considered a high art (Sugaya 2004; Gerow 2006; see also Chua B. 2012: 124).

In the late 1990s, the Japanese government started seriously formulating policies to help the domestic film industry catch up with the initiatives that neighbouring countries and territories had already taken (Gerow 2006).[22] In the meantime, Japan started to realign its internal film industry infrastructure and external connections with other countries to promote its film industry and film contents. It joined the Asian Film Commissions Network (AFCNet) in October 2004 as a founding and regular member.[23] In 2005, the government-founded Association for the Diffusion of Japanese Film Abroad[24] joined the organizers of the TIFF to form the Japan Association for International Promotion of the Moving Image (UNIJAPAN), which would be responsible for organizing the TIFF.

However, there has been no central governmental organization and at times no clear direction to implement any comprehensive scheme for supporting the Japanese film industry (Sugaya 2004: 9). One may argue that the spread of film-related activities among different government units and government-supported non-profit organizations allows the film industry in Japan to mould its own competitiveness without too much interference from the federal government. This practice certainly worked when Japan was the world's second-largest box-office territory (Pulver 2013). But when the film trade environment began to change, Japan's film industry would be exposed to a range of challenges. This has precisely been the case in Japan's Tokyo-led film sector since the 2000s. There is no doubt that Tokyo has been striving hard to catch up with other film industry and business pivots in East Asia, and has led a change of national attitude towards cross-border film business. But the changes have been carried out under the Japanese government's overall cautious attitude and swaying approach between seeing 'film as culture' and 'film as business' (Schilling 2003; Sugaya 2004: 15; Gerow 2006). This makes Tokyo appear as a relatively lacklustre node compared with other main cinematic nodes in the region, which are thoroughly equipped and prepared to engage in developing a sophisticated regional nexus of film business in the twenty-first century.

South Korea: Busan (Main Node)

South Korea offers an interesting case showing that a media capital might not necessarily accord with the popular rendezvous of international film executives. Although the capital city Seoul has been the favourite home for most segments of the South Korean film industry and related companies (Han 2010e: 21),[25] the second largest city Busan (with the annual Busan International Film Festival (BIFF) and its affiliated film market, Asian Film Market (AFM)[26]) is the preferred place for domestic/international investors, film executives and other film practitioners to gather annually to network, negotiate film deals and probe the latest trends of Asian films. The festival, known formerly as the Pusan International Film Festival (PIFF), was launched in 1996 and has become one of the most established film events in East Asia (Ahn 2012: 34, 38–42, 48–49).[27]

Experienced East Asian cinema journalist and critic Darcy Paquet (2009b) believes that the success of the PIFF has made it easy for the city of Pusan (now Busan) to launch itself as a filmmaking hub. Indeed, the intention of the present South Korean government to turn Busan into a fully integrated city of film in the twenty-first century is clearly revealed in a government document on national territorial planning, published in 2013 by the Ministry of Strategy and Finance and supervised by the Ministry of Land, Infrastructure and Transport. It shows that, for the period of 2006 to 2020, Busan has been chosen as an 'innovation city', which will be turned into the centre for ocean, film and finance in South Korea (Moon et al. 2013: 69).[28] One immediate result of this territorial plan was the move of the headquarters of the Korean Film Council (KOFIC) from Seoul to Busan in October 2013. This relocation is likely to have a far-reaching effect on South Korea's future film policies as well as on the development of film business in East Asia.

The KOFIC, formerly the Korean Motion Picture Promotion Corporation, was established in South Korea in 1973 under the auspices of the Ministry of Culture, Sports and Tourism in a period of authoritarian political rule (Ahn 2012: 115).[29] With the later changes in South Korea's political system, the organization changed its responsibilities from being a film censorship agency to supporting and promoting (South) Korean Cinema (Kim H-j. Circa 2006: 351). The current KOFIC was launched in 1999 as part of the promotional film policy. For a cinematic tradition that started in 1923 with the first feature, *The Border* (directed by Won San-man) but was not fully industrialized until the 1980s, the current KOFIC can be viewed as a particularly supportive governmental response in the aftermath of the Asian Financial Crisis to boost the local film industry (Kim H-j. Circa 2006: 352; Kim M. and An J. Circa 2006: 19; An Y. and E. Kim 2008: 22–24; Ahn 2012: 34).[30]

Among its major initiatives, the KOFIC supports South Korea's film production by building financial support programmes for independent feature films, short films and documentary films; running an online screenplay market; supporting research and development for film companies; subsidizing independent and art-house film theatres; financing co-productions between South Korea and other countries; and supporting South Korean films/filmmakers to attend international film festivals and film markets. The KOFIC also serves as a central point for supplying information on the South Korean film industry to international film practitioners and researchers (Davis and Yeh 2008: 20; Kim H-c. 2011: 10).[31]

Infrastructural changes have been made in Busan to coincide with the KOFIC's recent relocation to this city. New facilities will be built, such as a headquarters building, new Busan Cinema Studio, outdoor sets and other film production facilities (W. Kim 2013: 69). Seen in this context, while the physical move of the KOFIC from Seoul to Busan seems to be a decentralization of administration, it certainly also suggests the increasing importance of Busan not just in the South Korean film industry but also within the most recent East Asian film business network.

Taiwan: Taipei (Sub-node)

Taipei is where we can find the concentration of Taiwan's film industry. Historically, it was the seat of the then Government Information Office (GIO), the government unit whose major responsibilities included regulating domestic film and other media sectors. Taipei also hosts the annual prestigious film event, the Taipei Golden Horse Film Festival and Awards. The festival was created in 1962 by the GIO. However, without the support of consistent promotional film policies over the years and, more importantly, a proper film marketplace like those affiliated to the biggest international film festivals in East Asia,[32] Taipei is outcompeted by other film business nodes in facilitating international film business exchanges (Frater 2013c). Hence, I refer to Taipei as the sub-node, and not the main node, of the newest East Asian film business network.

Taiwan's film development has been closely related to its political sector. Although film was introduced to Taiwan in 1901 during the Japanese colonial period (1895–1945), it was not until 1925 that the first film was made by and for local Taiwanese, under the strict supervision and censorship of the Japanese colonial government (1925: Taiwan Gets into the Game: n.d.; R. Chen 1998: 48). The early films made in Taiwan were propaganda tools used by the Japanese colonizers to spread the culture of Japan among its Taiwanese subjects (R. Chen 1998: 47). They were produced by major Japanese film studios, such as Nikkatsu, Shochiku and Toho (Yeh and Davis 2005: 16).

In the post-Second World War era, the ruling Kuomintang (KMT, aka the Chinese Nationalist Party) of the Republic of China was defeated and forced to move out of mainland China by the Chinese communists in the civil war. After taking over Taiwan, the authoritarian KMT government established the major film studio, Central Motion Picture Company (CMPC), in Taipei in 1954. The early missions of the studio were mostly anti-communist.[33] However, there was a neglect of film policy (Yeh and Davis 2005: 17). In the 1960s, the KMT government began to devote more efforts to supporting Taiwan's local film industry.[34] In 1975 the government set up the Foundation for the Development of the Motion Picture Industry under the GIO. Taiwan's political-economic transformation from authoritarian rule to democratization in the mid 1970s through to the 1980s spurred the establishment of independent and privately owned film companies. This period also witnessed the golden period of Taiwan Cinema. A total of 2,150 Taiwan films were produced in the 1970s (R. Chen 1998: 54–55). In the 1980s, Taiwan films faced strong competition from Hong Kong films, which took away

much of Taiwan's domestic market share and Taiwanese private financial investments (R. Chen 1998: 56, 61). Although there was encouragement from the Taiwan
government for members of the New Taiwan Cinema movement (1982–86), such
as Hou Hsiao-hsien, Edward Yang and Wu Nien-jen among others who worked
on art-house films (M. Berry 2005: 253), their number of outputs remained small.
Taiwan's mainstream film industry continued to be fragile until recently.[35]

Entering the twenty-first century, Taiwan started to restructure its film
industry (Gao 2009: 432–33). Between 2003 and 2010, the Taiwan government
introduced a series of improved film funding schemes, subsidies, tax break
and related policies to help domestic mainstream film industry and art-house
cinema, to encourage Taiwan-foreign co-productions, and to make Taiwan an
attractive choice for foreign filmmakers to carry out location shooting in the
territory.[36] All these different kinds of financial support seem to have come at
the right time to rescue Taiwan's domestic film production from dying (domestic
production occupied 0.1 per cent of the Taiwan local market share in 2001; 3 per
cent of the Taiwan local market share in 2002; only twenty-three mainstream
Taiwan films were produced in 2004, as compared to 230 films in 1969 during the
golden period of Taiwan's film history (from the 1960s to the 1970s)) (R. Chen
1998: 61; Shackleton 2003; Gao 2009: 428). However, following the GIO's dis-
solution in 2012 and its replacement by the newly formed Taipei-based Ministry
of Culture, there was a series of severe film subsidy cuts.[37] The still fragile Taiwan
film industry would feel the negative effects immediately (Cremin 2013, n.d.).

Hong Kong as a Main Node in the Latest East Asian Film Business Network

Hong Kong Film Policy Overview

We have just seen how contemporary film-related policies in Beijing, Shanghai,
Tokyo, Busan and Taipei fit in their respective, current stages of film industry
and business development, and how each city's structural, infrastructural and
institutional arrangements have been modified so as to cope with the needs
of the film sector. Unlike these other nodes, Hong Kong has achieved its nodal
position in the latest East Asian film business network not as a result of any systematic and coherent local government support, but mostly through the persistent efforts of the local film practitioners over the years. Its being a major node in

this film business network reflects the way in which the New Hong Kong Cinema carves out a niche of its own astride and within this network's interstices left open (or sometimes covered up) by the workings of the other nodes. To justify my point, in the following I will take a look at Hong Kong's different sets of film-related policies in different time periods. This will be followed by an analysis of Hong Kong's most recent film-related policies and relevant conditions.

As part of the overall non-interventionist approach to administering Hong Kong during the colonial era, the British colonial government there adopted a type of laissez-faire policy towards the local film sector, which has been built by private enterprises on the principles of a market-oriented economy (J. Chan, Fung and C. Ng 2010: 24). *Zhuangzi Tests His Wife* was the first Hong Kong feature film ever made, directed by Lai Man-wai (aka Li Minwei) in 1913. The film was an adaption of a Cantonese opera. Lai Man-wai, his brother Lai Pak-hoi (aka Li Beihai), cousin Lai Hoi-san (aka Li Haishan) and theatre actor/director Liang Shaobo founded Minxin Film Company in Hong Kong in 1923. It was the first Chinese-owned film company in the territory. In the following year the company relocated to Canton (now Guangzhou) because of an unsuccessful land rent application with the colonial government, before moving further north to Shanghai in 1926 amid the Canton-Hong Kong strike. In 1930, Minxin became part of the Lianhua Film Company in Shanghai (Teo 1997: 3). Before the Japanese invasion of Shanghai in the Second World War, the Hong Kong film sector remained secondary to the more glamorous Shanghai film industry. The fall of Shanghai to the Japanese indirectly breathed new life into the Hong Kong film industry, for many Shanghai film practitioners moved their capital, talent, technologies and expertise to Hong Kong to continue their filmmaking ventures.

The 1950s and the 1960s saw the dominance of Chinese tycoon-led film studios such as Shaw Brothers in the Hong Kong film sector. These filmmakers also continued their personal film business networks they had built in East/ South East Asia in the pre-war period (Teo 1997: 7–8; S. Chung 2003). The lack of active government intervention together with the overall prosperity of the Hong Kong economy and other unique film industry elements represented the competitive edge of the Hong Kong film industry at that time (see also K. Ng 2009). The local film industry reached its pinnacle in the late 1980s and the early 1990s, with an annual output quantity comparable to Hollywood and Bollywood. The annual output peaked at 239 films in 1993 (Chan C. 2000: 457). This period also witnessed the structural change in the Hong Kong film industry from a domination of big film studios to a proliferation of small- to medium-sized independent film companies lacking huge capital backups. For various extrinsic and intrinsic reasons, however, the local film industry started to plummet in 1994. Since 2002, the number of local films released has been less than 100 annually, with an average of fifty films in recent years. In 2014, a total of fifty-one Hong Kong local films were released (S. Chan 2015).

Meanwhile, the British colonial government in Hong Kong continued to keep the local film industry at arm's length. Before the 1997 Handover, relatively limited administrative procedures such as the local film censorship and film classification system were carried out by the then Television and Entertainment Licensing Authority (TELA).[38] The Hong Kong International Film Festival (HKIFF), one of the important film events in the city, was organized and financially supported by different government units between 1977 and 2004 (R. Cheung 2009: 100–1). According to Li Cheuk-to, Artistic Director of the HKIFF, before the festival's corporatization in 2004 it was thought by many Hong Kong film industry practitioners as a government-sponsored event that served only a small number of cinéphiles. The festival was thus not considered a structural part of the local mainstream film industry that was there to produce grass-roots entertainment for the general public (R. Cheung 2011c: 205–6).[39]

After the Handover in 1997, Tung Chee-hwa, who was the first chief executive of the newly formed Hong Kong SAR government, started to show some signs of support for the deteriorating film sector following a persistent lobby of the local government by representatives from the mainstream film industry. A series of film-related policies as well as financial and infrastructural arrangements have accordingly been implemented since then. In the area of funding, in 1999 the Hong Kong government put together the Film Development Fund with an initial sum of HK$100 million (£7.9 million or U.S.$12.9 million) for enhancing the professional and technological capabilities of the local film industry (J. Chan, Fung and C. Ng 2010: 25–29). International marketing scholar Zhihong Gao (2009: 431) notes that '[r]ather than directly subsidising film production, the fund supports projects that promote dialogues and co-operation among film professionals'. In 2003, a sum of HK$50 million (£3.9 million or U.S.$6.4 million) was drawn from the Film Development Fund to form the Film Guarantee Fund, which is to be applied for by local film companies as backup funding when they take out loans from banks or lending institutions to cover their filmmaking costs.[40] In 2007, the government injected another HK$300 million (£23.7 million or U.S.$38.7 million) into the Film Development Fund so as to offer financial support to small- and medium-budget film productions.[41]

The Hong Kong SAR government has also made some structural adjustment within the government architecture for helping the local film industry. In April 1998, the government established the Film Services Office (FSO) to facilitate film production, building a database on location shooting and post-production facilities in Hong Kong.[42] In 2004, the HKIFF was corporatized after having been run by the local government for twenty-seven years, starting from 1977 (R. Cheung 2009; C. Wong 2011: 216–17). Its partner film marketplace, the Hong Kong International Film & TV Market (FILMART; launched in 1997),[43] remains an annual event organized by the Hong Kong Trade Development Council (HKTDC). The HKTDC is a statutory body in Hong Kong aiming to promote Hong Kong's trade, but it does not belong to the governmental structure, although some of the members of the council are current senior government officials (R. Cheung 2011c: 201–3).[44] In 2007, a non-statutory advisory committee, the Hong Kong Film Development Council (HKFDC), was founded to incorporate established film practitioners to provide strategic advice to the government. The council also administers the two government-controlled film funds via the FSO.[45] In June 2009, a new agency, the Create Hong Kong (CreateHK), was set up under the auspices of the Commerce and Economic Development Bureau of the government to overlook the policies and related arrangements for creative industries. Since then, film-related matters have been placed side by side with other local creative industries, such as design and digital entertainment, under the administration of this new agency. While the FSO now goes into the organization chart of the CreateHK, the HKFDC, still functional, is not included in the CreateHK's official profile (see Figure 5.1).[46]

To tap the mainland China market, in 2003 the Hong Kong SAR government and the PRC government signed the Mainland and Hong Kong Closer Economic Partnership Arrangement (CEPA). The CEPA was updated ten times between 2004 and 2013, allowing a total of twenty-eight sectors (including film) of Hong Kong to become 'partly liberalized' – that is, to be allowed to conduct business activities in mainland China, with conditions attached.[47] For the film sector, films co-produced by Hong Kong film companies with their mainland Chinese partners under the CEPA will be treated as mainland films when they are distributed in mainland China. Chinese-language films produced in Hong Kong are also allowed to be imported for distribution in the mainland on a quota-free

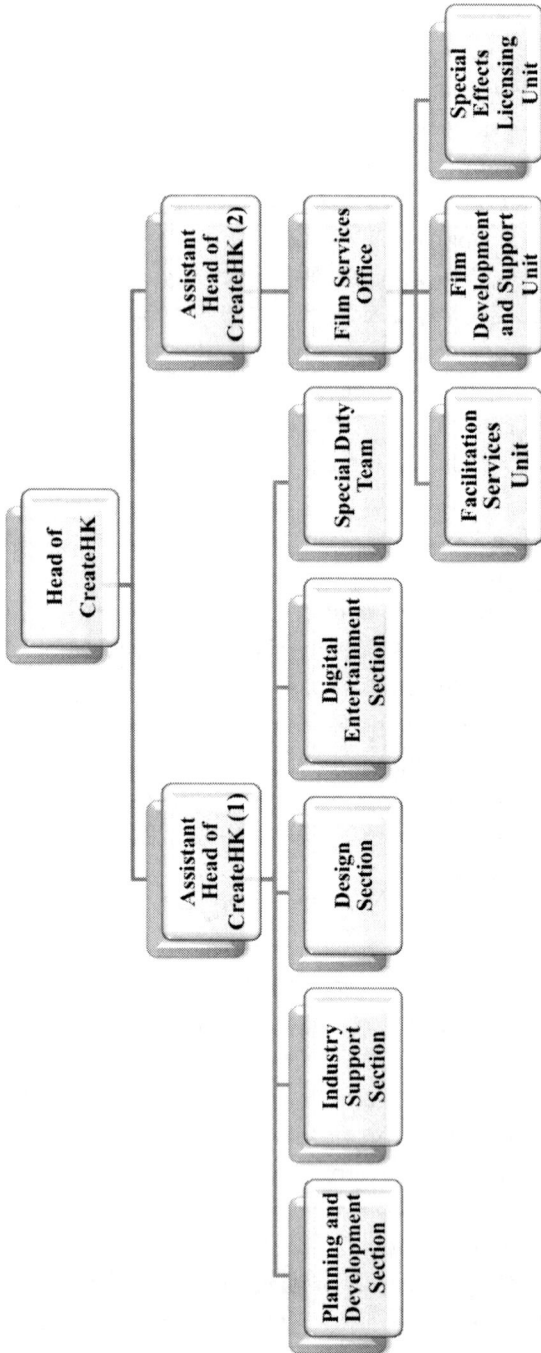

Figure 5.1 The Organization Chart of the CreateHK
Source: The CreateHK's official website (English), www.createhk.gov.hk (accessed 5 May 2015).

basis, after China's censorship approval (when distributed in China, Hong Kong-made films that were not co-produced were treated as foreign films in the time after the political reunification and before the signing and implementation of the CEPA) (J. Chan, Fung and C. Ng 2010: 72–74). Initially welcomed by Hong Kong's film practitioners, this series of government endeavours (being some of the newest elements in the development of the New Hong Kong Cinema) turned out not to be especially beneficial. Many critics and film professionals even view them negatively (V. Chow 2013). What has gone wrong?

Analysis

Ostensibly, the Hong Kong SAR government has been responding to the urgent requests of the film industry practitioners to save the industry from dwindling further. All these long overdue supportive measures in the form of financial setups, institutional arrangements and political infrastructures have been put in place since the new Hongkonger-led government was formed. However, it is worth noting that the Hong Kong SAR government has, from the outset, treated Hong Kong Cinema as a sector of the Hong Kong economy only (in particular, emphasizing its moneymaking ability). The local government has confusedly and narrowly defined the artistic and cultural sectors of Hong Kong, and there-fore has not considered film as part of these two sectors.[48] Hence, whatever kinds of measures the government implements with regard to the film sector, the first priority is always of economic and not cultural concern. These government interventions have thus met with severe criticisms from both within and outside the local film industry.

In examining the efficacies of Hong Kong's film-related policies, scholars of mass media Joseph Chan, Anthony Y.H. Fung and Chun Hung Ng (2010: 31) remark that these policies have thus far been 'mostly sporadic and passive responses to the industry's requests' and there is still 'no coherent long-term planning, nor any strong rationale underlying the measures'. To be more spe-cific, the Hong Kong SAR government has not made any ambitious plans to enable Hong Kong Cinema to take another major leap along the value chain in the global film business context. Also, understandably trying to avoid displeas-ing the Chinese authorities, the new set of Hong Kong film-related policies does not display a clear mission of facilitating Hong Kong film production in building distinctive local identities and ideologies for the Hongkongers. We can see, for example, that the objectives of the two film funds focus only on fulfilling the budgets, promotion, talent training and audience development of 'Hong Kong films'. They do not state clearly whether the sponsored films need to reflect the lives and thinking of the locals. The two funds have strict application criteria and only support feature films. A total sum of HK$4.13 million (£325,000 or U.S.$533,000) from the Film Development Fund was awarded to Hong Kong film projects between July 2007 and March 2013 for taking part in film festivals, and thereby generating publicity (V. Chow 2013). About half of this sum – that is, around HK$2.21 million (£174,000 or U.S.$285,000), went to forty-three films directed or co-directed by twelve filmmakers who were already very established. Five of these films were directed by Johnnie To, accounting for a total of HK$1.13 million (£89,000 or U.S.$146,000) of this award sum. Two films were directed by Ann Hui, accounting for HK$380,000 (£30,000 or U.S.$49,000). And two were directed by Wong Kar-wai, accounting for HK$190,000 (£15,000 or U.S.$25,000). Many of these films were produced and distributed by major film companies, which have strong capital reserves. They were not in urgent need of award money as might be the case with smaller film projects/companies. As it turns out, the government sees its role as an investor rather than a provider of subsidies (Chui and R. Wong 2010: 20). Those film projects that promise higher returns will get a better chance to win the government funds. Filmmakers having less directorial experience, small-budget films and non-feature films (e.g., shorts, microfilms and documentaries) that are also part of Hong Kong Cinema, on the other hand, have not had much chance to get governmental financial support, for the current system favours star-laden feature films (V. Chow 2013).

The ambiguity of Hong Kong's film-related policies points directly to the core of the problem – the government lacks a proactive attitude towards, and a forward-looking vision for, a truly diverse local film sector that has helped build Hong Kong's economy and identity over the past several decades. Even worse, the establishment of the HKFDC and, later, of the CreateHK reveals a deep-seated governance problem: there are constant changes being made to the direction of what the local government hopes it would be able to achieve for local filmmaking – a sector in the society that for ages has not been high on the government's political and administrative agendas. Yiu-Wai Chu (2013: 77–79) observes that the CreateHK was set up to show the Hong Kong SAR government's determination to 'make Hong Kong a creative capital', which is actually part of the Brand Hong Kong marketing strategy and not a campaign dedicated wholeheartedly to developing Hong Kong's creative industries.

Frequent changes to the newly established set of film-related policies there-fore often generate confusion rather than help for the local film professionals in Hong Kong. When we look at the membership list of the HKFDC (the term running from 1 April 2015 to 31 March 2017), more questions arise as to how rep-resentative these members are in a diverse society.[49] Whereas there are mostly government officials, film practitioners and business sector representatives on board, there is only one film professor, Cheuk Pak Tong,[50] representing the local film education sector (or filmmaking, as he was part of the first Hong Kong New Wave) and no representative from the viewing public (see Gerow (2006) for a similar criticism on the Committee on Film Promotion in Japan).

As a result, although there seems to be a set of film-related policies in Hong Kong, in effect it does not make a significant contribution to the rescue of the local film sector. Hong Kong film practitioners continue to do things accord-ing to the proven best industry practices, without resorting to the government's assistance. For example, most of the filmmakers in Hong Kong continue to seek film funding from equity investors and pre-sale agreements of distribution rights instead of making use of the Film Development Fund and the Film Guarantee Fund. The Hong Kong film industry continues to be dominated by several film-makers, such as Ann Hui, Johnnie To, Tsui Hark and Derek Yee, who established themselves during the golden period of the industry. The less successful Hong Kong film practitioners may have quit the Hong Kong film industry completely. Mainland China could be an option for them to restart their professions, but there is still no guarantee that they would succeed there because China tends to welcome those Hong Kong filmmakers who are already well known (Elley 2012; A Quarter 2013; Y-W. Chu 2013: 79). Film-talent training offered and supported by the Hong Kong government is far from adequate. Many newcomers (except a few of the better known, newest Hong Kong filmmakers) continue to drop out of the field after having worked on one or two local film projects (J. Chan, Fung and C. Ng 2010: 30–31).

The number of local film outputs continues to be low. Polarization in the film sector is getting more and more serious. Filmmaking is characterized by either mega blockbusters, which are usually China-Hong Kong co-production projects under the CEPA with a heavy dose of 'China' element and insufficient defin-ing characteristics/creativity of Hong Kong local films (A Quarter 2013; Y-W. Chu 2013: 104, 109–112; Xing 2014), or cheaply produced local films that lack overseas market potential. China-Hong Kong co-productions 'have become the predominant genre in the Hong Kong film industry' after the CEPA was signed, as Chu (2013: 105) observes. Even with the CEPA signed between Hong Kong and China, which on the surface has made it easier for Hong Kong films to reach the mainland audience market, many Hong Kong filmmakers still find it hard to truly incorporate themselves and their productions into the mainland film industry system. This is because these Hong Kong filmmakers are unfamiliar with the highly regulated and opaque mainland film distribution and exhibition network, film industry statistics, legal enforcement, censorship criteria and approval gateways (Gao 2009: 429–30; J. Chan, Fung and C. Ng 2010: 30). This is evident in the Supplement X to CEPA, signed in August 2013. It stipulates a vague condition for the audiovisual sector of Hong Kong, which might be interpreted differently by different parties:

> To allow the dialect version of motion pictures produced by Hong Kong and co-produced by Hong Kong and the Mainland to be distributed and screened in the Mainland, after being examined by and obtaining the approval of the relevant authorities in the Mainland, on the condition that standard Chinese subtitles are provided on screen.[51]

The Hong Kong SAR government continues to neglect the interests and the further development of the local audience. Yet, it cannot ignore the possibility that because of geolinguistic closeness, the Hong Kong mainstream film audience's likes and dislikes can easily influence other communities of audience based nearby on the mainland, such as the neighbouring areas within the Pearl River Delta region (Curtin 2003: 221; J. Chan, Fung and C. Ng 2010: 94–95). It follows that not fulfilling the interests of the local audience in Hong Kong would eventually also lead to dissatisfaction among other viewing communities residing in the south of China, thereby counteracting the positive results of opening the mainland audience market that the CEPA could normally bring to the Hong Kong film industry. Commenting on the local government's failure in nurturing a truly interested audience for creative industries, Chu (2013: 85) notes that '[w]ithout a solid audience base, creative industries cannot be fully developed'. Therefore, in terms of institutional, political-economic and cultural effectiveness, it is not difficult to conclude that the film-related policies in Hong Kong still have a long way to go before their missions are fully accomplished.

The incompetent film-related policies in Hong Kong may not help the local film sector immediately, but neither are they likely to hurt it further. I attribute this to the mature film business relationship that Hong Kong has built with its business partners over the decades. In the next section, I will explore the interrelationships of the cinematic nodes in the newest East Asian film business network, and how Hong Kong's resilience in transitional circumstances could possibly help the local film industry to renew and re-strengthen its position among other cinematic nodes in the region.

The Logics of a (Counter-)Imbalance of Power

China's rise and its huge audience market have created international film business hype for exploring this undertapped gold mine. The biggest beneficiaries seem to be the nearby cinematic nodes in China's home region in East Asia, where there is an ongoing high volume of cultural and film business traffic. These neighbouring nodes seem to rely on Beijing and Shanghai to sustain the long-term growth of their film sectors. We begin to see an asymmetry of power in the hexagonal film business relationships: Beijing and Shanghai seem to be the engines of growth of the newest East Asian film business network, while Busan, Hong Kong and Tokyo are just surviving (or struggling); Taipei is unfortunately fading away in importance in this network, despite the fact that major film funding in the East Asian region often comes from Taiwanese private investors. But can their relationships be read as simply as this?

Economic Arrangements and Co-production Treaties

In discussing the soft power configuration and confrontation of the three largest East Asian powers in the present era, Chua (2012) notes a certain inequality between China, Japan and South Korea in their use of pop culture to accomplish their missions. While Japan and South Korea are the two big exporters of pop culture, China as the major importer has the advantage of its huge consumer market. To exploit this biggest single market on earth, consisting of a population of over 1.3 billion people, regional cultural producers will need to co-produce with China in order to bypass its import quota, state bureaucracies and other business obstacles. South Korea seems to be allying with China because of the lingering effect of Japan's past colonization of Korea. Yet, China accuses South

Korea of stealing its cultural traditions and using them as their own in South Korea's television drama series. Japan is trying to maintain its superior position as the originator of the manga culture, but its government has failed to employ public policies to develop its soft power resources in a timely manner (Chua B. 2012: 7–8, 124, 127–28, 135).

Down at the level of individual cities, and focusing primarily on the film sector, we can detect yet another picture of power imbalance – or, we might even say, a power counter-imbalance among the identified regional cinematic nodes. As a whole, China is a magnet for international filmmakers, who use all sorts of ways to become part of the rising Chinese film empire. The ways they use to get involved range from building joint ventures with their mainland Chinese partners, to opening offices in strategic locations in China (staffed with Chinese employees). Their presence (mainly in Beijing and Shanghai) in turn helps China at the nascent stage of its international film business development in the post-WTO era, when China is requiring the know-how, management skills and funnelling of international film funding to its film business undertakings. Under such circumstances, China's two major cinematic nodes, Beijing and Shanghai, will be the first to benefit. Beijing in this context is in a better position than Shanghai, for the state-run National Film Capital Company Limited (NFC) is located in the capital city. According to a business partner of the NFC, the fund is deployed for financing 'larger projects with global commercial elements' (China's NFC 2012). It has recently announced a plan of injecting a sum of U.S.$230 million (£141 million) into a collection of film projects, a number of which have Hollywood partners (Frater 2012). Not surprisingly, a part of the amalgamation of funds was raised from Hong Kong, besides inputs from public and private investors in mainland China.

One of the formal procedures for working with China nowadays is for other countries/territories to sign special co-production treaties or economic arrangements with the Chinese authorities. Concluding such treaties has become a common phenomenon since the 2000s. As part of the Hong Kong film-related policies to support the ailing local film industry, the CEPA, first signed in 2003, enables Hong Kong filmmakers to make co-produced films with their mainland Chinese partners. The final products can then be categorized as mainland films, which will enjoy quota-free distribution in mainland China on the condition that they fulfil the approval requirements laid down by the Chinese authorities (the process of approval is, however, notoriously unclear to filmmakers, and is subject

to change). The part of the CEPA that is related to the film industry is not recip-
rocal, and there are no requirements or strings attached as to how many mainland Chinese films have to be imported into Hong Kong. Other kinds of trade
treaties, for example the Economic Cooperation Framework Agreement (ECFA)
signed between the Taipei and the Beijing governments, act as two-way tracks.
The ECFA was signed between the two governments in June 2010. It helps break
down the long-term political animosity, and open up mutual economic benefits
and trade opportunities on both sides of the Taiwan Strait. Under the ECFA,
Taiwan films are exempt from being subject to the foreign film import quota
that China imposes on foreign films entering the mainland audience market. In
return, ten mainland films are initially allowed to enter the Taiwan market every
year (China Opens up 2010; Liu W. 2012). This is likely to be a win-win situation.
On the one hand, Taiwan Chinese-language films will have a chance to tap the
huge mainland Chinese audience market. On the other hand, China can utilize
China-Taiwan co-production projects to absorb investments, young directors
and actors from Taiwan (Shackleton 2010a). However, it is still too early to conclude whether 'China' is the solution for sustaining Taiwan's film industry and
film business opportunities in the long run, given Taiwan residents' strong oppo-
sition in March–April 2014 against the ECFA's follow-up treaty on service trade
between China and Taiwan. Many protesters from Taiwan worried that such a
pact with China might 'harm the territory's small businesses and erode its political autonomy' (Kaiman 2014; see also J. Lee and Culpan 2014).

South Korea has also jumped on the bandwagon. In October 2013, the country signed a film and television co-production treaty with China, following a ten-
tative agreement signed in June of the same year. Co-produced films under this
treaty are expected to be treated as local or national by both countries.[52] This
treaty is likely to have similar results to that of the ECFA signed between Taiwan
and China: China opens the door of its huge domestic audience market to allow
South Korean films to enter it, in return for the opportunities to gain access
to the reserves of South Korea's film subsidies, talent, contents and technologies that are available only to South Korean national films (Frater 2013a; Lee H.
2013). The treaty can again be understood as part of China's strategy to build up
international film finances and other resources for its embryonic film business.
On the other hand, South Korea also shares the victory. After Korean cultural
products such as film and television series have entered into China, they will
likely be dubbed in the Chinese language or carry Chinese subtitles before being

redistributed via formal and informal (e.g., fan-based) channels to the diasporic Chinese communities worldwide. South Korea's soft power in the form of its pop culture (the Korean culture hype, dubbed the 'Korean Wave' by the mass media; or *hanliu* in Mandarin Chinese) will be further consolidated, albeit through indirect channels and at times through submission to China's Sinocentric ideology when South Korea is working to develop a pan-East Asian cultural identity (Chua B. 2012: 130, 140). A case in point is South Korea's participation in the Chinese-language pan-East Asian co-production film, *Red Cliff* (see my discussion in Chapter Four).

Film Commission Networks

While co-production treaties are signed by the central governments in the case of Taiwan and South Korea, the major cinematic cities of Taipei and Busan in these two territories are likely to be the first at the city level to benefit via the establishment of film commissions. Local film commissions started to become a distinguishable part of the East Asian cinematic structure in the 2000s, after the region-wide film industry redeployment in the 1980s and 1990s. Many film commissions are established as public non-profit organizations by local governments to provide assistance and support to international filmmaking teams that shoot their films on location in the corresponding cities and provincial areas. These film commissions may help the international teams to find the best possible locations, hire local talent to work on the crews, and carry out certain marketing tasks. They may also help the international teams to apply for local governmental licences and obtain tax-free incentives to do relevant filming. These commissions, then, indirectly also help the local residents, especially those local filmmakers who might obtain employment and development opportunities through working temporarily with these international teams, and local non-film business (e.g., advertising, marketing, equipment hiring, catering, tourism, hotel business and so on). Together with other local film commissions, they may form a nationwide network, such as that of Japan[53] or South Korea (Han 2010a, 2010b, 2010c, 2010d, 2010e).

Beyond the national boundaries, a regional film commission network, the Asian Film Commissions Network (AFCNet), was formed in October 2004. The AFCNet is the largest in Asia and was started by the Busan Film Commission. Interestingly, we can see another level of power structure among cities and countries by considering this official regional network's membership.[54] The member film commissions hail from East/South East Asia, Indo-China, the

Middle East and the Asian Pacific.[55] Japan and South Korea are the most strongly represented. They dominate this network with seventeen representative film commissions (both local and national) and ten representative local film commissions respectively. Beijing, Hong Kong and Shanghai do not have any representative film commissions in this network. On the current board of directors,[56] it is Busan that holds the lead with the network secretariat located in the city. The AFCNet president, Oh Seokgeun, is from the Busan Film Commission. One of the vice-presidents of the AFCNet, Terawaki Ken, is from the Japan Film Commission; the other vice-president, Kamil Othman, is from the National Film Development Corporation Malaysia. Jennifer Jao from the semi-governmental Taipei Film Commission, formed in 2007, serves as director of the network board, while Jiang Ping (a filmmaker working under the auspices of the SAPPRFT in China) serves as a member on the advisory board of the AFCNet.

Film Marketplaces

Platforms are necessary for conducting film business. Economic arrangements, co-production treaties and film commission networks may serve as platforms on paper at government level to facilitate film business. For actual business to happen, film buyers, sellers and investors alike need to come together face-to-face to negotiate deals. Film marketplaces (or simply 'film markets'), usually affiliated to corresponding film festivals in their host cities, are then preferred platforms offering convenient times and places for the film business community to gather. As the director of the International Promotion Center at the KOFIC, Daniel D.H. Park, remarks: 'Festivals are cultural but markets are about business ...' (Director 2012: 9). It is thus of paramount importance for film business executives to attend these events.

The sector of film marketplaces witnessed some of the fastest changes in the East Asian film business landscape in the 2000s (see Table 5.1). A few years ago I conducted a study comparing the levels of significance of four major East Asian film markets in terms of their schedules, numbers of attendees and reputation in global film business. Based upon my findings, I classified them into two tiers (see R. Cheung 2011a: 40–61). The more important tier one comprises FILMART in Hong Kong and the AFM in Busan. The less important tier two includes the TIFFCOM in Tokyo and the SIFF Market in Shanghai. Only FILMART, the most established one among them, was launched in the last century (in 1997). All the others started to appear in the new millennium. Since my study was published, there have been dramatic changes to their positioning. First of all, one more global-scale film market, the BFM in Beijing, sprang up in 2011. Secondly, my tier system has been challenged in terms of the numbers of film buyers/sellers officially recorded at the AFM, the TIFFCOM and the SIFF Market over the past several years. In particular, the AFM and the TIFFCOM have modified the ways they record the official volumes of human traffic at the events, making it diffi-cult to quantify and compare their importance in the minds of film executives/investors and other film professionals who participate in these events. From the data available, it shows that the AFM and the TIFFCOM have been major rivals hoping to reach and maintain the second rank among these major East Asian film markets (see Table A.5 in the Appendix).[57]

Table 5.1 East Asian Film Markets

Film market	Related film festival	Launch year	Period (annually)	Host city
Asian Film Market (AFM)	Busan International Film Festival	2006	Early October	Busan
Beijing Film Market (BFM)	Beijing International Film Festival	2011	April	Beijing
Hong Kong International Film & TV Market (FILMART)	Hong Kong International Film Festival	1997	March	Hong Kong
SIFF Market	Shanghai International Film Festival	2007	June	Shanghai
TIFFCOM	Tokyo International Film Festival	2004	Late October	Tokyo

What has remained unchanged and unchallenged is FILMART's position among these other major film markets in the region. Strategically scheduled for late March every year, after the important European Film Market at the Berlin International Film Festival in February, and before Marché du Film at the Cannes Film Festival in May, FILMART is one of the film markets most frequented by film executives. Participants in FILMART are usually from Hong Kong and other parts of Asia, though film buyers/sellers from Europe and the United States also go there (Shackleton 2011a). FILMART's status as a 'must-attend' film business event has become even more outstanding, as the travel budgets of film execu-tives diminished after the Global Financial Crisis; it has become less easy for them to hop from one major international film festival and market to another along the film festival circuit. The HKTDC notes FILMART's importance in a film industry research report published in 2015 (S. Chan 2015):

> FILMART (Hong Kong), Marche Du Film [sic: Marché du Film] (Cannes) and American Film Market (the US) have been chosen by film industry players as the top three most important global film events. FILMART is now the largest film and TV market event in Asia.

FILMART's importance is often further publicized by film trade magazines and individual journalists. The influential *Screen International* carries major and usually positive coverage of the HKIFF and FILMART around the festival period each year. For example, the title 'Beauty in the East: Filmart 2011' (Shackleton 2011a) was used in an article for the 2011 edition of this film market. Writing a regular column for the KOFIC's *Korean Cinema Today* (the official magazine for promoting the South Korean film industry), Paquet (2009b: 29) assesses the performance of the PIFF (now BIFF):

> The biggest challenge for any film festival is not to grow, or to become more famous, but to establish its niche. In the 1980s and 1990s, the Hong Kong film festival was known for its focus on Chinese language cinema. Now it is better known for its market, which is considered far more successful than Pusan's own Asian Film Market.

Paquet's praise is extraordinary not because it comes from an Asian film industry expert but because his essay was published in an official film magazine of the KOFIC, the very promoter of the PIFF and the AFM. The AFM, launched in 2006, has been FILMART's toughest competitor (R. Cheung 2011a: 49). The fact that *Korean Cinema Today* carried Paquet's article thus gives much greater authority and weight to the critic's recognition of FILMART than if the article had been published in some other trade magazines. Paquet's idea echoes that of Liz Shackleton, another experienced East Asian film trade journalist, who works for *Screen International* (its electronic and daily version is *Screen Daily*). Shackleton writes frequently about the HKIFF and FILMART. She comments, '[FILMART] ... continues to be a platform for Hong Kong and mainland Chinese companies to launch big-budget Chinese-language productions' (Shackleton 2011b). Another

Screen Daily journalist, Jean Noh (2014), writes about FILMART's increasing importance with regard to China: 'With China's box office continuing to grow – last year [2013] it increased by 27% to reach $3.6bn – Hong Kong Filmart is strengthening its position as a gateway to the mainland'. FILMART's well-established status and continuing importance in the minds of global film executives and critics enable Hong Kong as a cinematic node to stay afloat in a rough sea of power struggles and competition in the newest East Asian film business network. It is likely to continue channelling business and networking opportunities for film buyers and sellers from different countries and territories. Obviously, some of the major beneficiaries would be Hong Kong filmmakers and the Hong Kong film industry as a whole in a period of its transitional structural readjustment, when it is catching up with the changes happening to film industries in East Asia and regions further afield (J. Chan, Fung and C. Ng 2010: 92).

Concluding Remarks

In this chapter I have used the model of the 'newest East Asian film business network' as a prism to explore the most recent film industry and business evolvement in East Asia. My purpose was to understand how the New Hong Kong Cinema has strived/thrived astride and within the interstices between other identified film business nodes in the region. The superlative 'newest' I have employed to describe this network denotes that the phenomenon of intraregional film business relationships is not in itself something 'new' in East Asia. This model represents the most recent cycle of a relationship system that has been evolving over the past century. Neither did I mean the newest network is an overnight creation, for it has gradually built up through collaboration and competition at international, national, municipal and city levels over the past two decades. The network also refers to all kinds of discernible or obscure relationships among individual filmmakers, creative talent, funding providers and audiences, which have been continuously waxing and waning. In this system of relationships, what is highly emphasized is the self-sustenance of regional film business and individual film industries. Relationships within this newest East Asian film business network are therefore complicated, multilayered and multilateral.

In seeking to understand the relationships and operations within this network, I have identified Beijing, Busan, Hong Kong, Shanghai and Tokyo as the main nodes and Taipei as the sub-node. Within the region, the volumes of film business collaboration and competition are heaviest among them, while they may also forge connections with those up-and-coming non-nodes located nearby geographically. These cinematic nodes offer superior interconnectedness for binding this network together, leading and defining the film business activities within and outside of East Asia. Although I have mainly been concerned with the latest development of film business of these regional nodal points in the post-Asian Financial Crisis period, my discussion has also touched upon the cinematic history of each node. While these cinematic nodes are the brightest spots in this newest network, the imbalance of power due to their own strengths and weaknesses and to the political-economic power of the countries/territories they represent should not be forgotten. On the contrary, it is arguably the imbalance of power and the reflexive counter-imbalance of power among these cinematic nodes (and the respective countries/territories) being crystallized into economic and co-production arrangements, film commission networks and film marketplaces that help keep this film business network alive.

In the middle of these intertwining relationships, Hong Kong does not seem to be performing outstandingly well, given the fact that the local film industry has been suffering for two decades, but the most recent film-related public policies have not helped relieve the problems. We should, however, not forget that among the cinematic nodes in the region, Hong Kong's biggest advantage is that it is the host city of the most successful and the longest established film business platform FILMART. This film market has continuously been facilitating local, regional and global film trades and investment opportunities. As Yiu-Wai Chu (2013: 117) notes when commenting on the function of the Hong Kong-Asia Film Financing Forum (HAF), a related event of the FILMART under the Entertainment Expo Hong Kong: 'When Hong Kong no longer has the power to produce new film stars and directors, it can at best be a financing center for Chinese cinema, wherein Mainland-Hong Kong co-productions will have become Chinese films financed in Hong Kong'. Interestingly, the origin of FILMART was not part of the public policies deliberately designed to help the failing Hong Kong film industry. Moreover, FILMART's organizer, the HKTDC, operates outside the local governmental structure. As long as Hong Kong can maintain this local advantage of hosting FILMART, the city's flexibility and international outlook in film industry development, and as long as it avoids the danger of over-relying on 'China' as the sole solution to the film industry's deep-seated problems, Hong Kong and its cinematic practice will remain one of the sharpest frontiers of the newest East Asian film sphere when the local film industry goes through its transitional restructuring.

Notes

1. A close look at the workings of the latest East Asian film business network, where most of the East Asian films are traded and circulated, is further justified from the perspective of the global film trade. I am grateful to Thomas Gerstenmeyer of Aldeburgh Cinema and Chris Harris of Picturehouse Cinemas for sharing their profound knowledge of film distribution and exhibition business, and film programming respectively. During the discussion both of them shared with me their insights about why East Asian films, even if they are blockbusters in their home base, are not usually selected for general release in Europe. The taste of the local audiences, the presence/absence of distributors of these East Asian films in Europe and general economic decisions are some of the main influences on film distributors and exhibitors in determining what East Asian films are selected for showing to the European audiences.
    Founded in 1919, Aldeburgh Cinema is one of the longest running independent cinemas in the United Kingdom. Gerstenmeyer has over thirty years of management experience in international film exhibition business in continental Europe and the United Kingdom. Picturehouse Cinemas is a network of art-house cinemas in the United Kingdom that also provides programming services for its client cinemas (known internally as virtual cinemas) throughout the country. Harris works in the programming section, and deals with film distributors and exhibitors on a daily basis. The discussion with Gerstenmeyer took place on 27 October 2013 and with Harris on 16 November 2013, both in Aldeburgh, Suffolk, in the United Kingdom.
2. While Yau notes that the association's name is 'Southeast Asian Motion Pictures Producers Association', another researcher, Sangjoon Lee (2011), traces the name of the association to a different source, as the 'Federation of Motion Picture Producer's Association of Asia'. Here I adopt Yau's version, which forms part of my citation of her argument about the origins of the East Asian cinematic network.
3. Personal interview with Li Cheuk-to, Artistic Director of the Hong Kong International Film Festival (HKIFF), conducted by the author in Hong Kong on 7 July 2010 (within the context of the 'Dynamics of World Cinema' project at the University of St Andrews).
4. The main sponsors of the Beijing International Film Festival (BJIFF) and the Beijing Film Market (BFM) are the State Administration of Press, Publication, Radio, Film and Television (SAPPRFT) and the government of Beijing Municipality of the PRC. The Film Bureau of the SAPPRFT and the Beijing Municipal Bureau of Press,

Publication, Radio, Film and Television (Beijing Municipal Bureau of Copyright) undertake the festival and the film market. Source: 'About BJIFF', the BJIFF's official website (English), www.bjiff.com (accessed 5 May 2015).

5. The Chinese authorities consolidated the China Film Corporation in 1971 by combining China Film Distribution and Exhibition Corporation (formerly, China Film Management Corporation), China Film Archive and China Film Equipment (Yeh and Davis 2008: 39).

6. On the SAPPRFT's official website (simplified Chinese), www.sarft.gov.cn, China Film Group Corporation (CFGC) is placed under the category 'Units under Direct Supervision [of the SAPPRFT]' (accessed 5 May 2015).

7. Sino-foreign co-production is one of the possible ways for foreign film companies to bypass the strict quota on foreign films imported into China annually. It is thus important to understand that CFGC acts as the single most important gatekeeper of the mainland Chinese film industry, ensuring its development and flourishing. The actual work (approval, censorship, filmmaking and so on) involved in Sino-foreign co-productions is the responsibility of CFGC's subsidiary, China Film Co-Production Corporation, established in 1979.

8. See also the SAPPRFT's official website (simplified Chinese), www.sarft.gov.cn (accessed 5 May 2015).

9. CFGC was involved in the production and/or distribution of most of the expensively produced Chinese-language blockbusters released in the first decade of the new millennium (see Table A.1 in the Appendix).

10. The other two mainland Chinese municipalities are Chongqing and Tianjin.

11. The first film introduced to Qing China was referred to as 'shadow plays from the West' and was screened on 11 August 1896 at the teahouse Another Village in the Xu Garden in Shanghai. Xu Garden was privately built by silk merchant Xu Hongkui in 1883, and was used as an entertainment venue. For a fee of thirty cents, visitors could take a tour of the garden, see film projections and enjoy other entertainments, such as a magic show, fireworks and riddle competitions (Yao 2013).

12. The founder of the first film production studio in China was an American merchant who hired local Chinese to work for the company.

13. The first Chinese (partial) talkie *The Singing Girl Red Peony* (directed by Zhang Shichuan) was made in Shanghai by Mingxing company in 1929 with Pathé recording (Zhang Z. 2005: xxiv).

14. The founding companies of United Film Exchange included Mingxing, Shanghai Yingxi, Da Zhonghua-Baihe and Shenzhou. They were later joined by Minxin, Huaju and Youlian.

15. Different genres, such as detective stories, martial arts, fantasy, feminist, progressive and patriotic, etc., were developed in the early Chinese films in the 1920s and 1930s (S. Chung 2011; Sugawara 2011).

16. SFG consists of the former Shanghai Film Studio, Shanghai Animation Film Studio, Shanghai Dubbing Studio, Shanghai Documentary Film Studio, Shanghai Film

Technology Plant, Shanghai United Cinemas, East Film Distribution Company, Shanghai East Movie Channel, Shanghai Film Park, Shanghai Art Designing, and Crowne Plaza Hotel Shanghai. Source: 'About SFG', SFG's official website (English), www.sfs-cn.com (accessed 5 May 2015).

17. It was reported that by 2003, Shanghai had enjoyed 18 per cent of China's box-office returns (Goodridge 2003). In 2005, SFG already owned seventy-eight theatres with 241 screens (Noh 2006). SFG's exhibition networks include domestically owned and joint-venture cinemas (co-run by SFG's exhibition arm and major exhibitors from other countries, such as CJ CGV (South Korea) and Warner Bros. International Cinemas (United States)).

18. A mainland Chinese news report in 2001 suggested that, although the SARFT (now SAPPRFT) and the Shanghai Municipal government were the hosts of the Shanghai International Film Festival (SIFF), and the Shanghai Municipal Administration of Culture, Radio, Film & TV as the co-organizer, the actual planning, fund raising and implementation of the SIFF was carried out by a small-sized advertising company under the Shanghai Municipal Administration of Culture, Radio, Film & TV. The festival's daily operations were handled by SMEG Special Events Office (SSEO) under Shanghai Media & Entertainment Group (SMEG) before SMEG became part of the newly restructured Shanghai Media Group (SMG). The SIFF changed in 2004 from a biennial to an annual event held in June (Liu Y. and Tan Q. 2001; Davis and Yeh 2008: 143–45). See also 'About SMG', the Shanghai Media Group (SMG)'s official website (simplified Chinese), www.smg.cn (accessed 5 May 2015).

19. The year 2007 marked the birth of the SIFF Market (Noh 2013a). This film market not only serves the role of improving the chances of the SIFF's long-term self-sustenance (Shackleton 2008; R. Cheung 2011a: 50–51), but it also paves the way for this film market to carve out a space for international filmmakers, especially less experienced ones, to engage in real business. In 2012, the SIFF Market came to comprise the International Film Trade Market and Film Project Market, the latter consisting of the China Film Pitch and Catch (renamed in 2014 as New Talent Project), and Co-production Film Pitch and Catch. This move has allowed the SIFF as a whole to revise its identity into a more established and energetic festival that discovers new talent and independent films while facing fierce competition from the Beijing International Film Festival (BJIFF) established in April 2011 (Young Chinese Directors 2011; S-I. Yu 2011a, 2011b). See also 'About SIFF' and 'SIFFMART', the SIFF's official website (both English and simplified Chinese), www.siff.com (accessed 5 May 2015).

20. Source: 'About Us', the Japan Association for International Promotion of the Moving Image (UNIJAPAN)'s official website (English), unijapan.org (accessed 5 May 2015).

21. In terms of its position in the newest East Asian film business network, Tokyo, as representing Japan, does not show the extent of persistent proactivity and aggressiveness that Beijing, Shanghai or Busan have demonstrated through their film-related infrastructural arrangements. On the contrary, over the past one and half decades Tokyo has shown a continuously strong self-containment in hosting major

film industry events (e.g., re-concentrating the TIFF's focus on supporting local films after years of emphasizing a green environment) (Noh 2013b). The fact that these important events are scheduled in the middle of a busy autumn calendar of sizable international film festivals does not help Tokyo to hone its absolute uniqueness, except for a large concentration of Japanese film content business taking place at these events (Frater and Blair 2009). A further development in the 2012 and 2013 editions of the TIFF was that the TIFFCOM had been moved to a larger venue in the Odaiba area, far away from the main venue of the TIFF in Roppongi Hills (Noh 2012b). With a larger venue, chosen with the good intention of offering a combination of different creative industry products to potential buyers all under one roof, the TIFFCOM is no longer for film business only. Since 2012, the TIFFCOM has been held together with the Creative Market Tokyo, the Tokyo International Anime Festival (TIAF) and the Tokyo International Music Market (TIMM), all in one single location (TIFFCOM 2013: 2). This move inevitably defeats the purpose of facilitating the convenience of hosting the film festival and the film market side by side for the participants, and dilutes the sharp focus that used to be put on the film marketplace. With regard to all this, Tokyo seems easily overshadowed by Beijing or Busan in the minds of film executives, who are looking for transactions involving a wide array of Asian film contents instead of solely Japanese film contents at the TIFFCOM (Shackleton 2009a; Noh 2010; J. Gray 2012).

22. For example, in November 2001, the Fundamental Law for the Promotion of Culture and the Arts was formulated as 'the basic law for promoting culture and the arts' (Policy of Cultural Affairs in Japan 2014: 2). In 2002, the Committee on Film Promotion (made up mostly of film practitioners) was formed to investigate film-related measures, which resulted in the ¥2.5 billion Plan for Promoting Japanese Film and Image Media (i.e., worth about £14.6 million or U.S.$24 million), formulated in 2004 (Gerow 2006). Several other nationwide film-related public plans and policies were passed, including: the Basic Policy on the Promotion of Culture and the Arts (with the First Basic Policy approved by the cabinet in December 2002, the Second Basic Policy approved in February 2007 and the Third Basic Policy approved in February 2011) (Policy of Cultural Affairs in Japan 2014: 2); in 2003, the Plan for the Creation, Protection and Exploitation of Intellectual Property; and in 2004, the Content Promotion Law (Gerow 2006).

23. Sources: 'About AFCNet', the Japan Film Commission Promotion Council's official website (English), www.japanfc.org/film-com090329/en/about.html#08, and 'Successful Launching of AFCNet' (published on 12 October 2004) under 'News', the Asian Film Commissions Network (AFCNet)'s official website, www.afcnet.org (accessed 5 May 2015).

24. The Association for the Diffusion of Japanese Film Abroad was established in 1957 under the auspices of the Ministry of Foreign Affairs and the Ministry of Economy, Trade and Industry.

25. South Korea's biggest film conglomerates, such as CJ E&M Film Division (formerly CJ Entertainment), Lotte Entertainment and Showbox Mediaplex, set up their head-quarters in Seoul. Major American studios, like Twentieth Century Fox, also open distribution offices there.

26. The Asian Film Market (AFM) is an adjunct event to the Busan International Film Festival (BIFF). It was launched in 2006 and had two component parts, the Pusan Promotion Plan (PPP) and the Busan International Film Commission & Industry Showcase (BIFCOM) before 2011. Since the 2011 edition of the film festival, the PPP has been renamed as the Asian Project Market (APM) and listed directly under the umbrella event of the BIFF, instead of being a component of the AFM (R. Cheung 2011a: 48–50; see also the BIFF's official website (English), www.biff.kr, and 'Overview', the APM's official website (English), apm.asianfilmmarket.org (accessed 5 May 2015)).

27. The BIFF is now held annually in early October. Its name changed from the previous Pusan International Film Festival (PIFF) to the current one in February 2011, in order to align with the new version of the city name Busan, as a result of the revised Korean Romanization system adopted in 2000 (Ahn 2012: 165).

28. There are altogether ten such 'innovation cities' in South Korea, chosen to relieve the capital area Seoul of its excessive concentration of human resources and industry (Moon et al. 2013: 64).

29. Source: 'About KOFIC', Korean Film Biz Zone's official website (English), www.koreanfilm.or.kr (accessed 5 May 2015).

30. The current KOFIC comprises the former Korean Motion Picture Promotion Corporation (established in 1973), the Korean Academy of Film Arts (established in 1984) and Seoul (Namyangju) Studio complex (established in 1997) (Kim H-j. Circa 2006: 355; Davis and Yeh 2008: 21).

31. The KOFIC has published guidelines and industry updates (in English) for domestic and international film practitioners on a regular basis. The online English version of book-length publications such as the *Korean Cinema* series and *Korean Cinema: From Origins to Renaissance* introduces important aspects of South Korean Cinema to the world. The KOFIC's English-language online database, Korean Film Business Zone (KoBiz), www.koreanfilm.or.kr, was launched in April 2011.

32. There is only a film investment platform, the Golden Horse Film Project Promotion (established in 2007), affiliated to the Taipei Golden Horse Film Festival. Source: the Taipei Golden Horse Film Festival's official website (English), www.goldenhorse.org. tw (accessed 5 May 2015).

33. Central Motion Picture Company (CMPC) became privately run in 2003 and was renamed as Central Pictures Corporation (CPC) in 2009. Source: 'About Us', CPC's official website (traditional Chinese), www.movie.com.tw (accessed 5 May 2015).

34. In 1964, Taipei for the first time hosted the oldest film festival in East Asia, the Asian Film Festival (renamed from the Southeast Asian Film Festival in 1957; changing the name again to the Asia-Pacific Film Festival in 1982) (S. Lee 2011: 243). This film

festival has been run mainly by privately owned film studios in the region (R. Cheung 2011c: 203–4). In the inaugural edition of the festival, Taiwan won the Best Picture Award for *Oyster Girl* (Li Hsing and Li Chia, Taiwan, 1963).

35. Locally produced Taiwan films accounted for only 10 per cent of the domestic market share, whereas Hollywood films held more than 90 per cent of the share (after the attraction of Hong Kong films faded among the Taiwan audience); this was before some Taiwan local productions, such as romance drama *Cape No. 7* (Wei Te-sheng, Taiwan, 2009) and the semi-autobiographical youth romance film *You are the Apple of My Eye* (Giddens Ko, Taiwan, 2011) were box-office sensations (Taiwan's Summer Box Office Booming 2011).

36. The GIO announced in 2003 the plan to improve its funding policy to help both the mainstream film industry and art-house productions. A Domestic Film Guidance Fund was established to encourage co-productions between Taiwan and foreign collaborators (Shackleton 2003). A tax break of up to 20 per cent of the total budget of a film was introduced in 2005 to attract international filmmakers to shoot parts of their films in Taiwan (Shackleton 2005b). In 2006, a more comprehensive film development action plan was announced, which committed the government to putting in more money to support local film productions (Gao 2009: 432). In 2009, the GIO announced the Cultural Creative Development Policy, aimed at providing financial help to various creative industries, including filmmaking. This new support for local film production was expected to last for five years (Shackleton 2009c). In 2010, the Taiwan government announced an increase of subsidy for foreign filmmaking troops shooting films in Taiwan. This will indirectly increase their allowances for hiring Taiwanese film labourers (Taiwan to Increase Subsidy on Foreign Shoots 2010).

37. The GIO was dissolved in May 2012 as part of the government's restructuring ensuing from the democratization of Taiwan. The GIO's functions related to policies and matters of film and publications were transferred to the Ministry of Culture (Jennings 2012; L. Chung 2013).

38. Since April 2012, the Television and Entertainment Licensing Authority (TELA) has become part of the Office of the Communications Authority (OFCA). The TELA's previous functions are now shared by the Office for Film, Newspaper and Article Administration (OFNAA) under the OFCA and the Home Affairs Department (HAD). While the OFNAA handles film classification and obscenity control, the HAD is responsible for issuing entertainment licences. Source: the TELA's official website (English), www.tela.gov.hk (accessed 5 May 2015).

39. Personal interview with Li Cheuk-to, Artistic Director of the Hong Kong International Film Festival (HKIFF), conducted by the author in Hong Kong on 7 July 2010 (within the context of the 'Dynamics of World Cinema' project at the University of St Andrews).

40. According to Gao (2009: 431), 'The loan guarantee requires a qualified Hong Kong film production company to have equity of at least 30% of the film budget, and it guarantees 50% of the loan or a maximum of 35% of the film budget or $2.625 million

[£210,000 or U.S.$339,000], whichever is less'. See also 'Film Development Fund' and 'Film Guarantee Fund', the Hong Kong Film Development Council (HKFDC)'s official website (English), www.fdc.gov.hk (accessed 5 May 2015).

41. Source: 'Film Services', the Create Hong Kong (CreateHK)'s official website (English), www.createhk.gov.hk (accessed 5 May 2015).

42. Source: 'About Us', the Film Services Office (FSO)'s official website (English), www.fso-createhk.gov.hk (accessed 5 May 2015).

43. The Hong Kong International Film & TV Market (FILMART) was launched in 1997 by the Hong Kong Trade Development Council (HKTDC) and was initially held annually, in the month of June. Since March 2005, with the launch of the umbrella banner, the Entertainment Expo Hong Kong, FILMART has become a concurrent partner event of the HKIFF and six other formerly independent film and entertainment events. FILMART is not directly related to the structure and organization of the HKIFF, for they have different organizers. While FILMART's main organizer has always been the HKTDC, the HKIFF has gone through governmental direct supervision to currently being operated by a charitable, non-profit, non-governmental organization, the Hong Kong International Film Festival Society (HKIFFS). The two events have forged close working relationships over the years in areas such as programming (the HKIFF helps FILMART to programme its industry screening section on a payment basis) and venue sharing (FILMART shares the same venue with the Hong Kong-Asia Film Financing Forum (HAF). The HAF and the HKIFF have the same organizer, i.e., the HKIFFS) (R. Cheung 2011a: 47–48, 2011c: 201–3).

44. Personal interview with Li Cheuk-to, Artistic Director of the Hong Kong International Film Festival (HKIFF), conducted by the author in Hong Kong on 7 July 2010 (within the context of the 'Dynamics of World Cinema' project at the University of St Andrews). See also 'HKTDC Hong Kong International Film & TV Market (FILMART)', www.hktdc.com/fair/hkfilmart-en/Hong-Kong-International-Film---TV-Market--FILMART-.html, and 'About HKTDC', the HKTDC's official website (English), www.hktdc.com (accessed 5 May 2015).

45. Sources: the HKFDC's official website (English), www.fdc.gov.hk, and the FSO's official website (English), www.fso-createhk.gov.hk (accessed 5 May 2015).

46. Source: 'About Us', the CreateHK's official website (English), www.createhk.gov.hk (accessed 5 May 2015).

47. Source: 'CEPA', the Trade and Industry Department of the Hong Kong SAR government's official website (English), www.tid.gov.hk (accessed 5 May 2015).

48. During the Tung Chee-hwa's administration (1997–2005), the artistic sector of Hong Kong was to include only fine arts, gallery-bound visual arts and performing arts (1997 policy address). The cultural sector was vaguely identified, referring to the 'Chinese history and culture' (1997 policy address) and the 'protection of historic buildings and archaeological sites' (1998 policy address). Since Donald Tsang's administration (2005–12), the cultural sector has also included gallery and performing arts (2006–07, 2008–09, 2009–10 policy addresses). Source: 'Archives', the Hong Kong

SAR government chief executive's annual policy address official website (English), www.policyaddress.gov.hk (accessed 5 May 2015).

49. Source: 'Membership List of the Film Development Council (1 April 2015 – 31 March 2017)', the HKFDC's official website (English), www.fdc.gov.hk (accessed 5 May 2015).

50. Cheuk Pak Tong is a professor at the Academy of Film at the Hong Kong Baptist University.

51. Source: 'The Mainland and Hong Kong Closer Economic Partnership Arrangement Further Liberalization Measures in 2013', the Trade and Industry Department of the Hong Kong SAR government's official website (English), www.tid.gov.hk (accessed 5 May 2015).

52. The KOFIC opened a branch office, the Korean Business Center, in Beijing in April 2013 to facilitate joint ventures between the Chinese and the South Korean film industries (Lee H. 2013).

53. In February 2000, Japan established the Japan Film Commission Promotion Council (JFCPC) to offer location shooting support to international filmmakers through its local non-profit public film commissions. In April 2001, Tokyo Location Box was set up to be responsible for location shooting support in Tokyo. In April 2009, Japan Film Commission, with its main office based in Tokyo, was set up under several governmental ministries and agencies of the federal government to take over the previous tasks of the JFCPC. It united all the film commissions established in the previous eight years throughout Japan (J. Gray 2008; see also 'What is the Tokyo Location Box?' the Tokyo Location Box's official website (English), www.locationbox.metro.tokyo.jp (accessed 5 May 2015)).

54. Source: the AFCNet's official website, www.afcnet.org (accessed 5 May 2015).

55. The AFCNet has fifty regular members: one from the United Arab Emirates, one from Australia, two from Cambodia, two from China, two from Indonesia, seventeen from Japan, one from Jordan, two from Malaysia, one from Myanmar, one from Nepal, three from New Zealand, one from the Philippines, one from Russia, one from Singapore, ten from South Korea, one from Taiwan, one from Thailand, one from the United States, and one from Vietnam. These members include both local and national film commissions. Source: the AFCNet's official website, www.afcnet.org (accessed 5 May 2015).

56. There is no information on the AFCNet's official website showing how long the term is of the current president, vice-presidents and directors of the board. Source: the AFCNet's official website, www.afcnet.org (accessed 5 May 2015).

57. For more information on the SIFF Market, see note 19; for more information on the TIFFCOM, see note 21.

Conclusion

It was in the autumn of 2003, in my native Hong Kong, that I started serious academic research on contemporary Hong Kong Cinema; however, as I indicated in the Introduction to this monograph, I had been familiar with these films for most of my life. Now, in 2015, in my current home in the United Kingdom, I am completing the manuscript of this book. Looking back at these years of research on Hong Kong films that are so close to me (while it has always been a personal pleasure for me to watch these films, I can honestly say not all of them are objectively pleasing to watch), what strikes me most are not the films' aesthetic value or technical sophistication, but the fast pace of adaptation that the New Hong Kong Cinema displays towards changes in the larger environment, and the closeness of these films to the life of Hong Kong citizens. The latter point does not mean that all contemporary Hong Kong films fall under the category of realism. Far from that, many Hong Kong feature films made over the past thirty-plus years are human dramas that might or might not be true to life. The kind of closeness to life that the New Hong Kong Cinema perpetuates is more of an emotional kind. Moreover, the emotions involved in these films are connected to how people (filmmakers, target audiences, crews and casts, characters and so on) find themselves at home while not really being at home, and how they live at a historical crossroads – the effects of which are still unfolding before our eyes.

Studying the New Hong Kong Cinema as an exemplification of the Cinema of Transitions in a continuously changing East Asian region seems in itself to be a truism but we cannot afford to miss this perspective. I have employed the theoretical framework of accented cinema proposed by diaspora and film scholar Hamid Naficy (2001) in order to understand how 'transitions' are incorporated in Hong Kong filmmakers' specific ways of working. Their approaches to filmmaking, intentional or not, reflect individual concerns about transformations that have happened in the larger social, political, economic, cultural and film industry environments over the past several decades. Transitions are arguably what the New Hong Kong Cinema is made of. Yet, I should note that transitions are not exclusively the experience of Hong Kong citizens and filmmakers, nor did they happen to Hong Kong in a sudden and tragic fashion. On the contrary, the kind of terrible events we learn about from the international news every day (wars, tsunamis, earthquakes, bomb attacks, etc.) have never befallen Hong

Kong in all the thirty years since the news of the political Handover was first announced. By international standards, Hong Kong is still a metropolitan, and its sociopolitical conditions are more stable than in many comparable cities in the world. But the fears, anxieties and grievances, intermingled with a certain degree of excitement regarding all sorts of transitions revolving around and extending from the political Handover (transitions that are beyond the personal control of individuals), have been there among the ordinary people of the city and have been expressed in various cultural forms. As an agent and a reflecting lens of this society, the New Hong Kong Cinema provides a cathartic experience to people in front of and behind the screen, whether the films are human dramas, realistic depictions, animations, or documentaries, and whether they are comedies, tragedies or a mixture of both.

In writing this text, I have set out with several overarching questions (see Introduction) to guide my thinking. To answer these questions, I have discussed how Hong Kong filmmakers make use of 'journeys' and 'journeying' as common threads in feature films of different genres and natures. Journeys and journeying can be found in the subject matter of the films, in the routes by which the characters are developed, and in the narrative structure. Regardless of how journeys and journeying are employed in Hong Kong-related Chinese-language films, there is always a sense of rootlessness and helplessness just when people in and outside the films are facing the effects of the Handover and its related, ongoing transitions. I have also discussed how Hong Kong filmmakers feature foreigner and outsider characters in film to stand in for the Hongkongers, who in the 1980s and 1990s suddenly found themselves on the road to becoming 'Chinese' by nationality with or without their consent (Ang 2001: 36, 51). Some of these non-Hongkonger characters and their stories (e.g., Vietnamese refugees and illegal Chinese immigrants) were chosen during the time when they were heated topics in Hong Kong's sociopolitical domain. What these characters have in common, and what is of absolute importance for the Hong Kong Chinese audience to be able to identify with them and for other viewing publics to be able to recognize these films as Hong Kong films, is the fluent colloquial Cantonese they speak. Even more noticeable is their specific style of speaking the language that is exclusively used by the Hong Kong Cantonese speakers. The linguistic marker, then, immediately becomes the means for these Hong Kong-related Chinese-language films to intervene in the complexities of what it might possibly mean to become, and be, 'Chinese' once again. But the most direct device of all is when

Hong Kong filmmakers display their authorial vision by inscribing themselves in their films. I have examined how these filmmakers portray social underdogs in film to achieve such a goal, and thereby construct a space for revisiting certain collective memories shared among the locals in Hong Kong.

The exploration of how much, and how far, individual Hong Kong filmmakers display the consequences of sociopolitical changes in film has been balanced in this study by a consideration of the spectatorial responses of their ethnic Chinese audiences in East and South East Asia. Film audience reception involves complexities that are often neglected in the original filmmaking intentions. This is especially the case when film audiences in the Web 2.0 era are gradually taking over some of the traditional tasks of filmmakers and film marketers to reinterpret and spread around their views on the films via online platforms. The virtual Sinophone space that Sinitic-speaking/writing audiences have created for themselves adds yet another dimension to the intricacies of the transitions embodied in the New Hong Kong Cinema.

All these considerations and discourses regarding the state of transitions and interstitiality of the New Hong Kong Cinema would have been piecemeal and narrowly focused if we had only concentrated on Hong Kong itself without taking into account the conditions of the other parts of East Asia, especially in the post-Asian Financial Crisis era. I have thus inquired at another level into how Hong Kong's filmmaking and related film business environment have been experiencing structural transitions. Situating the New Hong Kong Cinema in East Asia has allowed me to interrogate how this cinematic practice fares astride and within the interstices among other East Asian cinematic systems. Hong Kong as a media capital maintains its distinct position in the region, while all the other cinematic nodes of the newest East Asian film business network are also trying to stay at, or return to, the peak levels of their competitiveness.[1] Yet, the distinctiveness of the New Hong Kong Cinema is honed not by the local government's film-related policies formulated recently, but by the persistent efforts of Hong Kong film professionals built up over the years. This quality is becoming most visible, and most paradoxical, when Hong Kong's film sector and the local identities it represents are moving towards a predominantly China-powered era, amid a realignment of power relations within the East Asian region. The regional restructuring in terms of hard and soft power, nonetheless, often hinges on other kinds of arrays and dis-arrays between East Asia and other regions. While researching the East Asian film business sphere, I noticed that there were new announcements being released in the film trade press about an increasing number of confirmed collaborations between East Asian and Euro-American film industry players. For the purpose of this book, I have deliberately limited my discussion of European and Hollywood influences in order to concentrate on what has been going on in East Asia. These interregional exchanges deserve close analyses, possibly using other paradigms that are beyond the scope of this book.

Under the China-led East Asian cinematic rearrangements, it is hard for me to say how long Hong Kong Cinema will continue to be called by that name, and I do not intend to speculate on the fate of the New Hong Kong Cinema in an unforeseeable future. It would be too pessimistic and unrealistic to do so. Instead, in this concluding note in my exploration of the New Hong Kong Cinema, let me recall what cultural theorist Ackbar Abbas advocated for the proposition of 'postculture' to understand Hong Kong's culture on the eve of its sovereignty shift. According to Abbas, '*postculture* ... is a culture that has developed in a situation where the available models of culture no longer work. In such a situation, culture cannot wait or follow social change in order to represent it; it must *anticipate* the paradoxes of hyphenation' (Abbas 1997: 145; emphasis in original), where the political mutant of 'hyphenation' embraces 'autonomy' and 'dependence' at the same time (Abbas 1997: 142). Anticipation here does not mean speculation; it signals a condition under which one is fully prepared for something unknown to come. In a similar vein, while the New Hong Kong Cinema can be read as a prime example of the Cinema of Transitions, which is haunted by human anxiety, uncertainties, fears, excitements, attachments, detachments, and so on, it is this alertness to changes that makes the New Hong Kong Cinema refuse to succumb easily to the negative effects of transitions. Based on the archetype of the New Hong Kong Cinema, I hope that the Cinema of Transitions model can provide a meaningful orientation for understanding other cinematic traditions and practices as well – cinemas that involve instabilities, possibilities and potentialities at given times of change in their corresponding social/cultural/political/economic/historical circumstances.

Note

1.   Except for China, which overall has maintained a steady growth in its film industry since the start of the new millennium, other major filmmaking countries and territories in East Asia suffered noticeable ups and downs in the 2000s. The Japanese

film industry recorded a historical low in the box-office earnings of its domestic films in 2002 (Gerow 2006). The South Korean film industry enjoyed a boom period between 1996 and 2006 before the bubble burst in around 2007. After that, volatility was noted in the South Korean film industry (Paquet 2009a: 28–29, 2010: 30–31). The performance of domestic Hong Kong and Taiwan films in their respective local box offices has been far from satisfactory (see Chapter Five for details). The mainland Chinese film industry is, however, not completely immune to negative factors. Piracy and strict government censorship are two major problems that have brought down its post-WTO growth (S. Wang 2003; L. Pang 2006a).

Appendix

Chinese-Language Blockbusters: Top Ten (2000–10) in Terms of Budget

Rank	Title	Release year	Budget (£ million)	Budget (U.S.$ million)
1	Red Cliff*	2008 and 2009	49	80
2	Curse of the Golden Flower	2006	27	45
3	The Promise*	2005	26	42
4	The Warlords*	2008	24	40
5	Hero*	2002	19	31
6	Aftershock*	2010	15	25
–	Three Kingdoms: Resurrection of the Dragon*	2008	15	25
7	Bodyguards and Assassins	2009	14	23
8	CJ7*	2008	12	20
–	Kung Fu Hustle*	2004	12	20
9	Battle of Wits	2006	10	16
10	Crouching Tiger, Hidden Dragon*	2000	9	15
–	Forever Enthralled*	2008	9	15
–	The Banquet	2006	9	15
–	The Myth*	2005	9	15
–	The Shinjuku Incident	2008	9	15

Notes

1. China Film Group Corporation (CFGC) was involved in the production and/or distribution of those films shown above with an asterisk.

2. Film information:
   Red Cliff (John Woo, China/Hong Kong/Japan/South Korea/Taiwan/United States, Part I in 2008 and Part II in 2009); Curse of the Golden Flower (Zhang Yimou, China/Hong Kong, 2006); The Promise (Chen Kaige, China/South Korea/United States, 2005); The Warlords (Peter Chan, China/Hong Kong, 2007); Hero (Zhang Yimou, China/Hong Kong, 2002); Aftershock (Feng Xiaogang, China, 2010); Three Kingdoms: Resurrection of the Dragon (Daniel Lee, China/Hong Kong/South Korea, 2008); Bodyguards and Assassins (Teddy Chan, China/Hong Kong, 2009); CJ7 (Stephen Chow, China/Hong Kong, 2008); Kung Fu Hustle (Stephen Chow, China/Hong Kong, 2004); Battle of Wits (Jacob Cheung, China/Hong Kong/Japan/South Korea, 2006); Crouching Tiger, Hidden Dragon (Ang Lee, China/Hong Kong/Taiwan/United States, 2000); Forever Enthralled (Chen Kaige, China/Hong Kong, 2008); The Banquet (Feng

Xiaogang, China, 2006); *The Myth* (Stanley Tong, China/Hong Kong, 2005); *The Shinjuku Incident* (Derek Yee, Hong Kong, 2009).

Source: budget figures mainly come from IMDb, www.imdb.com (accessed 5 May 2015) (see also Can Pricy Movie 2006).

Table A.2

Summary of Online Surveys of Interactive Websites Dedicated to *Red Cliff* (up until 24 August 2009)

Interactive platform on *Red Cliff's* official site (China) (chibi.sina.com.cn)
Total number of blog messages (written in simplified Chinese): 114   (hosted by sina.com.cn and linked to *Red Cliff's* China site)   • Number of positive comments: 73   • Number of negative comments: 41

Bebo/Friendster/MySpace
There were no messages about *Red Cliff*

Facebook
Total number of fan pages and member groups: 13   **Total number of fans/members registered with these pages: 3,738**   [Note: duplicate membership of the same fans/members is possible if they use different names to open more than one account on Facebook]   **Total number of posts about *Red Cliff*: 239**   • Number of messages in English and other languages: 233   • Number of messages in Chinese: 6   • Number of bilingual (English and Chinese) messages: 0   **Information of creators/administrators:**   • 1 based in LA, 1 based in Missouri, 2 based in Singapore, 9 with unknown locations   • All of these identified creators/administrators had Chinese surnames in their screen names

Twitter (15–24 August 2009)
Total number of tweets about *Red Cliff*: 153   • Number of tweets about *Red Cliff* (in English and other languages): 125   • Number of tweets about *Red Cliff* (in simplified/traditional Chinese): 28

Notes

1. This table was published as part of my piece 'Red Cliff: The Chinese-language Epic and Diasporic Chinese Spectators' (R. Cheung 2011b). It is reprinted here in a modified format for readers' easy reference. All statistics remain unchanged in this modified version.
2. No specific forum dedicated to Red Cliff was found online.

Table A.3
Summary of Online Survey of Interactive Websites Dedicated to Kaneshiro Takeshi (up until 24 August 2009)

Bebo
• **Total number of Bebo pages dedicated to Kaneshiro: 1 (in English)**
• **Total number of fans registered with that page: 24**
• **Total number of posts related to Red Cliff found on that page: 0**
Facebook
Total number of fan pages and member groups: 14
Total number of fans/members registered with these pages: 52,810
[Note: duplicate membership of the same fans/members is possible if they use different names to open more than one account on Facebook]
Total number of posts: 1,253
Total number of posts related to Red Cliff: 42
• Number of messages in English and other languages: 40
• Number of messages in Chinese: 2
• Number of bilingual (English and Chinese) messages: 1
Information of creators/administrators:
• 1 based in Australia, 1 based in France, 4 based in Hong Kong, 1 based in Massachusetts, 1 based in the United Kingdom, 6 with unknown locations
Friendster
There were no messages about Kaneshiro's role in Red Cliff
MySpace
• **Total number of pages dedicated to Kaneshiro: 10 (all in English)**
• **Total number of pages using Kaneshiro's name but not dedicated to him: 13**

Twitter (15–24 August 2009)

Total number of tweets about Kaneshiro's role in *Red Cliff*: 4

- Number of tweets about Kaneshiro's role in *Red Cliff* (in English and other languages): 4
- Number of tweets about Kaneshiro's role in *Red Cliff* (in simplified/traditional Chinese): 0

Individual fansites

---

9 individual fansites were found, with highlights as follows:

1) city.udn.com/1124

- Chinese-language site
- Taiwan-based forum but not interactive; information on the administrator not available
- Functioned as a Kaneshiro news portal

2) s7.invisionfree.com/SimplyTK

- English-language site with forum
- Hosted by a company in Virginia, the United States
- Administrator with Japanese background

3) tkaneshiro.net/site

- Chinese-language site
- Administrator (Maggie) with Chinese background, based in LA
- Forum inoperative

4) www.asianhunk.net/takeshi-kaneshiro
[Note: this website was found defunct in my 2013 survey]

- English-language site
- Information on the administrator not available
- Not updated since 22 March 2008; comments on Kaneshiro's role in *Red Cliff* not available

5) www.fulong.jp/kaneshiro/takeshi.html
[Note: this website was found defunct in my 2013 survey]

- Japanese-language site
- Official site hosted by Kaneshiro's agent company in Japan; without forum

6) www.geocities.com/Tokyo/Island/7258
[Note: this website was found defunct in my 2013 survey]

- English-language site
- Information on the administrator not available
- No forum

7) www.takeshikaneshiro.net

- Chinese-language site
- Administrator (Derrick Tao) with Chinese background, based in Hong Kong
- One of the most systematically organized fansites dedicated to Kaneshiro, consisting of an interactive forum that carries comprehensive thread messages written by fans (claimed to be based in different East/South East Asian territories)

8) www.takeshikaneshiro.org

- English-language site
- Information on the administrator not available
- Forum not utilized by the registered users (less than 50 registered users)
- Forum posts related to *Red Cliff* were written by the administrator only (all with nil reply)
  - 'Red Cliff Movie Review' (posted 17 July 2008) — views: 1,523
  - 'Red Cliff Movie New China Box-office Record' (posted 12 August 2008) — views: 1,570
  - 'Red Cliff Opens in Japan' (posted 25 October 2008) — views: 1,655
  - 'Red Cliff 2 to be Released on January 7th'(posted 30 December 2008) — views: 1,655
  - 'Red Cliff 2 Review' (posted 16 January 2009) — views: 1,022

9) www.takeshikaneshirocn.com
[Note: this website was found defunct in my 2013 survey]

- Chinese-language site based in mainland China
- Information on the administrator not available
- 19 news topics about *Red Cliff* (with a few replies) found on the forum

Note

This table was published as part of my piece '*Red Cliff*: The Chinese-language Epic and Diasporic Chinese Spectators' (R. Cheung 2011b). It is reprinted here in a modified format for readers' easy reference. All statistics remain unchanged in this modified version.

Table A.4

Summary of Follow-up Online Survey Related to *Red Cliff* (Conducted in 2013)

Sina Weibo

Total number of available posts about *Red Cliff* listed by Sina Weibo's search engine: 866,987

- All available posts listed had publication dates between 20 February 2013 and 24 August 2013
- No posts were archived before 20 February 2013
- All posts found were written in simplified Chinese characters within the word limit of 140 characters per post
- Sina Weibo had registration instructions page written in English, and simplified and traditional Chinese; internal web pages showed choices of simplified and traditional Chinese language interfaces only
- Most posts found were concerned with the stars on *Red Cliff*'s cast; others were about the film's topic of history and the lines in the film
- Many posts found were shared or forwarded posts

Tencent Weibo

Total number of available posts about *Red Cliff* listed by Tencent Weibo's search engine: 1,500

- All available posts listed had publication dates between 31 March 2010 and 2 August 2013
- Only 5 posts related to *Red Cliff* were posted during the surveyed period of 1 January to 24 August 2013
- All posts found were short and written in simplified Chinese characters (no word limit was clearly specified on the site)
- Tencent Weibo had registration instructions page written in traditional Chinese only, while its internal web pages showed the choices of English, and simplified and traditional Chinese language interfaces
- Most posts found were concerned with the stars on *Red Cliff*'s cast; others were about the film's topic of history and the lines in the film

Table A.5

Number of Sellers/Buyers/Visitors at Major East Asian Film Markets (2004–13): A Comparison

Year	AFM		BFM		FILMART		SIFF Market		TIFFCOM	
	No. of sellers	No. of buyers/ visitors	No. of sellers	No. of buyers/ visitors	No. of sellers	No. of buyers/ visitors	No. of sellers	No. of buyers/ visitors	No. of sellers	No. of buyers/ visitors
2004	-	-	-	-	306	2,023	-	-	No info	No info
2005	-	-	-	-	352	2,832	-	-	131	2,295 visitors
2006	562	3,500	-	-	407	3,706	-	-	163	2,923 visitors
2007	460	3,600	-	-	453	4,094	No info	No info	172	3,505 visitors
2008	508	4,640	-	-	483	4,196	No info	No info	201	4,006 visitors
2009	45* sales booths (BIFCOM excluded)	780	-	-	505	4,503	100	500	212	4,037 visitors
2010	51 sales booths	789	-	-	548	4,943	No info	800+	222	4,162 visitors
2011	109 sales booths (incl. BIFCOM)	1,080	No info	No info	596	5,073	143	2,015	226	800 buyers
2012	96 sales booths (incl. BIFCOM)	1,098	No info	4,000+	648	5,762	807	2,617	229	983 buyers
2013	92 sales booths (incl. BIFCOM)	1,272	200+	4,000+	710	6,317	819	2,718	261	**

*Since 2009, the AFM has recorded the attendance of the film sellers by the number of booths instead of by the number of exhibiting/selling companies.

**There is only combined data on the attendance of the buyers/sellers at the TIFFCOM, the TIAF and the TIMM of their 2013 editions, but no relevant information for separate events.

Sources: the official websites of the above film markets (see also Noh 2011b).

Filmography

English Title (Pinyin/Traditional Chinese/Simplified Chinese) (Director, Country, Main Market Release Year)
[Note: films shown with an asterisk do not have official titles written in Chinese scripts.]

2002 (Wilson Yip, Hong Kong, 2001)*

2046 (Wong Kar-wai, China/France/Germany/Hong Kong/Italy, 2004)*

300 (Zack Snyder, United States, 2007)*

4 Months, 3 Weeks and 2 Days (Cristian Mungiu, Belgium/Romania, 2007)*

A Beautiful Life (Bu Zai Rang Ni Gu Dan/不再讓你孤單/不再让你孤单) (Andrew Lau, China/Hong Kong, 2011)

A Better Tomorrow (Ying Xiong Ben Se/英雄本色/英雄本色) (John Woo, Hong Kong, 1986)

A Chinese Fairy Tale aka *A Chinese Ghost Story* (Qian Nu You Hun/倩女幽魂/倩女幽魂) (Wilson Yip, China/Hong Kong, 2011)

A Chinese Ghost Story (Qian Nu You Hun/倩女幽魂/倩女幽魂) (Tsui Hark, Hong Kong, 1987)

A Chinese Ghost Story II (Qian Nu You Hun II: Ren Jian Dao/倩女幽魂 II: 人間道/倩女幽魂 II: 人间道) (Ching Siu-tung, Hong Kong, 1990)

A Chinese Ghost Story III (Qian Nu You Hun III: Dao Dao Dao/倩女幽魂 III: 道道道/倩女幽魂 III: 道道道) (Ching Siu-tung, Hong Kong, 1991)

A Chinese Ghost Story: The Tsui Hark Animation (Xiao Qian/小倩/小倩) (Tsui Hark, Hong Kong, 1997)

A Simple Life (Tao Jie/桃姐/桃姐) (Ann Hui, Hong Kong, 2012)

After This Our Exile (Fu Zi/父子/父子) (Patrick Tam, Hong Kong, 2006)

Aftershock (Tang Shan Da Di Zhen/唐山大地震/唐山大地震) (Feng Xiaogang, China, 2010)

All about Ah-Long (A Lang De Gu Shi/阿郎的故事/阿郎的故事) (Johnnie To, Hong Kong, 1989)

All about Love (De Xian Chao Fan/得閒炒飯/得闲炒饭) (Ann Hui, Hong Kong, 2010)

An Autumn's Tale (Qiu Tian De Tong Hua/秋天的童話/秋天的童话) (Mabel Cheung, Hong Kong, 1987)

Arrest the Restless (Lan Jiang Zhuan Zhi Fan Fei Zu Feng Yun/藍江傳之反飛組風雲/蓝江传之反飞组风云) (Lawrence Ah Mon, Hong Kong, 1992)

As Tears Go by (Wang Jiao Kamen/旺角卡門/旺角卡门) (Wong Kar-wai, Hong Kong, 1988)

Au Revoir Mon Amour (He Ri Jun Zai Lai/何日君再來/何日君再来) (Tony Au, Hong Kong, 1991)

Back to 1942 (Yi Jiu Si Er/一九四二/一九四二) (Feng Xiaogang, China, 2012)

Bangkok Dangerous (Oxide and Danny Pang, Thailand, 1999)*

Bangkok Dangerous (Oxide and Danny Pang, United States, 2008)*

Battle of Wits (*Mo Gong*/墨攻/墨攻) (Jacob Cheung, China/Hong Kong/Japan/South Korea, 2006)

Beijing Rocks (*Beijing Le Yu Lu*/北京樂與路/北京乐与路) (Mabel Cheung, Hong Kong, 2001)

Blind Detective (*Mang Tan*/盲探/盲探) (Johnnie To, China/Hong Kong, 2013)

Boat People (*Tou Ben Nu Hai*/投奔怒海/投奔怒海) (Ann Hui, Hong Kong, 1982)

Bodyguards and Assassins (*Shi Yue Wei Cheng*/十月圍城/十月围城) (Teddy Chan, China/Hong Kong, 2009)

Born to be King (*Sheng Zhe Wei Wang*/勝者為王/胜者为王) (Andrew Lau, Hong Kong, 2000)

Breaking News (*Da Shi Jian*/大事件/大事件) (Johnnie To, China/Hong Kong, 2004)

Bruce Lee, My Brother (*Li Xiaolong*/李小龍/李小龙) (Manfred Wong and Raymond Yip, China/Hong Kong, 2010)

Buenos Aires Zero Degree: The Making of Happy Together (*She Shi Lin Du: Chun Guang Zha Xie*/攝氏零度: 春光乍洩/摄氏零度: 春光乍泄) (Kwan Pun-leung and Amos Lee, Hong Kong, 1999)

Cape No. 7 (*Hai Jiao Qi Hao*/海角七號/海角七号) (Wei Te-sheng, Taiwan, 2009)

Chengdu, I Love You (*Chengdu Wo Ai Ni*/成都我愛你/成都我爱你) (Cui Jian and Fruit Chan, China, 2009)

Chinese Box (Wayne Wong, France/Japan/United States, 1996)*

CJ7 (*Chang Jiang Qi Hao*/長江 7 號/长江 7 号) (Stephen Chow, China/Hong Kong, 2008)

Comrades, Almost a Love Story (*Tian Mi Mi*/甜蜜蜜/甜蜜蜜) (Peter Chan, Hong Kong, 1996)

Conspirators (*Tong Mou*/同謀/同谋) (Oxide Pang, Hong Kong, 2013)

Crossings (*Cuo Ai*/錯愛/错爱) (Evans Chan, Hong Kong, 1994)

Crouching Tiger, Hidden Dragon (*Wo Hu Cang Long*/臥虎藏龍/卧虎藏龙) (Ang Lee, China/Hong Kong/Taiwan/United States, 2000)

Curse of the Golden Flower (*Man Cheng Jin Dai Huang Jin Jia*/滿城盡帶黃金甲/满城尽带黄金甲) (Zhang Yimou, China/Hong Kong, 2006)

Days of Being Wild (*A Fei Zheng Zhuan*/阿飛正傳/阿飞正传) (Wong Kar-wai, Hong Kong, 1990)

Don't Go Breaking My Heart (*Dan Shen Nan Nu*/單身男女/单身男女) (Johnnie To and Wai Ka-fai, China/Hong Kong, 2011)

Don't Look up (Fruit Chan, Japan/South Africa/United States, 2009)*

Drug War (*Du Zhan*/毒戰/毒战) (Johnnie To, China/Hong Kong, 2012)

Drunken Master (*Zui Quan*/醉拳/醉拳) (Yuen Woo-ping, Hong Kong, 1978)

Dry Wood Fierce Fire (*Gan Chai Lie Huo*/乾柴烈火/乾柴烈火) (Wilson Yip, Hong Kong, 2002)

Dumplings (*Jiao Zi*/餃子/饺子) (Fruit Chan, Hong Kong, 2004)

Durian Durian (*Liu Lian Piao Piao*/榴槤飄飄/榴槤飄飄) (Fruit Chan, China/France/Hong Kong, 2000)

Echoes of the Rainbow (*Sui Yue Shen Tou*/歲月神偷/岁月神偷) (Alex Law, Hong Kong, 2010)

Eight Taels of Gold (*Ba Liang Jin*/八兩金/八两金) (Mabel Cheung, Hong Kong, 1989)

Eighteen Springs (*Ban Sheng Yuan*/半生緣/半生缘) (Ann Hui, China/Hong Kong, 1997)

Election (*Hei She Hui*/黑社會/黑社会) (Johnnie To, Hong Kong, 2005)

Election 2 aka *Triad Election* (*Hei She Hui: Yi He Wei Gui*/黑社會: 以和爲貴/黑社会: 以和为贵) (Johnnie To, Hong Kong, 2006)

Exiled (*Fang · Zhu*/放 · 逐/放 · 逐) (Johnnie To, Hong Kong, 2006)

Eye in the Sky (*Gen Zong*/跟蹤/跟踪) (Yau Nai-hoi, Hong Kong, 2007)

Farewell My Concubine (*Ba Wang Bie Ji*/霸王別姬/霸王别姬) (Chen Kaige, China/Hong Kong, 1993)

Finale in Blood (*Da Nao Guang Chang Long*/大鬧廣昌隆/大闹广昌隆) (Fruit Chan, Hong Kong, 1993)

Five Lonely Hearts (*Wu Ge Ji Mo De Xin*/五個寂寞的心/五个寂寞的心) (Fruit Chan, Hong Kong, 1991)

Floating Life (Clara Law, Australia, 1996)*

Flying Swords of Dragon Gate (*Long Men Fei Jia*/龍門飛甲/龙门飞甲) (Tsui Hark, China/Hong Kong, 2011)

Forever Enthralled (*Mei Lanfang*/梅蘭芳/梅兰芳) (Chen Kaige, China/Hong Kong, 2008)

From the Queen to the Chief Executive (*Deng Hou Dong Jian Hua Fa Luo*/ 等候董建華發落/等候董建华发落) (Herman Yau, Hong Kong, 2001)

Fulltime Killer (*Quan Zhi Sha Shou*/全職殺手/全职杀手) (Johnnie To and Wai Ka-fai, Hong Kong, 2001)

Gallants (*Da Lei Tai*/打擂台/打擂台) (Clement Cheng and Derek Kwok, Hong Kong, 2010)

Happy Together (*Chun Guang Zhe Xie*/春光乍洩/春光乍泄) (Wong Kar-wai, Hong Kong/Japan/South Korea, 1997)

He Ain't Heavy, He's My Father (*Xin Nan Xiong Nan Di*/新難兄難弟/新难兄难弟) (Peter Chan, Hong Kong, 1993)

Health Warning (*Da Lei Tai*/打擂台/打擂台) (Kirk Wong, Hong Kong, 1983)

Heaven and Earth (*Tian Yu Di*/天與地/天与地) (David Lai, China/Hong Kong, 1994)

Her Fatal Ways (*Biao Jie, Ni Hao Ye!*/表姐, 你好嘢!/表姐, 你好嘢!) (Alfred Cheung, Hong Kong, 1991)

Hero (*Ying Xiong*/英雄/英雄) (Zhang Yimou, China/Hong Kong, 2002)

Hollywood Hong Kong (*Xiang Gang You Ge He Li Huo*/香港有個荷里活/香港有个荷里活) (Fruit Chan, France/Hong Kong/Japan/United Kingdom, 2001)

Homecoming (*Si Shui Liu Nian*/似水流年/似水流年) (Yim Ho, Hong Kong, 1984)

Hong Kong, Hong Kong (*Nan Yu Nu*/男與女/男与女) (Clifford Choi, Hong Kong, 1983)

In the Mood for Love (*Hua Yang Nian Hua*/花樣年華/花样年华) (Wong Kar-wai, France/Hong Kong, 1999)

Infernal Affairs (*Wu Jian Dao*/無間道/无间道) (Andrew Lau and Alan Mak, Hong Kong, 2002)

Infernal Affairs II (Wu Jian Dao II/無間道 *II*/无间道 *II)* (Andrew Lau and Alan Mak, Hong Kong, 2003)

Infernal Affairs III (Wu Jian Dao III: Zhong Ji Wu Jian/無間道 *III:* 終極無間/无间道 *III:* 终极无间) (Andrew Lau and Alan Mak, Hong Kong, 2003)

Intruder (Kung Bu Ji/恐怖雞/恐怖鸡) (Tsang Kan-cheung, Hong Kong, 1997)

July Rhapsody (Nan Ren Si Shi/男人四十/男人四十) (Ann Hui, Hong Kong, 2002)

Just Like Weather (Mei Guo Xin/美國心/美国心) (Allen Fong, Hong Kong, 1986)

Kung Fu Hustle (Gong Fu/功夫/功夫) (Stephen Chow, China/Hong Kong, 2004)

Lan Yu (Lan Yu/藍宇/蓝宇) (Stanley Kwan, China/Hong Kong, 2001)

Leaving Me, Loving You (Da Cheng Xiao Shi/大城小事/大城小事) (Wilson Yip, Hong Kong, 2004)

Life without Principle (Duo Ming Jin/奪命金/夺命金) (Johnnie To, Hong Kong, 2011)

Lifeline (Shi Wan Huo Ji/十萬火急/十万火急) (Johnnie To, Hong Kong, 1997)

Little Cheung (Xi Lu Xiang/細路祥/细路祥) (Fruit Chan, Hong Kong, 2000)

Long Arm of the Law (Sheng Gang Qi Bing/省港旗兵/省港旗兵) (Johnny Mak, Hong Kong, 1984)

Love in a Fallen City (Qing Cheng Zhi Lian/傾城之戀/倾城之恋) (Ann Hui, Hong Kong, 1984)

Love in the Buff (Chunjiao Yu Zhiming/春嬌與志明/春娇与志明) (Edmond Pang Ho-cheung, China/Hong Kong, 2012)

Love on a Diet (Shou Shen Nan Nu/瘦身男女/瘦身男女) (Johnnie To and Wai Ka-fai, Hong Kong/Japan, 2001)

Made in Hong Kong (Xiang Gang Zhi Zao/香港製造/香港制造) (Fruit Chan, Hong Kong, 1997)

Mary from Beijing (Meng Xing Shi Fen/夢醒時分/梦醒时分) (Sylvia Chang, Hong Kong, 1992)

McDull, Kung Fu Kindergarten (Mai Dou Xiang Dang Dang/麥兜響噹噹/麦兜响噹噹) (Brian Tse, China/Hong Kong/Japan, 2009)

McDull. Me & My Mum (Mai Dou. Wo He Wo Ma Ma/麥兜・我和我媽媽/麦兜・我和我妈妈) (Brian Tse and Li Junmin, China/Hong Kong, 2014)

McDull, Prince de la Bun (Mai Dou Bo Luo You Wang Zi/麥兜菠蘿油王子/麦兜菠萝油王子) (Toe Yuen, Hong Kong, 2004)

McDull, The Alumni (Chun Tian Hua Hua Tong Xue Hui/春田花花同學會/春田花花同学会) (Samson Chiu, Hong Kong, 2006)

Men Suddenly in Black (Da Zhang Fu/大丈夫/大丈夫) (Edmond Pang Ho-cheung, Hong Kong, 2003)

My Left Eye Sees Ghosts (Wo Zuo Yan Jian Dao Gui/我左眼見到鬼/我左眼见到鬼) (Johnnie To and Wai Ka-fai, Hong Kong, 2002)

My Life as McDull (Mai Dao Gu Shi/麥兜故事/麦兜故事) (Toe Yuen, Hong Kong, 2001)

Needing You ... (Gu Nan Gua Nu/孤男寡女/孤男寡女) (Johnnie To and Wai Ka-fai, Hong Kong, 2000)

Night and Fog (Tian Shui Wei De Ye Yu Wu/天水圍的夜與霧/天水围的夜与雾) (Ann Hui, Hong Kong, 2009)

Once a Gangster (Fei Sha Feng Zhong Zhuan/飛砂風中轉/飞砂风中转) (Felix Chong, Hong Kong, 2010)

Once upon a Time in China and America (Huang Feihong Zhi Xi Yu Xiong Shi/ 黃飛鴻之西域雄獅/黄飞鸿之西域雄狮) (Sammo Hung, Hong Kong, 1997)

Ordinary Heroes (Qian Yan Wan Yu/千言萬語/千言万语) (Ann Hui, Hong Kong, 1999)

Oyster Girl (Ke Nu/蚵女/蚵女) (Li Hsing and Li Chia, Taiwan, 1963)

Painted Skin (Hua Pi/畫皮/画皮) (Gordon Chan, China/Hong Kong, 2008)

Perhaps Love (Ru Guo. Ai/如果 · 愛/如果 · 爱) (Peter Chan, China/Hong Kong/Malaysia, 2005)

Pirates of the Caribbean: At World's End (Gore Verbinski, United States, 2007)*

Pirates of the Caribbean: Dead Man's Chest (Gore Verbinski, United States, 2006)*

Pirates of the Caribbean: Dead Men Tell No Tales (Joachim Rønning and Espen Sandberg, United States, 2017)*

Pirates of the Caribbean: On Stranger Tides (Rob Marshall, United States, 2011)*

Pirates of the Caribbean: The Curse of the Black Pearl (Gore Verbinski, United States, 2003)*

Portland Street Blues (Gu Huo Zai Qing Yi Pian Zhi Hong Xing Shi San Mei/ 古惑仔情義篇之洪興十三妹/古惑仔情义篇之洪兴十三妹) (Raymond Yip, Hong Kong, 1998)

PTU (Johnnie To, Hong Kong, 2003)*

Public Toilet (Ren Min Gong Ce/人民公廁/人民公厕) (Fruit Chan, Hong Kong/Japan/South Korea, 2002)

Punished (Bao Ying/報應/报应) (Law Wing-cheong, Hong Kong, 2011)

Rebel Without a Cause (Nicholas Ray, United States, 1955)*

Red Cliff (Chi Bi/赤壁/赤壁) (John Woo, China/Hong Kong/Japan/South Korea/Taiwan/United States, 2008)

Red Cliff II (Chi Bi: Jue Zhan Tian Xia/赤壁: 決戰天下/赤壁: 决战天下) (John Woo, China/Hong Kong/Japan/South Korea/Taiwan/United States, 2009)

Ringu (Nakata Hideo, Japan, 1998)*

Romancing in Thin Air (Gao Hai Ba Zhi Lian II/高海拔之戀 II/高海拔之恋 II) (Johnnie To, China/Hong Kong, 2012)

Run and Kill (Wu Shu Ji Mi Dang An/烏鼠機密檔案/乌鼠机密档案) (Billy Tang Hin-sing, Hong Kong, 1993)

Running on Karma (Da Zhi Lao/大隻佬/大只佬) (Johnnie To and Wai Ka-fai, China/Hong Kong, 2003)

Running out of Time (An Zhan/暗戰/暗战) (Johnnie To, Hong Kong, 1999)

Shaolin Soccer (Shaolin Zu Qiu/少林足球/少林足球) (Stephen Chow, China/Hong Kong, 2001)

Skyline Cruisers (Shen Tou Ci Shi Dai/神偷次世代/神偷次世代) (Wilson Yip, Hong Kong, 2000)

Snake in the Eagle's Shadow (She Xing Diao Shou/蛇形刁手/蛇形刁手) (Yuen Woo-ping, Hong Kong, 1978)

Snakes on a Plane (David R. Ellis, United States, 2006)*

Song of the Exile (*Ke Tu Qiu Hen*/客途秋恨/客途秋恨) (Ann Hui, Hong Kong/Taiwan, 1990)

Sparrow (*Wen Que*/文雀/文雀) (Johnnie To, Hong Kong, 2008)

Spirited Away (Miyazaki Hayao, Japan, 2001)*

Starry is the Night (*Jin Ye Xing Guang Can Lan*/今夜星光燦爛/今夜星光灿烂) (Ann Hui, Hong Kong, 1988)

Summer Snow (*Nu Ren, Si Shi.*/女人，四十./女人，四十.) (Ann Hui, Hong Kong, 1995)

Tales from the Dark (Part 1) (*Li Bi Hua Gui Mei Xi Lie Mi Li Ye*/ 李碧華鬼魅系列《迷離夜》/李碧华鬼魅系列《迷离夜》) (Fruit Chan/Lee Chi-ngai/Simon Yam, Hong Kong, 2013)

Tales from the Dark (Part 1): Jing Zhe (*Li Bi Hua Gui Mei Xi Lie Mi Li Ye: Jing Zhe*/ 李碧華鬼魅系列《迷離夜》：《驚蟄》/李碧华鬼魅系列《迷离夜》：《惊蛰》) (Fruit Chan, Hong Kong, 2013)

Temptress Moon (*Feng Yue*/風月/风月) (Chen Kaige, China/Hong Kong, 1996)

The Banquet (*Ye Yan*/夜宴/夜宴) (Feng Xiaogang, China, 2006)

The Battle of Dingjunshan aka *Conquering Jun Mountain* (*Dingjunshan*/定軍山/定军山) (Ren Jingfeng, China, 1905)

The Border (Won San-man, Korea, 1923)*

The Crossing: Part 1 (*Tai Ping Lun (Shang)*/太平輪（上）/太平轮（上）) (John Woo, China/Hong Kong, 2014)

The Crossing: Part 2 (*Tai Ping Lun (Xia)*/太平輪（下）/太平轮（下）) (John Woo, China/Hong Kong, 2015)

The Detective (*C Jia Zhen Tan*/C+偵探/C+侦探) (Oxide Pang, Hong Kong, 2007)

The Detective 2 (*B Jia Zhen Tan*/B+偵探/B+侦探) (Oxide Pang, Hong Kong, 2011)

The Enchanting Shadow (*Qian Nu You Hun*/倩女幽魂/倩女幽魂) (Li Han-hsiang, Hong Kong, 1960)

The Enigmatic Case (*Bi Shui Han Shan Duo Ming Jin*/碧水寒山奪命金/碧水寒山夺命金) (Johnnie To, Hong Kong, 1980)

The Eye (*Jian Gui*/見鬼/见鬼) (Oxide and Danny Pang, Hong Kong/Singapore, 2002)

The Eye 2 (*Jian Gui 2*/見鬼 2/见鬼 2) (Oxide and Danny Pang, Hong Kong/Singapore, 2004)

The Eye 10 aka *The Eye Infinity* and *The Eye 3* (*Jian Gui 10*/見鬼 10/见鬼 10) (Oxide and Danny Pang, Hong Kong, 2005)

The Floating Landscape (*Lian Zhi Feng Jing*/戀之風景/恋之风景) (Carol Lai, Hong Kong, 2003)

The Flowers of War (*Jinling Shi San Chai*/金陵十三釵/金陵十三钗) (Zhang Yimou, China/Hong Kong, 2011)

The Grandmaster (*Yi Dai Zong Shi*/一代宗師/一代宗师) (Wong Kar-wai, China/Hong Kong, 2013)

The Last Supper (*Wang De Sheng Yan*/王的盛宴/王的盛宴) (Lu Chuan, China, 2012)

The Longest Summer (*Qu Nian Yan Hua Te Bie Duo*/去年煙花特別多/去年煙花特別多) (Fruit Chan, Hong Kong, 1998)

*The Man from Vietnam (Yue Nan Zai/*越南仔/越南仔*)* (Clarence Fok, Hong Kong, 1982)

*The Midnight After (Na Ye Ling Chen, Wo Zuo Shang Liao Wang Jiao Kai Wang Da Bu De Hong Van/*那夜凌晨, 我坐上了旺角開往大埔的紅*Van/*那夜凌晨, 我坐上了旺角开往大埔的紅*Van)* (Fruit Chan, Hong Kong, 2014)

*The Mission (Qiang Huo/*鎗火/枪火*)* (Johnnie To, Hong Kong, 1999)

*The Myth (Shen Hua/*神話/神话*)* (Stanley Tong, China/Hong Kong, 2005)

*The Pork of Music (Mai Dou. Dang Dang Ban Wo Xin/*麥兜‧噹噹伴我心/麦兜‧当当伴我心*)* (Brian Tse, China/Hong Kong, 2012)

The Postmodern Life of My Aunt (Yi Ma De Hou Xian Dai Sheng Huo/ 姨媽的後現代生活/姨妈的后现代生活*)* (Ann Hui, China/Hong Kong, 2006)

*The Promise (Wu Ji/*無極/无极*)* (Chen Kaige, China/South Korea/United States, 2005)

*The Secret (Feng Jie/*瘋劫/疯劫*)* (Ann Hui, Hong Kong, 1979)

*The Shinjuku Incident (Xin Su Shi Jian/*新宿事件/新宿事件*)* (Derek Yee, Hong Kong, 2009)

*The Singing Girl Red Peony (Ge Nu Hong Mu Dan/*歌女紅牡丹/歌女红牡丹*)* (Zhang Shichuan, China, 1929)

*The Stool Pigeon (Xian Ren/*綫人/线人*)* (Dante Lam, Hong Kong, 2010)

*The Story of Woo Viet (Hu Yue De Gu Shi/*胡越的故事/胡越的故事*)* (Ann Hui, Hong Kong, 1981)

*The Stunt Woman (A Jin/*阿金/阿金*)* (Ann Hui, Hong Kong, 1996)

The Umbrellas of Cherbourg (Jacques Demy, France/West Germany, 1964)*

*The Warlords (Tou Ming Zhuang/*投名狀/投名状*)* (Peter Chan, China/Hong Kong, 2007)

*The Way We Are (Tian Shui Wei De Ri Yu Ye/*天水圍的日與夜/天水围的日与夜*)* (Ann Hui, Hong Kong, 2008)

*Three (San Geng/*三更/三更*)* (Peter Chan/Kim Jee-won/Nonzee Nimibutr, Hong Kong/South Korea/Thailand, 2002)

*Three … Extremes (San Geng 2/*三更 2/三更 2*)* (Fruit Chan/Miike Takashi/Park Chan-wook, Hong Kong/Japan/South Korea, 2004)

*Three: Going Home (San Geng Zhi Hui Jia/*三更之回家/三更之回家*)* (Peter Chan, Hong Kong, 2002)

*Three Kingdoms: Resurrection of the Dragon (San Guo Zhi Jian Long Xie Jia/*三國之見龍卸甲/三国之见龙卸甲*)* (Daniel Lee, China/Hong Kong/South Korea, 2008)

*Thunderstorm (Lei Yu/*雷雨/雷雨*)* (Ng Wui, Hong Kong, 1957)

*Tiny Times 1.0 (Xiao Shi Dai/*小時代/小时代*)* (Guo Jingming, China, 2013)

*To Liv(e) (Fu Shi Lian Qu/*浮世戀曲/浮世恋曲*)* (Evans Chan, Hong Kong, 1991)

*Turn Left, Turn Right (Xiang Zuo Zou, Xiang You Zou/*向左走‧向右走/向左走‧向右走*)* (Johnnie To and Wai Ka-fai, Hong Kong/Singapore, 2003)

*Vulgaria (Di Su Xi Ju/*低俗喜劇/低俗喜剧*)* (Edmond Pang Ho-cheung, Hong Kong, 2012)

*Wong Fei-hung's Fight at Henan (Huang Fei-hong Henan Yu Xie Zhan/*黃飛鴻河南浴血戰/黄飞鸿河南浴血战*)* (Wu Pang, Hong Kong, 1957)

*Yesterday Once More (Long Feng Dou/*龍鳳鬥/龙凤斗*)* (Johnnie To, Hong Kong, 2004)

*You are the Apple of My Eye (Na Xie Nian, Wo Men Yi Qi Zhui De Nu Hai/*那些年, 我們一起追的女孩/那些年, 我们一起追的女孩*)* (Giddens Ko, Taiwan, 2011)

Young and Dangerous (*Gu Huo Zai Zhi Ren Zai Jiang Hu*/古惑仔之人在江湖/古惑仔之人在江湖) (Andrew Lau, Hong Kong, 1996)

Young and Dangerous 2 (*Gu Huo Zai 2 Zhi Meng Long Guo Jiang*/古惑仔 2 之猛龍過江/古惑仔 2 之猛龙过江) (Andrew Lau, Hong Kong, 1996)

Young and Dangerous 3 (*Gu Huo Zai 3 Zhi Zhi Shou Zhe Tian*/古惑仔 3 之隻手遮天/古惑仔 3 之只手遮天) (Andrew Lau, Hong Kong, 1996)

Young and Dangerous 4 (*97 Gu Huo Zai Zhan Wu Bu Sheng*/97 古惑仔戰無不勝/97 古惑仔战无不胜) (Andrew Lau, Hong Kong, 1997)

Young and Dangerous 5 (*98 Gu Huo Zai Zhi Long Zheng Hu Dou*/98 古惑仔之龍爭虎鬥/98 古惑仔之龙争虎斗) (Andrew Lau, Hong Kong, 1998)

Zhuangzi Tests His Wife (*Zhuangzi Shi Qi*/莊子試妻/莊子试妻) (Lai Man-wai, Hong Kong, 1913)

Bibliography

'10th Osian's-Cinefan Festival to Open with *The Sparrow*'. 2008. *Tribune Business News*, 9 July.

'1925: Taiwan Gets into the Game'. No date. *The Chinese Mirror: A Journal of Chinese Film History*. Retrieved 5 May 2015 from http://www.chinesemirror.com/index/taiwan.

'A Description of China's Film Industry'. 2007. *Variety*, 46(13), 14 May.

'A Quarter of Hong Kong Film Professionals Have Moved to Beijing' (in traditional Chinese). 2013. *Asia Pacific Daily*, 25 October. Retrieved 5 May 2015 from https://hk.news.yahoo.com/香港電影人才北移-1-4定居北京-074954494.html.

Abbas, Ackbar. 1994. 'The New Hong Kong Cinema and the "Déjà Disparu"', *Discourse* 16(3): 65–77.

———. 1997. *Hong Kong: Culture and the Politics of Disappearance*. Minnesota: University of Minnesota Press.

Acquarello. 2001. '*Liulian Piao Piao*, 2000 [*Durian Durian*]', *Strictly Film School* website. Retrieved 5 May 2015 from http://www.filmref.com/directors/dirpages/chan.html.

Ahn, SooJeong. 2009. 'Placing South Korean Cinema into the Pusan International Film Festival: Programming Strategy in the Global/Local Context', in Chris Berry, Nicola Liscutin and Jonathan D. Mackintosh (eds), *Cultural Studies and Cultural Industries in Northeast Asia: What a Difference a Region Makes*. Hong Kong: Hong Kong University Press, pp. 73–86.

———. 2012. *The Pusan International Film Festival, South Korean Cinema and Globalization*. Hong Kong: Hong Kong University Press.

Amato, Mary Jane, and J. Greenberg. 2000. 'Swimming in Winter: An Interview with Wong Kar-Wai', *Kabinet*, 5, Summer. Retrieved 8 April 2006 from http://www.kabinet.org/magazine/issue5/wkw1.html [now defunct].

Ambroisine, Fred. 2010. 'Clement Cheng: The "Gallants" Interview (Part 1)', *Twitch*, 3 June. Retrieved 5 May 2015 from http://twitchfilm.com/2010/06/clement-cheng-the-gallants-interview-part-1.html.

———. 2011. 'Clement Cheng: The "Gallants" Interview (Part 2)', *Twitch*, 16 January. Retrieved 5 May 2015 from http://twitchfilm.com/2011/01/clement-cheng-the-gallants-interview-part-2.html.

'An Interview with Ann Hui: A Period of Tumult and *Ordinary Heroes*' (in traditional Chinese). 1999. *City Entertainment*, 521, 1–14 April, 27–29.

An, Young-jin (Korean ed.), and Ellen Kim (English ed.). 2008. *The Guide to Korean Film Industry and Production*. Seoul: Korean Film Council.

Anderson, Benedict. 1983 (revised ed. 1991 and 2006). *Imagined Communities: Reflections on the Origin and Spread of Nationalism*. London: Verso.

Ang, Ien. 1991. *Desperately Seeking the Audience*. London and New York: Routledge.

———. 1998. 'Can One Say No to Chineseness? Pushing the Limits of the Diasporic Paradigm', *boundary 2* 25(3): 223–42.

———. 2001. *On Not Speaking Chinese: Living Between Asia and the West*. London: Routledge.

'Ann Hui' (in traditional Chinese). 1990. *City Entertainment*, 289, 26 April, 12–17.

Appadurai, Arjun. 1990. 'Disjuncture and Difference in the Global Cultural Economy', *Public Culture* 2(2): 1–24.

———. 1996. *Modernity at Large: Cultural Dimensions of Globalization*. Minnesota: University of Minnesota Press.

Asch, Mark. 2007. 'Sergio Leone, Hong Kong Cinema and Johnnie To's *Exiled*', *Stopsmiling*, 4 September. Retrieved 5 May 2015 from http://www.stopsmilingonline.com/story_detail.php?id=879.

Ash, Robert, Peter Ferdinand, Brian Hook, and Robin Porter (eds). 2000. *Hong Kong in Transition: The Handover Years*. Hampshire and London: Macmillan Press; New York: St. Martin's Press.

———. (eds). 2003. *Hong Kong in Transition: One Country, Two Systems*. London and New York: RoutledgeCurzon.

'At the Box Office: My Generation'. 2013. *The Economist*, 20 July. Retrieved 5 May 2015 from http://www.economist.com/news/china/21582049-new-film-divides-public-opinion-my-generation.

Austin, Thomas. 2002. *Hollywood, Hype and Audiences: Selling and Watching Popular Film in the 1990s*. Manchester and New York: Manchester University Press.

Barker, Martin, with Thomas Austin. 2000. *From Antz to Titanic: Reinventing Film Analysis*. Virginia: Pluto Press.

Berry, Chris (ed.). 1985. *Perspectives on Chinese Cinema*. New York: Cornell University Press. Reprinted 1991 and 2003. London: BFI.

Berry, Chris, and Mary Farquhar. 2006. *China on Screen: Cinema and Nation*. New York: Columbia University Press.

Berry, Chris, Nicola Liscutin, and Jonathan D. Mackintosh (eds). 2009. *Cultural Studies and Cultural Industries in Northeast Asia: What a Difference a Region Makes*. Hong Kong: Hong Kong University Press.

Berry, Michael. 2005. *Speaking in Images: Interviews with Contemporary Chinese Filmmakers*. New York: Columbia University Press.

'Between Human and Pig: *Hollywood Hong Kong*' (in traditional Chinese). 2002. *City Entertainment*, 610, 29 August–11 September, 96.

Bhabha, Homi K. 1994. 'How Newness Enters the World: Postmodern Space, Postcolonial Times and the Trials of Cultural Translation', in Homi K. Bhabha, *The Location of Culture*. London and New York: Routledge, pp. 212–56.

'*Boat People* Reappears after Ten Years of Shelving' (in traditional Chinese). 1992. *City Entertainment*, 338, 19 March–1 April, 26.

Bordwell, David. 1979. 'The Art Cinema as a Mode of Film Practice', *Film Criticism* 4(1): 56–64.

———. 2000. *Planet Hong Kong: Popular Cinema and the Art of Entertainment.* Massachusetts: Harvard University Press.

———. 2003. 'The Films of Johnnie To Louder than Words', *Artforum* 41(9), May, 155–57.

Braziel, Jana Evans, and Anita Mannur (eds). 2003. *Theorizing Diaspora: A Reader.* Massachusetts: Blackwell Publishing.

Browne, Nick, Paul G. Pickowicz, Vivian Sobchack, and Esther Yau (eds). 1994. *New Chinese Cinemas: Forms, Identities, Politics.* Cambridge: Cambridge University Press.

Brunette, Peter. 2005. *Wong Kar-wai.* Illinois: University of Illinois Press.

Bunch, Sonny. 2009. 'Movie Review: "Red Cliff"', *The Washington Times,* 27 November. Retrieved 5 May 2015 from http://www.washingtontimes.com/news/2009/nov/27/movie-review-red-cliff.

Burgoyne, Robert (ed.). 2011. *The Epic Film in World Culture.* New York: Routledge.

Busse, Kristina. 2009. 'In Focus: Fandom and Feminism: Gender and the Politics of Fan Production: Introduction', *Cinema Journal* 48(4): 104–7.

———. 2013. 'Geek Hierarchies, Boundary Policing, and the Gendering of the Good Fan', *Participations* 10(1), May: 73–91. Retrieved 5 May 2015 from http://www.participations.org/Volume 10/Issue 1/6 Busse 10.1.pdf.

Campbell, Kurt M. 2011. 'Asia Overview: Protecting American Interests in China and Asia', Testimony before the House Committee on Foreign Affairs Subcommittee on Asia and the Pacific, U.S. Department of State, 31 March. Retrieved 5 May 2015 from http://www.state.gov/p/eap/rls/rm/2011/03/159450.htm.

Camper, Fred. 2007. 'The Blood and the Beauty: The Visual Poetry of Johnnie To's Gangster Films Counters their Nihilism', *Chicago Reader,* 6 September. Retrieved 5 May 2015 from http://www.chicagoreader.com/chicago/the-blood-and-the-beauty/Content?oid=925884.

'Can Pricy Movie Produce Profit?'. 2006. *Xinhuanet* (source: *Shanghai Daily*), 9 February. Retrieved 5 May 2015 from http://news.xinhuanet.com/english/2006-02/09/content_4156217.htm.

Cavicchi, Daniel. 1998. *Tramps Like Us: Music and Meaning among Springsteen Fans.* Oxford and New York: Oxford University Press.

Chakrabarty, Dipesh. 1998. 'Reconstructing Liberalism? Notes toward a Conversation between Area Studies and Diasporic Studies', *Public Culture* 10(3): 457–81.

Chan, Ching-wai. 2000. *The Structure and Marketing Analysis of the Hong Kong Film Industry* (in traditional Chinese). Hong Kong: Film Biweekly Publishing House Limited.

Chan, Fruit. 2000. 'Director's Note: *Durian Durian*' (in traditional Chinese), *City Entertainment,* 546, 16 March, 51.

Chan, Joseph, Anthony Y.H. Fung, and Chun Hung Ng. 2010. *Policies for the Sustainable Development of the Hong Kong Film Industry.* Hong Kong: Chinese University of Hong Kong.

Chan, Stephen. 1999. 'What is This Thing Called a Chinese Diaspora?', *Contemporary Review* February: 81–83.

Chan, Steve. 2015. 'Film Entertainment Industry in Hong Kong', Hong Kong Trade Development Council, 6 March. Retrieved 5 May 2015 from http://hong-kong-economy-research.hktdc.com/business-news/article/Hong-Kong-Industry-Profiles/Film-Entertainment-Industry-in-Hong-Kong/hkip/en/1/1X000000/1X0018PN.htm.

Chan, Suet-ling. 2012a. 'Beijing Officials and Mass Media Threaten the Chinese University of Hong Kong' (in traditional Chinese), *Apple Daily*, 14 November, A1.

———. 2012b. 'Conflicts Intensified between Hong Kong and Mainland China: Identification Falls to the Historic Low since Handover' (in traditional Chinese), *Apple Daily*, 12 November, A2.

Chang, Bryan. 2002. '*Hollywood Hong Kong*: Fruit Chan's Heaven and Hell', trans. Maggie Lee, *Hong Kong Panorama 2001-2002*, 26th Hong Kong International Film Festival. Hong Kong: Hong Kong Arts Development Council, pp. 86–88.

Chen, Ru-shou Robert. 1998. 'Taiwan Cinema', in Yingjin Zhang and Zhiwei Xiao (eds), *Encyclopedia of Chinese Film*. London and New York: Routledge, pp. 47–62.

Cheng, Shui-kam. 2002. 'The Change in the Prostitute Identity in Fruit Chan's Films: From *Durian Durian* to *Hollywood Hong Kong*' (in traditional Chinese), *Twenty-First Century* 73, October: 85–89.

Cheng, Tin-yee. 2014. 'Big Spender: Johnnie To and Fun' (in traditional Chinese), *Apple Daily*, 28 August. Retrieved 5 May 2015 from http://hk.apple.nextmedia.com/supplement/big_spender/art/20140828/18845415.

Cheuk, Pak Tong. 2008. *Hong Kong New Wave Cinema (1978-2000)*. Bristol: Intellect.

———. 2012. 'Ann Hui and Cheuk Pak Tong on Hong Kong New Wave' (in traditional Chinese), in Kwong Po-wai (ed.), *Director Ann Hui*. Hong Kong: Eucalyptus House, pp. 457–72.

Cheung, Carmen. 1998. 'HK Chasing $1.6b Debt from UN', *Hong Kong Standard*, 25 August. Retrieved 5 May 2015 from http://www.thestandard.com.hk/news_detail.asp?pp_cat=&art_id=40740&sid=&con_type=1&d_str=19980825&sear_year=1998.

Cheung, Esther M.K. 2008. 'Durian Durian: Defamiliarisation of the "Real"', in Chris Berry (ed.), *Chinese Films in Focus II*. Hampshire and New York: Palgrave Macmillan/BFI, pp. 90–97.

———. 2009. *Fruit Chan's Made in Hong Kong*. Hong Kong: Hong Kong University Press.

Cheung, Esther M.K., and Chu Yiu-wai (eds). 2004. *Between Home and World: A Reader in Hong Kong Cinema*. Hong Kong: Oxford University Press.

Cheung, Esther M.K., Gina Marchetti, and Tan See-Kam. 2011. 'Interview with Ann Hui: On the Edge of the Mainstream', in Esther M.K. Cheung, Gina Marchetti and Tan See-Kam (eds), *Hong Kong Screenscapes: From the New Wave to the Digital Frontier*. Hong Kong: Hong Kong University Press, pp. 67–74.

Cheung, Jimmy, and Klaudia Lee. 2003. '500,000 Take to the Street', *South China Morning Post*, 2 July.

Cheung, Ruby. 2009. 'Corporatising a Film Festival: Hong Kong', in Dina Iordanova with Ragan Rhyne (eds), *Film Festival Yearbook 1: The Festival Circuit*. St Andrews: St Andrews Film Studies with College Gate Press, pp. 99–115.

———. 2011a. 'East Asian Film Festivals: Film Markets', in Dina Iordanova and Ruby Cheung (eds), *Film Festival Yearbook 3: Film Festivals and East Asia*. St Andrews: St Andrews Film Studies, pp. 40–61.

———. 2011b. '*Red Cliff*: The Chinese-Language Epic and Diasporic Chinese Spectators', in Robert Burgoyne (ed.), *The Epic Film in World Culture*. New York: Routledge, pp. 176–204.

———. 2011c. '"We believe in 'film as art'" An Interview with Li Cheuk-to, Artistic Director of the Hong Kong International Film Festival (HKIFF)', in Dina Iordanova and Ruby Cheung (eds), *Film Festival Yearbook 3: Film Festivals and East Asia*. St Andrews: St Andrews Film Studies, pp. 196–207.

———. 2013. 'Film and Migration, East Asia', in Immanuel Ness and Peter Bellwood (eds), *The Encyclopedia of Global Human Migration*. Chichester: Wiley-Blackwell.

Cheung, Wai Yee Ruby. 2007. 'Hong Kong Cinema 1982–2002: The Quest for Identity during Transition', Ph.D. thesis. St Andrews: University of St Andrews.

Chiao, Peggy Hsiung-ping. 1997. '*Happy Together*: Hong Kong's Absence', trans. Clara Shroff, *Cinemaya*, 38, Autumn, 17–21.

Chin, Bertha. 2007. 'Beyond Kung-Fu and Violence: Locating East Asian Cinema Fandom', in Jonathan Gray, Cornel Sandvoss and C. Lee Harrington (eds), *Fandom: Identities and Communities in a Mediated World*. New York and London: New York University Press, pp. 210–19.

Chin, Bertha, and Lori Hitchcock Morimoto. 2013. 'Towards a Theory of Transcultural Fandom', *Participations* 10(1): 92–108. Retrieved 5 May 2015 from http://www.participations.org/Volume 10/Issue 1/7 Chin & Morimoto 10.1.pdf.

'China Agrees to Widen Market Access for US Films'. 2012. *Screen International*, 18 February.

'China Becomes New Base for Runaway Productions'. 2002. *Screen International*, 1 October.

'China Eases Foreign Film Restrictions'. 2012. *BBC News*, 20 February. Retrieved 5 May 2015 from http://www.bbc.co.uk/news/entertainment-arts-17099980.

'China Media: White Paper on Hong Kong'. 2014. *BBC News*, 11 June. Retrieved 5 May 2015 from http://www.bbc.co.uk/news/world-asia-china-27790302.

'China Opens Up – Sort Of'. 2012. *Variety*, 5–11 March, 1 and 10.

'China Opens Up to Taiwanese Films'. 2010. *Screen Daily*, 5 July. Retrieved 5 May 2015 from http://www.screendaily.com/china-opens-up-to-taiwanese-films/5015724.article.

'China's New Global Strategy'. 2012. *Screen International*, 7 June.

'China's NFC to Back *The Annihilator*'. 2012. *Screen International*, 19 June.

'China's Wanda Group Buys AMC Entertainment'. 2012. *Screen International*, 21 May.

Choi, Jinhee, and Mitsuyo Wada-Marciano (eds). 2009. *Horror to the Extreme: Changing Boundaries in Asian Cinema*. Hong Kong: Hong Kong University Press.

Chow, Ching-yin. 2009. 'John Woo on Rationale behind *Red Cliff*' (in traditional Chinese), *Sing Tao Daily*, east of U.S. ed., 13 October. Retrieved 31 August 2013 from http://ny.stgloballink.com/community/200910/t20091013_1141863.html [now defunct].

Chow, Rey. 1993. *Writing Diaspora: Tactics of Intervention in Contemporary Cultural Studies.* Indiana: Indiana University Press.

———. 1995. *Primitive Passions: Visuality, Sexuality, Ethnography, and Contemporary Chinese Cinema.* New York: Columbia University Press.

———. 1998. 'Introduction: On Chineseness as a Theoretical Problem', *boundary 2* 25(3): 1–24.

Chow, Vivienne. 2013. 'Fund Fails Young Movie Makers, Says Hong Kong Film Community amid Calls for Overhaul', *South China Morning Post*, 3 September. Retrieved 5 May 2015 from http://www.scmp.com/news/hong-kong/article/1302063/filmmakers-call-funding-overhaul.

Chow, Yiu Fai, and Jeroen de Kloet. 2008. 'The Production of Locality in Global Pop – A Comparative Study of Pop Fans in the Netherlands and Hong Kong', *Participations* 5(2). Retrieved 5 May 2015 from http://www.participations.org/Volume 5/Issue 2/5_02_chowdekloet.htm.

Choy, Howard Y.F. 2007. 'Schizophrenic Hong Kong: Postcolonial Identity Crisis in the *Infernal Affairs* Trilogy', *Journal of Global Cultural Studies* 3: 52–66. Retrieved 5 May 2015 from http://transtexts.revues.org/138?lang=en.

Chu, Yingchi. 2003. *Hong Kong Cinema: Coloniser, Motherland and Self.* London and New York: Curzon.

Chu, Yiu-Wai. 2001. 'Whose Chineseness? Postcolonial Studies in the Mainland, Hong Kong and Taiwan in the 1990s' (in traditional Chinese), *Hong Kong Journal of Social Sciences* 19: 137–40.

———. 2013. *Lost in Transition: Hong Kong Culture in the Age of China.* New York: State University of New York Press.

Chua, Beng Huat. 2012. *Structure, Audience and Soft Power in East Asian Pop Culture.* Hong Kong: Hong Kong University Press.

Chua, Siew Keng. 1998. 'Song of the Exile: The Politics of "Home"', *Jump Cut* 42: 90–93.

Chugani, Michael. 1984. 'Council Raps Refugee Policy', *South China Morning Post*, 7 December.

Chui, Crystal Tsz-ying, and Rebecca Wong Wing-yan. 2010. 'A Lifeline for Hong Kong Films', *Varsity*, 116, May, 20–22. Retrieved 5 May 2015 from http://www.com.cuhk.edu.hk/varsity/1005/fund.pdf.

Chun, Allen. 1996. 'Fuck Chineseness: On the Ambiguities of Ethnicity as Culture as Identity', *boundary 2* 23(2): 111–38.

Chung, Hom-kwok. 1999. '1990s Hong Kong Films – Recession in Hong Kong Films' Development' (in traditional Chinese), *City Entertainment*, 539, 9–22 December, 21–23.

Chung, Lawrence. 2013. 'Taiwan Media Shake-up Gets its Wires Crossed', *South China Morning Post*, 13 February. Retrieved 5 May 2015 from http://www.scmp.com/news/china/article/1148927/shake-gets-its-wires-crossed.

Chung, Robert Ting-yiu. 2012. 'Survey on Ethnic Identity of Hong Kong People (full version)' (in traditional Chinese), Public Opinion Programme, University of

Hong Kong. Retrieved 5 May 2015 from http://hkupop.hku.hk/chinese/columns/columns127.html.

Chung, Stephanie Po-yin. 2003. 'The Industrial Evolution of a Fraternal Enterprise: The Shaw Brothers and the Shaw Organisation', in Wong Ain-ling (ed.), *The Shaw Screen: A Preliminary Study*. Hong Kong: Hong Kong Film Archive, pp. 1–17.

———. 2011. 'Connecting Shanghai, Hong Kong, and Singapore: The Story of the Shaw Brothers (1920s–1950s)' (in simplified Chinese), in Emilie Yueh-yu Yeh (ed.), *Rethinking Chinese Film Industry: New Histories New Methods*. Beijing: Peking University Press, pp. 152–68.

Ciecko, Anne, and Hunju Lee. 2007. 'Han Suk-kyu and the Gendered Cultural Economy of Stardom and Fandom', in Jonathan Gray, Cornel Sandvoss and C. Lee Harrington (eds), *Fandom: Identities and Communities in a Mediated World*. New York and London: New York University Press, pp. 220–31.

'CJ, Bona Start Strategic Partnership for Chinese Films'. 2010. *Screen Daily*, 14 June. Retrieved 5 May 2015 from http://www.screendaily.com/cj-bona-start-strategic-partnership-for-chinese-films/5014954.article.

Clarke, Roger. 2012. 'Domestic Service: *A Simple Life*', *Sight & Sound*, 22(8), August, 50–51.

Clifford, James. 1994. 'Diasporas', *Cultural Anthropology* 9(3): 302–38.

Cohen, Robin. 1997. *Global Diasporas: An Introduction*. Washington: University of Washington Press.

———. 2008. *Global Diasporas: An Introduction*, 2nd ed. London and New York: Routledge.

Coonan, Clifford. 2009. 'Hong Kong in Tune with Mainland Biz', *Variety*, 415(9), 20 July.

Coppa, Francesca. 2009. 'A Fannish Taxonomy of Hotness', *Cinema Journal* 48(4): 107–13.

Cremin, Stephen. 2013. 'Taiwan Cinema: North or South?', *Film Business Asia*, 20 March. Retrieved 5 May 2015 from http://www.filmbiz.asia/news/taiwan-cinema-north-or-south.

———. No date. 'Looking North and South: Taiwan Cinema in 2012', 15th Far East Film Festival, 19–27 April 2013 (online introduction to 'Taiwan' section). Retrieved 5 May 2015 from http://www.fareastfilm.com/easyne2/LYT.aspx?IDLYT=7803&CODE=FEFJ&ST=SQL&SQL=ID_Documento=4082.

Cresswell, Tim, and Deborah Dixon. 2002. 'Introduction: Engaging Film', in Tim Cresswell and Deborah Dixon (eds), *Engaging Film: Geographies of Mobility and Identity*. Oxford: Rowman & Littlefield, pp. 1–10.

Curtin, Michael. 2003. 'Media Capital: Towards the Study of Spatial Flows', *International Journal of Cultural Studies* 6(2): 202–28.

———. 2007. *Playing to the World's Biggest Audience: The Globalization of Chinese Film and TV*. California: University of California Press.

Davis, Darrell William. 2010. 'Market and Marketization in the China Film Business', *Cinema Journal* 49(3): 121–26.

Davis, Darrell William, and Emilie Yueh-yu Yeh. 2008. *East Asian Screen Industries*. London: BFI.

De Kosnik, Abigail. 2009. 'Should Fan Fiction be Free?', *Cinema Journal* 48(4): 118–24.

DeBoer, Stephanie. 2014. *Coproducing Asia: Locating Japanese-Chinese Regional Film and Media*. Minnesota: University of Minnesota Press.

'Director of International Promotion Center: Daniel D.H. Park'. 2012. *Korean Cinema Today*, Berlin special ed., 12, February, 8–9.

'Disney Forms Chinese Partnership to Develop Animation Content'. 2012. *Screen International*, 10 April.

Dissanayake, Wimal, and Dorothy Wong. 2003. *Wong Kar-wai's Ashes of Time*. Hong Kong: Hong Kong University Press.

Elley, Derek. 2002–3. 'My Life as McDull', *Variety*, 389(6), 26.

———. 2004. 'Mcdull, Prince de la Bun (Makdau Boloyau Wongchi)', *Variety*, 396(7), 117.

———. 2008. 'Sparrow', *Variety*, 410(1), 29.

———. 2012. 'Drug War', *Film Business Asia*, 16 November. Retrieved 5 May 2015 from http://www.filmbiz.asia/reviews/drug-war.

Elsaesser, Thomas. [2005] 2005. 'Double Occupancy and Small Adjustments: Space, Place and Policy in the New European Cinema since the 1990s', in Thomas Elsaesser, *European Cinema: Face to Face with Hollywood*. Amsterdam: Amsterdam University Press, pp. 108–30.

England, Vaudine. 2012. 'Hong Kong Suffers Identity Crisis as China's Influence Grows', *The Guardian*, 23 March. Retrieved 5 May 2015 from http://www.theguardian.com/world/2012/mar/23/china-hong-kong-identity-crisis.

Erens, Patricia Brett. 2000a. 'Crossing Borders: Time, Memory, and the Construction of Identity in *Song of the Exile*', *Cinema Journal* 39(4): 43–59.

———. 2000b. 'The Film Work of Ann Hui', in Poshek Fu and David Desser (eds), *The Cinema of Hong Kong: History, Arts, Identity*. Cambridge: Cambridge University Press, pp. 176–95.

Feng, Pin-chia. 2011. 'Reimagining the *Femme Fatale*: Gender and Nation in Fruit Chan's *Hollywood Hong Kong*', in Esther M.K. Cheung, Gina Marchetti and Tan See-Kam (eds). *Hong Kong Screenscapes: From the New Wave to the Digital Frontier*. Hong Kong: Hong Kong University Press, pp. 253–62.

Feng, Xiaocai. 2011. 'Between Research Questions and Historical Materials: The Reconstruction and Rewriting of Contemporary Mainland Chinese Film History' (in simplified Chinese), in Emilie Yueh-yu Yeh (ed.), *Rethinking Chinese Film Industry: New Histories New Methods*. Beijing: Peking University Press, pp. 135–50.

Files, Gemma. 1997. 'Review: *Floating Life*', *Eye Weekly*, 26 June. Retrieved 18 November 2006 from http://www.eye.net/eye/issue/issue_06.26.97/film/files.html [now defunct].

'Film Development Fund of Hong Kong Being Abused by Hong Kong Film Industry' (in traditional Chinese). 2012. *Apple Daily*, 15 November.

'FILMART 2007 Seminar Series: Romancing the Mid-Budget Film'. 2007. Hong Kong International Film & TV Market (FILMART), press release, 21 March. Retrieved 5 May 2015 from http://www.hkfilmart.com/filmart/release16b.htm.

Finney, Angus. 2010. *The International Film Business: A Market Guide beyond Hollywood*. London and New York: Routledge.

Fiske, John. 1992. 'The Cultural Economy of Fandom', in Lisa A. Lewis (ed.), *The Adoring Audience: Fan Culture and Popular Media*. London and New York: Routledge, pp. 30–49.

Fitzpatrick, Liam. 2003. 'The Long March', *TIME*, 14 July. Retrieved 5 May 2015 from http://content.time.com/time/world/article/0,8599,2047553,00.html.

Fong, Cochran. 1999. 'Middle-aged and Jobless in 1997: Fruit Chan on *The Longest Summer*', trans. Ranchof Cong, *Hong Kong Panorama 98–99*, 23rd Hong Kong International Film Festival. Hong Kong: Provisional Urban Council of Hong Kong, pp. 51–54.

Fore, Steve. 1999. 'Introduction: Hong Kong Movies, Critical Time Warps, and Shapes of Things to Come', *Post Script* 19(1): 2–9.

Frater, Patrick. 2000. 'Applause Sets Hur's Spring Day as First Project', *Screen International*, 14 April.

———. 2008. 'Asia Piggy Bank Has Gobs of Gold: India, China, Japan All Show Financial Strength during Cannes', *Variety*, 411(2), 26 May.

———. 2012. 'National Fund Unveils Multinational Slate', *Film Business Asia*, 19 June. Retrieved 5 May 2015 from http://www.filmbiz.asia/news/national-fund-unveils-multinational-slate.

———. 2013a. 'China-Korea to Sign Co-production Pact this Month', *Variety*, 6 October. Retrieved 5 May 2015 from http://variety.com/2013/film/news/china-korea-to-sign-co-prod-pact-this-month-1200701056.

———. 2013b. 'John Woo Sets Sail on "The Crossing"', *Variety*, 8 July. Retrieved 5 May 2015 from http://variety.com/2013/film/international/john-woo-sets-sail-on-the-crossing-1200555003.

———. 2013c. 'Taiwan to Tax Cinema Tickets', *Variety*, 10 October. Retrieved 5 May 2015 from http://variety.com/2013/film/news/taiwan-to-tax-cinema-tickets-1200711081.

Frater, Patrick, and Gavin J. Blair. 2009. 'Quiet TIFFCOM Wraps with Few Sales', *The Hollywood Reporter*, 22 October. Retrieved 5 May 2015 from http://www.hollywoodreporter.com/news/quiet-tiffcom-wraps-sales-90381.

Fu, Poshek. 2003. *Between Shanghai and Hong Kong: The Politics of Chinese Cinemas*. California: Stanford University Press.

Fu, Poshek, and David Desser (eds). 2000. *The Cinema of Hong Kong: History, Arts, Identity*. Cambridge: Cambridge University Press.

Fu, Poshek (ed.). 2008. *China Forever: The Shaw Brothers and Diasporic Cinema*. Illinois: University of Illinois Press.

'Full Text: The Practice of the "One Country, Two Systems" Policy in the Hong Kong Special Administrative Region'. 2014. *Xinhuanet*, 10 June. Retrieved 5 May 2015 from http://news.xinhuanet.com/english/china/2014-06/10/c_133396891_2.htm.

Fung, Anthony, and Joseph M. Chan. 2010. 'Towards a Global Blockbuster: The Political Economy of *Hero*'s Nationalism', in Gary D. Rawnsley and Ming-Yeh T. Rawnsley (eds), *Global Chinese Cinema: The Culture and Politics of Hero*. London and New York: Routledge, pp. 198–211.

Gan, Wendy. 2005. *Fruit Chan's Durian Durian*. Hong Kong: Hong Kong University Press.

Gao, Zhihong. 2009. 'Serving a Stir-Fry of Market, Culture and Politics – On Globalisation and Film Policy in Greater China', *Policy Studies* 30(4): 423–38.

Gerow, Aaron. 2006. 'Recent Film Policy and the Fate of Film Criticism in Japan', *Midnight Eye*, 11 July. Retrieved 5 May 2015 from http://www.midnighteye.com/features/recent-film-policy-and-the-fate-of-film-criticism-in-japan.

Gittings, John. 2000. 'Gate Slams on Last of the Boat People: Camp Shuts 25 Years after First Vietnamese Refugees Arrived in Hong Kong', *The Guardian*, 1 June. Retrieved 5 May 2015 from http://www.guardian.co.uk/china/story/0,,468017,00.html.

Goodridge, Mike. 2003. 'Warner Gets China Greenlight for Multiplex Opening in Shanghai', *Screen International*, 11 July.

Gray, Jason. 2008. 'Japan to Launch Film Commission as Part of Policy Shift', *Screen Daily*, 5 October. Retrieved 5 May 2015 from http://www.screendaily.com/japan-to-launch-film-commission-as-part-of-policy-shift/4041235.article.

──────. 2012. 'The Tokyo Connection', *Screen Daily*, 18 October. Retrieved 5 May 2015 from http://www.screendaily.com/reports/in-focus/the-tokyo-connection/5047602.article.

Gray, Jonathan, Cornel Sandvoss, and C. Lee Harrington (eds). 2007. *Fandom: Identities and Communities in a Mediated World*. New York and London: New York University Press.

Greiner, Clemens, and Patrick Sakdapolrak. 2013. 'Translocality: Concepts, Applications and Emerging Research Perspectives', *Geography Compass* 7(5): 373–84.

Guback, Thomas H. 1969. *The International Film Industry: Western Europe and America since 1945*. Indiana: Indiana University Press.

H., Andy. 2012. 'Roger Lee Interview: A Not-So-Simple Life', *easternkicks.com*, 16 November. Retrieved 5 May 2015 from http://www.easternkicks.com/features/roger-lee-interview-a-not-so-simple-life.

Hall, Stuart. 1990. 'Cultural Identity and Diaspora', in Jonathan Rutherford (ed.), *Identity: Community, Culture, Difference*. London: Lawrence & Wishart, pp. 222–37 (first published in 1989 in *Framework* 36: 68–82).

──────. 1993. 'Encoding, Decoding', in Simon During (ed.), *The Cultural Studies Reader*. London and New York: Routledge, pp. 90–103.

'Han Sanping: Biography' (in simplified Chinese). 2009. *sina.com.cn*, 21 January. Retrieved 5 May 2015 from http://ent.sina.com.cn/m/2009-01-21/00562351461.shtml.

Han, Sunhee. 2010a. 'Busan: Hub of the Asian Film and Television Industry', *Korean Cinema Today*, Berlin ed., 5, January–February, 22–23.

──────. 2010b. 'From Incheon to Jeju', *Korean Cinema Today*, Berlin ed., 5, January–February, 28–29.

──────. 2010c. 'Gyeonggi-Do: A Region Balancing the Urban and the Natural', *Korean Cinema Today*, Berlin ed., 5, January–February, 24–25.

──────. 2010d. 'Jeonju: A City of Art', *Korean Cinema Today*, Berlin ed., 5, January–February, 26–27.

──────. 2010e. 'Seoul: Crossroads of Tradition and Modernity', *Korean Cinema Today*, Berlin ed., 5, January–February, 20–21.

Harrington, C. Lee, and Denise D. Bielby. 2007. 'Global Fandom/Global Fan Studies', in Jonathan Gray, Cornel Sandvoss and C. Lee Harrington (eds), *Fandom: Identities and Communities in a Mediated World*. New York and London: New York University Press, pp. 179–97.

Hau, Caroline S. 2012. 'Becoming "Chinese" – But What "Chinese"? – in Southeast Asia', *Asia-Pacific Journal: Japan Focus* 26, June. Retrieved 5 May 2015 from http://japanfocus.org/-Caroline_S_-Hau/3777/article.html.

Havis, Richard James. 1997. 'Wong Kar-wai: One Entrance Many Exits', *Cinemaya*, 38, Autumn, 15–16.

He, Hilary Hongjin. 2012. '"Chinesenesses" Outside Mainland China: Macao and Taiwan through Post-1997 Hong Kong Cinema', *Culture Unbound: Journal of Current Cultural Research* 4: 297–325.

Hellekson, Karen. 2009. 'A Fannish Field of Value: Online Fan Gift Culture', *Cinema Journal* 48(4): 113–18.

Higson, Andrew. 1989. 'The Concept of National Cinema', *Screen* 30(4): 36–46.

———. 1997. *Waving the Flag: Constructing a National Cinema in Britain*. New York: Oxford University Press.

Hills, Matt. 2002. *Fan Cultures*. Oxon: Routledge.

Hjort, Mette, and Scott MacKenzie (eds). 2000. *Cinema and Nation*. London and New York: Routledge.

'HK Government Respects Court's Right of Abode Ruling'. 2001. *People's Daily Online*, 21 July. Retrieved 5 May 2015 from http://english.peopledaily.com.cn/english/200107/21/eng20010721_75525.html.

Ho, Elaine Yee-lin. 1999. 'Women on the Edges of Hong Kong Modernity: The Films of Ann Hui', in Mayfair Mei-hui Yang (ed.), *Spaces of their Own: Women's Public Sphere in Transnational China*. Minnesota: University of Minnesota Press, pp. 162–87. Reprinted 2001, in Esther C.M. Yau (ed.), *At Full Speed: Hong Kong Cinema in a Borderless World*. Minnesota: University of Minnesota Press, pp. 177–206.

Ho, Sam. 1999. 'As Time Goes By: Ann Hui's *Ordinary Heroes*', *Hong Kong Panorama 98–99*, 23rd Hong Kong International Film Festival. Hong Kong: Provisional Urban Council of Hong Kong, pp. 18–19.

'Hong Kong 1990: A Review of 1989'. 1990. Hong Kong: Hong Kong Census and Statistics Department.

'Hong Kong 1991: A Review of 1990'. 1991. Hong Kong: Census and Statistics Department.

'Hong Kong 1992: A Review of 1991'. 1992. Hong Kong: Census and Statistics Department.

'Hong Kong 1993: A Review of 1992'. 1993. Hong Kong: Census and Statistics Department.

'Hong Kong 1994: A Review of 1993'. 1994. Hong Kong: Census and Statistics Department.

'Hong Kong 1995: A Review of 1994'. 1995. Hong Kong: Census and Statistics Department/Government Information Services.

'Hong Kong 1996: A Review of 1995 and a Pictorial Review of the Past Fifty Years'. 1996. Hong Kong: Census and Statistics Department/Government Information Services.

'Hong Kong 1997: A Review of 1996'. 1997. Hong Kong: Census and Statistics Department/ Government Information Services.

'Hong Kong 1998'. 1998. Hong Kong: Census and Statistics Department/Government Information Services.

'Hong Kong 1999'. 1999. Hong Kong: Census and Statistics Department/Government Information Services.

'Hong Kong 2000'. 2000. Hong Kong: Census and Statistics Department/Government Information Services.

'Hong Kong Government's Sponsorship for Hong Kong Film Industry Recording a Loss of 55 Per Cent' (in traditional Chinese). 2012. *Ming Pao*, 15 November.

Horlemann, Ralf. 2003. *Hong Kong's Transition to Chinese Rule: The Limits of Autonomy*. London and New York: RoutledgeCurzon.

'How Bad Did Chinese Films Perform in the First Half [of 2012]?' (in simplified Chinese). No date. *ent.163.com*. Retrieved 5 May 2015 from http://ent.163.com/special/ zmhollywood.

'How Come There's a Hollywood in Hong Kong?' (in traditional Chinese). 2002. *City Entertainment*, 600, 11–24 April, 40–42.

'How Does *Made in Hong Kong* Produce the Legend of Independents – Made by Fruit Chan?' (in traditional Chinese). 1997. *City Entertainment*, 481, 18 September–1 October, 47–48.

Hu, Jubin. 2003. *Projecting a Nation: Chinese National Cinema before 1949*. Hong Kong: Hong Kong University Press.

Huang, Yunte. 1999. 'Writing against the Chinese Diaspora', *boundary 2* 26(1): 145–46.

Hughes, Richard. 1968. *Hong Kong: Borrowed Place – Borrowed Time*. London: Andre Deutsch.

Hui, Ann. 1998. '*Boat People*' (interview conducted in 1996) (in traditional Chinese), in Kwong Po-wai (ed.), *Ann Hui on Ann Hui*. Hong Kong: Hong Kong Arts Development Council, pp. 21–25.

———. 1999. '*Ordinary Heroes*: Director's Note', 23rd Hong Kong International Film Festival. Hong Kong: Provisional Urban Council, p. 15.

———. 2012a. '*Ordinary Heroes*' (interview conducted in June 1998) (in traditional Chinese), in Kwong Po-wai (ed.), *Director Ann Hui*. Hong Kong: Eucalyptus House, pp. 85–97.

———. 2012b. '*Song of the Exile*' (interview conducted in June 1996) (in traditional Chinese), in Kwong Po-wai (ed.), *Director Ann Hui*. Hong Kong: Eucalyptus House, pp. 141–48.

Hume, Tim. 2014. 'Alarm in Hong Kong at Chinese White Paper Affirming Beijing Control', *CNN*, 13 June. Retrieved 5 May 2015 from http://edition.cnn.com/2014/06/11/world/ asia/hong-kong-beijing-two-systems-paper.

Hung, Jude, and Zoe Li. 2010. 'Aarif Lee: "I Don't Look Like Bruce Lee"', *CNN*, 29 November. Retrieved 5 May 2015 from http://travel.cnn.com/hong-kong/play/bruce-lee-my-brother-113914.

'Immigration Department Annual Report 2011'. 2011. Hong Kong: Hong Kong SAR Government. Retrieved 5 May 2015 from http://www.immd.gov.hk/publications/a_report_2011/index.htm.

'In the Dock: China's Man in Hong Kong Has Been Humiliated by Popular Protest'. 2003. *The Economist*, 10 July. Retrieved 5 May 2015 from http://www.economist.com/node/1908354.

Iordanova, Dina. 2011. 'East Asia and Film Festivals: Transnational Clusters for Creativity and Commerce', in Dina Iordanova and Ruby Cheung (eds), *Film Festival Yearbook 3: Film Festivals and East Asia*. St Andrews: St Andrews Film Studies, pp. 1–33.

Iwabuchi, Kōichi. 2009. 'Reconsidering East Asian Connectivity and the Usefulness of Media and Cultural Studies', in Chris Berry, Nicola Liscutin and Jonathan D. Mackintosh (eds), *Cultural Studies and Cultural Industries in Northeast Asia: What a Difference a Region Makes*. Hong Kong: Hong Kong University Press, pp. 25–36.

Jacques, Martin. 2012. *When China Rules the World: The End of the Western World and the Birth of a New Global Order*. London: Penguin.

Jaffe, Gabrielle. 2011. 'Will the Great Film Quota Wall of China Come Down?', *The Guardian*, 24 March. Retrieved 5 May 2015 from http://www.guardian.co.uk/business/2011/mar/24/china-film-quota.

Jenkins, Henry. 1992a. '"Strangers No More, We Sing": Filking and the Social Construction of the Science Fiction Fan Community', in Lisa A. Lewis (ed.), *The Adoring Audience: Fan Culture and Popular Media*. London and New York: Routledge, pp. 208–36.

_____. 1992b. *Textual Poachers: Television Fans & Participatory Culture*. New York: Routledge.

_____. 2006. *Fans, Bloggers, and Gamers: Exploring Participatory Culture*. New York and London: New York University Press.

_____. 2008. *Convergence Culture: Where Old and New Media Collide* (updated and with a new Afterword). New York and London: New York University Press.

_____. 2013. *Textual Poachers: Television Fans and Participatory Culture*, updated 20th anniversary ed., kindle ed. New York and London: Routledge.

Jenkins, Henry, Sam Ford, and Joshua Green. 2013. *Spreadable Media: Creating Value and Meaning in a Networked Culture*, kindle ed. New York and London: New York University Press.

Jennings, Ralph. 2012. 'Taiwan Government Information Office Closes its Doors', *Voice of America*, 18 May. Retrieved 5 May 2015 from http://www.voanews.com/content/taiwan-government-information-office-closes-its-doors/667298.html.

'John Woo: I am not Making History Film' (in simplified Chinese). 2009. *QQ.com*, shared 8 January. Retrieved 5 May 2015 from http://ent.qq.com/a/20090108/000258.htm.

Jones, Arthur. 2007. 'Fest Traveller: Shanghai: Chinese Studio Participation Swells with Fest's Market Launch', *Variety*, 407(4), 11 June.

Jost, Marie. 2011. *The Rise of Johnnie To* (E-book). *HKCinemagic.com*. Retrieved 5 May 2015 from http://www.hkcinemagic.com/fr/pdf/The-Rise-of-Johnnie-To-Marie-Jost-HKCinemagic-PDF-version.rar.

Kaiman, Jonathan. 2014. 'Taiwan Protesters to End Occupation of Legislature', *The Guardian*, 8 April. Retrieved 5 May 2015 from http://www.theguardian.com/world/2014/apr/08/taiwan-protesters-end-occupation-legislature-china-trade.

Katzenstein, Peter J. 2000. 'Regionalism and Asia', *New Political Economy* 5(3): 353–68.

Keane, Michael. 2006. 'Once Were Peripheral: Creating Media Capacity in East Asia', *Media, Culture & Society* 28(6): 835–55.

Kim, Hong-chun. 2011. 'KoBiz, the Gateway to Korean Films', *Korean Cinema Today*, special ed., Cannes Film Festival, 10, May, 10.

Kim, Hyae-joon. Circa 2006. 'A History of Korean Film Policies', in Kim Mee-hyun and An Jae-seok (eds), *Korean Cinema: From Origins to Renaissance*. The Korean Film Council (KOFIC)'s official website (English), pp. 351–55. Retrieved 5 May 2015 from http://www.koreanfilm.or.kr/jsp/publications/history.jsp.

Kim, Mee-hyun, and An Jae-seok (eds). Circa 2006. *Korean Cinema: From Origins to Renaissance*. The Korean Film Council (KOFIC)'s official website (English). Retrieved 5 May 2015 from http://www.koreanfilm.or.kr/jsp/publications/history.jsp.

Kim, Woody. 2013. 'KOFIC to Call Busan Home Soon', *Korean Cinema Today*, 17, October, 69.

Klein, Christina. 2004. '*Crouching Tiger, Hidden Dragon*: A Diasporic Reading', *Cinema Journal* 43(4): 18–42.

Kraicer, Shelly. 2002. 'My Life as McDull', *A Chinese Cinema Site*, April. Retrieved 5 May 2015 from http://www.chinesecinemas.org/mcdull.html.

Kronengold, Charles. 2013. 'Multitemporality and the Speed(s) of Thought in Johnnie To's Action Films', *Journal of Chinese Cinemas* 7(3): 277–95.

Kuan, Hsin-chi. 1999. 'Is the "One Country, Two Systems" Formula Working?', in Wang Gungwu and John Wong (eds), *Hong Kong in China: The Challenges of Transition*. Singapore: Times Academic Press, pp. 23–46.

Kuhn, Annette, and Guy Westwell. 2012. *A Dictionary of Film Studies*. Oxford: Oxford University Press.

Lam, Jeffie. 2014. '"Hongkonger" Makes It to World Stage with Place in the Oxford English Dictionary', *South China Morning Post*, 19 March. Retrieved 5 May 2015 from http://www.scmp.com/news/hong-kong/article/1451929/finally-hongkonger-arrives-world-stage.

Larsen, Katherine, and Lynn Zubernis (eds). 2012. *Fan Culture: Theory/Practice*. Newcastle upon Tyne: Cambridge Scholars Publishing.

Lau, Chris. 2012. 'Movie Star Piglet on Song', *Young Post of South China Morning Post*, 14 August. Retrieved 5 May 2015 from http://yp.scmp.com/article/4205/movie-star-piglet-song.

Lee, Bono. 2002. 'A Good Man is Hard to Find: Herman Yau on *From the Queen to the Chief Executive*', trans. Piera Chen, *Hong Kong Panorama 2001–2002*, 26th Hong Kong International Film Festival. Hong Kong: Hong Kong Arts Development Council, pp. 24–27.

Lee, Hyo-won. 2013. 'Busan: South Korea Taps China Film Boom', *The Hollywood Reporter*, 6 October. Retrieved 5 May 2015 from http://www.hollywoodreporter.com/news/busan-south-korea-taps-china-643966.

Lee, Justina, and Tim Culpan. 2014. 'Taiwan Students End 24-Day Occupation over China Trade Deal', *Bloomberg*, 10 April. Retrieved 5 May 2015 from http://www.bloomberg.com/news/2014-04-10/taiwan-students-to-end-24-day-occupation-of-legislature-today.html.

Lee, Maggie. 2008. 'Red Cliff', *The Hollywood Reporter*, 10 July. Retrieved 5 May 2015 from http://www.hollywoodreporter.com/review/red-cliff-125483.

Lee, Sangjoon. 2011. 'Table 1: The Asia-Pacific Film Festival (from 1954)', in Dina Iordanova and Ruby Cheung (eds), *Film Festival Yearbook 3: Film Festivals and East Asia*. St Andrews: St Andrews Film Studies, pp. 242–46.

Lee, Vivian P.Y. 2009. *Hong Kong Cinema Since 1997: The Post-Nostalgic Imagination*. London: Palgrave Macmillan.

_____. 2011a. 'Introduction: Mapping East Asia's Cinemascape', in Vivian P.Y. Lee (ed.), *East Asian Cinemas: Regional Flows and Global Transformations*. New York: Palgrave Macmillan, pp. 1–12.

_____. 2011b. '"Working through China" in the Pan-Asian Film Network: Perspectives from Hong Kong and Singapore', in Vivian P.Y. Lee (ed.), *East Asian Cinemas: Regional Flows and Global Transformations*. New York: Palgrave Macmillan, pp. 235–48.

Lent, John A. 1990. *The Asian Film Industry*. London: Christopher Helm.

Leung, Grace L.K., and Joseph M. Chan. 1997. 'The Hong Kong Cinema and its Overseas Market: A Historical Review, 1950–1995', in *Hong Kong Cinema Retrospective: Fifty Years of Electric Shadows*, 21st Hong Kong International Film Festival. Hong Kong: Urban Council, pp. 143–51.

Leung, Ping-kwan. 2000. 'Urban Cinema and the Cultural Identity of Hong Kong', in Poshek Fu and David Desser (eds), *The Cinema of Hong Kong: History, Arts, Identity*. Cambridge: Cambridge University Press, pp. 227–51.

Lewis, Lisa A. (ed.). 1992. *The Adoring Audience: Fan Culture and Popular Media*. London and New York: Routledge.

Ley, David, and Audrey Kobayashi. 2005. 'Back to Hong Kong: Return Migration or Transnational Sojourn?', *Global Networks: A Journal of Transnational Affairs* 5(2): 111–27.

Li, Cheuk-to. 1994. 'The Return of the Father: Hong Kong New Wave and its Chinese Context in the 1980s', in Nick Browne, Paul G. Pickowicz, Vivian Sobchack and Esther Yau (eds), *New Chinese Cinemas: Forms, Identities, Politics*. Cambridge: Cambridge University Press, pp. 160–79.

_____. 1999. 'Ordinary Heroes' (in traditional Chinese), *Hong Kong Panorama 98–99*, 23rd Hong Kong International Film Festival. Hong Kong: Provisional Urban Council of Hong Kong, p. 20.

———. 2000. 'Asian Bearings and Post-97 Mentalities', trans. Sam Ho, *Hong Kong Panorama 1999–2000*, 24th Hong Kong International Film Festival. Hong Kong: Leisure and Cultural Services Department, pp. 13–15.

———. (ed.). 2012. *Peter Ho-sun Chan: My Way* (in traditional Chinese). Hong Kong: Joint Publishing.

Li, Li, and Chen Xiao. 2008. 'Original Scriptwriter: John Woo is Serious but He Lacks Deep Cultural Background' (in simplified Chinese), *QQ.com*, shared 26 July. Retrieved 5 May 2015 from http://ent.qq.com/a/20080728/000102.htm.

'Life in the Shadows'. 2006. *South China Morning Post*, 26 June.

Lim, Marcus. 2008. 'Golden Horse Disqualifies Thesp: Takeshi Kaneshiro Nixed after Nationality Mix-up', *Variety*, 31 October. Retrieved 5 May 2015 from http://variety.com/2008/film/news/golden-horse-disqualifies-thesp-1117995079.

Lim, Song Hwee. 2011. 'Transnational Trajectories in Contemporary East Asian Cinemas', in Vivian P.Y. Lee (ed.), *East Asian Cinemas: Regional Flows and Global Transformations*. New York: Palgrave Macmillan, pp. 15–32.

Liu, Eric. 2004a. 'An Exclusive Interview with Oxide Pang (Part I)', *Cinespot*, November. Retrieved 5 May 2015 from http://www.cinespot.com/einterviews06.html.

———. 2004b. 'An Exclusive Interview with Oxide Pang (Part II)', *Cinespot*, November. Retrieved 5 May 2015 from http://www.cinespot.com/einterviews06b.html.

Liu, Juliana. 2012. 'Surge in Anti-China Sentiment in Hong Kong', *BBC News*, 8 February. Retrieved 5 May 2015 from http://www.bbc.co.uk/news/world-asia-china-16941652.

Liu, Wei. 2012. 'Policy Issued for Mainland-Taiwan Film Co-productions', *China Daily*, 4 December. Retrieved 5 May 2015 from http://usa.chinadaily.com.cn/culture/2012-12/04/content_15984791.htm.

Liu, Yang. 2012. 'The China Film Group Corporation in the Making of the Flagship of China's Film Industry' (in simplified Chinese), *people.com.cn*, 14 August. Retrieved 5 May 2015 from http://media.people.com.cn/n/2012/0814/c40606-18737300.html.

Liu, Yin, and Tan Qin. 2001. 'Deficit of More than RMB 1 Million, Shanghai International Film Festival in Red' (in simplified Chinese), *Zhongguo Jingying Bao*, 27 June. Retrieved 26 April 2010 from http://ent.sina.com.cn/48237.html [now defunct].

Lo, Kwai-Cheung. 2005. *Chinese Face/Off: The Transnational Popular Culture of Hong Kong*. Illinois: University of Illinois Press.

———. 2009. 'Reconfiguring Chinese Diaspora through the Eyes of Ethnic Minorities: Tibetan Films by Exiles and Residents in People's Republic of China'. Paper Number: 94, Working Paper Series, David C. Lam Institute for East-West Studies, Hong Kong Baptist University.

Lo, Yu-lai. 1997. 'Some Notes about Film Censorship in Hong Kong', *The 21st Hong Kong International Film Festival*. Hong Kong: Urban Council, pp. 60–63.

Lok, Fung. 2002. *City on the Edge of Time* (in traditional Chinese). Hong Kong: Oxford University Press.

Long, Tin. 2003. *Post-97 and Hong Kong Cinema* (in traditional Chinese). Hong Kong: Hong Kong Film Critics Society.

Lothian, Alexis. 2009. 'Living in a Den of Thieves: Fan Video and Digital Challenges to Ownership', *Cinema Journal* 48(4): 130–36.

Louie, Kam. 2003. '*Floating Life*: Nostalgia for the Confucian Way in Suburban Sydney', in Chris Berry (ed.), *Chinese Films in Focus: 25 New Takes*. London: BFI, pp. 97–103.

Lu, Sheldon. 2000. 'Filming Diaspora and Identity: Hong Kong and 1997', in Poshek Fu and David Desser (eds), *The Cinema of Hong Kong: History, Arts, Identity*. Cambridge: Cambridge University Press, pp. 273–88.

Lu, Sheldon H., and Emilie Yueh-yu Yeh (eds). 2005. *Chinese-Language Film: Historiography, Poetics, Politics*. Hawaii: University of Hawai'i Press.

Lu, Sheldon Hsiao-peng (ed.). 1997. *Transnational Chinese Cinemas: Identity, Nationhood, Gender*. Hawaii: University of Hawai'i Press.

Mackintosh, Jonathan D., Chris Berry, and Nicola Liscutin. 2009. 'Introduction', in Chris Berry, Nicola Liscutin and Jonathan D. Mackintosh (eds), *Cultural Studies and Cultural Industries in Northeast Asia: What a Difference a Region Makes*. Hong Kong: Hong Kong University Press, pp. 1–22.

'Mainland Girl Eating Caused Controversy in Hong Kong MTR' (with traditional Chinese subtitles). 2012. *appledaily.com.hk*, uploaded 17 January by shamhing5's channel. Retrieved 5 May 2015 from http://www.youtube.com/watch?v=NJydwlhvvcc.

Mannur, Anita. 2003. 'Postscript: Cyberspaces and the Interfacing of Diasporas', in Jana Evans Braziel and Anita Mannur (eds), *Therorizing Diaspora: A Reader*. Massachusetts: Blackwell Publishing, pp. 283–90.

Marchetti, Gina. 2006. *From Tian'anmen to Times Square: Transnational China and the Chinese Diaspora on Global Screens, 1989–1997*. Pennsylvania: Temple University Press.

_____. 2007. *Andrew Lau and Alan Mak's Infernal Affairs – The Trilogy*. Hong Kong: Hong Kong University Press.

Marchetti, Gina, and Tan See Kam (eds). 2007. *Hong Kong Film, Hollywood and New Global Cinema: No Film is an Island*. Oxon and New York: Routledge.

Martin, Peter. 2007. 'Hong Kong's "The Detective" Opens Strong in Asia', *Moviefone*, 5 October. Retrieved 5 May 2015 from http://blog.moviefone.com/2007/10/05/hong-kongs-the-detective-opens-strong-in-asia.

Mazaj, Meta. 2011. 'Freewheeling on the Margins: The Discourse of Transition in the New Slovenian Cinema', *Studies in Eastern European Cinema* 2(1): 7–20.

Mazurkewich, Karen. 2000. 'Chan Sets Off Applause to Boost Asian Production', *Screen International*, 21 March.

McQuail, Denis. 1994. *Mass Communication Theory: An Introduction*, 3rd ed. London: Sage.

Meng, Angela. 2014. 'State-Owned China Film Group Invest Millions in Hollywood Productions Seventh Son and Warcraft', *South China Morning Post*, 16 April. Retrieved 5 May 2015 from http://www.scmp.com/news/china/article/1483334/state-owned-china-film-group-invest-millions-hollywood-productions.

Miller, Adam. 2011. 'The Birth of Japanese Cinema', *Axiom Magazine*, 6 April. Retrieved 5 May 2015 from http://www.axiommagazine.jp/2011/04/06/the-birth-of-japanese-cinema.

Monk, Claire. 2011. 'Heritage Film Audiences 2.0: Period Film Audiences and Online Fan Cultures', *Participations* 8(2): 431–77. Retrieved 5 May 2015 from http://www.participations.org/Volume 8/Issue 2/3h Monk.pdf.

Moon, Jeong Ho, Eun Gyo Jang, Jung Ho Park, and Min Jung Kang. 2013. '2012 Modularization of Korea's Development Experience: National Territorial and Regional Development Policy: Focusing on Comprehensive National Territorial Plan'. Sejong Special Self-Governing City, South Korea: Ministry of Strategy and Finance, Republic of Korea.

Mor, Jessica Stites. 2012. *Transition Cinema: Political Filmmaking and the Argentine Left since 1968*. Pennsylvania: University of Pittsburgh Press.

Moran, Albert. 1996. 'Terms for a Reader: Film, Hollywood, National Cinema, Cultural Identity and Film Policy', in Albert Moran (ed.), *Film Policy: International, National and Regional Perspectives*. London and New York: Routledge, pp. 1–19.

Morris, Meaghan, Siu Leung Li, and Stephen Chan Ching-kiu (eds). 2005. *Hong Kong Connections: Transnational Imagination in Action Cinema*. Durham, North Carolina: Duke University Press; Hong Kong: Hong Kong University Press.

Naficy, Hamid. 2001. *An Accented Cinema: Exilic and Diasporic Filmmaking*. New Jersey: Princeton University Press.

———. 2008. 'Iranian Émigré Cinema as a Component of Iranian National Cinema', in Mehdi Semati (ed.), *Media, Culture and Society in Iran: Living with Globalization and the Islamic State*. Oxon and New York: Routledge, pp. 167–92.

Napier, Susan J. 2007. *From Impressionism to Anime: Japan as Fantasy and Fan Cult in the Mind of the West*. New York: Palgrave Macmillan.

Newman, David. 1995. 'The Road to China: Hong Kong's Transition to Chinese Sovereignty' (working paper). Hong Kong: Faculty of Social Sciences, Lingnan College.

Ng, Kenny K.K. 2009. 'Political Censorship of Hong Kong Cinema in the Cold War Period' (in traditional Chinese), in Wong Ain-ling and Lee Pui-tak (eds), *The Cold War and Hong Kong Cinema*. Hong Kong: Hong Kong Film Archive, pp. 53–69.

Ngai, Jimmy. 1990. 'All About *Days of Being Wild*: A Dialogue with Wong Kar-wai' (in traditional Chinese), *City Entertainment*, 305, 6–19 December, 38–39.

Ngai, Jimmy, and Wong Kar-wai. 1997. 'A Dialogue with Wong Kar-wai: Cutting between Time and Two Cities', in Jean-Marc Lalanne, David Martinez, Ackbar Abbas and Jimmy Ngai, *Wong Kar-wai*. Paris: Editions Dis Voir, pp. 83–117.

Nochimson, Martha P. 2005. 'Lies and Loneliness: An Interview with Tony Leung Chiu Wai', *Cineaste*, Fall, 16–17.

Nochimson, Martha P., and Robert Cashill. 2007. 'One Country, Two Visions: An Interview with Johnnie To', *Cineaste*, Spring, 36–39.

Noh, Jean. 2006. 'CJ CGV to Build Multiplexes with Shanghai Film Group', *Screen International*, 15 February.

———. 2010. '"Busy" TIFFCOM Sees Visitors and Exhibitors Increase', *Screen Daily*, 28 October. Retrieved 5 May 2015 from http://www.screendaily.com/festivals/other-festivals/busy-tiffcom-sees-visitors-and-exhibitors-increase/5019925.article.

———. 2011a. 'ScreenSingapore Wraps with Larry Crowne, Attracts 700 Trade Attendees', *Screen Daily*, 13 June. Retrieved 5 May 2015 from http://www.screendaily.com/other-festivals/screensingapore-wraps-with-larry-crowne-attracts-700-trade-attendees/5028690.article.

———. 2011b. 'TIFFCOM Kicks off with Buyer Attendance up 12%', *Screen Daily*, 24 October. Retrieved 5 May 2015 from http://www.screendaily.com/tiffcom-kicks-off-with-buyer-attendance-up-12/5033683.article.

———. 2012a. 'ScreenSingapore's New Format Wins Industry Approval', *Screen Daily*, 11 December. Retrieved 5 May 2015 from http://www.screendaily.com/screensingapores-new-format-wins-industry-approval/5049854.article.

———. 2012b. 'TIFFCOM Closes with Mixed Reactions to New Venue', *Screen Daily*, 26 October. Retrieved 5 May 2015 from http://www.screendaily.com/tiffcom-closes-with-mixed-reactions-to-new-venue/5048238.article.

———. 2013a. 'Shanghai Film Market Launches', *Screen International*, 17 June.

———. 2013b. 'Tokyo's Show of Support', *Screen Daily*, 9 October. Retrieved 5 May 2015 from http://www.screendaily.com/features/tokyos-show-of-support/5062233.article.

———. 2014. 'Filmart 2014: Destination Hong Kong', *Screen Daily*, 24 March. Retrieved 5 May 2015 from http://www.screendaily.com/features/filmart-2014-destination-hong-kong/5069891.article.

Nye, Joseph S., Jr. 2004. *Soft Power: The Means to Success in World Politics*. New York: PublicAffairs.

Ong, Aihwa. 1999. *Flexible Citizenship: The Cultural Logics of Transnationality*. North Carolina and London: Duke University Press.

Pan, Lynn (ed.). 1999. *The Encyclopedia of the Chinese Overseas*. Richmond: Curzon.

Pang, Laikwan. 2006a. *Cultural Control and Globalization in Asia: Copyright, Piracy and Cinema*. London and New York: Routledge.

———. 2006b. 'Walking Into and Out of the Spectacle: China's Earliest Film Scene', *Screen* 47(1): 66–80.

———. 2007. 'Postcolonial Hong Kong Cinema: Utilitarianism and (Trans)Local', *Postcolonial Studies* 10(4): 413–30.

———. 2009. 'Trans-national Cinema, Creative Labor, and New Directors in Hong Kong', *Asia Japan Journal* 4: 79–87.

———. 2010. 'Hong Kong Cinema as a Dialect Cinema?', *Cinema Journal* 49(3): 140–43.

Pang, Yi-ping. 1997. '*Happy Together*: Let's be Happy Together before 1997' (in traditional Chinese), *City Entertainment*, 473, 29 May–11 June, 40–50.

Paquet, Darcy. 2006. 'Asian Animation Outfits Drawing Attention', *Variety*, 403(2), A10.

_____. 2009a. 'A Dark Era for Korean Cinema?', *Korean Cinema Today*, special ed., Cannes Film Festival, 1, May–June, 28–29.

_____. 2009b. 'The Meaning of PIFF', *Korean Cinema Today*, 3, September–October, 28–29.

_____. 2010. 'Expectations, Fears, Predictions for 2010', *Korean Cinema Today*, Berlin ed., 5, January–February, 30–31.

'Parallel Importers Bulk Purchasing Baby Milk Powder in Hong Kong's Pharmacies' (in traditional Chinese). 2013. *Sing Tao Daily*, 24 January. Retrieved 5 May 2015 from http://hk.news.yahoo.com/水客攻陷全港藥房掃奶粉-220356607.html.

Peters, John Durham. 1999. 'Exile, Nomadism, and Diaspora: The Stakes of Mobility in the Western Canon', in Hamid Naficy (ed.), *Home, Exile, Homeland: Film, Media, and the Politics of Place*. New York: Routledge, pp. 17–41.

Petkovic, Silvana. 2009. *The Guide to Japanese Film Industry and Co-production 2009*. Tokyo: UNIJAPAN.

Petrie, Duncan. 2000. 'The Scottish Cinema', in Mette Hjort and Scott MacKenzie (eds), *Cinema and Nation*. London and New York: Routledge, pp. 153–69.

Po, Fung. 2002. 'The Helpless Sympathizer in Ann Hui's Films', trans. Maggie Lee, *Hong Kong Panorama 2001–2002*, 26th Hong Kong International Film Festival. Hong Kong: Hong Kong Arts Development Council, pp. 121–23.

'Policy of Cultural Affairs in Japan: Fiscal 2014'. 2014. Tokyo: Agency for Cultural Affairs. Retrieved 5 May 2015 from http://www.bunka.go.jp/english/index.html.

Pulver, Andrew. 2013. 'China Confirmed as World's Largest Film Market outside US', *The Guardian*, 22 March. Retrieved 10 May 2015 from http://www.theguardian.com/film/2013/mar/22/china-largest-film-market-outside-us.

Punathambekar, Aswin. 2007. 'Between Rowdies and *Rasikas*: Rethinking Fan Activity in Indian Film Culture', in Jonathan Gray, Cornel Sandvoss and C. Lee Harrington (eds), *Fandom: Identities and Communities in a Mediated World*. New York and London: New York University Press, pp. 198–209.

Rayns, Tony. 1995. 'Poet of Time', *Sight & Sound*, 5(9), September, 12–16.

_____. 1999. '*Made in Hong Kong*: Hong Kong 1997', *Sight & Sound*, 9(8), August, 47–48.

'Renowned Director John Woo: The Global Outlook of Chinese Traditional Values' (in traditional Chinese). 2005. *Xinhuanet*, 19 May. Retrieved 5 May 2015 from http://big5.xinhuanet.com/gate/big5/news.xinhuanet.com/overseas/2005-05/19/content_2976369.htm.

Reynaud, Bérénice. 1999. 'Three Chinas … : Societies in Motion Culture, Culture in Commotion', *Cinemaya*, 43, Spring, 4–10.

Richards, Terry. 1999. '*Made in Hong Kong (Xianggang Zhizao)*', *Film Review*, July, 34.

Robbins, Bruce. 1995. 'Some Versions of US Internationalism', *Social Text* 45(14): 97–123.

Rosenstone, Robert A. 2006. *History on Film/Film on History*. Harlow: Pearson Education Limited.

Russo, Julie Levin. 2009. 'User-Penetrated Content: Fan Video in the Age of Convergence', *Cinema Journal* 48(4): 125–30.

Safran, William. 1991. 'Diasporas in Modern Societies: Myths of Homeland and Return', *Diaspora* 1(1): 83–99.

Sanjek, David. 2007. 'Exiled/Fongchuk', *Senses of Cinema* 43, May. Retrieved 5 May 2015 from http://sensesofcinema.com/2007/cteq/exiled.

Sarris, Andrew. 1981. 'Andrew Sarris', in John Caughie (ed.), *Theories of Authorship: A Reader*. London: Routledge & Kegan Paul, pp. 61–67.

Sassen, Saskia. 2001. *The Global City: New York, London, Tokyo*, 2nd ed. New Jersey: Princeton University Press.

Schilling, Mark. 2003. 'Planning Group Proposes Studio City Tokyo', *Screen Daily*, 21 January. Retrieved 5 May 2015 from http://www.screendaily.com/planning-group-proposes-studio-city-tokyo/4011877.article.

Sek, Kei. 1988. 'The Social Psychology of Hongkong Cinema', *Changes in Hongkong Society through Cinema*, 10th Hong Kong International Film Festival. Hong Kong: Urban Council, pp. 15–20.

———. 2013. 'Is Hong Kong Becoming Like the Mainland, or Vice Versa?', *The 37th Hong Kong International Film Festival*. Hong Kong: Hong Kong International Film Festival Society, pp. 120–25.

'SFG to Launch Joint Venture with Technicolor'. 2010. *Screen International*, 12 June.

Shackleton, Liz. 2003. 'Taiwan Overhauls Film Funding Policy', *Screen Daily*, 19 May. Retrieved 5 May 2015 from http://www.screendaily.com/taiwan-overhauls-film-funding-policy/4013458.article.

———. 2005a. 'Endeavour Tries China with Shanghai Media Group', *Screen International*, 13 May.

———. 2005b. 'Taiwan Launches First Asian Tax Finance Incentives', *Screen Daily*, 16 May. Retrieved 5 May 2015 from http://www.screendaily.com/taiwan-launches-first-asian-tax-finance-incentives/4023130.article.

———. 2006a. 'Hong Kong's EMP Teams with Shanghai Film Studio', *Screen International*, 19 June.

———. 2006b. 'Shanghai Unveils Plans for New Studio Facility', *Screen International*, 19 June.

———. 2008. 'Filmart: Asia Gets down to Business', *Screen Daily*, 7 March. Retrieved 5 May 2015 from http://www.screendaily.com/filmart-asia-gets-down-to-business/4037674.article.

———. 2009a. 'Far East Festivals Compete for Market Attention', *Screen Daily*, 29 October. Retrieved 5 May 2015 from http://www.screendaily.com/reports/in-focus/far-east-festivals-compete-for-market-attention/5007485.article.

———. 2009b. 'Mainland Mission', *Screen Daily*, 4 May. Retrieved 5 May 2015 from http://www.screendaily.com/mainland-mission/5000759.article.

———. 2009c. 'Taiwan Pumps $228m into Local Film and Co-productions', *Screen Daily*, 20 May. Retrieved 5 May 2015 from http://www.screendaily.com/taiwan-pumps-228m-into-local-film-and-co-productions/5001411.article.

———. 2010a. 'A Tale of Three Cities', *Screen Daily*, 16 April. Retrieved 5 May 2015 from http://www.screendaily.com/reports/opinion/a-tale-of-three-cities/5012830.article.

———. 2010b. 'Leung, Chung Join Cast of Bruce Lee, My Brother', *Screen International*, 22 July.

———. 2011a. 'Beauty in the East: Filmart 2011', *Screen Daily*, 16 March. Retrieved 5 May 2015 from http://www.screendaily.com/features/territory-focus/beauty-in-the-east-filmart-2011/5024554.article.

———. 2011b. 'Filmart 2011: Growing Confidence in Pan-Chinese Market', *Screen Daily*, 24 March. Retrieved 5 May 2015 from http://www.screendaily.com/reports/in-focus/filmart-2011-growing-confidence-in-pan-chinese-market/5025337.article.

———. 2012a. 'A Change of Image', *Screen International*, 2 November.

———. 2012b. 'Hong Kong Box Office Soars by 19% in First Half of 2012', *Screen Daily*, 6 July. Retrieved 5 May 2015 from http://www.screendaily.com/news/asia-pacific/hong-kong-box-office-soars-by-19-in-first-half-of-2012/5044112.article.

———. 2012c. 'Hong Kong Films to Gain Greater Access to Guangdong', *Screen International*, 18 July.

Sharp, Jasper, and Michael Arnold. 2002. 'Forgotten Fragments: An Introduction to Japanese Silent Cinema', *Midnight Eye*, 16 July. Retrieved 5 May 2015 from http://www.midnighteye.com/features/forgotten-fragments-an-introduction-to-japanese-silent-cinema.

Shih, Shu-mei. 2007. *Visuality and Identity: Sinophone Articulations across the Pacific*. California: University of California Press.

———. 2011. 'The Concept of the Sinophone', *PMLA* 126(3), May: 709–18.

Shin, Thomas, and Keeto Lam. 2003. 'Public Toilet: Fruit Chan: Life and Death in a Global Cesspool', *Hong Kong Panorama 2002-2003*, 27th Hong Kong International Film Festival. Hong Kong: Hong Kong Arts Development Council, pp. 88–90.

Shu, Kei. 1988. 'The Television Work of Ann Hui', *Changes in Hongkong Society through Cinema*, 10th Hong Kong International Film Festival. Hong Kong: Urban Council, pp. 47–52.

Sida, Michael. 1994. *Hong Kong towards 1997: History, Development and Transition*. Hong Kong: Victoria Press.

'SIFF Debates Declining Market Share of Chinese Films'. 2012. *Screen International*, 18 June.

Skeldon, Ronald. 1994a. 'Hong Kong is an International Migration System', in Ronald Skeldon (ed.), *Reluctant Exiles?: Migration from Hong Kong and the New Overseas Chinese*. New York: An East Gate Book, pp. 21–51.

———. 1994b. 'Reluctant Exiles or Bold Pioneers: An Introduction to Migration from Hong Kong', in Ronald Skeldon (ed.), *Reluctant Exiles?: Migration from Hong Kong and the New Overseas Chinese*. New York: An East Gate Book, pp. 3–18.

———. (ed.). 1994c. *Reluctant Exiles?: Migration from Hong Kong and the New Overseas Chinese*. New York: An East Gate Book.

'Snapshots: Eight Years of Hong Kong Cinema' (in traditional Chinese). 1986. *City Entertainment*, 200, 6 November, 6–8.

Solomons, Jason. 2009. 'Red Cliff', *The Guardian/The Observer*, 14 June. Retrieved 5 May 2015 from http://www.theguardian.com/film/2009/jun/14/red-cliff-john-woo.

Sosnowski, Alexandra. 1996. 'Cinema in Transition: The Polish Film Today', *Journal of Popular Film & Television* 24(1): 10–16.

Squire, Jason E. (ed.). 2006. *The Movie Business Book*, international 3rd ed. Berkshire: Open University Press.

Stein, Michael. 2002. 'Dir. Clara Law, *Floating Life* [fu sheng]', *Intersections*, 8, October. Retrieved 5 May 2015 from http://wwwsshe.murdoch.edu.au/intersections/issue8/stein_review.html.

Stephens, Chuck. 1996. 'Time Pieces: Wong Kar-wai and the Persistence of Memory', *Film Comment*, 32(1), January–February, 12–18.

Stokes, Lisa Odham, and Michael Hoover. 1999. *City on Fire: Hong Kong Cinema*. London: Verso.

Stringer, Julian. 1997. '"Your Tender Smiles Give Me Strength": Paradigms of Masculinity in John Woo's *A Better Tomorrow* and *The Killer*', *Screen* 38(1): 25–41.

_____. 2003. '*Boat People*: Second Thoughts on Text and Context', in Chris Berry (ed.), *Chinese Films in Focus: 25 New Takes*. London: BFI, pp. 15–22.

Sugawara, Yoshino. 2011. 'Liuhe (United Six) Film Company Revisited' (in simplified Chinese), in Emilie Yueh-yu Yeh (ed.), *Rethinking Chinese Film Industry: New Histories New Methods*. Beijing: Peking University Press, pp. 95–120.

Sugaya, Minoru. 2004. 'The Policy Analysis of the Film and Video Market in Japan', *Keio Communication Review* 26: 3–16.

Sussman, Nan M. 2011. *Return Migration and Identity: A Global Phenomenon, A Hong Kong Case*. Hong Kong: Hong Kong University Press.

Szeto, Mirana M. 2011. 'Ann Hui at the Margin of Mainstream Hong Kong Cinema', in Esther. M.K. Cheung, Gina Marchetti and Tan See-Kam (eds), *Hong Kong Screenscapes: From the New Wave to the Digital Frontier*. Hong Kong: Hong Kong University Press, pp. 51–66.

Szeto, Mirana M., and Yun-chung Chen. 2012. 'Mainlandization or Sinophone Translocality? Challenges for Hong Kong SAR New Wave Cinema', *Journal of Chinese Cinemas* 6(2): 115–34.

_____. 2013. 'To Work or Not to Work: The Dilemma of Hong Kong Film Labor in the Age of Mainlandization', *Jump Cut* 55, Fall. Retrieved 5 May 2015 from http://ejumpcut.org/archive/jc55.2013/SzetoChenHongKong/index.html.

T., Susanna. 1998. 'No Future! No Future!: Fruit Chan Speaks about *Made in Hong Kong*' (both English and traditional Chinese versions), *Hong Kong Panorama 97–98*, 22nd Hong Kong International Film Festival. Hong Kong: Provisional Urban Council, pp. 54–57.

'Taiwan to Increase Subsidy on Foreign Shoots'. 2010. *Screen Daily*, 22 March. Retrieved 5 May 2015 from http://www.screendaily.com/taiwan-to-increase-subsidy-on-foreign-shoots/5011961.article.

'Taiwan's Summer Box Office Booming, Led by Record-Setting Apple of My Eye'. 2011. *Screen Daily*, 25 August. Retrieved 5 May 2015 from http://www.screendaily.com/taiwans-summer-box-office-booming-led-by-record-setting-apple-of-my-eye/5031233.article.

Tambling, Jeremy. 2003. *Wong Kar-wai's Happy Together*. Hong Kong: Hong Kong University Press.

Tan, See Kam, Justin Clemens, and Eleanor Hogan. 1994–95. 'Interview: Clara Law', *Cinemaya*, 25–26, Autumn–Winter, 50–54.

Tan, See-Kam, Peter X. Feng, and Gina Marchetti (eds). 2009. *Chinese Connections: Critical Perspectives on Film, Identity and Diaspora*. Pennsylvania: Temple University Press.

Teo, Stephen. 1988. 'Politics and Social Issues in Hongkong Cinema', *Changes in Hongkong Society through Cinema*, 10th Hong Kong International Film Festival. Hong Kong: Urban Council, pp. 38–41.

———. 1997. *Hong Kong Cinema: The Extra Dimensions*. London: BFI.

———. 2001. '*Floating Life*: The Heaviness of Moving', *Senses of Cinema* 12, February–March. Retrieved 5 May 2015 from http://sensesofcinema.com/2001/director-clara-law/floating.

———. 2005. *Wong Kar-wai*. London: BFI.

———. 2007. *Director in Action: Johnnie To and the Hong Kong Action Film*. Hong Kong: Hong Kong University Press.

'Textbooks Round the World: It Ain't Necessarily So'. 2012. *The Economist*, 13 October. Retrieved 5 May 2015 from http://www.economist.com/node/21564554.

The Centre for Cultural Policy Research of the University of Hong Kong. 2003. 'Baseline Study on Hong Kong's Creative Industries'. Hong Kong: University of Hong Kong.

'*The Detective 2*'s Box Office Earnings Surpasses *The Detective*'s' (in traditional Chinese). 2011. *paper.wenweipo.com*, 14 May. Retrieved 5 May 2015 from http://paper.wenweipo.com/2011/05/14/EN1105140008.htm.

'The Identity and National Identification of Hong Kong People – Survey Findings' (in traditional Chinese). 2012. Centre for Communication and Public Opinion Survey, Chinese University of Hong Kong, press release, November.

'Thematic Report: Ethnic Minorities'. 2012. Hong Kong: 2011 Population Census Office, Census and Statistics Department, Hong Kong SAR Government.

Thompson, Anne. 2008. 'H'wood in Thrall of Great Wall', *Variety*, 410(3), 3 March.

'TIFFCOM 2012 Market Report'. 2013. Tokyo: TIFFCOM.

Tölölyan, Khachig. 1991. 'The Nation-State and its Others: In Lieu of Preface', *Diaspora* 1(1): 3–7.

———. 1996. 'Rethinking Diaspora(s): Stateless Power in the Transnational Moment', *Diaspora* 5(1): 3–36.

Tsui, Clarence. 2000. 'Sex, Cash and Videotape', *HKiMail*, 16 November.

———. 2013. 'Chinese Box Office Hit "Tiny Times" Bumps up Sequel Release to August 9', *The Hollywood Reporter*, 12 July. Retrieved 5 May 2015 from http://www.hollywoodreporter.com/news/chinese-box-office-hit-tiny-584068.

Tu, Wei-ming (ed.). 1994. *The Living Tree: Changing Meaning of Being Chinese Today*. California: Stanford University Press.

Veg, Sebastian. 2014. 'Anatomy of the Ordinary: New Perspectives in Hong Kong Independent Cinema', *Journal of Chinese Cinemas* 8(1): 73–92.

Verrier, Richard. 2009. 'MPAA Stops Disclosing Average Costs of Making and Marketing Movies', *Los Angeles Times*, 1 April. Retrieved 5 May 2015 from http://articles.latimes.com/2009/apr/01/business/fi-cotown-mpaa1.

Wang, Enbao. 1995. *Hong Kong, 1997: The Politics of Transition*. Colorado: Lynne Rienner.

Wang, Gungwu. 1991a. *China and the Chinese Overseas*. Singapore: Times Academic Press.

———. 1991b. *The Chineseness of China*. Hong Kong: Oxford University Press.

Wang, Gungwu, and John Wong (eds). 1999. *Hong Kong in China: The Challenges of Transition*. Singapore: Times Academic Press.

Wang, Gungwu, and Wong Siu-lun (eds). 1995. *Hong Kong's Transition: A Decade after the Deal*. Hong Kong: Oxford University Press.

Wang, Shujen. 2003. *Framing Piracy: Globalization and Film Distribution in Greater China*. Maryland: Rowman & Littlefield.

Wesley-Smith, Peter (ed.). 1993. *Hong Kong in Transition: Problems and Prospects*. Hong Kong: Faculty of Law, University of Hong Kong.

'Who to Know in China'. 2011. *Screen Daily*, 7 February. Retrieved 5 May 2015 from http://www.screendaily.com/reports/territory-focus/who-to-know-in-china/5023298.article.

Williams, Tony. 1998. 'Song of the Exile: Border-Crossing Melodrama', *Jump Cut* 42: 94–100.

———. 2000. 'Hong Kong Cinema, the Boat People, and *To Liv(e)*', *Asian Cinema* 11(1): 131–42.

Wong, Ain-ling (ed.). 2003. *The Shaw Screen: A Preliminary Study*. Hong Kong: Hong Kong Film Archive.

Wong, Chi-fai. 2012. 'Three: Going Home: Hong Kong's Death and Resurrection' (in traditional Chinese), in Li Cheuk-to (ed.), *Peter Ho-sun Chan: My Way*. Hong Kong: Joint Publishing, pp. 202–3.

Wong, Cindy Hing-Yuk. 2011. *Film Festivals: Culture, People, and Power on the Global Screen*. New Jersey and London: Rutgers University Press.

Wong, David. 1983. 'Cost of Housing Viet Refugees Expected to Soar', *Hong Kong Standard*, 3 February.

Wong, Siu-lun. 1997. 'Issues Paper from Hong Kong', in Patrick Brownlee and Colleen Mitchell (eds), 'Asia Pacific Migration Research Network: Migration Issues in the Asia Pacific'. Australia: APMRN Secretariat, Centre for Multicultural Studies, Institute for Social Change & Critical Inquiry, University of Wollongong. Retrieved 5 May 2015 from http://www.unesco.org/most/apmrnwp7.htm.

———. 1999. 'Changing Hong Kong Identities', in Wang Gungwu and John Wong (eds), *Hong Kong in China: The Challenges of Transition*. Singapore: Times Academic Press, pp. 181–202.

Wu, David Yen-ho. 1994. 'The Construction of Chinese and Non-Chinese Identities', in Tu Wei-ming (ed.), *The Living Tree: The Changing Meaning of Being Chinese Today*. California: Stanford University Press, pp. 148–67.

Xing, Liyu. 2014. 'Chairman of the Hong Kong Film Development Council on the Future Development of Hong Kong Films with Local Characteristics' (in simplified Chinese), *China News Service*, 20 July. Retrieved 5 May 2015 from http://www.chinanews.com/ga/2014/07-20/6404645.shtml.

Xiong, Yuezhi. 1996. 'The Image and Identity of the Shanghainese', in Tao Tao Liu and David Faure (eds), *Unity and Diversity: Local Cultures and Identities in China*. Hong Kong: Hong Kong University Press, pp. 99–106.

Yano, Christine R. 2004. 'Letters from the Heart: Negotiating Fan-Star Relationships in Japanese Popular Music', in William W. Kelly (ed.), *Fanning the Flames: Fans and Consumer Culture in Contemporary Japan*. New York: State University of New York Press, pp. 41–58.

Yao, Minji. 2013. 'Cradle of Cinema Rocked by Creativity', *ShanghaiDaily.com*, 2 November. Retrieved 5 May 2015 from http://www.shanghaidaily.com/Feature/art-and-culture/Cradle-of-cinema-rocked-by-creativity/shdaily.shtml.

Yau, Esther C.M. (ed.). 2001. *At Full Speed: Hong Kong Cinema in a Borderless World*. Minnesota: University of Minnesota Press.

Yau, Kinnia Shuk-ting. 2003. 'Shaws' Japanese Collaboration and Competition as Seen through the Asian Film Festival Evolution', in Wong Ain-ling (ed.), *The Shaw Screen: A Preliminary Study*. Hong Kong: Hong Kong Film Archive, pp. 279–91.

Yau, Shuk-ting, Kinnia. 2010. *Japanese and Hong Kong Film Industries: Understanding the Origins of East Asian Film Networks*. London and New York: Routledge.

Ye, Nienchen. 2000. 'Can't Pass up a Good Story: From *Little Cheung* to *Durian Durian*', trans. Au Jing-wong, *Hong Kong Panorama 1999–2000*, 24th Hong Kong International Film Festival. Hong Kong: Leisure and Cultural Services Department, pp. 20–24.

Yeh, Emilie Yueh-yu. 2010. 'The Deferral of Pan-Asian: A Critical Appraisal of Film Marketization in China', in Michael Curtin and Hemant Shah (eds), *Reorienting Global Communication: Indian and Chinese Media: Beyond Borders*. Illinois: University of Illinois Press, pp. 183–200.

Yeh, Emilie Yueh-yu, and Darrell William Davis. 2005. *Taiwan Film Directors: A Treasure Island*. New York: Columbia University Press.

———. 2008. 'Re-nationalizing China's Film Industry: Case Study on the China Film Group and Film Marketization', *Journal of Chinese Cinemas* 2(1): 37–51.

Yeung, Linda. 2000. 'A Magnet for Mainland Sex', *South China Morning Post*, 25 October.

'Young Chinese Directors Dominate Shanghai's Golden Goblets'. 2011. *Screen Daily*, 19 June. Retrieved 5 May 2015 from http://www.screendaily.com/young-chinese-directors-dominate-shanghais-golden-goblets/5028921.article.

Yu, Sabrina Qiong. 2010. 'Camp Pleasure in an Era of Chinese Blockbusters: Internet Reception of *Hero* in Mainland China', in Gary D. Rawnsley and Ming-Yeh T. Rawnsley (eds), *Global Chinese Cinema: The Culture and Politics of* Hero. London and New York: Routledge, pp. 135–51.

Yu, Sen-lun. 2011a. 'China in their Hands', *Screen Daily*, 7 June. Retrieved 5 May 2015 from http://www.screendaily.com/features/features/china-in-their-hands/5028304. article.

———. 2011b. 'New Chinese Talent', *Screen Daily*, 7 June. Retrieved 5 May 2015 from http://www.screendaily.com/features/features/new-chinese-talent/5028305.article.

Yue, Audrey. 2010. *Ann Hui's Song of the Exile*. Hong Kong: Hong Kong University Press.

Zhang, April. 2012. 'Hong Kong Identity Caught between Political Reality and Insecurity', *South China Morning Post*, 17 October. Retrieved 5 May 2015 from http://www.scmp.com/comment/insight-opinion/article/1062558/hong-kong-identity-caught-between-political-reality-and?page=all.

Zhang, Yingjin. 1999. *Cinema and Urban Culture in Shanghai, 1922–43*. California: Stanford University Press.

———. 2002. *Screening China: Critical Interventions, Cinematic Reconfigurations, and the Transnational Imaginary in Contemporary Chinese Cinema*. Michigan: Center for Chinese Studies, University of Michigan.

———. 2011. 'Preface', in Vivian P.Y. Lee (ed.), *East Asian Cinemas: Regional Flows and Global Transformations*. New York: Palgrave Macmillan, pp. viii–x.

Zhang, Zhen. 2005. *An Amorous History of the Silver Screen: Shanghai Cinema 1896–1937*. Illinois: University of Chicago Press.

Index

South Korea: film industry (*see* South Korean film industry (*under* film industries)); film policy (*see* film policies)

Sparrow, 57, 90, 106, 123–27. *See also* To, Johnnie

State Administration of Press, Publication, Radio, Film and Television (formerly, State Administration of Radio, Film and Television) (People's Republic of China), 187, 207

Sussman, Nan M., 79–80

Szeto, Mirana M., 18, 85, 107, 111

T

Taiwan: film industry (*see* Taiwan film industry (*under* film industries)); film policy (*see* film policies); Republic of China (*see* China)

Tan, See Kam (also Tan See-Kam), 107

Television Broadcasts Limited, 10, 56, 85, 89, 112–13

Teo, Stephen, 3, 13, 54, 112, 114

The Detective (series), 82, 96–99. *See also* Pang, Danny and Oxide

To, Johnnie, 33, 56–58, 105–6, 111–14, 119, 123–27, 200–1. *See also Exiled; Milkyway Image; Sparrow*

transitions, 2, 4, 14–21, 31, 33–34, 42, 47, 55–56, 65, 70–71, 76, 78, 80, 82, 103, 120, 136, 139, 163, 170–71, 176, 183, 203, 210, 212, 220–23

Tsui, Hark, 19–20, 114, 201. *See also A Chinese Ghost Story*; first New Wave (*under* Hong Kong New Waves)

Tu, Wei-ming, 25, 77

W

Wai, Ka-fai, 113–14. *See also* Milkyway Image

Wang, Gungwu, 7, 16–17, 41, 76

Wong, John, 16–17

Wong, Kar-wai, 27, 53–56, 59–61, 64, 110, 200. *See also Days of Being Wild; Happy Together*

Wong, Siu-lun, 18

Wong, Tin-lam, 112, 119

Woo, John, 4, 34, 139, 146–48, 150–51, 153, 157, 159–62, 165, 167, 170–71. *See also Red Cliff*

Y

Yeh, Emilie Yueh-yu, 27–28, 179, 188

Z

Zhang, Yimou, 28, 109, 186